INDIAN COUNCIL OF HISTORICAL RESEARCH
MONOGRAPH SERIES 3

We Lived Together

We Lived Together

edited by
S. SETTAR
P. K. V. KAIMAL

1999
PRAGATI PUBLICATIONS
INDIAN COUNCIL OF HISTORICAL RESEARCH
DELHI

First Published: 2000

Published by

PRAGATI PUBLICATIONS
9926 Library Road,
Azad Market, Delhi 110006

in association with

INDIAN COUNCIL OF
HISTORICAL RESEARCH
35 Ferozeshah Road,
New Delhi 110001

ISBN: 81-7307-062-8

Printed in India

Printed and published by Vinod Kapoor for Pragati Publications,
9926 Library Road, Azad Market, Delhi 110006

Contents

Foreword

This is the third in the series of monographs, published by the Indian Council of Historical Research since March 1999. As indicated by the title, the papers presented in this volume reflect on the Indian life through the ages, highlighting unity in diversity. India's vast and varied experience is not easy to capture in all its entirety – hence, only a selective effort could be made towards this.

This Council published a volume titled *We Fought Together for Freedom* in 1995. *We Lived Together* is inspired by its success. The 1995 publication was limited to the freedom struggle and it had also a limited framework. The present volume covers experiences of all periods of time, but only select aspects of Indian life. Of the twenty-one papers, some relate to a specific period of time, region and society, while the majority transcend the chronological and geographical barriers to capture the collective consciousness.

At no time the contributors to this volume were instructed to tailor their papers to suit the theme – in fact, each contribution is the choice of the author for which his scholarship alone is responsible. I thank all contributors and the members of this Council who helped bring out this volume.

S. Settar
Chairman

ICHR
New Delhi
30 June 1999

ONE

Ladders and Snakes: Cyclical Shifts in Culture Process

M. K. DHAVALIKAR

A PEEP INTO THE five thousand years of Indian history reveals that there were phases of prosperity and decline almost in a cyclical order. The glorious Indus or the Harappan civilization covered the thousand years of the entire third millennium whereas the second millennium and the first half of the first millennium BC are characterized by extreme degeneration. This is followed by the rise of urbanism – referred to as the second urbanization from *c.* 300 BC to AD 500 which witnessed the rise of empires – the Mauryan, the Sungas, the Satavahanas, the Kushans and the Guptas. The undreamt of prosperity of this period was in a large measure due to the extremely profitable trade with Roman empire. But again decline set in from AD 500 to 1000, so much so that this phase can rightly be called the 'second deurbanization'. There is some improvement between AD 1000–1400, but again the decline set in between AD 1400–1800. It must be stated in this context that these cyclical shifts were not peculiar to India only: in fact, the same situation prevailed in other part of the Old World – more or less.

Why did it happen? Although historians have sought to explain this curious phenomenon in their own way, their explanations do not fully account for it. The principal cause appears to be environment. The role of environment in the evolution of human culture is now well recognized and the New or Processual archaeologists define culture as an extra-somatic means of adaptation with environment (Binford 1972: 20). According to Fernand Braudel, a leading proponent of the *Annales* school of French historians, 'the history of man is the history of his relationship with environment. To him 'environment is a hindrance beyond which man and his experience cannot go. . . . For centuries, man has been a prisoner of the climate, of the animal population, of a particular agriculture, of a gradually established balance system from which we cannot escape without the risk of upsetting everything' (Braudel 1980: 30). This almost amounts to ecological determinism, and Braudel's views may appear rather extreme, but they are justifiably valid for India where our entire life cycle is dependent on the erratic monsoon. Our agriculture is a gamble with nature, for every third year is a bad year, and every fourth a famine.

II

Environment

How do we reconstruct the past environment? Some scientific methods are now available, such as pollen analysis. This is a most reliable method because of the scientific rigour employed in collecting and interpreting the data. Palynological investigations have been carried out by Gurdip Singh (1971) in the lake sediments of Rajasthan, D. P. Agarwal (1992) in Kashmir and S.N. Rajguru (1993) in western India. We, therefore, have a fair idea of the past environment in eastern India during the last 5,00,000 years.

Another important piece of evidence is furnished by Nile floods in Egypt. It may be asked as to how this data can be useful to us. It is pertinent to note in this context that the southwest monsoon that we get in India, also falls in east Africa, especially Ethiopia. Egypt itself does not get any rain but the Nile is flooded when rain falls in Ethiopia through which the Blue Nile flows before reaching Egypt. Records of Nile floods are available for ancient times, the earliest one going back to *c.* 2900 BC (Bell 1970) and an almost complete year to year record is available from AD 622 when an Egyptian prince installed a mechanical device called 'Nilometer' on the island of Roda at Cairo. Sir Gilbert Wallker (1986), a former Director General of Indian Meteorological Department, analyzed the rainfall data from the north and east Africa and India from 1840 to 1910 and discovered a close correspondence between Nile floods and the monsoon rainfall in India. The *Imperial Gazetteer of India* (1908: I, 127) records:

> It is now fully established that years of drought in Western or north Western India are almost invariably years of low Nile flood. The relation is further confirmed by the fact that years of heavier rain than usual in Western India are also years of high Nile flood.

It is, therefore, needless to state that the data of Nile floods is of immense help to us in reconstructing the past environment in India.

It also deserves a special mention that scientists have noted that whenever there is an immensely cold phase in Europe, tropical countries like India suffer droughts. Sulman (1982: II, 118) has clearly mentioned that 'whenever the high latitudes cool, monsoons tend to fail.' Similarly, it appears that whenever the temperate lands experience a warmer phase countries like India enjoy a good rainfall. (Currie and Fairbridge 1985 of 111). This is probably due to the fact that 'climate is a world-wide system. Significant changes cannot take place in one part without changes occurring in other places. There are dynamic connections that interlink climate changes in various parts of the globe' (Bryson and Ross 1977: 509). In Europe the past environment has been reconstructed very thoroughly on the basis of scientific evidence and written records and this data goes a long way in the reconstruction of our past environment. It has been rightly observed that 'climatic world is one world' (Bryson *et al* 1947: 49).

In India another important source is our ancient literature like the *Puranas* which have recorded climatic shifts such as droughts and the disappearance of the river Saraswati. But far more important is the *Brhatsamhita* of Varahamihira which predicts natural calamities like droughts, floods, famines, earthquakes, etc. The predictions made by the celebrated astronomer appear to have been proved correct to a great extent as the testimony of the great Chinese pilgrim Hieun Tsang shows. Besides there are heart-rending descriptions of prolonged droughts as in Dandin's *Dasa-Kumara-charita* (Ch. VI).

III

Some 15000 years ago the environment almost all over the Old World is said to have been so congenial as never before or since. The last Ice Age had ended, the warmer phase began in temperate zones, and India enjoyed adequate rainfall. Plant and animal food was plenty and hence the population grew very fast during the Mesolithic period. But aridity set in between 7500–3000 BC and hence man was forced to produce his own food. Thus began agriculture, the earliest evidence of which is now available at Mehragarh near Quetta in Pakistan. Investigations carried out on the Sambar, Lunkaransar, and Didwana, which are salt water lakes, and on Pushkar, a fresh water lake, indicate that climate improved from 3000–2000 BC to wetter conditions in the area which is now a desert in Rajasthan, where rainfall may have been around 600 mm or 24 inches (Gurdip Singh 1971). From the satellite photographs it appears that the river Saraswati was then a mighty river, as much as 8 km wide, and flowed independently into the Gulf of Kutch (Misra 1993). It was during this period, the third millennium, that the Harappan civilization flourished in the sub-continent. It had the widest distribution of the Old World civilizations as it was spread over a large area of about 1500 × 1500 km. Over 1000 settlements of this great civilization have so far been brought to light, about 700 in India and the remaining in Pakistan. The recent evidence from excavations indicates that it evolved in the Saraswati valley (present Ghaggar) where there is a heavy concentration of Harappan settlements.

The antecedents of this great civilization are now clear. The Early Harappan phase (*c.* 3200–2600 BC) had contributed considerably to the make up of the Indus civilization which is now dated to *c.* 2600–2000 BC. This was the mature phase characterized by immaculate town planning, brick built houses laid out on the typical Indian *chatuhsala* plan, underground drainage system, elaborate bathrooms, and wells for water. It has now been revealed that Mohenjodaro was probably the largest city of the ancient world (Jansen 1993). An important feature of Harappan towns and cities is that they were divided into three different localities as the evidence from Kalibangan and other urban centres shows, and at Dholavira in Kutch, the city was divided into four watertight compartments. They suggest that it was a class-structured society and we may not be far off the mark if we infer that this arrangement was the precursor to the *varna* system of the Vedic period. In that case we cannot blame the Vedic Aryans for creating this evil in India.

The prosperity of the Harappan civilization was in a large measure based on the profitable trade with West Asia. There is evidence to show that the trade had begun much earlier around 2800 BC (Durante 1979) but received a tremendous boost from the time of the Sargon of Agade in *c*. 2350 BC as the evidence from tablet inscriptions in Mesopotamia shows. Indian exports included carnalian beads, ivory, shells, textiles, timber, copper, etc. which were probably paid for in silver. India did not have much silver, and the evidence from Indus cities, more particularly from the recent excavations at Kunal (Haryana), is corroborative. Our knowledge of this trade is solely derived from cuniform inscriptions in West Asia which refer to India as Meluhha (Leeman 1960). It appears that the demand for luxuries probably increased in the middle of the third millennium and hence the Harappans from Sindh, Punjab and Rajasthan ventured into Kutch and Saurashtra for procuring raw materials such as agates, shell, ivory and even copper. They first came to Kutch where they built forts as at Pabumath, Surkotada and Dholavira which afforded succour and protection to the itinerant merchant traders. In a short period of time they established their specialized manufacturing centres as at Lothal (bead making, copper artifacts), Nageshwar (shall cutting), Kuntasi (bead making and pottery), etc.

The strong agrarian base supported the large population of Harappan urban centres. Their staple food in Punjab, Sindh and Rajasthan was wheat and barley, but when they came to Saurashtra, they had to adapt to the local environment. They had to subsist on coarser grains like finger millet (*Ragi, Eleusine coracana*) and Italian millet (*Setaria italica*). Slightly later, they began to cultivate bajra (*pennisetum typhoides*) and jowar (Sorghum bicolour) which were probably introduced from the Gulf region. They are hardy crops which could be raised on monsoon rains and are suitable for dry farming.

IV

The third millennium witnessed the rise of civilizations all over West Asia and even in Greece and China for which the favourable environment was largely responsible. But towards the close of the millennium the climate change occurred and aridity set in. The palynological studies carried out by Gurdip Singh (1971) suggest that 1800 BC (calibrated 2000 BC) to 1500 BC was a dry period. This was the time when the Saraswati began to dry up in its lower course, probably because of shifts in the hydraulic regime (Misra 1993). The Sutlej and the Yamuna, which were the tributaries of the Saraswati, changed their courses and joined, respectively, the Indus and the Ganga systems. The lowering of the sea levels caused silting of ports which in turn affected trade. Yet another cause which has recently come to light is tectonic movements in different parts of the Old World during 2200–1900 BC as is evident from Dholavira, Kalibangan, Bansvali, etc (Courty 1994).

The late Harappan phase (*c.* 2200–1800 BC) is marked by decline in trade and agriculture which in turn led to deurbanization. The prosperous cities were now a thing of the past, large-scale migrations began, with people settling in villages, and many even resorted to pastoral nomadism leading a seasonally settled life as the archaeological evidence from Saurashtra suggests. (Dhavalikar 1994: 94ft). This phenomenon, however, was not peculiar to India only but occurred in many parts of the Old World. Everywhere, early civilizations received a setback, and the second millennium is therefore styled as the Dark Age of history. In Egypt there was disturbance during Middle Kingdom and in the intermediate period from 1991–1570 BC. There was a considerable fall in Nile levels (Bell 1975), and droughts became frequent occurrences in Greece, Anatolia, Egypt and Mesopotamia (Bell 1973).

The second half of the third millennium and first half of the second millennium BC witnessed the rise of early farming cultures in different parts of the country, as for instance the Ahar (Rajasthan), Kayatha and Malwa (MP), the Prabhas and Rangpur (Gujarat) and the Jorwe (Maharashtra) as also in the south and north India. These were all rural cultures which never attained the urban status. Their mixed economy was based on subsistence agriculture, stock-raising and hunting and fishing. Their habitations were small, spread over an area of about 2–3 ha, and were self sufficient. But the entire second millennium, if the palynological evidence from Rajasthan lake sediments is any indication, was marked by aridity which was getting intensely severe in the latter half of the second millennium (Gurdip Singh 1971). In consequence many of the Chalcolithic people vanished from the scene by 1400–1200 BC. In the Ganga Valley, however, the climate probably was better and hence the people continued to live. This period (1400–900 BC) has been compared with the 'Nuclear Winter' that will follow a nuclear war when the climate in Europe will be intensely cold and the tropical countries like India will suffer severe droughts (Burgess 1989). In central and western India and the Deccan, the settlements were deserted and the evidence from

Inamgaon shows that the people were gradually resorting to pastoral nomadism and leading a seasonally settled life (Dhavalikar 1984). We do not know what happened to the people between 1000 and 600 BC. It is likely that they may have become hunter-gatherers. This period labelled as the Sub-Atlantic phase in Europe was characterized by extremely cold climate which forced people to resort to pastoral nomadism. Khazanov, a leading authority, states:

> Almost all palaeo-climatists accept that the second millennium BC was characterised by a dry climate which, it would appear, was at its driest at the turn of the second and the first millennium BC. Archaeological data would confirm this suggestion (Khazanov 1986:85).

V

This period has been dubbed as the 'Centuries of Darkness' (James *et al* 1991) and it has been found to be a global phenomenon. The early farming communities in south India probably came under the influence of megalithism and resorted to pastoral nomadism, but they had by this time acquired the knowledge of iron technology. In north India too the advent of iron can be placed in the latter half of the second millennium. D.D. Kosambi (1965: 108) was the first to argue that iron was the prime mover of our second urbanization which occurred in the sixth to fifth century BC when our historical period begins. But this argument is no longer tenable as there is clear evidence of iron dating back to the latter half of the second millennium. It appears that in spite of the knowledge of iron technology, no significant progress could be made as the environment was not congenial. It could only be achieved when the climate improved from the sixth to fifth BC when Europe began to enjoy a warmer climate and we began to have adequate rainfall. It led to agrarian development, and the production increased because of such iron implements as plough, sickles, etc. The period from fifth century BC to fifth century AD witnessed the rise of empires in India: the Mauryans, the Sangas the Satavahanas, the Kushans and the Guptas. This was also the age of empires in other parts of the world – the Hellenistic and the Roman empire in Europe, the Achaemenid and Sassanian in West Asia, and the Han in China. High floods have been recorded in the Nile indicating a vigorous monsoon in the upper reaches of the river and this suggests a very strong monsoon in India. Kautilya (*Arthaśāshtra* II 24, 116) has given the quantity of rainfall in different parts of the country.

Much of the prosperity of the early historical period was due to India's flourishing and highly profitable trade with the Roman empire which has been well documented. There was a great demand for Indian luxuries in the Roman world and many towns prospered. Roman gold started flowing into India as imports into India from the West were relatively quite small. There was a marked development in craft specialization as is attested by literary evidence which is corroborated by archaeological evidence. Arts and crafts received considerable patronage, and we come across references to guilds of artisans whose economic condition is evident from their donations to Buddhist establishments. Many new settlements came into being during this period and so also urban centres. The fruits of the flowering economy also reached rural areas where a new class of well-to-do *gahapatis* (householders) emerged. They frequently figure in epigraphs as donors to Buddhist shrines, more particularly in Western India. The *Kuḍubins* – the cultivators – appear to be on a lower level and their status was the same as that of the Kunbis today.

VI

The period from sixth to fifth century BC is very well represented in archaeological deposits almost all over the country. There was considerable peace and prosperity for about a thousand years from fifth century BC to fifth century AD which witnessed the rise of strong imperial powers. They ruled with an iron hand and the flourishing trade brought undreamt of prosperity. This was largely due to the favourable environment. But the decline begins with the downfall of the Kushans in the north and the Satavahanas in the Deccan, and the period from *c.* AD 400–1000 is marked by decline and degeneration almost all over the country save in the lower Ganga basin. This further leads to deurbanization for which there is evidence from archaeology and the same is confirmed by the eye-witness accounts of foreign travellers.

The signs of degeneration are visible from the fourth century AD in some parts, particularly in the north-west and western India and the Deccan where settlements were abandoned after the third century AD. Habitation continued albeit on a reduced scale at some sites in the north and eastern India. This period from AD 400–1000 is marked by degeneration in other parts of the Old World also. It witnessed the downfall of early empires and the consequent decline and degeneration for which the Huna invasion, not only in India but in Europe also, was to a great extent responsible. In India, the Golden Age of the Guptas was losing all its glitter, the empire was tottering after Skandagupta (AD 455–67), the highly profitable trade with the Roman empire had become a thing of the past, a new social order was emerging, regionalism was coming to the fore with the rise of petty kingdoms and the consequent internecine conflicts among rival regional powers. The frequent battles between the Pallavas and the Chalukyas and the tripartite struggle between the Palas, the Pratiharas and the Rashtrakutas are well documented. In short it was a period of upheavals and an era of social crisis which is supposed to be the beginning of the Kaliyuga (Sharma 1987).

Archaeological evidence from excavations carried out in different parts of the country indicates that the Kushan levels in the north and the Satavahana levels in the west and the Deccan are well represented, but the post-Kushan and post-Satavahana deposits are conspicuously lacking. In Punjab and Haryana there are a few sites where habitation of the Gupta period is represented, and when present, the decline is evident in cultural equipment. Among those excavated sites mention should be made of Rupar, Sanghol and Sugh which have yielded evidence of Gupta habitation, but the material culture is very poor as compared to that of the Kushan times. As against the few Gupta sites, there are scores of sites where there is no trace of habitation during the fourth to the tenth century AD; many of them were occupied again in the early medieval or Mughal period. More or less the same is the situation in western UP; even as extensive a settlement as Hastinapur has not revealed any evidence of habitation during the Gupta and the post-Gupta times. This hiatus during the fourth to the tenth century AD is hard to explain. Surface exploration of several sites also supplies corroborative evidence. There are, however, a few sites like Mathura, Sonkh, Sravasti, etc., where the habitation continued in the Gupta period, but the evidence suggests they were losing their urban character. This was possibly due to decrease in population. But many of these sites too were deserted after the Gupta period around AD 600. A good example of this is Sravasti, a booming township. When Fa-Hien (AD 393–414) visited it, he found that much of the population had deserted the city; there were only 200 families, and they too were scattered (Legge 1965: 30), and later, when Hieun Tsang (629–42) went there, it was already in ruins. (Watters 1904–5: I,377). Marshall found that Bhita near Allahabad had met the same fate (ARASI 1911–12: 30). This appears puzzling in the light of life size terracotta Ganga-Yamuna statues and other figurines of great beauty from several Gupta sites. Fa-Hien found even Kapilavastu 'desolate and barren with few inhabitants' (Legge 1965: 67), and Hieun Tsang records that not only Kapilavastu but many other towns in its vicinity were in ruins and even the country-side was sparsely occupied. He states that there was no king in the region and the city had become dirty and the pods had dried up and there were vast empty spaces (Watters 1904–5: II, 1).

There are some sites in UP which have provided evidence of habitation during the Gupta period. One among these is Kanauj (ancient Kanuakubia) which was the capital of emperor Harsha. It was in a flourishing state even in the post-Gupta epoch if we accept the testimony of Hieun Tsang. He described its imposing buildings, strong defences, carefully laid out gardens and tanks, etc and its wealthy, prosperous people (Watters 1904–5: I,340). But in sharp contrast to this vivid description, the excavations at Kanauj revealed that there is a great hiatus of about a thousand years between the Kushan habitation and that at the mediaeval times (IAR 1955–56; 19–20). It is highly likely that the occupation during the Gupta and post-Gupta period was located in some other area, for, Hieun Tsang cannot supply us false information.

The Gupta habitation, however, was in a flourishing state in the lower Ganga basin. Nalanda, a great educational centre, which was founded on the munificence of Gupta kings, and was later supported by the Palas, received lavish donations of hundreds of villages and hence the life of the people was not affected. In Bengal too Gupta and post-Gupta epochs are well represented at ancient sites. Sites like Chandraketugarh (Dt. 24 Parganas) and Bangarh (Dt. Dinajpur) were occupied from the Mauryan to the Pala times without any break, and many urban centres flourished in Bengal in the early mediaeval times (Mukherjee 1884–85). In Rajasthan Gupta remains occur only at a few sites and a vast majority of the settlements were deserted after the Kushan period. In Madhya Pradesh, there is a hiatus between the Satavahana and the mediaeval deposits, particularly in its western part which is the Malwa region, but in the eastern part there is some evidence of habitation during the Gupta period. In western India and the Deccan in general most of the sites were abandoned after the third century AD and were reoccupied only in the mediaeval times, In south India, too, there is very poor evidence of habitation from the fourth to the tenth century AD.

Why did this happen? R.S. Sharma (1987) has made an exhaustive study of this state of degeneration which can be referred to as the 'Second deurbanization' (Dhavalikar 1989–90). Among the several factors which have been cited as responsible for this economic decline, cessation of trade over-exploitation of resources and the beginning of feudalism (Sharma 1987) were the most dominent. It may be noted that after the decline of the Roman empire in the fifth century even Europe was passing through troubled times whereas slightly later from the seventh century West Asia witnessed the rise of Islam and the consequent turmoil. It was thus a period of stress and strain everywhere in the Old World from the fourth to the tenth century AD.

It appears that probably the most important cause of this decline and degeneration was the adverse environment. We have some literary evidence to indicate that the period was marked by frequent famines and droughts. Varahamihira had predicted it and Hieun Tsang's testimony corroborates it. Even the *Javanese Chronicles* record that because of the impending famine, a king in Western India sent his son along with an army which included even artisans. They all migrated to Indonesia (Mookerjee 1957: 105). Perhaps the most severe was a prolonged drought lasting for twelve years, of which Dandin has given a heart rending description in his *Daśa-kumāra-charita* which belongs to the eighth century AD. The *Brhan-Nāradīya Purāṇa* (38.87), a contemporary work, states that people will migrate to other areas because of droughts. The *Vāmana Purāṇa* (seventh century), which was compiled in the Kurukshetra region, states that several holy places, having lakes and tanks, were now getting filled up with sand because of severe aridity.

We have already observed that the Nile flood records are immensely useful to us in drawing inferences about the rainfall pattern in India. Fortunately for us these records are available continuously, almost yearly, from AD 622. They show that the flood levels of the Nile were among the lowest during two prolonged phases, once from AD 683–696 and the other from 770–782 (Taussoon 1925). The former may be the period of droughts mentioned in the *Vāmana Purāṇa* and the latter that described in the *Daśa-kumāra-charitam* of Dandin. Incidentally, it may be noted that this was a period of intense cold in Europe, which was so severe that sometimes there was snow in the Nile (Lamb 1977: II, 426–27, f. n-2)

Feudalism has been cited as one of the chief factors responsible for the decline from the Gupta period onwards (Sharma 1987). But it seems that Feudalism was not the cause but the consequence of the degeneration. There was no trade worth the name, neither external nor internal. There was almost total absence of coinage and therefore the state officers were being paid in the form of land grants. Hieun Tsang (Watters 1904–5: I,340) has recorded that this is how Harsha paid the salaries of his officers. Rulers began to make donations to religious establishments (*brahmadeya*) and educational institutes (*agrahāra*) in the form of land grants. Consequently people began to migrate from towns and cities to the interior where the grant lands were situated. Merchants and traders had no occupation in cites and artisans had lost patronage; they applied to the government for permission to purchase land. Thus migrations began on a large scale, which resulted in depopulation and the consequent deurbanization. Several new villages came into being and vast stretches of virgin lands were brought under cultivation, but agrarian production did not increase because of frequent droughts and famines.

In this period of prolonged drought a new goddess came to be worshipped. She was a new form of Durga who is supposed to have assumed the name Sakambhari. There are literary descriptions of the goddess in ancient texts which connect her with vegetative fertility, and probably because of her association with vegetation, she was worshipped to ward off droughts. The *Devi-Bhāgavata* section of the *Mārkaṇḍeya Purāṇa* (91: 43–44), a sixth century text refers to a period of hundred years during which people suffered untold misery because of failure of rain and the goddess Durga had therefore to assume the form of Sakambhari who caused rain to fall and cover the earth with vegetation (Dhavalikar 1987). Hence her name Sakambhari which literally means 'one who covers (the earth) with vegetation'. This goddess is associated with Lakshmi who is sometimes described as 'lotus-headed' (*Padma Purāṇa*: I, 9, 117–32). There are quite a few sculptures answering to this description which depict the goddess with outstretched legs with the pudenda marked prominently; she is headless or lotus-headed. She is connected with fertility and is presently worshipped by barren women for procuring an offspring.

VII

It seems that conditions began to improve from the ninth to tenth century AD onwards, but this again was a period of Muslim invasions and in spite of favourable environment during AD 1000–1400 much progress could not be made. This period is represented at some sites as at Hastinapur. Some improvement is visible for minor dynasties like the Gahadavalas in UP, the Paramaras in MP, the Chalukyas in Gujarat, the Yadavas in the Deccan who issued gold and silver coinage. External trade picked up a little with West Asia and Central Asia, but more importantly with China as is evident from the occurrence of the Celadon ware and the Ming blue-and-white porcelain at several sites (Mohammed 1984–85). The onslaught of Islam forced people into insularity and consequently the caste system got cemented with ideas of commensality and pollution reaching extremes. People became more religious and more resources were expended on temples than on improving the lot of the common man. Some of the loftiest temples like the sun temple at Konarak, and those of Khajuraho belong to this period.

The period from AD 950–1250 has been referred to as the 'minimum optimum' because the climate had improved in Europe. It had become warmer, and we probably had a slightly better rainfall. This inference is strengthened by the evidence of the Nile floods data which shows that between AD 1000–1400 there were hardly some fifty years when the Nile flood levels were low. But again in the temperate lands there is a drastic change in climate and the period from AD 1400–1800 has been labelled as the 'Little Ice Age', India appears to have suffered prolonged phases of droughts which are recorded by eye-witness accounts and are also corroborated by the Nile flood records. One prolonged drought which is still lingering in our memory is that which came to be known as the 'Durga-Devi famine which lasted for twelve years from 1396–1408 continuously. The Nile flood records show that the river levels were very low for the years AD 1393–94, 1399, 1401–3 and 1408. This goes to show that the Nile flood records are reliable to a considerable extent for the reconstruction of our past environment. The recently published *Cambridge Economic History of India.* (Raychaudhury and Habib, 1982) presents a very dismal picture of the economic condition of the people. The accounts of foreign visitors give harrowing details of the sufferings of the people. People were dying of hunger on roadside-children were sold for a pittance, and there were cases of cannibalism (Grove 1997).

For the mediaeval period from the fourteenth to eighteenth centuries, the Nile flood data is corroborated by the evidence of EI Nino which is supposed to be playing the most important role in the pattern of monsoon behaviour. This has been very well established by scientists who have now traced back the history of EI Nino by a few centuries.

BIBLIOGRAPHY

Agravala, V.S., (1963), *Devi Māhātma – The Glorification of the Great Goddess*. Ramnagar, Varanasi, All India Kashiraj Trust.

Agrawala, D.P., (1992), *Man and Environment in India through the Ages*. New Delhi, Books & Books.

Bell, Barbara, (1970), the Oldest Records of the Nile Floods, *Geogr, Jr.* 136, pp. 569–73.

———, (1975), Climate and the History of Egypt - The Middlex Kingdom, *American Jr. of Archaeology* 79, pp. 223–69.

Binford, L.R., (1972), *An Archaeological Perspective*, New York, Seminar Press.

Braudel, Fernand, (1980), *On History*. Chicago, Chicago University Press.

Bryson, R.A., (1989), Modelling the northwest monsoon for the last 40,000 years. *Climate Dynamics*, 39, pp. 169–77.

Bryson, R.A., *et al.*, (1974), Drought and the decline of Mycenae. *Antiquity*, 48, pp. 46–50.

Bryson, R.A. and J.E. Ross, (1977), Climate variations and the global crisis for world food production. *World Development*, 5, pp. 507–18.

Burgess, C., (1989), Volcanoes, Catastrophe and the global crisis of late Second millennium BC. *Current Archaeology* 5, pp. 325–29.

Courty, M.A., (1994), Spatial and temporal dynamics of the late third millennium abrupt climatic change and socio-economic collapse: Problems, evidence, skepticism and more questions. Paper read at *III World Archaeology Congress*, New Delhi.

Currie, G and R.W. Fairbridge, (1995), Periodic 18.6 year and Cyclic II year induced drought and flood in northeast China and some global implications. *Quaternary Science Review* 4, pp. 104–34.

Dhavalikar, M.K., (1984), Toward an ecological model for central and western India. *Jr. of Anthropological Archaeology*, 3, pp. 133–58.

———, (1987), Śākambharī, The headless goddess *ABORI* 68, pp. 281–93.

———, (1989–90), The second deurbanization. *IHR* 16, pp. 211–17.

———, (1994), *Cultural Imperialism: Indus Civilization in Western India*. New Delhi, Books & Books.

Durante, S., (1979), The utilization of *Xancus pyram* (L) at Shahr-i-Sokhta - Further evidence of cultural contacts between India and Iran in the 4th-3rd mill. BC. *South Asian Archaeology* 1975, pp. 27–42, E. J. Brill.

Grove, Richard Leiden (1997), The East India Company, the Australian and the El Nino: colonial scientists and ideas about global climatic change and teleconnections between 1770 and 1930. Paper read at the Seminar on *Ecological History*. New Delhi, unpublished.

Gurdip Singh, (1971), The Indus valley culture as seen in the context of post-glacial ecological studies in northwest India. *Archaeology and physical Anthropology in Oceania* 6, pp. 177–89.

———, *Imperial Gazetteer of India* (1908) *The Indian Empire*. 3 vols. Oxford: The Clarendon Press.

James, P., *et al.* (1991) *Centuries of Darkness*, London, Jonathan Cape.

Jansen, M., (1993), *Mohenjodaro*, Berlin, Bergisch Gladbach.

Khazanov, A.M., (1986), *Nomadism and the Outside World*. Cambridge, Cambridge University Press.

Kosambi, D.D., (1965) *Culture and Civilization of India*, London, Routlage & Kegan Paul.

Lamb, H.H., (1972 & 1977), *Climate – Past Present and Future*. 2 Vols. London, Methuen.

Leeman, W.F., (1960), *Foreign Trade in the Old Babylonian Period*. Leiden, E. J. Brill.

Legge, J., (1965), *A Record of Buddhist Kingdoms* (being an account by the Chinese monk Fa-Hien of his travels in India and Ceylon (AD 399–414) in search of Buddhist Books of Discipline), New York, Dover Publications.

Misra, V.N., (1993), Indus civilization and the Rgvedic Saraswati. *South Asian Archaeology* 2, pp. 511–26. Helsinki, Suomalaiken Tideakatemia.

Mohammad, I.K.A., (1984–85), Glazed ware in India, *Puratattva* 15, pp. 105–10.

Mookerjee, R.K., (1957), *Indian Shipping*, Bombay: Asia.

Mukherjee, B.N., (1984–85), A note on 'Archaeology of Early Mediaeval Towns in Bengal'. *Puratattva* 15, pp. 117–18.

Rajguru, S.N., (1993), Changs in Physical Environment in Western India during the last 2 m. years: A Geo-Chronolocial approach. In *Progs of Int. Group on Global Change*, pp. 599–613. Tokyo.

Raychaudhuri T. and Habib, Irfan, (1982), *Cambridge Economic History of India. Vol. I, c. 1200–1750*, Cambridge, Cambridge University Press.

Sharma, R.S., (1965), *Indian Feudalism: c. 300–1200*, Calcutta, University of Calcutta.

——(1987) *Urban Decay*, Delhi, Munshiram Manoharlal.

Sulman, F.G., (1982), *Short and Long term Changes in Climate*, 2 vols. Boca Raton, F10, CNC Press.

Toussoon, O., (1925), *Memoirs sur Histoire du Nil, in Memoires a L'lustitute D'Egypte*. Cairo, Impremeire de l'Institute Francaise de Archaeologie Orientale.

Walker, Gilbert, (1986), *Long Range Forcasting of Monsoon Rainfall – Collected papers of Sir Gilbert Walker*. New Delhi, Indian Meteorological society.

Watters, T., (1904–5), *On Yuan Chwang's Travels in India*. 2 vols. London, Royal Asiatic society.

TWO

❖ Social Life of the Early Tamils: Random Reflection on the Components

T. K. VENKATASUBRAMANIAN

By the middle of the twentieth century, a sizable corpus of 'social history' has projected the question, 'What is social history?' When 'dynastic history' was popular, it was perhaps enough to define social history as 'history with politics left out'. This is a residual definition, and 'residual social history' is often criticised as 'an invertebrate subject' lacking a framework or structure'; in other words, without a means of linking different pieces of information about social life in the past into a coherent description, narrative or analysis.

'Social cognition' is the cognition of human history in all its diversity. Certain specifics of social life are always distinguishable. This concept of cognition attracted a few scholars. The Neo-Kantians took it for granted that all social sciences are 'ideographic', that is, descriptive. Neo-Kantism includes a number of trends and schools like the Baden school (late 19 / 20 centuries) which concentrated on methodology. According to them specifics are to be identified on certain premises such as 'Men act under the influence of passion, reflection or at worst whim'. Specifics of concrete history in the region reveal much more that is general and recurrent than may appear at first sight.

The relationship between the 'general' (pan-Indian) and the 'Individual' (Tamiḻakam) as applied to History is yet to be unambiguously drawn. In attempting the fixation of norms, many challenges are to be met, since scientific investigation is the expert's domain. 'Social life' is something original, *sui-generis*. There is no logic in treating it as an aspect of a line of evolution.[1] Society, as an object of cognition, differs very substantially. Components of a society are individualistic.

Reconstruction of the social life of the Tamils is a challenging premise, since it is primarily religion-oriented in character.[2] A belief in supernatural agency dominates the vision and affords little scope for accuracy of perception in the mundane activities. Inadequate references to the impact of pan-Indian characteristics on Tamiḻakam hold that such dispersal had started as early as 1000 BC. It is held that the Vindhyas mark the limit of travelling, the regions south of the Vindhyas being described as 'Pari yatra'. Manu, the law-giver, confines Āryavarthā to trans-Vindhyan north. The south is called as 'Yamyā dik' or 'Yamā-Dik' or that which points to the abode of death. 'Dakṣhiṇapatha' seems to be a condemned region, a convict settlement. Aitréya Brāhmana states that Viswamitra condemned his fifty sons to 'live on the borders of Āryavartha' and that 'their descendants are Dasyuṡ like the Āndhras, Pundaras, Sabaras, and Pulindas'! So far as the extreme south is concerned, apart from the reference to 'Çērapada' in Aitréya Brāhmaṇa, the earliest reference known so far is in the Vārtikas of Kātyāyana, the grammarian of the fourth century BC.[4] Pāṇini (sixth century BC) mentions only the Kalingas as the farthest people of the south. Evidently, in Pāṇini's time regions south of Kalinga had been 'hidden areas'.[5] Kātyāyaṇa (sometimes spoken of as a southern Brahmin!) refers to the Çōḷa kingdom. The epics *Ramāyaṇa, Mahabhārata* and later Aśōkan edicts refer to the kingdoms of the south. Will it be logical to guess that by the third or fourth century BC many had migrated to the south? If the premise is granted, the migration should have been sporadic. At present, the Śaṅgam age is the earliest known epoch of Tamil history. Many attempts have been made to 'discover the laws of motion of Śaṅgam society'.[6] The present endeavour is to reassess the components projected and examine the validity of claims already made in this regard. Śaṅgam age is the earliest known epoch of Tamil history.

Historical evolution is normally obscure and elaborately complex. At least part of it could have originated in centuries old theologies. 'The gulf between a grandfather's ghost in a Neolithic village and a modern deity is wide but not absolute.'[7] Knowledge, thought and art are valued in terms of social context. Religion is a group activity though in most cases spearheaded by a messiah. All religions are 'fantastic reflections in men's minds of external forces which control their day-to-day routine, a reflection in which terrestrial forces assume the form of supernatural forces.'[8] That Hinduism, Buddhism and Jainism do reflect terrestrial forces is an axiomatic truth.

Age of the Śaṅgam of Tamil history forms a transitional stage in the evolution of the life of the Tamils from the prehistoric to the historic period. The Śaṅgam anthologies (Pāttu and Tokai) deal with contemporary life and the remnant of the life that had preceded.[9] They are not stratified as the Védas, and consequently attempts at determining the chronological sequence of the evolution of Tamil society (corpus) continues to be elusive. Human thought is not independent of the time-space continuum. Three important trends seem to have shaped the social milieu, namely, Freedom, Limitation and Faith. The Śaṅgam, post-Śaṅgam and Pallava age mark the crystallisation of these trends. 'Freedom' and 'Limitation' overlap, yet the concepts are valid with respect to the social milieu.

Many scholars make us believe that the influence of Hindu tenets preceded those of Jainism and Buddhism in Tamiḻakam, but there seems to be nothing improbable that the reverse order had taken place. Tangible evidence prove that the Jains and Buddhists had reached so far down south as Madurai and Tirunelvéli by the third century BC. Brahmi inscriptions have been found in these places. May be it is by no means easy to decide as to who came first.[11] In this context, it is necessary to remember that after the third century BC there were several waves of migration to the south.

A survey of the cosmographical information provided by Hindu, Jain and Buddhist literature provides the clue to assess the knowledge of the universe by all the three religionists. The Buddha did not encourage speculations on the universe which according to him were nothing but foolish questions.[12] But in course of time Buddhists developed a systematic cosmographical outlook. The most systematic work on Buddhist cosmography is the second treatise on Abidhamma of the Sarvāstivādin school entitled Prajnāpathi sāra, the first section of which is called 'Lōkaprajnāpathi'.[13] 'Vasu-bhandu', in which we find the description of the two worlds (lōkas) – Bhājnalōka and Sattvalōka – is based on this work.[14] The former suggests a 'Receptacle world' (the abode of gods) while the latter 'a world of beings'.[15] Pāli texts make mention of 'Sankhāra lōka' (material world) and 'Okāsalōka' or 'Avakāsalōka' (The Room world).[16] According to Buddhist conception, there are thousands of small universes (lōkadāthūs or çakravāḻas). It appears that the Buddhists originally conceived of a small universe, following the pre-Buddhistic brahmanical notions. With efflux of time the number seems to have increased.[17] In the 'Visuddhimagga' we find three kṣétras (field, domain) of a Buddha: Jana kṣétra (birth domain) consisting of ten thousand worlds, Ājnākṣétra (authority domain) consisting of hundred thousand times ten millions of worlds and 'Jnanakṣétra' (knowledge domain) consisting of infinite number of worlds.[18]

These worlds are grouped into innumerable small universes and in this way a number of great 'Çakravaḻas' are formed.[19] Three great Çakravaḻas' are connected with one another with tangent circles and such groups are separated from one another by a dark region.[20]

Ray Chaudhuri observes, "The description of the Dvīpas in the extant puranas marks them out as things of fairy land comparable to the 'Isles of the blessed' or the 'Spanish Eldorado'. The very conception of the Earth as an aggregate of such concentric islands surrounded by sea is pure mythology".[21] Purānic conceptions of Earth are conflicting, that is, Earth consisting of Four or Seven islands. The conception of the Earth as consisting of four island continents is found in Buddhist literature. These island continents are the abodes of mankind.[22] 'Jambudvīpa' occurs in puranic Buddhist and Jain scriptures. Buddhists call it as Jambuṣandha.[23] It derives the name from the Jambu tree (also called Nāga) which grows there. Jambudvīpa looks like a chariot. The number of cities in Jambudvīpa during Asōka's reign was eighty four thousand and in each one of them he built a monastery. The Buddhas and Çakravartins are born only in this dvīpa.[24]

Jain canons conceive the central continent as Jambudvīpa, which covers fifty per cent of the continental ring. Jambudvīpa is surrounded by some sort of a wall eight yōjanas in height. The purānic conception of 'Jambudvīpas is that it is one of the seven island continents constituting the world. It is the continent in which India is situated.[25] It is also called Sudarśanadvīpa 'low on the south and north and highly elevated in the middle'.[26] The name is derived from Jambu tree, the branches of which are often said to have expanded over a space of hundred yōjanas.[27]

Some references make Jambudvīpa appear like lotus with Mount Méru or its kāṛika (pericarp) and the varṣas entitled Badráśva, Bhāratha, Kétumāla and Uttarākuru as its four petals.[28] Jambudvīpa is circular in shape so that the northern most and southernmost varṣas (Uttarākuru and Bharatha) are each shaped like a bow.[29] Information about Vindhyas or the land south is not to be traced in the early literature of Hinduism Buddhism or Jainism.

S. Vaiyapuri Pillai, the well-known Tamil scholar observed: 'judging from the vocabulary contributed by the religionists, we might conclude that Hinduism (Brahmanism) powerfully held the imagination of the people and was predominant in every walk of life.'[30] Sir John Evans said in his presidential address to the British Association, 'Southern India is probably the cradle of the human race'. Fergusson admits 'They have no tradition which points to any seat of their race outside India or of their having migrated from any country with whose inhabitants they can claim kindred. So far as I know they are indigenous and aboriginal.'[31] The commentary on *sutra* 395 in Śollathikāram of *Tolkāppiyam* informs us that the home of the Tamils was the territory which was bounded by the river Vaigai in the south and the river Mārudam in the north and by Karuvoor on the west and Maruvoor on the east. This is the home of 'sen-Tamil'. Tamil literature describes Tamiḻakam as being situated between Vada Véṅkatam (north) and Tenkumari (south). This is clear from the panegyric verses by Panampāraṉar in *Tolkāppiyam*, verses in Śikandiar and Kākkaipātininyar and a verse in *Śilappathikāram*.[32] Sanskrit literature refers to Tamilnādu (Tamiḻakam) as 'Drāvidadésa'.

Impact of incoming impulses on the indigenous matrix of the Tamil society, the quantum and extent had been favourite themes of researchers on Tamil civilisation and culture. Despite the abundance of findings by researchers – they seem to be variedly represented and interpreted – the entire literature is a bundle of contradiction. Bases are many, yet touchstones used are few and can be listed: (*a*) Sage Agastya as the first migrant to create a school in Tamiḻakam (going as far back as sixth century BC); (*b*) Epic hero Arjuna's visit to Madurai and his marriage with one of the princess there; (*c*) Māmūlanār's (Saṇgam literature) mention of the southern invasion of Mauryans and the advance of the army of Vadugar; (*d*) Mention of Çéra, Çōḷa and Pāṇdyan kingdoms in Aśokan inscriptions; (*e*) The Çēra ruler Imayavarampan's expedition to Himālayas; (*f*) the carving of Pāṇdyan emblem of Fish in the Himālayas. (Nālayira Prabandham (vaishṅavite) 'Paruppataṭtu-kayal poṟitta Pāṇdyan kulapathi pōr)'.

Of the touchstones cited two may be examined *in extenso*: the epic *Rāmāyaṇa* refers to various 'āsramas' (habitats) at Daṇdakāraṇya including that of Agastya. That of Agastya is taken as significant by researchers who contend that he is the earliest Brahmin migrant to settle in the Tamil country. There is no mention of Agastya either in *Tolkāppiyam* or in the preface to it by Panambāranār. The earliest reference to Agastya occurs only about the ninth century AD, and that is also the time when the Pāṇdyan charters begin to proclaim the preceptorship of Agastya to the Pāṇdyas.

Tamil anthologies of the early centuries of the Christian era do not mention Agastya. In Naççinārkiniyar's commentary on *Tolkāppiyam*, there occurs a statement that when Agastya sang, the rocks of Podiyil hills were moved and in consequence they melted". *Puṟanāṇūṟu*, the Saṇgam anthology mentions a festival in honour of Indra, the God of Marutam.[33] In the epic *Śilappathikāram* (Indraviḻavūreduttakātai) we get an elaborate account of Indraviḻa at Puhār. A slightly less glowing but nevertheless vivid picture of the festival is found in the Viḻāvaṛaikkātai of the epic *Maṇimékalai*. Here it is reported that on the advice of Agastya, the Çōḷa king prayed to Indra direct to "grace the festival dedicated to him during the 28 days of celebration. At the same time, epic Maṇimékalai adverts to the prediction of Buddhist monk that the day this annual festival dedicated to Indra is neglected, the city of Puhār would be consumed by the sea. The larger Śinnamanūr plates state that the Indraviḻa was performed by the Pāṇdyan king Nedunchеḻiyan at Madurai.

An elaborate body of legends is found in Tamil purāṇic literature and Agastya is believed to be a resident in the Podiyil hill in the extreme south. Later, he is elevated to the rank of divinity, taken to be Siva in the form of a guru. A critical examination of the legends reveal existence of several Agastyas. The story of Agastya's birth postulates a system of biandry. Urvaśi, the mother of Agastya, is shared by Mitra and Varuṇa. Agastya is frequently associated with the mountains. Bhāgavatha and Matśya Purāṇas describe Agastya as a resident of Mount Malaya, while the Vāyu Purāṇa locates his abode on the Mandara mountain in the Malayadvīpa across the seas. Agastya's residence is sometimes also stated to be Mount Kunjara in Kerala, while Tamil tradition loates it on the Podiyil hill. Agastya is associated with witchraft. Ṛg véda itself connects Agastya with spells and charms. In the Atharvavéda, there are references to the association of Agastya with witchcraft. According to Tamil tradition many works on alchemy and medicine and also tantricism are ascribed to Agastya. Agastya is also spoken of as a hunter and archer. Purāṇas describe 'Agastyas' as 'Rākṣasas'. In the Vāyu Purāṇa Agastya as also Vaiśvāmitras and Pulastyas are listed as subjects of Kubéra. In the Matsya Purāṇa Agastyas are counted as Brahmarākṣasas. Agastya is mentioned as the son of Pulastya who is registered as the progenitor of tribes.

In the present context our concern is with the claim that Agastya spread northern culture into the Tamil region. He is claimed to be a Brahmin. Saṅgam anthologies do testify the fact that Brahmins lived in Tamiḻakam during the epoch.[34] Occurrence of terms like 'Uyarndōr, Mélōr, and Arivōr' in Tamil anthologies have been subjected to microscopic analysis. Iḷampūraṇar, the commentator of *Tolkāppiyam* takes 'Antaṇar and Arasar' as Uyarndōr.[35] But in respect of two rhymes (sūtras) which follow, he takes Uyarndōr to refer to Brahmins and traders. Pérāśiriyar, another commentator defining 'Uyarndōr' states that the term includes Brahmins and other learned persons. Regarding the term 'Melōr', *Tolkappiyam* itself lists Brahmins, traders, ascetics.[36] While Iḷampūraṇar interprets Mélōr as Devas, Nachchinārkkiniyar takes them to be traders. Nachchinārkkiniyar goes on to state that the code prescribed for earning wealth for vaṇikar (trader) holds good for the Antaṇar, Araśar and two kinds of Véḷaḷar. Apparently, 'Arivōr' were the men of learning among Tamils irrespective of the section to which they belonged. It is well-known that during the earliest epoch (Saṅgam) of Tamil history Brahmins occupied a lofty position in society. In that epoch itself, Brahmins began to live in separate streets.[37] Some Brahmins lived by cutting conch shells and they are described as 'Velappārpar' (Ūrpārppar).[38] The commentator of *Patiṟṟuppattu* says that certain Brahmins were skilled artisans, capable of making fine ornaments.[39] The commentator adds that these Brahmins were also well-versed in the art of conducting yagna (sacrifice). Brahmins engaged in various other professions, rather than simply following Védic injunctions, lived in a segregated portion described as 'Puṟanchēri'.[40]

Kapilar a Brahmin poet of the Śaṅgam epoch, admits that he is accustomed to taking meat and liquor.[41] A controversy has appeared over the question. *Perumpāṇāṟṟuppatai* and *Peruṅkātai* provide positive evidence of the vegetarian diet of the Brahmins.[42] The conflicting evidences are sought to be explained by suggesting that Brahmins must have changed over to vegetarianism due to the influence of Jainism and Buddhism! K.K. Pillai writes, 'Though it is difficult to determine the date of the change, it is clear that it must have appeared but gradually. Therefore, it is not inexplicable that during first and second centuries AD, some including Brahmins, continued the old habit, while others changed over to a complete vegetarian diet.'[43]

Such observations which confuse the issue make it appear that Brahmins (identified with northern impulse) spread a 'novel culture.' The word 'Brahman' first meant 'prayer', then ceremonies at sacrifices, and when speculation had made prayer into an ultimate universal principle, those who desired 'Brahman' and tended to identify with Brahman came to be called Brahmins. There are evidences to indicate that similar traditions existed in Tamiḻakam too prior to the so-called protracted advent of Brahmins.[44] The thesis of Winternitz (Aryan), though largely discredited has some validity. The Ṛg véda is 'earlier' but still a good deal of it belongs to a time of later vedic texts. There could have been compositions contemporaneous with or later than the first Ṛg védic compilation.[45] There are many indirect references in Saṅgam anthologies to various divinities and cults. Agastya could as well have been an indigenous Tamilian.

Knowledge, Thought and Art are the three main categories of 'culture'. They are valued in terms of social context. Social identities are relevant to the performance within the concept of particular situations and events. The esoteric dimensions of legends make it an instrument for maintaining stability of behaviour, integrating society and maintaining social cohesion: a collective representation of a unitary social group in its esoteric dimension. A legend originating in a particular social environment is bound to differ according to the innovator's preoccupation and conclusion. Legend is an 'ideological discipline, its methods and aims are determined by and reflect the outlook of the age'.[46] The legend of a certain group may not be the creation of one person, but it certainly has a great identity. A religion-based legend is a reflection in which 'terrestrial forces assume the form of supernatural forces.'[47]

Claude Levi–Strauss ascribed similarity in folk-lore and particularly myth to the sameness of logical structure of human thought. Strauss did not consider what is in a myth (legend) but only 'a system of axioms and postulates defining the best possible code capable of conferring a common significance or unconscious formulations which are the works of minds, societies and civilisations'.[48] Strauss ignores 'structure' of a narrative and looks for the general laws of structure. 'Structuralism' is the system of elements engaged in a particular pattern and their manifestation. Various Agastyan legends available to us do not manifest identical pattern. They differ in construction and objectives, though the subject matter hovers round Agastya.

In the formulation of a legend (myth), belief, religion and ritual are intertwined. It has the goal of representing 'reality' characterised in historical forms.[49] Form and content differ according to the period and genre. Pertaining to Agastyan legends of Tamil literature, two questions arise: (*a*) Do similar historical environs produce identical myths? (*b*) Do myths arise at a certain stage of political advancement of a dynastic rule? If myth is taken as a mediator of contradiction, the contents (structure) must portray the contradictions. Tamil works of the early centuries of the Christian era do not mention Agastya. Ptolemy refers to Bettigo, that is, *Pothikai*, but passes on without an allusion to the sage who is believed to have resided there. *Paripātal*, the Śaṅgam anthology which refers to the sage, is considered a later work by a number of scholars. Reference to 'Potiyil' is made by works like Tirumurukāṟṟuppatai and Maduraikkāṇchi.[50] Wherever anthologies *Puṟanāṇūru* and *Naṟṟiṇai* refer to Potiyil hill, Agastya's name does not appear.[51] Non-mention of Agastya by name suggests that perhaps Agastyan myths (legends) are of later origin. They must have come into circulation sometime after the fourth or fifth century AD.[52] The Tamil language commanded a position of enviable status during that time. Some legends are created to extoll the glory of Tamil. Agastyan legends (myths) come under this category and the object is sought to be realised by importing information provided by Védas and Puranas (Sanskrit). 'Agastyan' tradition gains recognition. The most ancient Tamil anthologies speak mostly of love and warfare. There are ample indirect references to beliefs and superstitions of the people about various divinities and cults. With the formulation of Agastyan legends too much of sentiment gain entry into the problem of interaction of cultures and the legends have not been appreciated in their right perspective by later scholars. The historian is invariably forced to depend on literary evidences (internal) to draw conclusions.

The assessment of the spread of Jain influence into Tamiḻakam too is a distorted proposition. The migration of Jains under Sruta kévali Bhadrabāhu due to a 12-year famine in the north (variously placed in Magadha or Ujjain), predicted by Sruta kévali himself dated third century BC, is on uncertain evidence. Jain traditions regarding the migration are of very later origin. They are found in works datable to the tenth century (Bṛhat katha kōsa), seventeenth century (Munivamśābtyudhaya) and nineteenth century (Rājāvali katha). Epigraphic evidences (substantial) are available from the seventh century onwards (Sravana Belgola inscriptions).[53] Statements in literary records (Jain) are themselves conflicting except on a few points relating to the names of the leader and the cause of migration. At best Jain migration of the third century could be admitted only as a working hypothesis. Indirect evidences of their presence in Tamiḻakam are afforded by early Brahmi inscriptions in the natural caverns of Madurai and Tirunelvéli areas. Jains are not characterised by the same missionary zeal as others. Jain settlers had meagre opportunities to spread 'Northern Culture'. 'Heterodox sects' –

Jainism and Buddhism – are non-Brahmanic in origin to the extent that they questioned the effectiveness of 'sacrificial religions'.

The growing influence of Jainism and Buddhism is reflected in the epics of *Śilappathikāram* and *Manimékalai*. Iḷaṅkō Atikal, a (Chéra prince), the accredited author of *Śilappathikāram* is a Jain.[54] Buddhists too appear to have reached Tamiḷakam in the third century BC. Buddhism had spread to various parts of Tamiḷakam. In the Çéra territory (present Kéraḷa) several Buddhist shrines and establishments have been found. Though Jainism also had found its way into the west coast region particularly southern most region abutting the Pāṇdyan zone, Buddhism had probably found wider acceptance in the Çéra zone of ancient Tamiḷakam. It is notable that some of the Bhagavathi temples in Kerala are Buddhist in origin.[55] Tamiḷakam shrines dedicated to Buddhist goddesses like Maṇimékalai and Śampāpati were transformed into Kāḷi or Durga temples sometime after the seventh century AD.

'Śāttar' were Buddhist monks. They are referred to in Tamil literature. It is likely that they became influential in the fourth century AD. Buddadata, a benefactor of Açyuthavikkānta speaks of Buddhist religious establishments called 'Chaityas' (Paḷḷis, Vihāras). The epic Maṇimékalai refers to a large 'Saivam' (śédium) in Kāvirippūmpattiṇam.[56] Çakravāḷakkōttam was a Buddhist temple near a burial ground.[57] Kuççarakuḍikai is a small Buddhist shrine which is stated to have housed Sāmpapati (deity).[58] Temples of 'Śattan' and 'Pāṣāṇda Śattan' were in the outskirts of Kāvirippūmpattiṇam.[59]

Hemmed in by Buddhist Ceylon on one side and the Deccan (which was Buddhist and Jain from early times till the eleventh century AD) on the other, Tamiḷakam also had to give way to the peaceful penetration of the two religions. They inevitably must have thrown the gauntlet. The necessary stimulus was given by Hinduism. Later events prove that it is the south that began the Hindu revival and gave it the impress of 'Bhakti'.[60] The lacunae on the plane of religion and cults could be explained. Chronological arrangement of the early literature of the Tamils eludes the linguist and the historian. Information provided to make a critical assessment within the framework of chronology of fortunes of religions and cults of early Tamiḷakam is inadequate. In *Tolkāppiyam*, the influence of Brahmanism is traceable but not Buddhism. *Śilappathikāram* and *Maṇimékalai* convey that Buddhism and Jainism were popular. Brahmanism and primitive faiths existed side-by-side in the time of the epics. Buddhism referred to in *Maṇimékalai* is Hināyana.

People of Tamiḷakam with their great attachment to indigenous religious faiths were in the beginning loth to give them up and adopt new ones. No Aśōkan mission visited Tamiḷakam though Tissa of Ceylon claims to have sent a few preachers. There was no Tamil representative in the assembly of *Dattagāmani Abhaya* BC. A number of Tamil invasions of Ceylon hostile to Buddhism are recorded.[61] Except in the two Tamil epics, there are few references to the 'anti-védic religions' in Śaṇgam literature. There is no evidence of royal patronage to 'non-vedic' religions. The cause of dispersal therefore is to be located elsewhere.

Religious history cannot bypass 'social thought' and action. 'Social condition' and 'social needs' are the criteria.[62] Society is subject to objective laws, social science recognises these laws; it can certainly do more than to describe the historical process; it can explain as well. Social thought and action are incentives to the progress of dispersal of religious ideas and ideals. Forms of religious life could not be detached from their social basis. 'Religious history is certainly not a limbo of human errors . . . a spiritual view is sustained not only by insight but also by a rational philosophy and sound social institutions.'[63] A distinguishing feature of Saṅgam polity is that 'it was not priest-dominated though the priests were slowly trying to assume powers of advice and supervision. Social-life seems to be on the heroic scale.'[64] Like all primitive societies the Tamils were accustomed to totems, tutelary trees, *bali* (sacrifice), music, rituals, etc. As days rolled by 'magic' disappeared but rituals continued to have their sway. Rituals came to be linked with divinity.[65]

That serpent cult of the Nāgas had immense diffusion potential is an established axiom. It attracted the Śaṅgam Tamils since it had dynamism to aid the activities of the Tamilian and fulfil his needs. 'Ophiolatry' (serpent worship) is one of the oldest, the most remarkable and widespread forms of religion the world has ever known. A serpent is worshipped not only in an independent individual capacity, but also in association with superhuman gods and godmen. One of the popular beliefs is that Balarāma, the brother of Kṛṣṇa was an 'Amśa of Nāga' (aspect of Snake).[66] R.G. Bhandarkar may be right in holding that Saṅkarshana or Baladéva was originally a god outside the Vaiṣṇava pantheon. J. Gonda thinks that the club and plough point to association with agriculture and with the fertility of the soil.[67] Saṅgam anthologies contain references to Balarāma, thereby illustrating his popularity.[68] The God bearing the plough so closely associated with the Nāgas got himself ingrained in the imagination of the Tamils whose mainstay was an agricultural economy. The Tamil expression 'Yérin vaḷnar' meaning 'Uḻuthu uṇbār' (live by the plough) is expressive of the subsistence on the plough. The patent symbol (Nāga) of Buddhism too could have struck the imagination of the Tamils.

The Nāga symbol combined the King, ancestors and God. Buddhist relic worship has its origin in the Nāga ancestor worship. The Tamilian equated the King with God. The snake cult of the Nāgas must have had a large share in the evolution in Tamiḻakam of other equally ancient and interwoven cults. The Tamil Āḷvārs and Nāyannārs of a later date too made full use of the cult to contend with 'non-védic' religions. Epigraphic evidences bear testimony to the popularity of Vaiṣṇavism in south India.[69] This was the 'Gupta brand of Vaiṣṇavism.' The features of 'Gupta Vaiṣṇavism' are given by H.C. Raychaudhuri as follows: 'Viṣṇu became the supreme deity and Kriṣṇa was merely his next perfect incarnation. In other words Bhāgavatism had now lost itself in Vaiṣṇavism. This is because of the fact of the greater association of Viṣṇu with the great serpent Ādiséṣa who serves as his bed. The Bhāgavata purāṇa informs that the devotees of Viṣṇu will appear in the south, on the banks of Tampraparṇi, Kṛtamāla (Vaikai); the Payaśvini (Pālār); Kāvéri and Mahānadi (Periyār). The Āḻvārs Nammāḻvārs and Madurakavi Āḻvār were born in the Tāmpraparṇi country, Periāḻvār and his adopted daughter Āṇḍaḷ in the Kṛtamāla, Poykaiāḻvār, Būtattu Āḻvār and Tondaradipod Āḻvār, Triuppāṇāḻvār and Tirumaikai Āḻvār in the Kāvéri; and Periāḻvār and Kulaśékara Āḻvār (perumān) in the Mahānada country.'[70] Southern India was the stronghold of Bhakti cult and the distribution of savants significantly coincides with centres of Buddhist activities. Saivite Nāyannārs too highlighted the particular interest of Siva in snakes. The Snake cult, the Buddhist medium of propaganda could not be dispensed with by the Vaiṣṇavites and Saivites.

The earliest inscriptions that we have in the Tamil country are the Brahmi inscriptions of the third century BC.[71] The inscriptions furnish scattered information about rock-cut beds in the Pāṇḍyan zone of ancient Tamiḻakam.[72] The nature of the remains that resemble those of Ceylon and few terms in the inscriptions themselves suggest their Buddhist origin. The inscriptions record the names of those who built monasteries and caves and those who caused them to be made. The Tirupparaṅkunṟam inscription names a husbandsman from Ceylon. At Kaḻugumalai (Tirunelvéli Dt.) an excavation had been undertaken to unearth a stone relic chamber at the instance of the husbandsman (chief) Sri Yaksa. At Arittapatti, Yakṣasithi, daughter of a citizen of Veḻḻodai caused a cave to be cut for the benefit of Bikṣūs. Donors hailed from Véṇādu (Kerala), Ettiyūr (Ettayāpuram), Madirai (Madura), Tittai (Thanjāvūr Dt.) and Podinūr (Coimbatore Dt). Such discoveries give the impression that Buddhist influence had already spread to those places. The image of Buddha found at Tenkarai is only a random sample, and if efforts are made, more probably could be found in the Tiruçcendur taluk of Tirunelvéli district.[73]

'Ethical works' are believed to be post-Śaṅgam works. The post-Śaṅgam age witnessed Kaḷabra inroads.[74] The ruler and ruled belonged to different cultural milieu. The ruled admired the rulers. To water down this fascination, ethical works arose. If the people were really satisfied with the social values of Puṟanāṉūṟu, *Tirukkuṟaḷ* could not have appeared. The age of 'unlimited freedom' wrought havoc, imposed lot of restrictions on the day-to-day life of the people.[75] The 'heretical religions' did yeoman service in converting 'brahmanical religion' into a 'folk-religion' that is 'popular Hinduism' Kāñçi (Kāñçipuram) was the centre of the evangelical activities of Buddhists. It is therefore not surprising to notice prominence of ethical ideas in didactic works. Enlightened self-interest and the larger interest of the society gave them social approval. 'Ethical ideas are praised because of social sanctions or tradition. Or else the people were taught to venerate them because of political, economic and social conditions.'[76]

The *Dhammapada* is the second book of the Khuddakanikāya of the *Suttapitaka*. It contains the sublime teachings of the Buddha.[77] There are many teachings common to both *Dhammapada* and *Tirukkuṟaḷ*. According to *Dhammapada* he who takes refuge in the Buddha is free from all pain.[78] *Tirukkuṟaḷ* also states that those who have attained the feet of the Lord will be free from all troubles.[79] *Tirukkuṟaḷ* says that the Dharma should be practised by one to the best of his ability.[80] *Dhammapada* declares 'one who is the driniker of Dharma lives happily with a serene mind. . . . Do not cease to practise Dharma on all possible occasions to the best of your ability.'[81] In the *Tirukkuṟaḷ* we find the injunction that whatever else you may not control, control your tongue lest you should repent for your indiscreet words.[82] 'A word of evil will lead one to trouble. One should give up all offence of speech and practise virtue with his speech', declared *Dhammapada*.[83] Many more parallels could be cited. Similarities abound so that Buddhists claim that 'Ādi Bhagavan' the expression in the first couplet of *Tirukkuṟaḷ* refers to Buddha. Like other leading religions like Hinduism and Jainism, Buddhism too approximates whole cultures or compresses social ways of life. It is inclined to interpret human history in terms of their particular doctrine and judge social progress according to the realisation of their own ideals. In this respect the views of history are actually conceptions of their own spiritual teleology. Historical and social science studies of Buddhist conceptions explain their origin and development rather than support them. Persual of such literary similarities tempt us to attempt a new interpretation of early Śaṅgam social history and cognition. It is through invasion of philosophical brains and religious hearts into the domain of each other that created fundamental similarities between *kuṟal* and *Dhammapada*. History of religion is one of constant conflict or compromise, the infinitude of the saint and limitation of man. *Tirukkuṟaḷ's* did differ from Śaṅgam way of life. By condemning robbery and prostitution Pālai and Marudam ways of life were at stake. By advocating vegetarianism, Neithal mode of life was placed in a disadvantageous position. By condemning war Mullai mode of life was put in jeopardy.

The role of the 'Vīran' (hero) in *Puṟanāṉūṟu* was usurped by the ascetic, and it is to be noted that Jains call their preceptor 'Mahāvīra.'[84] The author of *Tirukadugam* is a Vaiṣnavite! The author of *Nānmaṇikadigai* accepts Varṇa dharma when he says 'Antaṇar' is the highest birth.[85]

The work equates agriculture with 'Véḷvi' (sacrifice).[86] Of all the ethical works *Āçarakkōvai* regulates ablutions and rituals. According to S. Vaiyapuri

Pillai this work is based on several Sanskrit works.[87] Expressions (Tamil) like 'yāvaraum kaṇda neṟi', 'mikkavar kaṇda neṟi', 'nallaṟivāḷar thuṇivu' and 'péṟaṟivāḷar thuṇivu' suggest the worthiness of the work as a barometer of the social scales towards the close of the post Śaṇgam age. *Āçārakkōvai* affirms the superiority of the Brahmin.

Paripātal, one of the Ettuttokai collection includes twenty-four poems by different authors on various themes. The eleventh poem is on river 'vaiyai' by poet Nallantuvanār, L.D. Swamikkaṇṇu Pillai, the renowned astronomer, on the basis of the astronomical data contained in Paripātal ascribed seventh or eighth century AD to the third Tamil Śaṇgam (Academy). Other scholars pointed out that the details found in *Paripātal* are hardly adequate for the purpose of calculating the dates of events mentioned therein. The term 'mantarāja' figuring in the Allahabad pillar inscription of Samudragupta is equated with Māntaramçéral Irumpoṟai of Śaṅgam anthologies. The identification is based on little more than a verbal similarity between the names of these kings and on a distorted interpretation of the term 'Vamba Mōriyar' to mean 'Neo-Mauryans' or Guptas. Subsequently, N.P. Chakravarti partially dealt with such earlier attempts at fixing chronology.[88]

M.G.S. Narayanan gives a chronological scheme and draws certain conclusions.[89] He attempts 'a reconstruction of the story of contract and conflict between the Mauryan empire and south India based on Śaṅgam testimony.' He claims that 'the findings, if accepted would suggest that Mauryan contacts played an important part in quickening the transformation of a semi-tribal society in Tamiḻakam into a caste-class society of the classical Indian type.'[90] He refers to Nannan ruler of Ezhilmalai and his territory adjacent to 'Çolpeyardéśam (Land with another speech).[91] He contends that Kōśar of Tuḷunadu were the allies of the Mauryans. Citing a reference in the anthology Patiṟṟuppattu (IV. 10) 'Vampa Mauryans (Vampa Moriyar) with Kōśar.

The anthology *Akanāṇūṟu* (349) speaks of the land beyond that ruled by Nannan as the 'region of alien tongue.' The land stretching south from the Konkan along the west-coast (Keraḷa region) was a part and parcel of Tamiḻakam throughout the early part of South Indian History. While all the Śaṅgam-classics as well as *Śilappathikāram* speak of the Arabian sea as the western boundary of Tamiḻakam, the Nannūl composed about twelfth century AD mentions Kuḍakam (Coorg) as its western limit.[92] However from about the Śaṅgam age, the Tamil dialect spoken in Kéraḷa has evolved itself into a variety of Tamil known as Koduntamil as distinct from Śentamiḻ, popular in other areas of Tamilnadu.[93]

References to Kōsar in the anthologies are innumerable.[94] Sometimes they are spoken of as 'Nālūr Kōsar'.[95] Kanakasabhai Pillai identifies them as Kushans.[96] Krishnaswami Ayyangar tries to connect them with Kōsa-kāras of epic *Rāmāyaṇa* and the Khāsas of *Mudrarākshasa* of Viśākadatta and that modern Assam is the ancient kingdom of Kōsa-kāras.[97] P.T. Srinivasa Iyengar suggested that the Kōśar are inhabitants of Tuḷu country[98] V.R. Ramachandra Dikshitar also locates them in the Tuḷu country[99] Literary sources make mention of 'Mutu-kōśar' and 'Iḷamkōśar'. *Śilappathikāram* speaks of the Kōśar of Kongunādu as Iḷamkōśar.

Kōśar have been identified with 'Sātiyaputras' of Asokan edicts. This identification, already a subject of keen controversy is to be given up as erroneous after the discovery of an inscription at Jambai village in South Arcot district Tamilnādu.[100] R. Nagaswami deciphers it as 'Satiyaputa Atiyan Netuman Ançi itta palri'. L.Y.D. Malli Karjuna deciphers it as 'Atiyan Neetuman Ançukō itha Bali' (Satyaputra Atiyar Netumān died in the battle). The utility of the discovery is that it helps to exclude the Kōśar from the title 'Satiyaputra'. The 'sequel' that M.G.S. Narayanan seeks to wave is in jeopardy.

The spread of Buddhism into Tamiḻakam is to be disentangled from the 'Mauryan problem.' The claim that Tamilian society was converted into a class-caste society cannot also be entertained unreservedly. Social organisation of the Śaṅgam epoch was based on occupations which were regional and hereditary. The farmers (Uḻavar) who owned cultivable land enjoyed high social esteem. Shepherds and hunters came next and they occupied pastoral region. Artisans formed the third group and are found all over. 'Pataiaççiyār' (military men) come next to the artisans. Fishermen (Valayar, Paratavar) come last in the order. Significant changes in the social set up occur chronologically later. There had been a fusion of religious beliefs, and social customs. The northern impulses dominated in respect of religious ideas. In the matter of social customs and linguistic development there had been a fusion of the indigenous and incoming impulses. The incoming impulses included Hindu, Buddhist and Jain tenets.

To Karl Marx 'Religion is a phantasmic aspect of social life, an illusory representation of the internal structure of social relations as well as a sphere in which man is alienated; that is where he represents himself in an imaginary way and his behaviour towards this reality is based upon an illusion.'[101]

Religious thought and practice are the products of specific social relations and can openly change with the transformation of the social relations. Marx does not expect religion to disappear as a result of theoretical critique or struggle of ideas. A concrete social relation founded on the abolition of class-exploitation when producers take control of the production process and social organisation is yet to be located. Few Marxists seem to have taken cognizance of this reality about 'Sangam society'.

'Reciprocal dependence' (Tinai's) is too complex to be ascertained. There exists a net work of unintentional casualties between the productive forces and social relations of production, constituting the infrastructure which acts upon all the other levels and aspects of social cognition.

To group conditions of change we need an understanding of its nature and foundations. This paper has tried to provide the fabric of foundation. The study of sociological attitudes to economic development with particular reference to the impact of occupational rigidity could be a subject of objective inquiry, but one may then have to make clear that material values are given prominence and that the spiritual, ethnic or sociological implications are ignored. Such an approach is objective from the purely economic angle but biased from the stand point of a social cognition or spiritual historical approach. 'Objectivity' is a relative term and hence, in this paper 'social condition' and 'social needs' figure prominently.

The texture of the culture of the early Tamils is its composite character – a blending of two distinct 'cultures' into a composite one. The process of fusion must have lasted over a long period of time. Yet, it may be asserted that early Tamils had perfected the 'Art of living together' and cognition of it in all its diversity is a desideratum.

Notes and References

1. Some scholars do so:
   Burton Stein: *Peasant-state and society in Medieval South India* (Oxford University Press, Delhi 1980).
   George W. Spencer: *The Politics of Expansion – The Çōḷa conquest of Sri Lanka and Sri Vijaya.*
   (New era publications, Madras 1983).
2. Dr K.K. Pillay made a gallant attempt Ref: *A social history of the Tamils – Part I* (Madras University Historical series No. 25. University of Madras, 1969).
3. *Aitreya Brahamaṇa*: VII: 18.
4. 'Çerapada' is variously interpreted sayana, the commentator takes 'Çēra' to mean 'Snake'. P.T. Srinivasa Iyengar (*History of the Tamils. p. 29*) thinks that it refers to a royal dynasty and that Çēras had appeared as early as the Age of Āraṃyakas. Also K.G. Sesha Iyer: *Çéra kings of the Śaṅgam period* (Luzac, 1931) p. 132.
5. R.G. Bhandarkar: *Early History of the Dekkan*, (Bombay 1957) pp. 12–13.
6. It was Engels who declared that 'Modern materialism saw history as a process of evolution of humanity, it being its task to discover the laws of motion thereof' *Anti Duhring*, (Moscow, 1969), p. 135.
7. Henry Frankfort, *Kingship and the Gods* (University of Chicago Press, 1948), p. 65–69.
8. Eugen Dāhrung, *Revolution in Science* (International Publishers, Moscow, Gopalitizdat, N.Y. 1961) p. 54.
9. U.V. Swaminatha Iyer made them available (1904).
10. T.V. Kuppuswami, *Śaṇgam chieftains and their times*, (Thanjāvūr) ch. I & II.

11. Jain inscription at Sravaṇa Belgola is customarily quoted to support 'Exodus of Bhadrabāhu' in 3rd century BC.
12. *Digha* I. 215.
Rhys Davids: *Dialogues of Buddha* I. pp. 280.
cf: Milinda (*SBE* XXXVI, 153)
13. Ref: Takasusa in '*Journal of Pāli Tripitaka Society*' (1905) pp. 77, 117, 142.
14. Vasubhandu, *Abidharmakōsa*, III, pp. 1–44, 45–102.
15. Childers, *Dictionary of Pāli language*, p. 453.
16. Anguttara I. 227.
17. Digha Nikāya refers to ten universes (Daśāsa lōka chhatu) Elsewhere in the same text thousand Brahma worlds are mentioned. In Mazzhima and Sanyukta Nikayas, we find reference to 10,000 universes (Dasasahasi Lōkadhāthu).
18. 'Hardy, *Legends and theories of the Buddhists*.
19. The name Çakravāḷa is also applied to a particular mountain range. 'Çakravāḷakköttam' is a Buddhist temple near the burial ground.
Maṇimékalai, VI. 002
Śilappatikāram, IX 20
The earlier shrine was 'Śudukāṭtukkōtram!' Perhaps it was converted into a Buddhist one. From the laboured explanation supposed to have been ordained by goddess Maṇimékalai to Sudamati, this is suggestive (*Mani.* VI cited). Location of the temple is at the outskirts of Kāvérippūm-pattiṇam. (Puhār)
20. Hardy, *Legends and theories of the Buddhists*, p. 110 Beal: *Catena of Buddhist scriptures*. p. 64.
21. *Studies in Indian Antiquities*, p. 68.
22. Hardy, *Legends and Theories of Buddhists*, *op. cit.*, p. 85.
23. Aṅguttara, IV, 90.
24. Malalasekara: Dictionary of Pāli proper names, *op. cit.*
25. Jamubudvīpa is identified with 'Bhāratha varsha' or S.V. Jambudviha, India Proper.
26. Mārkaṇdéya Purāṇam. LIV, 129.
27. *Matsya purāṇam*, CXIV, 65–74.
Brahmāṇda purāṇam XXXVII, 28–34.
Mahābhāratha, V, 13–16.
28. *Brahmāṇda Purāṇam*, XLIV, 35–41
Mārkaṇdéya Purāṇam, LV, 206.
29. *Mahābhāratha*, VI, 6, 38.
Matsya purāṇam, CXIII, 32.
Brahmāṇda purāṇam XXXV, 33.
30. *History of Tamil language and literature*. pp. 42–43 (Beginning to AD 1000) (Madras, 1954)
31. James Fergusson: *Tree and Serpent worship* (London 1868).
32. *Tolkāppiyam*. Pāyiram
Puṟanāṉūṟu: 6, 17
Silappatihkāram, canto VIII; Nūṟkatturai
Kākkaipātiniyār quoted in *Tolkāppiyam*. Cheyaḷ Iyal urai by pérāśinriyar.
33. *Puṟanāṉūṟu*: 241.
Aiṅkuṟunūṟu: 62:1.
34. T.V. Kuppuswami, Brahmin and Brahmanism in the Śaṅgam Age (*Bulletin of the Institute of Traditional Cultue, Madras, 1980)*.

35. *Tolkāppiyam,* Sūtram 27.
36. *Tolkāppiyam*: Sūtram 3.
37. *Kuruntokai*: 277, 272. (streets called 'Aśil Teruvu')
Perumpāṇārruppatai: 30
Śirupāṇārruppatai: 187–88. (The village Āmūr in Ōymānādu is a brahmin village)
38. *Akanāṇūru,* 24: 1–3.
39. *Patirruppattu,* 74: 10–4.
40. *Śilappathikāram,* Puranchiri Iruntha kādai. 38–39.
41. *Puranāṇūru,* 113, 119.
42. *Perumpāṇārrappatai*: 306:10.
43. *A Social history of the Tamils.* Part I. *op. cit.*, p. 294.
44. 'Māmudu Pārpan Maraivaḷi kātta' (*Kurinjippāttu*)
'Poyyum vaḷuvum Tōnriya pinnar Ayyar Yātta Kāraṇam' (*Kurinjippātta*)
Ayyar and pārpān in the context are indigenous
Is véḷvi derived from northern impulse?
'Arumarai nāvin Antaṇakāyānār' (*Sirupāṇārruppatai*)
'Arumarai' could also be taken as indigenous
45. D.R. Bhandarkar, (ed.) *Indian Culture,* vol. III, no. 1 (July 1936. pg. ff)
46. Vladimir propp, Theory and History of Folk-lore (Tr. Aridha V. Martin and Richard P. Martin Manchester University Press, Manchester, 1984)
47. *Ibid.*, p. 214.
48. Claud Levi Strauss, *The naked man* (original French edition L'vionne nu – vol. IV Mythologies, Paris, 1971. Tr. London 1981)
49. Mary Douglas, *The structural study of Myth and Totemism.* As a monograph (ed.) Leach Edmund Michael Banton (Tavistock Publication 1967).
50. Curiously Nachchinārkkiniyar interprets the term 'Mudu kadavul' occurring in Maduraikkānchi to mean Agasthya. This is not sustained. 'Potiyil' in all such references means a 'common place of meeting'.
51. *Puranāṇūru*, 2, 128
Narriṇai, 379.
52. Earliest reference to Agasthya is in ninth century AD. The Pāṇdyas (charters) claim that Agasthya is their perceptor.
53. Spread of ascetic Jainism is claimed to be earlier to Buddhism in Tamilnādu. Rock-cut beds of Jain asctics in Tamiḷakam are pointed as proofs (S. Viyapuri pillai, *History of Tamil language and literature, op. cit.*). Apparently Jainism had reached the less habitable hill-tracts of Tamilakam. Chittoor and North Arcot districts of Tamilnādu contain vestiges. (Veḷḷimalai, Ārpakkam, Tirumalai etc.)
Also Lewis Rice, *Mysore and Coorg from the inscriptions* p. 467.
V. Smith, *Early history of India* (4th edn.) p. 154, 458.
54. The view of S. Vaiyapur Pillai regarding the date of Silappathikāram (fifth century AD) has not gained acceptance of most historians. (ref. *History of Tamil-language and literature, op. cit.*, pp. 139–55). Also K.K. Pillay, *A social history of the Tamils –* Part I, *op. cit.*, pp. 145–50.
55. Chitarāl near Kuḷitturai, ThirçcCānāthumalai, etc. V. Nagama Aiya, The Travancore State Manual, vol. II, pp. 224–26.
56. *Manimékalai*: XXVIII:131. The description indicates that it was a well-constructed building. It is also called 'Sédyam' (Maṇimékalai XXVIII: 175)

57. *Maṇimēkalai*, VI, 002
    Śilappatikāram, IX: 20
58. *Maṇimēkalai,* XVII: 145. Also known as 'Muḍivālkkōttam'. Sampapati was a tutelar deity of the Buddhists.
    Probably the name 'Kuchcharakudikar' indicates a small thatched structure.
59. *Silappatikāram,* IX, 15: 23. It is said that 'Pāṣāndasāsta' belongs to the category of defined Buddha
60. cf: Freedom enjoyed by women in Buddhistic age to give charity, become nuns and the privilege of donating to the shrines (e.g., Chāmār in Amarāvati)
61. Karikāl Çōḷa is said top have brought back Buddha's bowl and other relics from Ceylon 'displaying great enmity to the religion of the enlightened one.'
62. Engels *Anti-Durhing* (Moscow, 1969), *op. cit.*, p. 35.
63. R. Radhakrishnan, *Eastern religions and western-thought* (Oxford University Press, Oxford, 1940), p. 76.
64. N. Subrahmanian, *Śaṅgam polity* (Ennes publications, Madurai, 1980) p. 291.
65. This led Burton Stein to speak of 'Ritual Sovereignty', Ref: *Peasant state and society*, *op. cit.*
66. Mahābhāratha, Anuśāsana Parvan, XIII 132, 8–11 (Poona Edn)
67. Quoted by Sudhakar Chattopadhyāya (*Evolution of Hindu sects*). (Munshiram Manōharlal, New Delhi, 1970), pp. 44–46.
68. Ibid.
69. Rithpur Copper-plates.
    Prabhāvathi Gupta Chemmak Inscription of Pravarasēna II.
70. A.C. Ray Chaudhuri, Materials for the study of the early history of the Vaishṇava sect. (2nd edn. Calcutta. 1936) p. 172 ff.
    Chronology of Āḷvārs is a moot question. Most of them could have lived after the period of Saṅkarāchārya. A concise account of the reformers is given by Farquhar. (outline of the Religious literature of India. pp. 187–88. Also James Fergusson, Tree and Serpent worship, London. 1868)
71. K.V. Subramania Iyer deciphered them – paper. Proceedings of the Oriental Congress 1924. p. 275.
72. M.A.R. 1913–14. p. 6; 1915, p. 86.
    M.E.R. 1907, p. 60; 1910, pp. 76–80; 1912, p. 57 etc.
73. M.A.R. 1916–17. p.
    Indian Antiquary, vol. IV, p. 272.
74. Despite controversies the consensus of opinion is in favour of 'Kalabra interregnum'.
75. A. Velu Pillai, *Tamiḷ Ilakkiyattil kālamum and karuthum* (Tamil Pari putthaka paṇṇai, Madras, II, edn. 1978) pp. 39–40.
76. A. Velu Pillai, *Tamil Ilakkiyattil kālamum karutthum* (Tamil Pari Putthaka paṇṇai, Madras, II. edn. 1978) *op. cit.*, p. 49.
77. B.C. Law, *History of Pāli literature* vol. I. pp. 215–22.
78. *Dh. Pada*, VV 190, 192.
79. *Thirukkuṟaḷ:* VV. 4, 7, 10.
80. *Ibid.*, V. 33.
81. *Dh. Pada*, V. 79. cf. Milinda: p. 345.
82. *Tirukkuṟaḷ* VV. pp. 127–28.
83. *Dh. Pada:* V. 232.

84. A. Velu Pillai, *Tamiḻ Ilakkiyattil kālamum and karuthum* (Tamil pari putthaka paṇṇai, Madras, II, edn. 1978), *op. cit.*, p. 60.
85. *Nānmaṇikadtigai*, 32.
86. *Ibid.*, 51.
87. This work is said to be Tamil rendering of the Sanskrit 'Śagarasmṛthi' Ref.: A Velupillai, *Tamiḻ Ilakkiyattil kālamum and karuṭhum* (Tamil Pari putthaka paṇṇai, Madras, 2nd edn. 1978), *op. cit.*, p. 63.
88. N.P. Chakravarti, Presidential address, 17th session of the Indian History congress, Ahmedabad 1954.
89. 'The Mauryan problem in the Śaṅgam-age' (*Foundations of South Indian Society and Culture*. Bharatiya Book Corporation, Delhi, 1994), pp. 69–79.
90. *Ibid.*, p. 69.
91. *Ibid.*, p. 73.
92. Kuṇakadal Kumari Kuḍakam, Vérikatam eru Nānkrllriyirirunda Tamiḻ kaal (Nannūl-Śirappuppāyiram)
93. After a time Śentamiḻ acquired certain local peculiarities to become koduntamiḻ (cf.: expressions like viḷikkunnu, karaiyunnu in Malayāḷam)
94. Kuṟuntokai 15, 73; Akanāṇūṟu, 15, 90, 113, 196, 205, 216, 261–62; Maduraikkāñci, 508, 519, 772–73.
95. Kuṟuntokai, 15–3.
96. The Tamils 1800 years ago, p. 51
97. *Beginnings of South-Indian History*, p. 94.
98. History of the Tamils, p. 521. This inference is based on categorical assumption in Akanāṇūru 15.
99. *Indian Culture*. 'The Kōsar – their place in South Indian History', p. 493.
100. T.V. Kuppuswami, *Śaṅgam chieftains and their times* (Thanjavur 1984) ch. V.
100. Karl Marx, *Capital*, vol. I, (New York. 1973) pp. 15304; 372–73.

THREE ❖ Kāñchi Through the Ages

V. BALAMBAL

KĀÑCHIPURAM, THE CAPITAL OF Pallavas, a powerful dynasty in South India, was a very great and flourishing city noted for learning, art, architecture, political power and trade. It had its own political, social and cultural significance. It is considered as one of the seven sacred cities in India, others being Ayōdhyā, Avanti, Dvārakā, Kāsi, Mathurā and Māyā. It was believed that death in any of these cities would give *mōksha* to an individual. It is interesting to note that among these, Kāñchi is the only city in South India, while all the other six are in North India. Though all are religious centres, Avanti, Kāsi, and Māyā are sacred to Siva, while Ayōdhyā, Dvārakā and Mathurā are the abodes of Vishṇu. But Kāñchi alone is scared not only to Siva and Vishṇu but also to Shakthi (Kāmākshi), Shaṇmukha (Muruga), Buddha and Jīṇa. It is one of the eighteen *Shakthi pīṭas* in India. Apart from being a Hindu religious centre, Kāñchi has been a centre of Jainism and Buddhism. Great seers of various religions like Sankara, Buddhaghosha, Dharmapāla, Āḻvārs and Nāyaṉnārs were associated with the Kāñchi. As all religious centres promote education and learning, Kāñchi was also a great centre of learning. Being the capital of the great Pallavas, Kāñchi had witnessed many political activities. It had attracted tourists, pilgrims and traders from various parts of the world as it promoted different religious philosophies, culture, art, architecture, learning and trade. In spite of political and social changes, Kāñchi retains its significance as a great religious centre for Saivites, Vaishnavites, Jains and Buddhists. Kāñchi was a part of the ancient political unit known as Toṇḍaimaṇḍalam,[1] the principal land of the Pallavas. *Perumpāṇāṟṟuppaḍai*, a Saṅgam work, makes the earliest reference to Kāñchi as Kaççi.[2] It is also known as Kāñchinagar and Kāñchimānagar in *Maṇimēkalai*.[3] Appar, Sundarar, Āḻvārs in *Nālāyirapra-bhandam* and *Nandikkalambakam* refer to Kāñchi in various ways. It is believed that Kāñchi got this name because Brahma worshipped Siva here (Ka = Brahma; anci = Worship). *Ka* also means bliss and Kāñchi means the place where one gets supreme bliss. Kāñchi is the name of a tree and it is believed that there was a forest of such trees there and hence the name Kāñchi. Kāñchi in

Sanskrit means girdle and because of its cultural value it was believed that the city was like a girdle to the earth.

Because of its religious sanctity, Kāñchi was known in very many terms. *i.e.*, Praḷayasindhu, Sivapuram, Vindhupuram, Mummūrtivāsam, Brahmapuram, Kāmapīṭam, Kāmeḳḳōṭṭa, Tapōmayam, Sakalasuddhi, Kannikappu, Tūndirapuram, Daṇḍakapuram and Satyavratakshetra.

The Buddhist pilgrim Hiuen-Tsang mentions in his *Siyaki* about Kāñchi. He says that Talopitu (Tondaimandalam) had been frequently visited by Buddha and near Kanchihpu-lo (Kāñchi) were traces of a sitting place and exercise walk of the four past Buddhas.[4] He also states that during Asoka's period, not far to the east of Kanchihpu-lo, was an old saṅgharama (monastery) of which the vestibule and court were then covered with wild shrubs, built by Mahendra, the younger brother of Asokaraja.[5]

The earliest Pallava record issued from Kāñchipuram is the Mayidavolu copper plates of Sivaskandavarnan.[6] Allahabad pillar inscription of Samudra Gupta mentions about Vishnugopa of Kāñchi.[7]

There are various inscriptional and literary sources which give a clear picture of Kāñchi as a centre of various religions. Parts of it were also known as *Siva Kāñchi*, *Vishṇu Kāñchi*, and *Jīṇa Kāñchi*. Based on primary sources, it is interesting to study Kāñchi as a religious centre in ancient India with reference to Saivism, Vaishnavism, Jainism and Buddhism and how in spite of differences Kāñchi proved to be an integrated whole.

Saivism: Though not known as Saivism, the worship of Siva dates back to the Sangam age in South India, and Harappa culture in the north. The Eight Anthologies and Ten Idylls mention Siva in the form of Mukkaṭselvaṉ, Ālamarselvaṉ, Talsaḍaipolinda Aruntavatōn, Karaimiḍaṟṟu Aṇṇal, Jalādari, etc. *Maṇimēkalai* mentions some Saivite festivals such as *Kārthigaiviḷakku*, *Taiviḻā*, *Indiraviḻā*, *Ādiraiviḻā*, etc. Worship of Liṅga was also known to the ancient Tamils. Siva was worshipped in the form of Dakshiṇāmūrthi, perhaps the earliest form of Siva.[8] The earliest work on *Saivasiddhanta* is *Tirumandiram* by Tirumūlar. He is said to have visited the Ēkāmbarēsvara at Kāñchi. *Tirurmandiram* beautifully narrates the six branches of Saivism, *i.e.*, Pāsupatam, Mahāvartam, Kāpālikam, Vāmaṉ, Bhairavam and Saivism.

There are some references to Saivism in Kāñchi in the pre-Pallavan era. Paranadevanayanar, the author of *Sivaperumanandadi* refers to the Saiva shrine Ēkāmbaram, identified with the Ēkāmbaranātha temple of Kāñchi. *Kshētraveṇbā*, written by Aiyaḍigal Kāḍavarkōṉ, a Pallava ruler and a great Saiva and one of the sixty-three Nāyaṇṇārs who refers to the Ēkāmbaranātha temple as one of the twenty-two shrines visited by the Saint Appar, refers to Saiva mathas at Kāñchi.[9] A hymn on *Tiruḳkachchiyakambam*[10] by Sambandar and Tiruvālaṅgāḍu copper plates of Rāśēndrachōḷa I[11] associate Karikālachōḷa as the conqueror and renovator of Kāñchi with gold.

During the reign of the Pallava rulers, Kāñchi became a popular and powerful city. Some Pallava rulers bore names like Sivaskandavarmaṉ, Skandasishya, Nandivarmaṉ, etc. to show their affinity to Saivism. They had bull as their royal emblem and flag. Mahēndravarmaṉ I, one of the powerful rulers of the Pallava dynasty, followed Jainism and ill-treated the Saivites. But Appar, one of the sixty-three Nāyaṇnārs, realised the greatness of Saivism after his being converted to Saivism from Jainism and appealed to the Mahēndravarmaṉ I, and succeeded in converting the Pallava ruler to Saivism. This was a great turning point in the history of Saivism in South India. After his conversion, Mahēndravarmaṉ I showed a keen interest in curbing Jainism in his kingdom while helping with the propagation of Saivism. He built many temples and donated for the proper upkeep of the temples and spread of Saivism. Appar, with his patronage, spread the Bhakti cult all over the Tamil country. Mahēndravarmaṉ I built a *maṇḍapa* in the Ēkāmbaranātha temple.[12] Appar sang about a *Mēṟṟaḷi* temple in the weavers' quarters in Kāñchi. Mahēndravarmaṉ I built cave temples for Brahma, Vishṇu and Siva at Mandagapattu. Ēkāmbaranātha, Kailāsanatha, Kāmākshi, and Muktīsvara temples of Kāñchi have many lithic records which describe the religious attitude of the Pallava rulers. Mahēndravarman I's son Narasimhavarman I was a great devotee of Siva. He contributed to the maintenance of the temples in various parts of his empire. Paramēsvaravarmaṉ I, the grandson of Narasimhavarman I, was compared with Siva in the Kāsakuḍi copper plates of Nandivarmaṉ II.[13] The Kūram plates of Paramēsvaravarmaṉ I[14] refer the king's interest in temple construction and allotment of land for burning titles for the same. The first verse of the Kūram plates is the earliest epigraphical reference to the Sadasiva aspect of Siva in South India giving in considerable details his iconographic features. Paramēsvaravarmaṉ I was also described as Paramamahēsvara and Paramabrahmaṇya. The Kailāsanātha temple inscription compares him and his son Rānasimha to Siva and Gulia respectively.[15]

His period was one of Hindu revival. The temple at Kūram was known as Vidyāvinitapallavēśvara griham and there was a *maṇḍapa* to recite *Mahābhārata*. Lands were donated for the upkeep and repair of the temple and provision for daily worship. Narasimhavarmaṉ II, also known as Rājasimha, was a great Siva devotee and temple builder. He was a great conqueror and administrator. He sought the help of pious Vajrabōdhi to relieve Kāñchi of a severe drought. The latter's sincere prayers brought rains in Kāñchi. Hiuen Tsang refers to him as the preceptor of the ruler[16] of Kāñchi. The Kāsakuḍi plates of Nandivarmaṉ II state that Rājasimha bestowed his wealth on temples and brahmanas, and devoutly caused the goddess of Earth to be enjoyed by those families well versed in four vedas.[16a] The Vālūrpālayam copper plates of Nandivarmaṉ III describe Rājasimaha as a builder of a stone abode in Kāñchi for the moon crested Siva which was comparable with the mount Kailāsa. His queen Raṅgapatāka constructed a small shrine in the Rājasimhēsvaram also known as Kailāsanātha temple.[17] His son Mahendra III built the Mahēndresvara (Siva) shrine in front of Rājasimhēsvara shrine.[18] During the reign of Nandivarmaṉ III (846–69), the Muktīsvara temple at Kāñchi was known as Dharmamahādēviśvaram, perhaps after the queen of Nandivarmaṉ.[19]

Rājasimhā's (690–729) titles Sivachūḍāmaṇi, Saṅkarabhakta, Rahabhalañchaṇa, Īsāṇasarana, Dēvadēvabhakta, Īsvarabhakta, etc. are self explanatory of his devotion to Siva. Along with Kailāsanātha temple, he built Airāvatēśvara and Mātaṅgīśvara temples in Kāñchi.

In *Pūsalārpurāṇam*, Sēkkiḻar, the author of *Periyapurāṇam* says that Lord Siva gave preference to the temple built by Pūsalār in his heart than to the stone temple built by the Kāḍava (Pallava King) who has been identified with Rājasimha, the builder of Kailāsanātha temple. The Kailāsanātha temple inscription talks about the heavenly voice heard by the King praising the devotion of Pūsalār.

Rājasimha is said to have subdued a Kalabhra chief Kūṟṟuva who later turned to be a great Saiva devotee (Kuruvanayanar).

Rajasimha's shore temples, Panamalei temple and other temples stand testimony to his devotion to Siva and his patronage of Vaishnavism.

The Tiruchirāpaḷḷi inscription of Rajasimha[20] testifies to the practice of *Ḳrtva Sivam Sirasi* (carrying on one's head the figure of Siva) as the Pallava ruler assumed the titles Chandradhasēkara Sihāmani, Dīptamauḷi, Sivachūḍāmaṇi, Mahēsvara Sihāmi, etc.

Sōmaskanda panel became popular during the Pallava period. *Avaṇisundarikathāsāya* states that Rajasimha's queen worshipped Guha in the cave temple and saw the wall painting of Guha along with his parents Siva and Parvathi and as a result of her devout prayers, a son was born to her.[21] Sōmaskanda panels are seen in the Siva temples in Kāñchi.

Being a great devotee, he installed his portrait sculptures in Kāñchi temple and Mallai. A few sculptures in small shrines surrounding the sanctum sanctorum in the Kailāsanātha temple seem to be the portrait figures of Rajasimha and Raṅgapatāka.

Inside the Kailāsanātha temple there are fifty-eight miniature shrines in the compound wall encircling the sanctum and the *maṇḍapa* in front. Siva is seen in several forms in softstone. Though a Saivite, Rājasimha showed his religious toleration in many ways. The shore temple at Māmallapuram is a complex of three shrines, of which the largest one facing the sea is Kshatriyasimhēswara and the smaller shrine facing the shore is called Rajasimhēswara; the third without a superstructure contains a rock cut image of Anantasayi (*Pallikondaruliyatēvar*). There are monolithics like five Pāṇḍavarathas, the

Ganēsaratha, Valayankuttai and Pidariratha. There are cave temples like Varāha cave, Ādivarāha cave, Trimūrthi cave, Mahishāsuramardiṇi cave and Dharmarāji Maṇḍapa and a few bar reliefs like Arjuna's penance.

Sri Saṅkarāchārya, the founder of Advaita Siddhanta, was closely associated with Kāñchipuram. There is lot of controversy regarding his date but his contribution to Saivism is not doubted. He is said to have established *saṇmatha* (six creeds) – Saiva, Vaishnava, Gānapatya, Kaumara, Saura and Sākta, which were getting systematised during the period. Saṅkarāchārya ascended the *Sarvajnapītam* at Kāñchi and worshipped till last the Yōgaliṅga and Kāmākshi.[22] A life size stone image of Saṅkarāchārya is kept very close to the sanctum in the Kāmākshi temple.

The stone images of an ascetic with a staff (*Ēkadaṇḍa Saṇyāsi*) found in Kachchāpēsvara, Ēkāmbaranātha, Irāvatēśvara temples and Kumarakkōṭṭam in Kāñchi are identified with the figure of Adisaṅkara himself.

Mūkakavi, the twentieth āchārya of Kāñchi matha, born dumb, got the power of speech on reciting *panchasati*, in praise of Kāmākshi.[23]

Sundaramurthi, one of the sixty-three Nāyaṇnārs, is said to have lost his eyesight for breaking his promise to his wife. He later regained the sight partially at Kāñchi by his sincere prayers to Lord Siva.[24] Sundra has also sung to Siva in Kāñchi.

Following the Pallavas, the Chōḷas also had shown keen interest in religious activities and they patronised Saivism in a very special way. They built Siva temples all over their empire and donated enormously for the maintenance of the same. As they conquered the Tondaimandalam, Kāñchi also became a part of the Chōḷa region.

Āditya Chōḷa I and his successors rebuilt in stone the old brick structures. The simple structure of the temple was changed into a big one with many *maṇḍapas, prakāras* and *parivāradēvatas*. Parānkaka I (AD 907–955), Pārthivēndra, a feudatory of the Chōḷas and Uthamachōḷa had contributed to Kailāsanātha, Ēkambaranātha, Phanimanisvara, Sokkanāthēśvara temples at Kāñchi. It is not known why the early Chōḷas had not donated anything to Muktīśvara, Kachchisvara and Kāmākshi temples. It may be due to constant warfare between the Chōḷas and Rāshtrakuṭas as Toṇḍaimaṇḍalam became the bone of contention.

Rajaraja I, also known as Sivapātasēkhara, was an ardent Siva devotee. Not only in Chōḷa but also in all the conquered regions, including Srilanka, Rajaraja I showed his interest in patronising Saivism. After a long break, he donated nine hundred sheep for ten perpetual lamps to be burnt in his name in the Kachchesvara temple at Kāñchi. It is interesting to note that he utilized the spoils of war for this purpose. Gold was also donated for the same purpose to the temple of Aiñjājandi Durgaiyar.[26] An inscription from Kāmākshi temple refers to the land donation in the name of the king to the temple. Not only the royal persons, but also the commoners made land, gold and sheep donations to the Durgai temple in Kāñchi during the reign of Rājēndra I.

Another interesting contribution of Rājēndra Chōḻa I to Saivism was that he brought Saiva Brahmanas from the banks of the Ganges to his empire and settled them in Kāñchipuram.[27] They played an important role in spreading Saivism in the region of the Chōḻas. Sitēśvara temple, which was not popular earlier, received good attention from Rājadhirāja I (AD 1018–54) who gave tax free lands for its maintenance.[28] He also contributed land for the maintenance of other temples in Kāñchi.

Toṇḍaimaṇḍalam, especially Kāñchi, received more attention from the Chōḻa and Chāḷukya rulers, as there were constant interactions in these regions.

Their epigraphs, seen in large numbers in Kāñchi temples, record various donations made for different purposes, one of them being thirty-two cows and one bull for instituting perpetual twilight lamps in the respective temples. When the Chōḻa empire started disintegrating, many chieftains like the Sambuvarāyas, Gaṅgās, Chēdirāyas and dancing girls and weavers also made independent donations to the temples.

Kulōttuṅga I (AD 1070–1122) contributed liberally to Sitēśvara, Kachchisvara, Kārnīśvara and Anēkataṅgapādam temples in Kāñchi.[29] His successors Vikramachōḻa, Kulōtuṅga II, Rājarāja II, Rājādhirāja II, Kulōthuṅga III were great devotees of Siva and made donations for various purposes. Kulōthuṅga II showed special attention to Ēkāmbarēśvara temple.

Rājādhirāja II and Kulōttuṅga III were responsible for the construction and maintenance of Tiruvīrattānēśvara temple. As Rājarāja III was unable to control his feudatories, the Vaidumpas, Gaṅgas, and Telugu chiefs became independent and donated independently to many temples in Kāñchi. Many inscriptions of these chieftains are seen in these temples. Later, a Sivāchārya by name Kachchiyappa, authored *Kandapurāṇam* in Tamil and served in Kumarakkōṭṭam in Kāñchi. He is said to have released *Kandapurāṇam* in the thousand pillared *maṇḍapa* of Ēkāmbarēśvara temple.

When the Pāṇḍyas and Kākatīyas succeeded the Chōḻas in the Toṇḍaimaṇḍalam region, they also made liberal donations to Kāmākshi and other temples.

During the reigns of Māṟavarmaṉ Kulasēkhara (1268–1310) and Māṟavarmaṉ Parākrama Pandya (1335–52) cows were donated to the Kāmākshi temple[30] and during that of Jatāvarmaṉ Sundara Pāṇḍya II (1276–90) two *vēli* of land to Ēkāmbaranātha temple.[31] During the reign of Kākatīya ruler Ganapathi (1199–1262) donations were made for daily offerings in the Ēkāmbarēśvara temple.

During the reign of Vijayagaṇḍagōpāladēva (1250–85), a powerful Telugu chief, many epigraphs were issued in his name. Siva temples in Kāñchi were patronised not only by the members of his family but by the commoners too. Donations were made in the form of cows, land, sheep, gold, etc. Villages were given as dēvadāṉa[32] for various services in the Kāmākshi temple; cows for supply of ghee to lamps by the members of the royal family in the Mahākāḷiśvara temple.[33] Devotees made offerings for various purposes during Gaṇḍagōpāla's period. For conducting morning offerings, and maintaining a watershed, and payment to sculptors in the form of money and paddy in the Kachchisvara temple, donations were made by private individuals.[33a]

It is interesting to note that Vidyatirtha (1296–1384), who was responsible for the foundation of the Vijayanagar empire and who was the preceptor of Harihara and Bukka, lived in Kāñchi for seventy-three years.[34]

Ēkāmbaranātharula in praise of the chief deity was composed by the twin poets known as *Iraṭṭaipulavarkaḷ* in the fourteenth century. They were under the patronage of the Veṉṟumankoṇḍaṉ (1321–39), as Samburaya chieftain.

It is learnt from an inscription that the Rājasimhēśvara shrine which was closed from the time of Kulōttuṅga was reopened by the minister of Kampana II, worship resumed and the properties belonging to the temple were restored.[33] Kumara Kampana showed keen interest in temple administration too.

He appointed an official to supervise all the Siva temples[36] and Kāmākshi temple. Kāmākshi temple received the attention of Harihara II who covered its Srivimana with copper.[37]

For the daily services of Sri Kāmākshi, a village was donated around AD 1408.[38] An inscription of Devaraya II in Kāmākshi temple clearly indicates the steps taken by the king to safeguard the temple properties.[39]

The establishment of Alala Sundara matha near Ēkāmbarēśvara temple and land donations for its maintenance by an individual also shows the religious attitude of the time in Kāñchi.[40] During the reign of Mallikārjuṉa (146–65), two villages were gifted for the performance of mahāpūja and lighting of lamp in the Ēkāmbarēśvara and Kāmākshi temples and the sixteen pillared *maṇḍapa* was donated and the king's daughter Trayambakādēvi constructed a shrine for Trayambakēśvara.[41] As Durga worship also became popular, land was offered for the mahāpūja and necessary offerings to be made in the Kāmākshi temple.[42] In the fifteenth century, lands were given as *vēdavrtti* and for offering to Sri Kāmākshi.

During Krishṇadēvarāya's period, donations of Kunnathur village to Ēkāmbarēśvara temple[43] and Aruvrthi Ilavantangel and Nallur to Kāmākshi temple were made by the king. As most of the Vijayanagar kings were Vaishnavites their contribution to Siva temples was comparatively less. Achyutaraya's (1529–42) inscriptions are found in large number in Kāñchi. He performed *tulabharaṁahadana* and gave eight villages to the Kāmākshi temple. As the auspicious married women (*sumangalis*) were well respected during the period, part of the offerings made by the ruler was distributed among them.[45] The king settled the disputes in the distribution of lands between the Ēkāmbarēśvara temple and Aruḷāḷaperumal temple in a smooth manner.[46]

He also donated the village Aruṅguṉṟam to the Kāmākshi temple for various offerings. He offered a land and house site to the great poet, Srinivasayajvan after adjudication by a sabha, for the composition of *Sivabhaktavilāsa*, the story of sixty-three Nāyaṉnārs, *Ēkāmbarēśvarastava*, a devotional poem on Ēkāmbarēśvara, and two other works.

Even during Sadāsivarāya's period, many donations were made by his officials for various purposes to Kāmākshi and Ēkāmbarēśvara temples. During Srīraṅgarāya's reign, the Kāmakōtipītha was built and fine stones were used to beautify the temple.[47]

Thus from the very early times, Kāñchipuram seems to have been a great Saiva centre. Many Saivamathas such as Gōlakimatha and Īsāṉadēvarmatha[48] found their places in Kāñchi. Great teachers, scholars, and students also flourished in the city. All Siva temples and the Kāmākshi temple received innumerable endowments for various purposes relating to temple activities. Among the four indigenous religions, Saivism received more patronage in Kāñchi.

Vaishnavism

A part of Kāñchipuram was known as Vishṇukāñchi. It covers the region adjacent to Srīvaradarājaperumāḷ and up to the place where temple car is kept. Yathōktakāri and Aṣṭabhujam temples are also found in this area. Though it was Vishṇukāñchi, it is interesting to note that Sivakāñchi accommodated many Vishṇu temples like Vaikuṇḍaperumāḷ, Ūragam, Pāḍagam, Ulagaḷandaperumāḷ, Nīlatiṅgaḷtuṇḍam, etc. It is not clearly known when the demarcation had taken place. There were disputes between the Saivites and Vaishnavites of Kāñchi but Krishnadevaraya met the representatives of Ēkāmbarēśvara and Varadarāja temples and settled them in AD 1516. The routes to be taken by the respective temple chariots were decided by the king.[49]

The earliest reference to Kāñchi is found in *Perumpanarruppadai*, a Sangam work. Uruttiraṅkaṉṉaṉār, the author of the work, praised his patron Tiraiyaṉ, the ruler of Kāñchi. The literature makes a reference to the shrine Vēhka where the God is seen sleeping on the serpent couch, like an elephant resting on a hill.[50] Tiraiyaṉ was described as a descendant of Vishṇu and he resembled the colour of the sea.[51] These references clearly show that the Tamils worshipped Vishṇu in the Sangam age itself. Vishṇu was referred to as Māyōn, Māl, Neḍiyan in Sangam literature. His abode was known as

Nīlamaṇineḍiyōṉkōyil. Some Pallava rulers bore the names of Vishṇu (Vishnugōpa, Kumāravishnu, Simhavishnu, Narasimha, etc.). Vaishnavism as a different sect was gaining momentum during the Pallava period and the Āḻvārs and Nāyaṉnārs contributed to the same. The early three Āḻvārs had contacts with Kāñchi. Poygaialvar, the first of the Āḻvārs, was born in Kāñchi. He and Peyāḻvār make references to the Tiruvēhka temples in their hymns.[52] Tirumaṅgai Āḻvār and Tirumaḻisai Āḻvār had good contacts with Kāñchipuram and were antagonistic towards Saivism, Buddhism and Jainism. Tirumaṅgai Āḻvār had sung at six of the Vishṇu temples at Kāñchi. Nammāḻvār and Nathamuni had also sung at Kāñchi Vishṇu temples.

Because of the patronage of the Pallavas and Chōḻas, Saivism flourished in Kāñchi and Vaishnavism had only a secondary place. Of course alongwith the Siva temples, the Vishṇu temples also got donations for various purposes. Vaikuntaperumāl temple received high attention from the time of Nandivarmaṉ II. Later Dantivarmaṉ (AD 796–846) gave 10000 *Kalañju* of gold to the temple.[53]

Rājasimha Pallava, though a staunch Saivite, was very tolerant towards Vaishnavism and assumed the titles Paramabhagavata, Paramamahēsvara and Paramabrahamanya to show his devotion to Trimūrtis. The Udayēndiram copper plates of Nandivarmaṉ I mention that Simhavishnu, the father of Mahendravarman I, was a devout Vaishnava.[54]

Nandivarmaṉ II Pallavamalla was a devotee of Vishṇu. Vaikuṇṭaperumāl temple of Kāñchi received his attention and he gave many endowments for various purposes. The sculptures on the walls of the raised verandas running round the central shrine of the temple depict the whole history of the Pallavas from their mythical progenitor Brahma upto the time of the construction of the temple by Pallavamalla.[55]

It is also interesting to note that no inscription of the Pallavas could be found in the Vishṇu temples at Kāñchi prior to the reign of Hiraṇyavarmaṉ. It may denote that Vaikuṇṭaperumāl temple was perhaps the first structural temple of the Pallavas of the collateral branch at Kāñchi.[56] Dantivarmaṉ (796–846) donated ten thousand *Kaḻanju* of gold to the Vaikuṇṭaperumāl[57] temple. Even the Aruḷāḷaperumāḷ temple, which is one of the ancient Vishṇu temples in Kāñchi does not contain any inscription of the Pallavas and early Chōḻas.

Tirumaṅgai Āḻvār sang ten verses on Paramēśvare Viṇṇagaram (Vaikuṇṭaperumāl temple), but of the fourteen Vishṇu temples sung at by the Āḻvārs, six were sung at by this Āḻvār.

Ulagalanda perumal temple was the second most ancient temple in Kāñchi.[57a] Sri Vardarājaswāmy temple at Vishṇukāñchi was sung at by Bhudattāḻvār, one of the earliest Āḻvārs. The god was known as Attiyuran after Attiyur, also known as Hastigiri. It became popular because of Rāmānuja

Tirukachchinambi and Kūrathāḻvār. Rāmānuja ranked Hastigiri as one of the four important places for the Srivaishnavites to meditate. Vedantadesika Manavala Mahamuni popularised Srivaradaraja.

Tirukachchinambi, a great Vaishnavite, used to walk to Kāñchi every day from Pūndamalli bringing flowers to Srivaradaraja. For his devotion and service to the Lord, he was conferred the title *dasyamana pēraruḷāḷadāsa* (Servant of Pēraruḷāḷa). It is believed that Sri Varadaraja chose Tirukachchinambi as his medium to convey to Ramanuja, the six famous tenets of Visishtadvaita. Rāmānuja brought Periyanambi of Sriraṅgam to his house in Kāñchi and learnt Tamil *Prabhandams* from him. Later Rāmānuja (1017–1137) renounced family life and became an ascetic and had Kandādi Mudali Āṇḍān and Kūrattāḻvār as his disciples. Yādavaprakāsa also accepted Rāmānuja's philosophy and became a Vaishnavite.

Guruparamarai talks about the plucking of the eyes of Kūrattāḻvār by the Chōḻa king and Rāmānuja asking the former to compose poems in praise of Lord Varadaraja. Kūrattāḻvār succeeded in composing *Varadarājastvam.*

Ramanuja converted many to Vaishnavism. He introduced in this temple various ritualistic practices followed in Sriraṅgam temple. For the services rendered by Rāmānuja, he was deified in the Varadarāja temple and two villages were donated to meet the expenses for the offerings.[57b] Provisions were made for the exposition of *Rāmānujabhāṣya.*

Kōyilōlugu, which gives details about the Srīraṅgam temple says that Alavandar, the pontiff of Srirangam temple, sent Āḻvār Tiruvaraṅgaperumāḷ Arayar to Kāñchi to bring Rāmānuja to Śrīraṅgam which he fulfilled by his musical talents. He obtained the divine permission of Lord Varadarāja by singing in praise of the Lord.[58] Periyanambi, another disciple of Ālavandar sent to Kāñchi for the same purpose, composed *śtōtraratṇa* in praise of the Lord Rāmānuja accompanied Periyanambi to Śriraṅgam and succeeded Āḷavandar as the pontiff of Srirangam temple.[59] Rāmānuja had contributed for the spread of Vaishnavism and Varadarājaperumāḷ temple proved to be the great nerve centre in this regard.

The Chōḻas were great Saivites but were very tolerant towards the other religionists. Vaishnavism was also patronised by them. Parāntka I made a lot of endowments to the Yathōktakāri temple. It is surprising to note that not even a single grant of Rājarāja I was registered in any of the Vishṇu temples in Kāñchi. But his son's records are found in two of the Vishṇu temples. The Asthtabhujaperumal temple was gifted with 3600 *kuḻi* of land as *devadāna* during the reign of Rājendra I (1012–44) for offerings and lighting a perpetual lamp by the people of Kāñchi.[60]

Rajendra I's records state about his grant of 127 *kaḻanju* of gold and a tax-free grant of 1000 *kuḻi* of land to the temple by some individuals.[61] During the reign of his son Rājādhirāja I, certain Nuḷambamahādēviyār donated an ear ornament and sheep for ghee to Lord Varadarāja.

Most of the records of Kulōttuṅga I are found in the Ashṭabhujaperumal, Pāṇḍavaperumal, Aruḷāḷaperumāḷ, Ulagaḷandaperumāḷ and Vikuṇṭaperumāḷ temples. Perhaps he and his queens were great devotees of Vishṇu. For the kitchen expenses of the Asṭabhuja temple, the *Mahāsabha* of the Rājasundari Chaturvēdimaṅgalam donated lands.[62] Kulōttuṅga I granted the village Kampādēvinallur as a tax free grant at the request of his queen for the celebration of festivals in the Ulagaḷandaperumāḷ. The king is said to have visited the temple with his two queens. The weavers donated some lands to the temple.[64] There are references to the grant of lands for feeding the Vaishnava Brahmanas of the Vishṇu temples in Kāñchi. Aruḷāḷaperumāḷ temple was extended with a kitchen, *maṇḍapa*, *prakara* walls and garden by his commander Naralōkavira.[66] He also set up an image of the Lord and donated lamps and the gold pinnacle for the new shrine.

Vikramachola (118–36) made donations only to Aruḷāḷaperumāḷ temple in Kāñchi. During his time the Lord of the temple was known as Vikramasola Viṇṇagarperumāḷ.[67] The Chōḻas used such nomenclatures to show their close identity with the Lord. To have a 13 day celebrations on the day of the natal star (Jyeshṭa) of Bhūtattalvar and Poygaialvar, paddy was donated by an individual.[68] An officer of Kulōttuṅga II (1133–1150) made endowments to maintain a *maṭha* and feed the Srivaishnavas who came to witness the Vaigasi and Masi festivals.[69]

Sheep, cows and land were donated during the Chōḻa period for perpetual lamps, maintenance of *matha* and garden. Pāṇḍavaperumāḷ, Ulagalandaperumāl and Aruḷaḷaperumāḷ temples were well patronised by Rājādhirāja II.[70]

Kulōttuṅga III's (1178–1216) records are found in Aruḷāḷapermāḷ and Yathōktakāri temples. Sambavarayas, Chedirayas, Yadavaraya, Telugu Chōḷas and Gangas and the chieftains of the king donated to the Aruḷāḷaperumāḷ temple. Cattle for milk to the god,[71] land for daily worship,[72] villages for daily worship and services and for brahmanas,[73] lamp and construction of Amantāḷvār shrine with stone,[74] were their endowments. The most interesting feature of Kulōttuṅga's endowments was the one made to the two hundred *talippendir* known as *tribhuvaṉavīraṉ patiyilār* in the form of the houses and land for performing their duty to the god of the temple.[75] This reminds of Rājarāja's contribution to Tañjāvūr Rājarājēśvaram in appointing 400 *taḷippeṇḍir* and endowing a house and land to each one of them for their services to the god of the temple. A powerful Telugu Chōḷa chief Gaṇḍagōpāla instituted *gaṇḍagōpālaṉ sandi* in the Aruḷāḷaperumāḷ temple during Rājarāja III's turn.[76] Many records state that fourteen villages were donated for the maintenance of their services.

The Telugu Chōḷa chieftain's great devotion to Aruḷāḷaperumāḷ is known from the fact that this service was conducted in no other Vishṇu temple in

Kāñchi. Not only the Chieftain but his queen, officials, servants, etc. also figure as donors. He called himself as the servant at the feet of Aruḷāḷaperumāḷ (Sri Arulalapadalan Chhamasya) and respected the devotees of Vishṇu as his parents and gurus.[77]

Srivaishnavas in the Aruḷāḷaperumāḷ temple *matha* were fed, and *bashyavritti* was expounded during the reign of certain Kōnērimeikoṇḍāṉ. Vīragaṇḍagōpāla I, Vijayagaṇḍagōpala, and Viragaṇḍagōpāla II were great devotees of Arulalaperumāḷ. Not only these rulers but commoners also donated tax free lands for various services, maintaining flower gardens, supply of garlands, etc. to this god.

Prakāra walls known as *gaṇḍagōpālan madil* were constructed and land was also given for a flower garden.[78]

During the reign of Jatāvarmaṉ Sundarapāṇḍya I, a tax free village was granted for offerings to the image of Tiruvalialvar in Arulala temple. Certain Rājanārāyaṇa Sambuvarāya (1339–63), put in order the route to be followed in taking the image of Aruḷāḷaperumāḷ during the festivals.[79] For *Vēdavritti* land was granted to a learned teacher.[80] Land was donated for rearing flower garden and supplying garlands to the Lord during Sundara Pandya's time (AD 1251).[81]

When the Hoysalas came to power, the Vishṇu temples of Kāñchi received their attention from the thirteenth century. Even the officials and commoners made endowments.

For reciting *Tiruvaymoḻi* (Vaishnavite hymns) in the Aruḷāḷaperumāḷ temple, land was donated to fifty-eight Brahmanas and provisions were made for lighting lamps and supply of garlands to the same god around AD 1242.[82] During the reign of Ballala III (1291–1342), Kāñchi turned to be a great centre of Teṉkalai Vaishnavism because of the presence of Varadāchārya, Appiḷḷar and Vēdāntadēsika. The king honoured the āchāryas with titles and endowments. Vijayanagar rulers were great Vaishnavites. Kampaṇa was respected by his people as incarnation of Vishṇu in *Madurāvijayam*. Later, during the time of Jiyar Aḻagiyamaṇavāḷar (1420–68) there was great progress in Vaishnavism in Kāñchi.[83]

Tulāpurushadāṇa was made by Tirumala I (AD 1472) at Kāñchi and some other places. Virupāksha, a great commander of Saḷuva Narasimha (1486–91), reconsecrated the images of Peraruḷāḷar, Perundēviyār and Nāchchiyār in the Aruḷāḷaperumāḷ temple and for various offerings he specified the lands allotted to the *Rāmānujakūtamatha*.[84]

Krishṇadēvarāya (1509–29) was a Vaishnavite and his southern military operations had their impact on Kāñchi too. His love and regard for his parents was reflected in the form of a golden *Vimāṇa* to the Aruḷāḷa temple.[85] Following the king, his officials and subjects also endowed lands for various purposes such as supply of sacred thread, champaka flowers, camphor, lime fruit, and for other offerings and feeding of brahmanas. Krishṇadēvarāya donated a village to *Vyāsa Tīrtha*, the pontiff, who in turn gifted the same for conducting festivals in the name of the king in the Aruḷāḷa temple and serpent vehicle to be used for the fourth day of all the festivals of the temple.[86] As the king respected the Vishṇu devotees, he honoured Veṅkaṭa Tātāchārya to receive the first holy water (*tirtha*) and *prasada* in all the Vishṇu temples in his empire including Kāñchi, and to have the judicial powers to deal with the cases of the followers of Rāmānuja. During his period, the Yathōktakāri temple received good attention. Nearer to the temple, a tank was dug, a village was founded, and a *maṇḍapa* and watershed were constructed.[87] A more interesting statement from *Amukatamalyoda* of the king is that Kāñchi was an important centre of pilgrimage.[88] Pilgrims from various parts of the country came in palanquins, on horses or on foot to this holy city. Achyutarāya followed the footsteps of his predecessors in patronising Vaishnavism, Aruḷālaperumāḷ temple was granted more lands and for making festival offerings. The Jiyars were well respected.

Rāmānujakuṭa *matha* was well taken care of. A big donation of seventeen villages and thousand cows was made to the Aruḷāḷaperumāḷ temple by the king on his coronation day. He made pearl *tulābhāra* along with his queen and son, and distributed the same among the brahmanas.[89] It is interesting to note the religious toleration of Achyutarāya, who equally distributed the villages to Ēkāmbaranātha temple and Varadarāja temple. During his reign, a *matha* was dedicated to Tirukachchinambi, and gold was donated for the maintenance of the *matha* and the offerings to be made.[91] Provision was made for the singing of *Tiruppallāṇḍu*, the hymns of Periyāḻvār in the Aruḷāḷaperumāḷ temple.[92] For the celebration of *Sri Jayanthi* festival, money was donated to the temple.[93]

During Sadāsivarāya's (1542–76) reign, Aḻagiyamaṇavāḷa Jīyar strengthened the influence of Vaishnavism in Kāñchi. Even the smaller shrines of Toṇḍaraḍipodi Āḻvār, Aḻagiyasiṅgar Tiruppāṇāḻvār received offerings from the lands allotted to them.[94] This Jiyar donated four villages to the Aruḷāḷaperumāḷ temple and built *prakāras* and *maṇḍapās* in the Dīpaprakāsa temple.[95] Various food offerings, services, celebrations and festivals related to the temple are known from many epigraphs.

The Yathōktakāri, Aruḷāḷaperumāḷ and Aḷgiyasiṅgaperumāḷ temples attracted the attention of King Śrīraṅga I (1572–85). Separate officials were appointed to look into the construction work in these temples. During his time many endowments were made to the Vishṇu temples at Kāñchi for various purposes. Tātāchārya family enjoyed high respect and privileges during this period and the family members contributed a lot to the Vishṇu temples in Kāñchi. During the reign of Veṅkaṭa II (1586–87), lands were donated for the floating and summer festivals in the Yathōktakāri temple.[96]

Appaiyadīkshita, a great scholar of this time, was a great Siva devotee but he wrote *Varadarajastava* in praise of Varadarājaperumāḷ. Thus Kāñchi continued to be a great centre of Vaishnavism all through the ages, in spite of religious differences.

JAINISM

A part of Kāñchi was known as Jīṉakāñchi as that was a great Jaina centre. Digambaras of Mysore included Jīṇa Kāñchi as one of the four seats of learning. There are references in later literary works to the religious activities of Visākhachārya, the disciple of Bhadrabāhu, a great Jaiṉa monk of third century in the Tamil region. Brahmi inscriptions in Tamilnadu belonging to early centuries refer to the abodes of the Jain monks. Drāviḍasangha or Mūla saṅgha was founded by Kundakundāchārya in the first century AD. Sāmantabhadra of Digambara school of the second century was referred to as the naked ascetic of Kāñchi in the *Kathākōsa* or Prabhāchandra and Nēmidatta.[97] His religious activities were centred round Kāñchi. When there was a debate between the Buddhists and Jains, Akalāṅka, a Jain philosopher from Belgola, belonging to the third century, won over the Buddhists.[98] Many Jains migrated to Toṇḍaimaṇḍalam and other parts of South India. He wrote a commentary of Samantabhadra's *Āptamīmāmsa*. It is interesting to note that the Jain monks were great exponents of Tamil. They had authored some of the eighteen minor works. They were great grammarians too. Ilango Adigal, the author of *Silappadikāram,* was a Jain. *Maṇimēkalai* states that Kāñchi was a great centre of Jaina philosophy.

The Kaḷabhras who ruled the Tamil country for three centuries after the Saṅgam age were Jains. Though there is no specific reference to Kāñchi during their rule, Tamil country which included Kāñchi was under their control. The Pallavas, who established their rule in Toṇḍaimaṇḍalam by overthrowing the Kaḷabhras, had Kāñchi as their capital. Though most of the rulers were Saivites and a few Vaishnavites generally, they showed their tolerance to other religions. The Paḷḷaṇkōvil copper plates[99] refer to the royal grant of a village, by Pallava Simhavarman to Vajranandi, a Jain monk, for the worship of Jainēndras and Munindras at the holy place of Vardhamanēsvara dharmatirtha. It was known as Paruttikkuṇru or Tirupanuttikkuṉṟam or Jīṇakāñchi.

Pallava Simhavishṇu's mother followed Jainism and she built a temple for Arhat for the benefit of her husband's family. Even the Hasakote plates state that Mahendra I's grandmother was a Jain. During the early Pallava period two Jain temples were built. At the request of two Jaina teachers, the kings built two temples. Mahēndravarmaṉ I, son and successor of Simhavishnu was a staunch Jain and ill-treated the Hindus. Similarly, his contemporary Tirunavukkarasar, also known as Appar, followed Jainism and was later reconverted to Saivism by his sister Tilakavathi.

Before conversion, Appar lived in the midst of Digambaras in Monastery. He was known as Dharmasēṉa and become the head of the monastery too. Appar was able to convince and influence Mahēndravarmaṉ I who reconverted himself to Saivism and became a great devotee of Siva. Forgetting his earlier stand, Mahēndravarmaṉ I ill-treated the Jains of Kāñchi, who lost the royal patronage. Appar also denounced the Jains in his *Devaram* hymns. Sekkilar's *Periyapurāṉam* also says about the destruction of the monastery at Pataliputra (Cuddalore) and construction of a Siva temple at Tiruvadigai with the same materials.[100]

Another reason for the decline of Jainism was the Bhakti movement and the role of Nāyaṉnārs and Āḻvārs. Jains and Buddhists were strongly opposed by the Saivites and Vaishnavites. The hymns of Āḻvārs and Nāyaṉnārs clearly show the conflict between them and the Jains and how the latter had to face the antagonism of the former. In spite of these onslaughts Jainism continued to have its place unlike Buddhism in and around Kāñchi. Even the Chinese pilgrim Hiuen-Tsang states that there were many Jains in Kāñchi and it continued to be a popular religion.[101] Pallava Rājasimha built a temple for Chandraprabha Tirtaṅkara at Tirupparuttikuṉṟam.[102] An inscription of Rājasimha in the Kāmākshi temple tells us about a land given to a Jain temple. It also refers to the fact that his queen Lōkamādēvi was affected by a brhamarākshasa.[103] Perhaps the donation was made to get a relief for the queen. The Chōḻas and Vijayanagara rulers extended the temple complex, added sculptures, Vimanas, and beautified the temple with the paintings.[104] The lives of Dharmanātha, Nēminātha and other Thirtankaras were painted. Even though the Chōlas and Vijayanagar rulers were staunch Saivites and Vaishnavites respectively, because of their tolerant attitudes Jainism retained its place in the South, especially in Kāñchipuram. *Iṟaiyili paḻḻichandam* (tax free temple grants) were made to Jain temples during the period, even by the Sabhas and individuals.

The Trailōkyanātha or Vardhamana temple at Tirupparuttikuṉṟam contains the records of the later Chōḻas. The forty-sixth regnal year record of Kulōttuṅga I records the purchase of land by a certain monk, Rishimudāyattar, for digging a channel.[105]

Tirupparuttikuṉṟam was a *paḻḻichandam*.[106] Kanippakkam was revived as Pallichandam to the god Sempoṟkuṉṟāḻvār in Tirupparuttikuṉṟam.[107] Endowment was also made for food offerings during the early morning service (*tiruppaḻḻieluchi*) to the god and the construction of a *maṇḍapa*.[108]

During the Hoysāla period, a certain Achchambike, the Jaina wife of Chandramauli, the Hindu minister of Ballala II and a great devotee of Vishṇu donated liberally to many Jaina bastis.[109] Kōpperuñjinga II is said to have constructed the compound wall of Trailōkyanātha temple at Jīṉakāñchi.[110]

The Vijayanagar rulers were also tolerant towards Jainism. During the reign of Bukka II, Mahendramaṅgalam was given as *Paḻḻichandam* to Trailokyavallabhar for offerings, maintaining an alms house, repairs of the *maṇḍapa* and for the construction of a *maṇḍapa* for conducting concerts in Jīnavardhan temple by his minister Irugappa, a staunch Jain. He had great respect for his Guru Pushpasena who instructed him to make the above grants.[111]

Similarly, during the rule of Krishṇadēvarāya, land transactions in relation to the Trailōkyanātha temple were made for regular offerings to the god. A Jaina village was transferred to an *agrahara* and another village replaced the transferred village.[112] Though not in detail, there are some references to preceptors like Vāmanāchārya, Mallishēṉamāmuni and Pushpasēṉa in some records of the Vijayanagar rulers.

Hence it is very clear that though Kāñchi witnessed different religious tides, Jainism continued to have the patronage of the rulers and people sometimes on a bigger and sometimes on a smaller scale.

BUDDHISM

Buddhism, a religion of India, was followed in the Tamil country even in the pre-Christian era. But the earliest reference where Kāñchi is associated with Buddhism is found in *Maṇimēkalai*, one of the five Tamil epics.[113] The heroine of the epic, Maṇimēkalai, was accommodated by Ilankilli in the south western corner of Kāñchi in a grove known as Dharmadavana.

When the people of Kāñchi suffered due to hunger, Maṇimēkalai fed them with the help of *Amudhasurabhi*. Ilankilli provided her a Vihāra for her and charty for enshrining the footprints of the Buddha. He also built a big monastery at Kāñchi. Staying in Kāñchi, Maṇimēkalai, the daughter of Mādhavi, learnt various tenets of Buddhism from Aravana Adigal who converted her to the ascetic order. He died in Kāñchi. During that period Buddhism was popular in all parts of Tamilnadu and Kāñchi was a great centre of all religions and learning. It is believed that people of Kaveripumpattinam migrated to Kāñchi when the city was engulfed by sea.[114]

As Kāñchi was a great centre of learning, without any conflict all religions benefitted and contributed to it. A certain Aryadeva (AD second–third century), who was considered by Hiuen-Tsang as one of the four suns which illuminated the world, spent his last years in Kāñchi. He authored Chatuhsataka and succeeded Nagarjuna at the Nalanda University. Later in the sixth century, Chandrakirti, a disciple of Dharmapala wrote a commentary on Aryadeva's masterpiece.

Buddhadatta, another monk and scholar of the fifth century, makes a mention of important places in Tamilnadu where Buddhism flourished. In that, along with Uriayur, Buddhamangalam, and Kāveripūmpaṭṭiṇam, Kāñchi also finds a place. Achchuta Vikkanata, the Kalabhra ruler, patronised Buddhadatta. The Buddhist scholars of his time stayed in various monasteries in the above mentioned places. Buddhadatta wrote *Viṇayaviṇīchchaya, Uttaravīnīchchaya, Jīnālaṅkara,* a commentery on Buddhavamsa *Abhidammavatāra, Buddhavamsattagatha,* etc.

During the Kaḷabhra period, there was good contact between the Buddhists and Srilanka. Buddhadatta, Buddhaghosha and others visited many Buddhist Viharas in Srilanka. Buddhaghosa also visited Kāñchi which was a centre of Pāli Buddhism.[115]

Itsing states that a certain Bodhi Dharma, a prince of Kāñchi went to China around AD 520 and converted emperor Wu-Ti of the Lyang dynasty to Buddhism. Dyāṇamārga was introduced by him in Buddhism which came to be known as 'Chan' by Chinese and 'Zenshu' by the Japanese.

Dinnaga (AD sixth century), originally a staunch Vedic Brahmin, belonged to a village near Kāñchi. He became a Hinayanist and later changed to Mahayanism. He was a great scholar and author. His works were included in the curriculum of the Nalanda University which around AD 671 was rated by Itsing as equal to the educational centres at Kāñchi, Taxila, Ujjain and Vikramasila.

Dharmapala, who became the head of the Nalanda University, is said to have hailed from this place. Some of the Burmese sources also confirm his association with Kāñchi and specify that Kāñchi was a great Hinayana centre promoting Pali Buddhism.

Kāñchi played a prominent role in spreading Buddhism and Buddhist art in South East Asia.

Another Buddhist, who was a native of Kāñchi, was Vajrabodhi (661–730). His father was a teacher of the King of Kāñchi. He travelled to Nalanda, Kapilavastu, Srilanka and China. He was also responsible for propagating the faith in China.

Siddha Nagarjuna (AD seventh century) born at Kahōra, a part of Kāñchi, was originally a Brahmana; he became a great exponent of Buddhism and had his higher religious education at Nalanda. He was one of the eighty-four siddhas. He is said to have got the blessing of the goddess Tārā at Kāñchi.

Even today scholars believe that the present Kāmākshi temple was a Buddhist temple for Tārā Devi, and due to Bhakti movement and decline of Buddhism, Tārā Devi, was replaced by Kāmākshi. There are references to Sri Sankarāchārya who had to face some opposition of the Buddhists in Kāñchi.[116] During the reign of the Pallavas and Chōḷas, unlike Jainism, there was a steady decline of Buddhism in the Tamil country; so also in Kāñchi. Sambandar and other saints and Vaishnavite seers had confrontations with Jains and

Buddhists and succeeded in overpowering them. Even though Buddhism was on the decline, Kāñchi housed innumerable statues of the Buddha.

Hiuen-Tsang visited Kāñchi in the AD seventh century and for twelve years he was in India visiting places connected with the Buddha. He talks in his *Siyuki* about the presence of other religions in India and how Buddhism continued to have its place in Kāñchi. He was in Kāñchi around AD 639 and he had the opportunity of meeting three hundred Buddhist monks from Srilanka due to political upheaval in their country. It is believed that in the seventh century, there were innumerable Buddhist monasteries in Kāñchi. When excavations were conducted, Kāñchi proved to have been a great Buddhist centre. In the Ēkāmbaranātha temple, many statues of Buddha were found. Hiuen-Tsang refers to the visit of the Buddha of Kāñchi where he convinced and converted the local people to his faith, and how Asōka, the Mauryan emperor, erected stupas at various spots where Buddha had preached and taken many people into his fold. He also states that to the east of Kāñchi, there was an old monastery built by Mahēndra, the younger brother of Asōka.[117]

Another monastery, south of Kanchipu-lo (Kanchipuram), was big enough to accommodate eminent men. There were more than a hundred monasteries with 10,000 monks belonging to *Sthavira* school. Most of the Buddhist temples belonged to the Digambaras. Panna's *Gandhavamsa* (seventeenth century) specifies that Kāñchi was one of the three main centres of Pāli Buddhism, the other two being Avnati and Arimaddana.[118]

Being an orthodox Buddhist, Hiuen-Tsang does not mention anything about the Pallavas or Chalukyas, the mighty rulers of the time. But his mention of Kāñchi was mainly because of his Buddhist interest. He very authentically states that Dharmapala of Nalanda university was born in Kāñchi.[119] Kanchi-pu-lo, a big city of the time, was the capital of Ta-lo-pitu (Dravida) and was about thirty *li* in circuit. The Rājvihāra in Kāñchi was the meeting place of learned monks. Mahendra I's *Rājavihāra* mentioned in *Mattavilāsaprahasana* could be identified with the Rājavihāra mentioned by Hiuen-Tsang. It received revenues for other monasrteries.

During the Pallava period, the *ghaṭika* at Kāñchi imparted different types of education to pupils. There were not only religious studies but secular studies also here. Hiuen-Tsang has mentioned about the Kāñchi *ghatika* and the importance of yoga school of philosophy.

The Buddhist monks made great efforts to propagate the religion in the South, South-east and Far east regions and succeeded a great deal. But though there were Buddha statues, Pallichandam, etc. in Tamilnadu Buddhism declined gradually. Rajasimha Pallava, though a staunch Saivite, was tolerant towards other religions. Buddhism also caught his attention. He built a Vihāra at Nāgapattinam for the Buddhists. Even the Chōḷa ruler Rājarāja I donated to the Buddhist Vihāra at Nagai.

The coming of the Āḷvārs and Nāyaṇnārs gave a death knell to Buddhism. Appar, Sambandar and Tirumangai Ālvār showed their indifference to Buddhism and Jainism. *Periyapuranam* gives a detailed account of the debate between the Buddhist leaders Sariputta and Buddhanandi and Sambandar.[120]

During the Chōḷa, Pandya, Hoysala and Vijayanagar reigns, Kāñchi had a low profile as far as Buddhism was concerned. The seats of Buddhist learning in the monasteries were losing their significance from the seventh to eighth centuries.

Buddhist influence in art and architecture is well known from the sculptures of Buddha and description of the Vihāras in Kāñchi. Buddha in various poses could be seen in Kāñchi collections. One could find the Javanese and Burmese influence in it. As the *ghaṭika* of Kāñchi was a famous one, it attracted students and teachers from various parts of the country.

Conclusion

Kāñchi, an ancient pilgrim city of India, accommodated all the four indigenous religions, *i.e.*, Saivism, Vaishnavism, Jainism and Buddhism, of India. From Sangam age to the time of Vijayanagar rulers, Kāñchi had witnessed many political vicissitudes. As it was ruled by tolerant rulers, there was not much bigotry. Along with Saivism and Vaishnavism, the worship of Shakti, Vinayaka, Skanta, Saptamātrikās, Navagrahas, Parivāradēvatas, etc., was followed in the Tamil country. The Kasakudi copper plates open with nine verses of invocation, one each to Parabrahman, Tiruvikrama, Hara, Tiruvikram and Hari jointly, Lakshmi, Parvathi, Vinayaka, God in heaven and earth, *i.e.*, brahmanas, and the last one to Brahma, Vishnu, and Siva.

Except a few, many rulers were tolerant ones making endowments of different types to all religious institutions. Education, learning, literary works, fine arts, etc. were patronised by the rulers and people of Kāñchi. It was one of the unique cities in India where one could see the establishment and growth of four important religions of India. Though Buddhism later became extinct, it along with the other religions contributed to the cultural growth of the city. No wonder that Kāñchi was considered as a centre of all religions which promoted religious integration or secular attitude. It accommodated a composite culture too.

Notes and References

1. Ahananura 213.
2. 1 420.
3. XXVIII 156; XXI 154.

4. T. Watters, *Yuvan Chwangs's Travels in India*, Vol. II, 1905, p. 226.
5. *Ibid.*, p. 228
6. *Epigraphia India* VI, pp. 84–91.
7. Fleet, *Corpus Inscriptionum Indicarum III, Gupta Inscription,* p. 8.
8. *Sirupāṇārṟuppaḍai*, L. 97.
9. *Taḍuttatkkonda Purānam*, V. 83.
10. V. 7.
11. *South Indian Inscription,* Vol. III, p. 395, V. 42.
12. ARE, 82/1921.
13. SII, I, p. 357.
14. E.I. XXXII, p. 97.
15. SII, I, p. 13.
16. Watters, Vol. II, p. 231.

16a. SII, p. 349.

17. ARE, 6/1888.
18. ARE, 4/1888.
19. SII, IV, no. 82.
20. SII, I, no. 34.
21. III, VV. 37–38.
22. *Journal of Oriental Research*, Vol. I, pp. 330–35.
23. *Classical Sankrit Literature*, p. 324.
24. *Periyapurranam*, Sundaramurthy Nayanar, 63.3.
25. ARE, 79/1921.
26. ARE, 78/1921.
27. K.A. Nilakanta Sastri, *The Colas*, p. 210.
28. ARE, 420/195 & 263/1956.
29. ARE, 36 & 68/1921 1/1893, 69 & 58/1921, 24, 22/1890.
30. ARE, 302, 345/1955.
31. ARE, 310/1909.
32. ARE, 309/1955.
33. ARE, 51/1921.

33a. ARE, 278/1956.

34. C.R. Srinivasan, *Kanchipuram through the Ages*, p. 252.
35. ARE, 27 & 28/1888.
36. ARE, 52/1921.
37. ARE, 230/1920, 326, 327/1955.
38. ARE, 152/1923.
39. ARE, 313/1954–55.
40. ARE, 346/1940.
41. ARE, 349/1940, 315/1955, 348/1940.
42. ARE, 346/1955.
43. ARE, 275/1954–54.
44. ARE, 336 & 334/1955.
45. ARE, 303/1955.
46. ARE, 544, 547 & 584/1919.
47. ARE, 349/1954–59.
48. ARE, 343/1939–40.

49. ARE, 644/1919.
50. 11–371–73.
51. 11–29–30.
52. First Andadi, 77, Third Andadi, 62.
53. ARE, 34/1888.
54. E.I. XXIV, p. 296.
55. SII IV no. 135.
56. C.S. Srinivasan, *Kanchipuram through the Ages*, p. 259.
57. ARE, 34/1888.
57a. ARE, 12/1895.
57b. ARE, 493/1919.
58. p. 23.
59. pp. 25–26.
60. ARE, 1/1921.
61. ARE, 23 & 6/1921.
62. ARE, 8 & 9/1921.
63. ARE, 45/1921.
64. ARE, 39/1921.
65. ARE, 35, 36/1888 & 635/1919.
66. ARE, 473/1919.
67. ARE, 590/1919.
68. SII III no. 80.
69. ARE, 406/1919.
70. ARE, 37, 46/1921 & SII II no. 861.
71. ARE, 620/1919.
72. ARE, 626/1921.
73. ARE, 486/1919.
74. ARE, 589/1919.
75. ARE, 417/1919.
76. ARE, 446, 454, 458.
77. ARE, 556, 607, 609, 1919.
78. ARE, 654/1919.
79. ARE, 604/1919.
80. ARE, 30/1892.
81. ARE, 485/1919.
82. ARE, 618/1819.
83. Koyilolugu p. 49.
84. ARE, 648/1919.
85. ARE, 510/664/1919.
86. ARE, 370/1919.
87. ARE, 26/1921.
88. Canto II, V. 95.
89. SII, IX no. 547.
90. ARE, 544, 545, 548/1919.
91. ARE, 583/1919.
92. ARE, 657/1919.
93. ARE, 579/1919.

94. ARE, 447, 448/1919.
95. ARE, 13/1921.
96. ARE, 33 & 34/1921.
97. Chakravarti, *Jain literature in Tamil*, ed. K.V. Ramesh, p. VIII.
98. M.V. Krishna Rao, *Gangas of Talakad*, pp. 198, 272.
99. Thirty Pallava Copper Plates, p. 1, March 1938, p. 800ff.
99a. March 1938, p. 80ff.
100. Tirunavukkarasar Puranam, VV 145–146.
101. List of Antiquarian remain in Madras Presidency, p. 177.
102. R. Narayanaswamy, *Jain monument of Tamil Nadu*, Tamilarasu, November 1974, p. 16.
103. ARE, 360/1954–55.
104. A. Ghosh (Rd.) *Jaina Art & Architecture*, Vol. II, p. 211.
105. ARE, 382/1929.
106. ARE, 381/1929.
107. SII, IV, No. 367.
108. SII, IV, No. 363.
109. K.P. Venkatarama Iyer, *The Hoysalas in Tamil Country*, p. 64.
110. SII, XII No. 259.
111. SII, IV Nos. 364–65.
112. SII, IV, No. 368, VII No. 398.
113. V. LL 98–105.
114. *Maṇimēkalai* XXVIII.
115. Krishnaswami Aiyangar Commemoration Volume, p. 244.
116. C. Minakshi, *Administration and Social Life and under the Pallavas*, pp. 225–26.
117. Watters, *Yuan Chwang's travel in India*, Vol. II, pp. 226–28.
118. Krishnaswamy Aiyangar Commemoration Volume, p. 244.
119. Watters, Vol. II, p. 70.
120. Sambandar, VV 904–26.

FOUR ❖ # Baḷḷigāve: A Medieval Urban Mosaic of Multi-Religious Communities

S. SETTAR

'And there shine temples of Hari, Hara, Kamalāsana,
Vītarāga and Bauddha, like the five arrows of the World'

THEY LIVED TOGETHER, IN perfect harmony, and without ever losing their identity. They prospered as an urban community, respecting the individuality in others. They frequently met in an assembly to witness acts of piety in which they might or might not have a share of benefit. They even acted as trustees of others' property.

They often debated vigorously, not merely to prove their point, but also to understand that of others. They ended the debate without leaving behind bitter feelings, without causing disturbance to communal harmony, and without making the other feel that they are ignored. They were all committed to their convictions, individually, and they held them close to their conscience. They embraced lofty ideals, conducted discourses, and proclaimed them on lithic columns. Some of them were as follows:

'There is no friend like merit'

'This body is [meant] for doing good to others'. . .

'Dharma is the root of the vine of fame'

'It is beloved of both worlds'

'There is none worthy of reverence in the world
than he who defends the devoted to dharma'

'The good of others was the wealth he sought
The satisfaction of his dependents he reckoned as his own satisfaction'[1]

Inspired by such ideals, even the most materialist among them began to re-examine the priorities of his life. The merchants of the city, we are told, 'began to stock imperishable goods in their marts', realizing that 'the stock of perishable commodities . . . beget them neither this, nor the other world.'[2]

It was not a dormant community, the minority meekly submitting to the dominant majority; on the contrary, it was a dynamic society and, indeed a valued-based one. Each stuck to his ideology, almost fiercely, but never questioning the freedom of the other. There was never a clash of interest, not even once in the long history of three hundred years (*c.* 1100–1300) when this heterogeneous community enjoyed enviable prosperity in history. Among them were Vaidikas, Lākuḷīśas, Kāḷāmukhas, Vīraśaivas, Vaiṣṇavas, Kṣapaṇakas, Bauddhas, Śāktas, Bhāravis, Ekadaṇḍins, Tridaṇḍins, Haṁsas and Paramahaṁsas. They identified themselves with specific ideologies – as *Lokāyatas, Akaḷankas, Sānkhyas, Mīmāṁsakas, Sugatas, Nayyāyikas, Vaiśesikas, Lakuḷasiddhāntins* and *Syādvādins*. Some had attained scholarship in all the Vedas; some others obtained fame as commentators on *Kaumāra, Pāṇini, Śakaṭāyaṇa* and *Siddhānuśāsana*. There were those who digested Bauddha and six other *Darśanas, Patañjali* and other *Yogaśāstras*, eighteen *Purāṇas* and *Dharmaśāstras*. Some stuck to the *brahmacarya*; others to the four *āśramas*. All of them lived in one urban centre, comprising seven *brahmapurīs*, five *maṭhas* and three *puras*. They never let their community languish – they built endlessly for two hundred years (*c.* 1000–1200) to make their city second to none. More than a hundred and thirty records and fifty temples, which are salvaged from the ravages of time, reveal but only an aspect of the most romantic experience of the citizens of Baḷḷigāve.

I. Emergence of the City

'In the Banavāse country', *mahāmaṇḍaleśvara*-Cāmuṇḍarāya instructs his Jaina subordinate Nāgavarma, 'Jaina, Vaiṣṇava and Īśvara settlements as well as the settlements of all *munigaṇas* are maintained with equal distinction'.[3] What was true of Banavāse was also true of its royal city. 'The citizens of Baḷḷigāve', asserts a Kāḷāmukha record, 'are worshippers of Hari, Hara, Pañkajāsana, Jina and all other gods. . . .' and temples of 'Hari, Hara, Kamalāsana, Vītarāga and Bauddha as well as the five monasteries of this city shine like the five arrows in the world'.[4] This poetry appears to have its foundation in history, for the claim is borne out by the temples of all these sects. The Kāḷāmukhas held a leading position, but this position of predominance, privilege, wealth, numerical superiority and the commanding spiritual status enjoyed by its ācāryas, did not make them undermine others. On the contrary, the respect they had earned from all citizens in this 'home of all beauty and all dharmas', where temples were built 'as if all the immeasurable merit acquired by its citizens had combined into one abode',[5] made them humble, tolerant, generous and eclectic. This, in turn, seems to have transformed the very tenor of the community life. The history of Baḷḷigāve reveals the benefits accruing to the society which had the good fortune of the tolerant majority embracing with grace an insecure minority. In this urban mosaic of ministers, monks and merchants, the din of the market transactions merged with that of temple rituals and court regulations, but the language of communication, literal as well as symbolic, contained common vocabulary. After building a Jinālaya in 1173, for example, its patron declared that one who protects it would 'obtain the merit of giving away thousand tawny cows to Brāhmaṇas who are experts in Vedas at Vāraṇasī and Kurukṣetra'.[6] This adage is common and familiar, no doubt, but when the sanctity of the Vedas is endorsed by Jains with the same amount of respect as by the Hindus, its significance changes.

A Humble Village Becomes a Humming City: The present Baḷḷigāve (Shikaripura Tk. of Shimoga Dt.) in Karnataka is a modest village. Its wealth is its historical remains – temples, tanks, fort walls, pillars, gateways, memorial columns, sacrificial posts, dislocated sculptures and deserted lithic records. The entire village is covered with precious historical rubble at least a millennium old. Its recorded antiquity goes back to the times of the early-Chālukyas and Sendrakas. When it first stepped into history in AD 685,[7] it was known by the name Vaḷḷigāme. Then it was only a humble village; its prominent residents were *dāsas* (servants [of gods]), *devaḍis* (priests), *gāmuṇḍas* (village officers), and *gāmigas* (village folk). In other words, it was far from being an urban settlement. Even the stability of this humble village could not be maintained during the following three centuries, when Banavāse province passed under the Kadaṁbas, Rāṣṭrakūṭas and other local chieftains. Nothing remarkable perhaps occurred in Vaḷḷigāme which deserved to be recorded between *c.* 685 and *c.* 1019, or the little that happened and recorded is eluding us now.

The fortunes of this centre, however, changed in the early eleventh century, with the Chālukyas of Kalyāṇa extending their political hold on the Banavāse territory. Very soon it attained the status of a city (*nagara*), and a little later, the status of a metropolis (*mahā-nagara*). In the meantime, it had also been recognized as a great capital city (*mahārājdhānī-paṭṭaṇa*) and as a hoary city (*anādi-paṭṭaṇa*). With this beginning, its expansion continued unabated for almost about two hundred years. Then, for about another hundred years, (1200–1300), it continued to maintain its profile, without, however, attempting further expansion. Its existence during the subsequent six centuries (1300–1900) is reminded only by about six records, issued at wide intervals. It survives to the day, no doubt, with its glory stuck on its broken back.

During its days of prosperity (eleventh–twelfth century), Baḷḷigāve was hardly matched by any medieval urban centre in the lower Deccan. It is interesting to note that it never became the capital of a kingdom in the sense in which Banavāse, Badāmi, Māḷakheḍ, Kalyāṇa, Hānagal and Dorasamudra had served the causes of kingdoms. As a provincial headquarter, it remained a strong, stable, popular and prosperous city under the Chālukyas and Kaḷachūryas of Kalyāṇa, and, perhaps, under the later-Kadaṁbas, Hoysaḷas and Yādavas too. But even as a provincial head-quarter, Baḷḷigāve overshadowed Banavāse.

At the beginning of the eleventh century, Baḷḷigāve's transactions became so intense and so important as to warrant permanent preservation on lithic tablets.[8] These records reveal names of temples – about thirty-seven of Śiva, eight of Jina, five of Viṣṇu, two of Śakti and one of Buddha. To this, we may have to add several shrines and monuments of religious and civic significance. Besides temples, monasteries and brahmanical settlements, several groves, gardens, tanks, streets (*keris*), alms-houses, hospitals, schools and watersheds also figure in records. Specific references are made to the deer and tiger parks, *nandanavana, pergaṭṭa* (steep mound) with a stream at its foot.[9] By the close of the eleventh century, Baḷḷigāve had become a garden city with groves and gardens of mango, betel-vine, areca-nuts, begonia and *muchchukunda* flowers – all of which attracted swarms of bees, parrots and cuckoos. The *pergaṭṭa*, with its stream, and tanks like *gaṭṭadakere, benakanakoḷa, tāvaregere,* etc., added beauty to this city; they also met the utilitarian needs of the town. Some of these tanks were woven with lotus creepers.[10]

Three townships formed the core of this city, but it also had several hamlets, forming its satellites. About thirty-four hamlets attached to religious institutions are named in records.[11] Devīpura, Govindapura and Vīrakeśavapura were maintained as separate settlements within the city of Baḷḷigāve in the mid-twelfth century.[12]

As a temple-city, Baḷḷigāve expanded gradually between 1019 and 1194, each temple establishment bringing in an additional settlement and additional population. The immediate environs of some of the temples accommodated houses for priests, also for dancing girls (*pātra*) and for all those who depended on the latter, family wise and profession wise. Each street had rows of shops, while several traders hawked their goods in open space, on the 'footpaths' of cart-streets, within temple precincts, etc. The bazaars attracted traders from other centres of Banavāse and beyond, while the temples attracted donors from all parts of the kingdom and even beyond.

Thus, the city began to gain in importance; with this, it also attempted to secure a hoary and respectable antiquity. The original name Vaḷḷigāme (seventh century) was replaced by Balipura, suggesting its association with the legendary hero Bali, in the early eleventh century. In 1036, its links were established with the Pāṇḍavas. The latter are stated to have established the five lingas (*Pañcalinga*) here as a part of their *rājasūya* sacrifice, on their way back from the capital of Vibhīaṣaṇa. In the same year, it was fondly called Baḷḷi and in 1115 Bali-ūr.[13] It was recognised as the maternal abode of all cities (*paṭṭaṇagaḷa tavarmane*) and a great metropolis (*kaṭaka-mahānagara*). Its clear and captivating streets are compared to the glittering twin eyes of Samagralakṣmī.[14] In the twelfth century, it was hailed as a 'shining ornament of Banavāse-nāḍu', and as the 'Southern Kedāra'.[15] A poet of the mid-twelfth century noticed that 'progressing for many ages, this city had become famous for its alms-houses, pleasure gardens, temples, expansive tanks and lines of watersheds . . .'.[16] This city of divine lords and learned men, wealthy merchants and joyous citizens, appeared, at least to a poet, like another Amarāvati (with lords and learned), Alakāpuri (with its wealth) and Bhogāvati (with its happy people).[17] No wonder that it made poets lavish words of praise on it, for they were the privileged lot to transcend reality with impunity. It was even declared to be 'two-fold of Vāraṇasī, a hundred-fold of Kedāra and a thousand-fold of Śrīparvata'.[18] This 'new Kedāra' or 'southern Kedāra' attracted a large number of ruling kings, feudatories, merchants, monks and local officials to make grants. The kings and feudatories agreed with the poets on the latter's estimate of the greatness of this city. 'Scared of the severe cold and unable to make pilgrimage to the distant Kedāra of the Himālayas, some hastened here to get themselves absolved of their sins', states a poet. 'Visiting this sacred city and making gift here, even demon Bali was able to gain the prosperity of Indra', states another. It was 'famous for its thousand lingas set up by *devas* and *asuras*, resounding with recitation of the *śṛti* and the sounds of musical instruments at the three ceremonies of the day'. Thus, the fame of Baḷḷigāve spread on the wings of myths, legends and poetry, to be hailed as the 'mother (house) of Banavāse'.[19]

The Great Builders – Gurudeva, Pujāri and Brāhmaṇa: When the eighth century village of *gāmikas* and *dāsas* was transformed into a temple-town, about fifty temples, thirteen monasteries and seven agrahāras provided employment for a large number of settlers. At the apex of this society were *gurudevas*, the heads of maṭhas, their immediate disciples and priests of temples. Inscriptions identify brāhmaṇas, *pujāri* and *gurudevas* as the hub of this religious community. The brāhmaṇas engaged themselves in various occupations, of which *bhaṭṭa-vṛtti; khaṇḍika-vṛtti* and *agniṣṭhaka-vṛtti* are named.[20] Hosts of learned brahmins are stated to have engaged themselves in mastering and teaching the four Vedas, writing commentaries on a variety of texts, and acquiring knowledge in their own doctrine and in those of rival sects. There were creative writers and masters of theatre arts too. The records make it clear how the temples and maṭhas were engaged in social services, especially in the fields of education, alms-distribution and tending the sick. Nearly every temple-monastery maintained one or more schools, where the learned teachers imparted elementary and higher education; the alms-houses served free food to the disabled, dependent monks, nuns, and destitutes; the hospitals took care of the sick and the old.[21] Temple rituals required the services of a body of auxiliary staff. The *pātra* or dancers are named along with drummers, musicians, dance-teachers, who were all accommodated in the immediate environs of temples.[22] Besides this, there were resident or wandering minstrels – story tellers, singers, drummers, dramatists, comedians – who also received free food. Oil and flowers were regularly supplied to temples by those who were assigned with this responsibility. The regular *mālakāras* and *telligas*, like dancers, musicians and other *ranga-bhoga* staff attached to the temple, were looked after by the temple authorities.

Poets: The records of all these religious establishments were carefully maintained and preserved. The composers and engravers apart, they were protected by a body of officials. Poets of great reputations and skill often composed temple records; this was also sometimes done by local senabovas. One of the earliest poet-composers was Śāntināthakavi, 'the forehead mark of the Goddess of Learning' (*Sarasvatī-mukha-tilaka*), and the author of Kannada *Sukumāra carite*, which has survived to the day. A long record of about seventy-four lines, which narrates the initiative he provided for re-building the Śāntinātha basadi was obviously composed by him. (This portion of the record is effaced). His ability to compose poetry in several metres, his imaginative skill and high tastes, and his innate descriptive abilities, are highlighted in this record.[23] Another poet of the early twelfth century has provided more details about himself. An accomplished poet in composing the *Śiva-dharmma-śāsana*, Mallikārjunabhaṭṭa was hailed as 'emperor of mnemonics', 'the Nitalākṣa (Īśvara) among extempore (*asu-kavi*) poets', and a mathematical wizard. 'If two from two sides should together come writing it down from the end and reading it out, he would arrange the poem so read out, whether it might be, as a new poem; repeat four stories from hearing them related; and make calculations in any given figures – all by mental effort'.[24] How many more such poets lived in Baḷḷigāve cannot be estimated as not all the records are acknowledged, but they seem to have been in considerable number. We learn about *kavirājapaṇḍita*-Maleya, Cāvuṇḍamayya disciple of Guṇabhadradeva, *Pratikaṇṭha*-Kāmarāja, Recarasa and senabova-Cāvuṇḍamayya among them.[25]

Artists: The community of composer-poets was certainly outnumbered by the community of artisans. In fact, Baḷḷigāve was one of the foremost centres of arts in the eleventh-twelfth centuries, others in the neighbourhood being Tāḷagunda, Gadag, Lakkuṇḍi, Banavāse, Hoṁbuccha, etc. Construction, maintenance and renovation of more than fifty temples – not to mention of other establishments like tanks, monasteries, schools, civil and civic buildings including forts, etc., – should have required the services of a large numbers of stone-cutters, carvers, sculptors, engravers, masons, designers, planners, etc. The metal-casters, copper and goldsmiths and other members of the pāñcāla-community seem to have led a prosperous life in this city. The Pañcamaṭha(s) employed a body of chief metal-workers; they seem to have been the leading families of this community. These *kañcugāras* parade their professional attainments through their titles: 'the lords [masters] of five metals' (*pañca-lohādipatigaḷum*), 'the sons of great city' (*mahānagara-magam*). They were not only skilled workers but also wealthy craftsmen. They built a temple for Kāḷī from their own funds, led by their leader *kañcukāra*-Maloja in 1131;[26] Māroja, brazier of Baḷḷigāve. built another temple for Kalideva.[27]

The prosperity attained by the artisan community at Baḷḷigāve is borne out by another family of sculptors. 'Good workmen, observers of *dharmma*, friends of Gaurīśadāsas', the two brothers, Bāvaṇa and Rāvaṇa, claim to be disciples of the Kāḷāmukha preceptor Gautamārya, a saint of great repute. 'In order to clear an aspersion on their own race of sculptors', [perhaps the curse was that they worked for others and for monetary gain, and not for gaining merit on their own], they built a temple for Kusuveśvara in the precincts of the famous Kedāreśvara temple in 1139.[28]

Not only had the craftsmen emerged as a prosperous community, but they had also improved on their social status. The sculptors of the medieval times are commonly identified by the terms *oja* (*upādhyāya*) and *ācārya*, which they normally suffix to their personal names; but in Baḷḷigāve we meet some of them bearing the suffix *seṭṭi* (*śreṣṭin*). With this, they perhaps claimed social equality with the other communities of traders and merchants. For example, Guṇavarmaseṭṭi, who gave grants for sculptor Maloja, son of Bammoja and son-in-low of Maṇikoja, the builder of Kāḷī temple, belonged to one such prosperous family of Baḷḷigāve.[29] Their contributions were further strengthened by *kaṭakada*-Masaṇa(seṭṭi) and Yemmeyaseṭṭi, who claim to be masters of 'five metals' and also 'protectors of city'.[30] There was another family of two brothers, *maṇigāra* (jewellers) Mahādevaseṭṭi and Lakṣmīseṭṭi, who renovated the Sarveśvara temple in 1150 and who received two houses in the street of Mūlasthāna temple as wages, from the priest of Hiriyamaṭha.[31] Those who were more prosperous than these acted as trustees and managers of grants and temples, as did the forty Nakharaseṭṭis of the Telligeśvara temple (another community of professionals) in 1143.[32]

Among artists who were engaged in temple-construction, image-carving, metal-casting, and record-engraving, not many have left behind their names. Names like Kalloja-Chaṭṭayya, Somoja-Barmoja, *śāstrakarmi*-Cāvuṇḍoja,

Mala, Mammalloja, 'Nelave Śakha' (perhaps the pseudonym), Bisadoja, Cāvoja, Singoja,[33] etc., occur in records, but they appear to be only a few of the hundreds of sculptors who were resident-artists of this temple-town.

We have observed above that Baḷḷigāve was an art-centre and it produced some famous artists. One such artist was Dāsoja, the greatest of the early twelfth century sculptors in the Banavāse-Gangavāḍi region. He first appears as an engraver of a record of the Śāntīśvara temple to which we have made reference above. He distinguished himself as temple builder and carver in about half a dozen centres – Baḷḷigāve, Mattihaḷḷi, Hāvaṇagi (?), Belūr, Haḷebīḍu and Kaḷikaṭṭe.[34] Dāsoja and his son Cāvaṇa were invited to participate in the construction of the Cannakeśava temple at Belūr by king Viṣṇuvardhana of the Hoysaḷa dynasty, and on this temple we find their masterpieces even today. Dāsoja claims to be a *Sarasvatīgaṇadāsi*, and 'the smiter of the crowd of titled-sculptors' (*biruda-rūvāri-gondaḷa-baḍiva*), and more important than this was his other title: 'a double-headed eagle to the serpents, the rival sculptors' (*maccaripa-rūvāri-śarabha-bheruṇḍa*). The latter title was obviously derived from the Bheruṇḍeśvara at Baḷḷigāve. Interestingly enough, though Dāsoja claims that he was a devotee of Dharmeśvara at Baḷḷigāve, no temple of this name figures in the records of this city.[35]

Professional Groups and Traders: Baḷḷigāve housed several prosperous professional communities, like *kañcukāra* (braziers), *akkasāli* or *savaṇiga* (goldsmiths), *maṇigāra* (jewellers), *telligas* (oil-pressers), *mālakāras* (garland-makers), *sippiga-gottaḷi* (tailors), *kolika* or *magga* (weavers) *pātra* (dancer-musicians), *davasi-kottaḷis* (traders in grains), *gaveras* (sack-carriers) and *jagati-samūha*, not to mention of agriculturists, horticulturists, cultivators (of gardens of betel and areca), producers of sandal, incense, saffron, camphor, musk, sugar, dry ginger, cardamon, drugs, roots, etc. The records refer to 'fifty' families of oil-pressers, 'sixty' *kottaḷis*, 'four' *ovagal*, 'five' chief *kañcukāras*, etc. But the richest, most prosperous and immensely influential members of Baḷḷigāve were the *Vīrabaṇajjigas*, a community of traders.

The trading community seems to have expanded and consolidated its activity as and when Baḷḷigāve began to grow as a city. We rarely meet this class in the first half of the eleventh century, and the earliest to make his presence felt here is *sāvāsi*-Hampaseṭṭi, whose Buddhist wife Nāgiyakkā established the Tārābhagavatī temple and a Buddha Vihāra in 1067.[36] We are not sure whether Hampaseṭṭi was also a Buddhist, as marriages during this period of history did not always follow rigid religious or sectarian norms. Since Rūpabhaṭṭaya, brother of Hampaseṭṭi, was a Buddhist, we may presume that Nāgiyakkā's husband was also a follower of this religion. Surprisingly, the merchant community of Baḷḷigāve is hardly associated with any of the Jaina establishments, not even in the individual capacity, as member of this community. Neither did they build Jinālayas, nor contribute to their maintenance. Nonetheless, there was a section of Jains who held this centre sacred, for only such centres were generally chosen for termination of life by the *samādhi*-vow. The cases of the wife of *paṭṭaṇaseṭṭi* -Maliseṭṭi of 1186 and of Mādaiyya, son of Keśavaseṭṭi, of 1203, who took to *samādhi*-death at Baḷḷigāve, bear this out.[37] The majority of the trading communities were followers of Śiva and supporters of the Kālāmukha sect, while some were also devotees of Kāḷī.

The entry of the merchant community is noticed in AD 1080. Its influence was intensified with the passage of time, reaching its peak in the middle of the twelfth century.

The traders were controlling the local market, import and export of select goods, and promotion of sale of select consumer items, all of which necessitated implementation of rigid customs regulation by the State authorities during 1080–1096.[38] As a town (*nagara*), they witnessed, registered, regulated and reviewed gifts governing religious institutions from about the year 1094. Their leader was named *paṭṭaṇaseṭṭi*, who was sometimes assigned the status of the head of the 'district' (*nāḍ-svāmi*); he led the town (comprising professional groups like *maṇigāras, mummuridaṇḍa, jagati-samūha, kottaḷi,* etc.).[39] The community of *Vīrabaṇajjigas* (the heroic community of traders) claim to have had a flag of white hill. Their remote ancestors of 'five hundred' hailed from Ayyavoḷe; the later *baṇajjigas* seem to have only retained the memory of those 'Ayyavoḷe-500' till late medieval period. The original 'five-hundred' were associated once with eighteen cities, sixty-four *yogapīṭhas* and sixty-four *ghaṭikasthānas*.[40] They ensured and strengthened their place among 'townsmen' (*nagara* here and *mahājanas* elsewhere) by making generous contributions to religious institutions. 'They gave only to forget it', states a record which further informs that they were also 'trees of plenty to their dependents'.[40] Whenever the *nagara* (township) assembled to witness a religious event, it also made its contributions, perhaps to live up to its name, or responding to the subtle pressures of other members of the society. Such contributions were made individually as well as collectively. Among the former were *vaḍḍa-vyavahāri*-Soviseṭṭi, *maṇigāra*-Nāgaseṭṭi, Togare-Māciseṭṭi, *miṇḍaguddali*-Nāmaseṭṭi, Bammiśeṭṭi, Guṇavarmaseṭṭi, *maṇigāra*-Mahadevaseṭṭi and Lakṣmīseṭṭi, Caṇḍiseṭṭi, *paṭṭaṇaseṭṭi*-Maliseṭṭi, *kaṭakada*-Masaṇa(seṭṭi) and Yemmeyaseṭṭi.[42] Of their collective contributions, those registered in 1094 for Nakhareśvara, in 1139 for Kusuveśvara and in 1143 for Telligeśvara deserve to be noted.[43]

Since they owned vast stretches of farm lands and gardens, they parted with some of them for a price when they were required for the services of temples or monasteries. King Kāmadeva, a Pāṇḍya feudatory under the Chāḷukyas, purchased a piece of land from *paṭṭaṇaseṭṭi*-Bhuvanaikaseṭṭi in 1113 to make it available for the maintenance of the Kedāreśvara temple.[44] Sometimes they received grants from the temple authorities in recognition of the meritorious work rendered by them.[45] From their own funds they also renovated or built new temples.[46] They often named temples after their community or profession, such as Nakhareśvara, Telligeśvara, Gavereśvara, etc.[47]

The merchant class is claimed to have stood for some ideals. Irrespective of whether these were strictly followed or not, they are repeatedly reiterated in records. As stated earlier, 'they gave only to forget'. Merchant Gopati declared that his body was 'for doing good to others.'[48] They were a cultivated lot - stated to be 'honest, pure, righteous, gentle, courteous, and pious'; they were also bold and courageous, ready to lay down their lives for a cause.[49] They were disposed towards earning merit, not merely material gains. 'The merchants, being not satisfied with the stocking of perishable articles which got them neither this nor the next world,' states a record 'began to stock their shops with the imperishable [pious, permanent, goods]'.[50]

The 'Ayyavoḷe-500' of Baḷḷigāve reiterate the principles which their ancestors had stood for, but, in fact, they seem to have lived partly in the memory of the past glory, and partly in the present reality. By about twelfth century they had probably lost their individual guild status – army, flag, musical instruments;[51] their trade juridictions of 32-*veloma*, 18-*nagaras*, 64-*yogapīṭhas*, and *āśramas* at the four points of compass were only memories. A handful of them could have wandered as traders over a limited geographical area, but hardly 'over many countries'.[52] They could have been still spread over eight nāḍus and divided into *gaveragas, gatrigas, seṭṭis, seṭṭiguttas, aṅkakāras, bīras, bīra vaṇigas, gandigas, gāvuṇḍas* and *gāvuṇḍa-svāmis*. Their trading secrets were many: 'their sack, the earth; the cord, serpent race; secret packet, their betel pouch: their light, the horizon; the wood knife, their sword; their wealth, the innumerable articles in their bag'.[53] They probably continued to trade in superior elephants, well-bred horses, large sapphires, moonstones, pearls, rubies, diamonds, lapis lazuli, onyx, topaz, carbuncles, coral, emeralds, *karkketana* and other previous goods. They also dealt with cardamoms, cloves, bdellium, sandal, camphor, musk, saffron, *malegaja*, perfumes and drugs. The majority of these goods were perhaps continued to be traded even in the eleventh-twelfth centuries. In 1150, *paṭṭaṇasvāmi*-Māciseṭṭe, Kīrtiseṭṭi and others of the *nagara* made releases on their shops and goods which comprised shops of the *nagara*, shops of gold merchants, local *gaveras* who traded in sacks of goods, *gaveras* from outside who carried their sacks into this city, those who sold camphor, musk, saffron, sandal and pearls by weight, 'local' and 'foreign' cloth, black pepper, cumin-seed, mustard, *sada*-flower, bishops' weed, coriander; goods like sugar, asafoetida, dry-ginger, long pepper, cardamom, green ginger, turmeric, drugs and roots sold by weight.[54] Besides merchants who loaded local goods, the record also identifies those who came from abroad. The census conducted by the composer of this record identifies forty prominent families of flower sellers, fifty leading families of *telligas* and one thousand prosperous families of *tambuligas* (betel producer-sellers) at Baḷḷigāve in 1150.[55] From another record dated in 1145, we learn about forty prominent Nakharaseṭṭis.[56] The trading community of Baḷḷigāve was, no doubt, powerful, influential and rich. Whether they continued to maintain an army for their protection and for the protection of their city, we are not sure, but there were certainly some heroes among them, who laid down their lives for common causes. Facing a raider, a hero named Nāgiseṭṭi laid down his life in 1186; another hero Mediseṭṭi fought bravely against an elephant rider and laid down his life in 1284.[57] Referring to their martial acts, a poet says that 'they attacked and killed like elephant; they stood and killed like cow; they killed with poison like snake, and they sprang and killed like lion.[58] In the thirteenth century, these traders were addressed as *paṭṭaṇasvāmi* and *praje-basavas*.[59]

The Vaḍḍavyavahāris of Baḷḷigāve had declared that they would never go back on their words, to save themselves from any kind of losses. 'When the contents of their bags burst from weight and fell to ground, when their donkeys ran away with the laden goods, when one got wounded and died, when their carts were attacked and ransacked, when their 'blood-load' was pinched, when a bar of gold was burgled, when they suffered loss in the bargain, when they had to pay heavy tax 'which others evaded' and even when they had to face loot' – they did not seek excuses to escape from the deal. In other words, they could face any loss in trade, not the loss of word.

Not only did they make generous grants during their lifetime, they also made 'wills' to take care of their wealth after their death. A 'will' prepared by the entire community of traders in 1181 states that 'all property of baṇajjigas dying without sons, shall go for the festivals and sacred rites of the god Gavereśvara; the property of those dying sonless in the *nagara* [shall go] to god Nagareśvara, and any unclaimed property in the area of *pañcamaṭha*, three *puras*, seven *brahmapuris*, shall go to the gods of those quarters.'[60]

Thus the preceptors, priests, brāhmaṇas, poets, sculptors, craftsmen, traders and other sections of society contributed to make Baḷḷigāve a wealthy and an enviable city in the Banavāse province.

II. The Maṭhas

Puras, Maṭhas and Agrahāras: Though a record of the twelfth century states that Baḷḷigāve was a city of three *puras*, five *maṭhas* and seven *agrahāras*, none of these are explained, spelling out their constituent units. The three *puras* could be Baḷḷigāve, Kiru-Baḷḷigāve a complex around Kedāreśvara temple and Bheruṇḍeśvarapura or Devīpura. The seven *agrahāras* are also not specified, and even a careful search of the surviving records does not help us know them all. The closest we could go towards identifying them are: (1) Devīpura with eighteen settlements (of Bhagavatī Baḷḷiyabbe temple), (2) [Vaiṣṇava] brahmapuri (of Narasimha temple), (3) an agrahāra of twelve settlements, (4) Govindapura of twenty-five settlements, (5) [Siddheśvara] agrahāra of sixty-seven settlements, (6) Keśavapura agrahāra (of Vīrakeśava temple), and (7) Bheruṇḍeśvarapura agrahāra of Bheruṇḍeśvara-Jagadekamalleśvara temple complex.[61] How reliable is this list, I am not sure; but it appears to be not too wide as it covers three major establishments of Vaiṣṇavas (who did not have many maṭhas), three establishments of Śaivas (which either enjoyed independent status or served as adjuncts to the maṭhas) and one establishment of Devī (the earliest one and named after the village goddess Baḷḷiyabbe).

The records present not less than thirteen monastic orders which existed at one or the other periods of time and throughout the eleventh-twelfth centuries. They were as follows:

Nos.	Names	Dates	Preceptors	Sources
1.	Pañcalingeśvara [maṭha]: *Kāḷāmukha-brahmacāri-sthāna* (s.a. no.10 below)	1036	Kāḷāmukhācārya Lakṣmīśvarapaṇḍita	Sk. 126
2.	Bheruṇḍeśvara [Jagadeka-malleśvara Hiriyamaṭha] (s.a. no.10 below)	1047	Kāḷāmukha-Anataśivācārya	Sk. 151
3.	Bauddhavihāra of Jayanti Chief [of Tārā Bhagavatī Caityālaya]	1067	Bauddha-baḷāra	Sk. 169
4.	Mūlasangha-Desiyagaṇa of Koṇḍakundānvaya and Tālakolānvaya of Śāntinātha basadi	1068	Māghaṇandi-bhaṭṭāraka	Sk. 136
5.	Tripurāntakeśvara [matha] (s.a. no.10 below) of Bhujangāvaḷi of Śakti-Pariṣe	1070	Kāḷāmukha Trilocanapaṇḍita	*ASMAR* 1929, 63; *EC* VII & VIII(S) 342, 345
6.	Advaita maṭha [Hariharāditya Yogeśvara, '. . . vassāyana']		Guṇagaḷḷayogi-Nāgavarmmācārya	Sk. 129
7.	Brahmapuri of Keśavadeva [Narasimha temple-maṭha]	1072 1075	Purṇānanda-bhaṭṭāraka	Sk. 130
8.	Āvali of Citrakūṭāmnaya of Balatkāragaṇa [Śāntinātha Jinālaya]	1075	Anantakīrtideva d/o Municandra-Siddhāntadeva	Sk. 134

Nos.	Names	Dates	Preceptors	Sources
9.	Mūlasangha-Senagaṇa-Pogarigaccha	1077	----	Sk. 124
10.	*Piriyamaṭha-Bheruṇḍeśvaramaṭha (s.a. no.2 above)	1077	Gauḷapaṇḍitadeva	
	*Pañcalinga [maṭha] (s.a. no.1 above)	--	Srikaṇṭhapaṇḍitadeva	Sk. 106
	*Tripurāntaka [maṭha] (s.a. no.5 above)	--	Caturānanapaṇḍitadeva	
	Mūlastāna Pañcamaṭha	--	*mūliga* Honnajīya. (For changes in the names of ācāryas and for a combination of Hiriyamaṭha – Pāčamaṭha under one head. see Sk. 99 of 1113)	
11.	Jīyaramaṭha [Anantaśayana temple of Govindapura agrahāra]	1114	Vaiṣṇava	Sk. 137
12.	Maṭha of Mūvarukoṇyasantati of Parvvatāvaḷi [of Kedāreśvara]	1129	Kāḷāmukha Vidyābharaṇa Gautamārya	Sk. 100
13.	Koḍiyamaṭha [of Kedāreśvara-Kusuveśvara]	1139	Gautamārya	Sk. 112

Those bearing *indicate either the incidental references made to them, or repetition of those which occur earlier. s.a. means same as.

This list may not cover all the maṭhas of Baḷḷigāve and also it may be somewhat overlapping. Whether the Mūlasthāna-Nandikeśvara temple was the most ancient maṭha or whether this privilege was given to the Pañcaligamaṭha can not be made out, but the *ācāryas* of the first are often addressed as *mūligas*. This list, however, reveals one Bauddha, two Vaiṣṇava, three Jaina, one Advaita, one Śrotrīya, and six Kāḷāmukha maṭhas. The last comprised five (*Pañcamaṭhas*) until Koḍiyamaṭha replaced one of them, or, was added to the original five in the twelfth century). Of the Kāḷāmukha establishments, the Pañcalinga and Tripurāntaka maṭhas always maintained themselves independently unlike the Hiriyamaṭha, Pañcamaṭha and Mūvarukoṇeyasantatimaṭha (the last of which got merged in the Koḍiyamaṭha).

The Most Ancient Maṭha: We have referred above to ancient establishments, and preceptors who headed them bearing the suffix *mūliga* to their names. However, it is to be noted that the term *mūliga* was not attached to any particular head of the temple or maṭha all through. For example, *mūliga*-Śivaśaktideva was the head of the Mūlasthāna-Nandikeśvara temple (maṭha) in 1019, while *mūliga*-Jñānadeva was the head of the Abhinava-Someśvaradeva temple in 1054, and, at the turn of this century, *mūliga*-Honnajīya was incharge of the Hiriyamaṭha.[62] The management of both Pañacamaṭha and Hiriyamaṭha passed into the hands of *mūliga*-Dharmaśivadeva in 1181 and, then, in those of Padmaśivadeva in 1182.[63] The term *mūliga* literally means 'the hoary', 'the original', and it could also be used to indicate 'the most revered one's'; but, it is not clear whether this status was determined by (the age of, or, the respect commanded by) the preceptors or (the age of, or, the respect commanded by) the institutions. It appears that the senior-most among the preceptors was accorded this distinctive status, irrespective of the institution he headed.

Judging by names, the senior-most monastery should have been the Hiriyamaṭha, though the exact location of it is not disclosed. The Pañcalinga-maṭha is the oldest of the dated monasteries at Baḷḷigāve, but the Bheruṇḍeśvara-Jagadekamalleśvara maṭha has been given precedence over the former in records.[64] The Hiriyamaṭha is also stated to be an integral part of the Mūlasthāna god in 1150, and of Jagadekamalleśvara (same as Bheruṇḍeśvara) in 1159.[65] As seen earlier, the headship of the Pañcamaṭha and Hiriyamaṭha was often shouldered by one and the same preceptor, but the individuality of these two institutions was never effaced.

The Pañacamaṭhas: The details of the five *maṭhas* (*Pañcamaṭha*)[66] of Baḷḷigāve are more difficult to ascertain, though several records refer to them. Before attempting this, it is necessary to note that there were three different institutions which bore the near-identical names: (1) Pañcamaṭha (noun, singular) indicating a monastery of that name, (2) Pañacamaṭhas (noun, plural; also a collective term, meaning five monasteries), and (3) Pañcalinga-maṭha (noun, singular, indicating a monastery attached to the temple of Pañcalinga). There is no doubt that almost all monasteries at Baḷḷigāve were attached to temples, but to which of the temples the foremost of the maṭhas –the Pañcamaṭha – was affiliated has never been made clear. It appears that it enjoyed an independent status and, occasionally, got linked with one of the temples through the preceptor who was both the head-monk of this monastery as well as the head-priest of one of the major temples. There is no ambiguity as regards the Pañcalingamaṭha, for it was clearly an annexe of the temple of that name. Built in 1036 to house the Kāḷāmukha celibates, it was appropriately called *Kāḷāmukha-brahmacāri-sthāna*. The Pañcamaṭhas, which are frequently referred to in records, perhaps indicate five great monasteries, all of them Śaiva, and perhaps all of them Kāḷāmukha. The earliest reference to the *Pañcamaṭha-sthāna* in Baḷḷigāve occurs in a record of 1065,[67] and it is continued through the twelfth century, with the same or with some minor variations in its name such as *Pañcamaṭha-sthāna, Pañcamaṭha-sthāna-nagara*, and *Pañcamaṭha-nagaraṅgaḷ*, (the latter indicating the three *puras*).[68] The preceptors of Pañcamatha were also chief authorities of Baḷḷigāve. We have already noted how their presence and participation were considered imperative on all religious and social occasions and how they acted as witnesses, donors and donees. In their capacity as chiefs of the city, they supervised the transactions of Śaiva, Bauddha, Vaiṣṇava (strangely enough, not Jaina) establishments.[69] However, it does not mean that these 'five monasteries' represented five different religious or sectarian orders. In fact, from about the late eleventh century, the term '*pañcamaṭha-sthāna*' seems to have been used as a conventional 'term' (and a conventional 'number') and the popularity enjoyed by the five great Śaiva maṭhas seems to have provided sufficient compulsions for their frequent allusions. However, a record of 1165, found at Devasthāna Hakkalu, states that the *pañacamaṭhas* at Balipura were 'practising the rites of their own respective convictions and were free from deceit (*sva-daruśanānusāri-sadācāra-cāraṇadim-nissatyam-enip-pañca-maṭhagaliṁ*).[70] This may support the assumption that the *Pañcamaṭhas* of Baḷḷigāve represented five religions or sects.[71] Nonetheless, scholars like Lorenzen, who believed that they comprised the 'Hari, Hara, Kamalāsana, Vītarāga (Jina) and Bauddha'[72] seem to have overlooked the fact that the followers of Brahmā did not maintain a separate maṭha at Baḷḷigāve, that Jains were never involved in their transactions and that the headship of the Pañcamṭha rested always with the Kāḷāmukhas, allowing no share of claim on this monastery Vaiṣṇavas, Jains and Buddhists. It is also relevant to note that the Jaina involvement in this monastery was almost nil as they neither took part in the transactions of the Kāḷāmukhas, nor let the Kālāmukhas participate in those of Jains.

The Pañacamaṭha, as a 'single' separate monastic establishment, is noticed for the first time in 1098. It was one of the four major Kāḷāmukha monasteries attached to the temple of Mūlasthāna, the other three being Piriya-Bheruṇḍeśvaramaṭha, Pañcalingamaṭha, and Tripurāntakamaṭha.[73] Its first head was *mūliga*-Honnajīya in 1098 and it was headed in 1159 by Dharmaśiva.[74] Baḷḷigāve is identified as the *Pañcamaṭha-sthāna* (base of five maṭhas) beginning from AD 1065.[75] These 'five' supervised the establishment of the Bauddha vihāra in 1065, a Vaiṣṇava establishment in 1078,[76] and the transactions of Śaiva institutions in 1103, 1104 and 1143.[77] With all the importance the 'five' enjoyed, the names of all of them are never made clear in any of the eleventh and early twelfth century records. Even in the latter twelfth century records only four monasteries are generally named, not the five.[78] It appears that after the emergence of Koḍiyamaṭha, the list of five was completed and all the five could be named only in the year 1159.[79] The Pañcamatha(s), however, survived to the end of the twelfth century, even after the Koḍiyamaṭha ceased to be a force at Baḷḷigāve.[80]

Koḍiyamaṭha: The Koḍiyamaṭha scaled greater height than any other monasteries in the twelfth century, but for only a very short period of time. Its emergence in 1139 seems to have, to a considerable extent, undermined the status of Śaktiparise Mūvarukoṇeyasantati of Parvvatāvaḷi, as it usurped the latter's place in the Kedāreśvara temple.[81] It stood along with other four ancient maṭhas in 1159 when transactions of the Keśava temple and Vīrakeśavapura took place.[82] No doubt, Koḍiyamaṭha gained an unparalleled status under the Kaḷachūryas (1162–64), but only to fall into oblivion within a couple of decades. After the twelfth century, it is never heard of at Baḷḷigāve, though it seems to have led a feeble existence at the neighbourhood temple-town Bandaḷike till about 1250.[83]

III. Kāḷāmukhas: Sects, Preceptors and Maṭhas

The history and the composition of the Śaktiparise of Mūvarukoṇeyasantati of Parvvatāvaḷi, which was superseded in the twelfth century by the Koḍiyamaṭha, and the appropriation of both of these by the Vīraśaivas, sometime after this century, deserve to be studied. This study is best done by first understanding the character of the Kāḷāmukha order, and correcting the image of this order created by those who were not in sympathy with it.

(1) The records at Baḷḷigāve refer only to the Lākuḷīśa and Kālamukha orders, and not to Pāśupatas and Kāpālikas even once; also, hardly any distinction is made between the first two, implying that they were two names of the one and the same sect. The generally accepted view is that the Pāśupata sect was older than the rest, and that the Lākuḷīśa-Kāḷāmukha order originated from it. It is also believed that Lākuḷīśa was the founder-preceptor of the Pāśupata order.

(2) The Lākuḷīśa-Kāḷāmukhas at Baḷḷigāve were very liberal and eclectic. Though they were devoted to Śiva, they also worshipped Viṣṇu and Brahmā. They invoked Trimūrtis nearly as often as they invoke Śiva. They also accepted the *Vedas, Varṇas, Āśramas* and *Āgamas*. They not only tolerated but also supported the cause of other sects and other religions. This is in contrast to the view that they were an extremist sect, opposed to the Vedas – the view which was spread by the Vaiṣṇava critics Yāmunācārya and Rāmānujācārya in the eleventh century.

(3) The Lākuḷīśa-Kāḷāmukhas of Baḷḷigāve belonged to the Śaktiparise of Mūvarukoṇeyasantati of Parvvatāvaḷi (SMP); not even one record of this centre refers to the Siṁhaparise, which was popular in the neighbourhood as well as in Andhra Pradesh. The heart land of the Śaktiparise was the present Shimoga (its strongest centre being Baḷḷigāve) and Dharwad districts. It is sometimes called Śaktiparise of Mūvarukoṇeyasantati of Parvvatāmnāya. Elsewhere in the neighbourhood, the order is stated to have had Beḷḷiya-santāna, Bhujaṅgāvaḷi, Iṭṭige-santati etc.[84] We have also drawn attention to a doubtful reference to 'āneyasantati' made in one of the records of Baḷḷigāve.

(4) The Lākuḷīśa-Kāḷāmukha order at Baḷḷigāve aimed at integrating itself into society, co-existing with all other sects and religions, and never ever deliberately opposing the followers of rival faiths, except in occasional polemics. They liberally promoted all institutions which subserved their social and religious causes – temples, monasteries, alms-houses, hospitals, schools, orphanages, asylums, etc. They accumulated wealth given as gifts, but they also distributed it for the promotion of community causes. They had no reservations in accepting invitations from other sects and even officiating at their religious and ritual ceremonies. They not only preached tolerance, but practised it. It was probably this quality which endeared them to Vaiṣṇavas, Jains, Śāktas, Ājīvikas and Bauddhas.

(5) Though this extreme tolerance helped the Kāḷāmukhas to grow in popularity and earn respect and loyalty from others, in the long run, it also worked against their interest – one, it alienated the extremists among them who preferred an aggressive opposition of their rivals; two, it made them drift closer to the revolutionary reformists who had launched a vigorous movement under Basaveśvara at Kalyāṇa. That the Vīraśaivas also had to accommodate extremist sections of Kāḷāmukhas in their fold, perhaps much against their conviction, is another matter.

The Founder Preceptors of the Kāḷāmukha Sect: The earliest reference to the Kāḷāmukha ācāryas at Baḷḷigāve is made in a record of 1019, in which *mūliga*-Śivaśaktideva is mentioned. He is described as a saint of some attainments, adept in the *yama, niyama, svādhyāya, dhyāna, dhāraṇa, mauna, japa* and *samādhi.*[85] He seems to have controlled the affairs of the Kāḷāmukha establishments till the latter half of the eleventh century and passed on the responsibility to his disciple Rudraśaktideva. There is no reference to SMP during this period, nor to any maṭhas.

In the early eleventh century, the hierarchy of monks in the Kāḷāmukha order appears to have been loosely structured. Parallel to Śivaśaktideva, there was *vādirudragaṇa*-Lakulīśvarapaṇḍita. The latter asserted the *dharmma*, based on the supremacy of Śiva, Vedas, Varṇa and Āśrama. He was a great polemist and logician; under him, Baḷḷigāve became a reputed centre of Kāḷāmukha celibates – *Kālāmukha brahmacāristhāna.*[86] He was also the first *ācārya* to build and maintain the Pañcalinga temple at Baḷḷigāve. The fact that this saint took his name after the founder of the Lakuḷīśa-Kāḷāmukha order, and built a temple of Pañacalinga on his own, suggests that he may have been the 'founder' of the Lakulīśa-Kalamukha monastic order at Baḷḷigāve. His contemporaries were Kriyāśakti-paṇḍitadeva, priest of the Siddeśvara temple in 1039 and Anantaśivācārya, who was associated with the installation of the *gaṇḍhabheruṇḍa* pillar in front of the Jagadekamalleśvara temple in 1047, as the priest of the latter temple.[87]

The first half of the eleventh century appears to be a period of consolidation for the Kāḷāmukhas at Baḷḷigāve. None of the half-a-dozen temples of this period were attached with the *maṭhas*, which they began to acquire during the latter part of the eleventh century. Between 1019 and 1070, preceptors *paṭṭaṇada-mūliga*-Jñānadeva, (priest of Abhinava Someśvara temple), a *bhaṭāra*, (priest of Mañjeśvara), *Kāḷāmukhāgreśa*-Trilocanamuni, disciple of Kasmīradeva, and the priests of Sarvveśvara as well as of Tripurāntakeśvara, distinguished themselves, not as members of the order of SMP, but as saints of great attainments.[88]

Emergence of Saktiparise: When exactly the Kāḷāmukhas established themselves in the Lower Deccan and which of their schools gained popularity and where, are yet to be properly traced. But Śaktiparise was in a noticeable strength as early as the late ninth century, as borne out by a record found at Aṇaji, Hire Kerūr taluk, which formed part of the Banavāse province under the Rāṣṭrakūṭa Kriṣṇa II. In this record, reference in made to *sasti-parise-tonam* (*Śakti-parise-sthāna* which was perhaps the present Aṇaji village), but not to any Kāḷāmukha preceptor.[89] For the first time in the history of Baḷḷigāve, we encounter the *muni-santati* of SMP in a record dated in 1078, comprising Kedāraśakti, his disciple *Lakulasamaya-lalāmaṇi*-Rudrābharaṇa and his disciple Vālmīkimuni. It is generally believed to belong to the Kedāreśvara temple, but in all probability, it did not. Kedāraśakti had another line of disciples named Śrīkaṇṭhapaṇḍita and the latter's disciple Someśvara-paṇḍita.[90] From this we may infer that it was only Kedāraśakti's line that initially claimed affiliation to Śaktiparise, and not others. Even after 1070, preceptors like Kamaladevapaṇḍita lived independently of Śaktiparise.[91] Unlike all these, Vareśvaramuni claims himself as the disciple of Kāśmīradeva-Trilocanamuni, not affiliated to SMP.[92] All these enjoyed equal status. Gauḷapaṇḍitadeva, *ācārya* of Hiriyamatha (of Bheruṇḍeśvara), Śrīkaṇṭha-paṇḍitadeva, *ācārya* of Tripurāntaka, *mūliga*-Honnajīya, *ācārya* of the Mūlasthāna and Pañcamaṭhas jointly supervised the consecration of the Lokeśvara-Jogeśvara temple at the turn of the century.[93] Of these, only Śrīkaṇṭhapaṇḍita is named a disciple of Kedāraśakti of SMP, while the teachers of the other three are not mentioned.

Kedāreśvara Temple: Stronghold of SMP: The Kedāreśvara temple had no place in the list of prominent establishments of Baḷḷigāve during the eleventh century. It is possible that Someśvarapaṇḍita, spiritual descendant of Kedāraśakti, got this temple established in the early twelfth century (1103 AD?) in memory of his teacher. A record of 1129 identifies Someśvara, Vāmaśakti and Gautamārya as founder-fathers of Kedārasthāna.[94] The emergence of Kedāreśvara temple in the early years of the twelfth century appears to have changed the very complex of the Kāḷāmukha order. This 'threepinnacled temple' was attached with the Kāḷāmukha monastery and, the temple and the monastery together attracted the largest number of grants, throughout the twelfth century.[95] The preceptors attached to this complex were renowned for their attainments, learning, spiritual leadership and also social service. In about 1139, a new monastery, named Koḍiyamaṭha, was established in this temple, which proved to be a more significant milestone not only in the historv of this temple town but also in the history of Kaḷāmukhas.

Kāḷāmukha Sub-Units: The Saiva records reveal not only three different Saiva establishments, but also some sub-groups within the Kāḷāmukha order. As noticed above, the first reference to Śaktiparise is encountered in 1078, which means that even if we allow a margin of about twenty-five years, its entry into Baḷḷigāve cannot be dated earlier than the mid-eleventh century. During the latter half of this century, it was relevant only to the ācāryas who descended from Kedāraśakti, probably not to others. The same continued even during the twelfth century. The two outstanding spiritual descendants of Śaktiparise were Someśvarapaṇḍitadeva (who headed this order during the first twenty years of the twelfth century) and Vāmaśaktideva who, as *rājaguru* (of Kalachūryas), headed it between 1156 and 1192.

The SMP was perhaps brought to the Banavāse region by Kedaraśaktideva, but the records preserve only his memory, not his achievements. The main line of his successor-disciples and their contemporaries were as follows:

SMP-Line	Contemporary Kāḷāmukha preceptors outside of SMP-Line
Kedāraśaktideva	—
Srīkaṇṭhadeva (1113)	—
Someśvarapanḍitadeva (1103–1129)	—
Vidyābharana (1129)	Śāntīśvarapaṇḍita Kriyāśaktipaṇḍita (contemporaries of Śrīkaṇṭapaṇḍita)
Vidyābharaṇa (1129)	
Vāmaśakti	
Gautamārya (1139–1149)	Madhukeśvarapaṇḍita (1150)
Vāmaśakti (1156–1192)	Dharmaśivadeva (1180)
	Rudraśaktideva (1180)
	Jñānaśaktideva (1181)
	Padamaśivadeva (1182)

[One Rudraśaktipaṇḍita, disciple of Kriyāśakti II, who lived in about 1117, also claims to belong to this order.]

All the preceptors of the SMP were attached to the Kedāreśvara temple, while the rest of the Śaiva establishments at Baḷḷigāve were managed by other Kāḷāmukha monks, who seem to have had very little to do with the SMP. It is obvious that the major four maṭhas – Hiriyamaṭha, Bheruṇḍeśvara-maṭha, Pañcalingamaṭha, Tripurāntakamaṭha were controlled by the Kālāmukha preceptors who did not belong to the SMP. The Tripurāntaka-matha was affiliated to the Bhujangāvaḷi line.

Three Great Preceptors of Śaktiparise: The three outstanding spiritual leaders of Śaktiparise were Someśvara, Gautamārya and Vāmaśakti. The first of these consolidated himself through his order: the second promoted Koḍiyamaṭha and the third outgrew the Śaktiparise so much as to even distance himself from his remote ancestor, Kedāraśakti in his later days. But the contributions of all these were substantial and deserve to be recaptured here:

(1) *Someśvarapaṇḍita:* Disciple of Śrikaṇṭhapaṇḍitadeva, he headed the order during the last decade of the eleventh and the first decade of the twelfth century; with his base at Baḷḷigāve, he extended his activities to Ablūr and probably to Sūḍi in Dharwad Dt.[96] He was the priest of Nakhareśvara in 1094 and between 1103 and 1113, he concurrently held the priesthood of Kedāreśvara.[97] Someśvara appears to be instrumental in getting the Kedāreṣvara temple erected at Baḷḷigāve, in all probability in about 1103.[98] He was a monk of considerable attainments: 'an eminent Sārasvata'; he commanded respect both from the order as well as from the laity.[99] A poet of 1094 states that besides all ascetic virtues, he was proficient in philosophy, logic, grammar, poetry, drama, music and several branches of literature and learning . . .'.[100] Another poet of 1103 informs that he was '*the caitra* (spring) to the mango tree Akaḷanka, a moon to the ocean Lokāyata, a regent elephant to the earth Sānkhya, a pearl ornament for the conch-like neck of lady Mīmāṁsā, a sun to the lotus Sugata . . . the leader of Naiyyāyikas'.

'Some are learned logicians, some are clever in conversation and discourse, some are skilled in drama, some are able at good poems, some are versed in grammar, but if it be asked who is the master of all these? Who in the world is skilled in them all? The celebrated ocean of learning, Someśvara, a sun in unfolding the lotus garden, the *Nyāyaśāstra*, an autumn moon in raising the ocean, the *Vaiśesika*, jewelled ornament in proficiency in *Sānkhyāgama* . . . spring to the mango garden the *Śabdaśāstra*, with the rise of wisdom causing the *Lakuḷasiddhānta* to bloom . . . satisfying Parameśvara by the strength of his devotion . . .'.[101]

The unique services he rendered to the Kedārasthāna are recalled in the following words: 'The fortune of the Kedārasthāna was a *kalpa* vine born in the earth, raised on the soil of his unshaken penance by Someśvarāryya, afterwards well nourished and covered with branches and blossoms through Gautamārya, till its fame was spread over all the world through Vāmaśakti-munīndra.'[102]

All this makes clear that (a) Someśvarapaṇḍita was a great exponent of *Lakuḷāgama* and master of the doctrines expounded by Akaḷanka, Lokāyata, Sānkhya, Mīmāṁsa, Saugatḥa; that (b) his eclectic outlook made Baḷḷigāve become a common centre for Hari, Hara, Paṅkajāsana, Jina and Buddha; and (c) that he was the real founder of the Kedārasthāna, which was later developed and made universally known by his two successors, Gautamārya and Vāmaśakti.[103]

Gautamārya: If the credit of establishing the Kedārasthāna goes to Someśvarapaṇḍita, the credit of establishing Koḍiyamaṭha and integrating it with the Kedārasthāna goes to Gautamārya and Vāmaśakti. This new chapter in the history of Baḷḷigāve seems to have necessitated even modifications of the monastic genealogy: the line of Kedāraśakti being gradually overlapped and those of Someśvara, Gautamārya and Vāmaśakti emphasized.

Gautamārya held the reins of the Kedārasthāna in about 1129.[104] Obviously he made deliberate attempts to distance himself from his great ancestor Kedāraśakti, if not immediately after assuming the monastic seat in 1129, certainly a couple of years later. A record of 1129 associates him with the 'Mūvarakoṇeya-santati of devout Parvvatāvali' (Śaktiparise is missing here) and places him in the line of monks descending from Kedāraśakti, but it clearly lays emphasis on the services of Someśvara, undermining Kedāraśakti. We are informed that Gautamārya, like the Kamaṭha, supported all sects and took in his stride the followers of Hari, Hara, Kamalāsana, Vītarāga and Buddha. In 1139, he strengthened the Kedārasthāna by adding Koḍiyamaṭha and a shrine of Kusuveśvara. This led him to be reverenced by a multitude of munis, and the ācāryas of the Koḍiyamaṭha, not of Śaktiparise.[105] After this, Gautamārya never again once allied himself with either Kedāraśakti or with the Śaktiparise. In 1149, he merely acknowledged his immediate *guru*, and none others. Significantly enough, the record establishes his eminence in these words: 'The Veda its roots, the Nyāya and other śāstras its secure fence, the Smṛti and others its branches, the virtues and aspirations of the good its sprouts, their deeds its blossoms, the observance of the *Śiva-śāsana* its fruit – the tree of plenty his *Dharmma,* Śrī Gautamāryya . . .'.[106]

Vāmaśakti II: Gautamārya's dear disciple, Vāmaśakti II succeeded him in about 1156 as the head of the Kedārasthāna. Like his teacher, (who acknowledged his link with the SMP only once when he came to authority in 1129, and never again during the next twenty-seven years), Vāmaśakti also acknowledges the SMP (without referring to Śaktiparise) only in the first record issued on his behalf in 1156, and never again. But even in this, the genealogy of the preceptors is modified, for it begins with Someśvarapaṇḍita, then eliminating two intermediary names (Vidyābharaṇa and Vāmaśakti I), it refers only to Gautamārya who was the *guru* of Vāmaśkati II.[107] During the entire career of about half a century, Vāmaśakti recalls only once (in *c.* 1164) the Mūvarukoṇeyasantati (not Śaktiparise) and only once the Parvvatāvaḷi, hinting at some kind of a break in the order of the Śaktiparise during the latter half of the twelfth century.[108] In about ten occasions, Vāmaśakti refers only to his *guru* Gautamārya and none else. It is also reiterated that the Kedārasthāna was built by only Someśvara, Gautamārya and Vāmaśakti.

Vāmaśakti II was one of the greatest and the last of the Lakuḷa-Kāḷāmukha ācāryas at Baḷḷigāve. He seems to have concentrated his attention on promoting Koḍiyamaṭha rather than Śaktiparise; in fact, the latter is almost eliminated from the records issued during his lifetime. The ascent of Koḍiyamaṭha under Gautamārya and Vāmaśakti seems to have synchronized with the decline of the Śaktiparise in the latter half of the twelfth century. The monk who witnessed this, and perhaps who was responsible for it, was Vāmaśaktipaṇḍitadeva.

In 1156, 'the southern Kedāra was the means of the absolution of sin, the very presence of Śiva manifested to all citizens, visibly displaying all the glory of the Kṛitayuga, and the maṭha there was like the ancient Kamaṭha, a support for all the world. . . .' The maṭha is not named in this record, but it was obviously the Koḍiyamatha, which Vāmaśakti was heading according to another record issued in 1159.[109] In his capacity as the 'head of Koḍiyamaṭha', he joined preceptors of other Śaiva maṭhas, to supervise the creation of Vīrakeśava settlement. His contemporaries were Dharmaśiva, preceptor of Pañcamaṭha, *mūliga*-Madhukeśvarapaṇḍita, preceptor of Jagadekamalleśvara of Hiriyamaṭha, Sarveśvara-paṇḍitadeva, preceptor of Pañacalingamaṭha and Jñānaśaktipaṇḍitadeva, preceptor of Tripurāntaka. None of these, including the heads of Koḍiyamaṭha, acknowledge the Śaktiparise, nor recall Kedāraśakti.

Koḍiyamaṭha: Though the records of 1139 and 1159 provide references to Koḍiyamaṭha, it is in the record of 1162 that we get complete and vivid account of this monastery and of its ācāryas: 'as the lights of the line of *gurus*, many munīśvaras, abodes of the highest qualities, illuminated that [Koḍiyal] maṭha and in the line of these *gurus*, was Vāmaśakti-munīśvarācārya the disciple of Gautamārya'. In this long record of 116 lines, Kaḷachūrya Bijjaḷadeva's generous grants to the Koḍiyamaṭha are listed, but no reference is made to SMP, nor to Kedāraśakti. The dramatic events which followed the visit of Bijjaḷa are worth recalling here in the spirit in which the poet, who was an eyewitness, has captured it.[110]

'[When] Bijjaḷa-mahārāja . . . encamped in Baḷḷigāve, was in the enjoyment of peace and wisdom: they all [his courtiers] came united and seated themselves to discourse on the *dharmma* of the Koḍiyamaṭha. Then [one of his feudatories], Kaśyapanāyaka rose from his seat and stood before the king with folded hands and said, 'Deva, a petition', and, after being permitted, prayed as follows:

'There is the Koḍiyamaṭha, the place of Southern Kedara, being like a field (*kedāra*) the crops standing on which resemble the hair of the body standing erect from joy at the worship of the Śivalinga;

'[it is] the place appointed for performance of the rites of devotee-brahmacāri Śivamunis;

'[it is] the place for the recital of the four Vedas, the Rig, Yajur, Sāma and Atharva, with their angas;

'[it is] the place for [preparing] commentaries on the Kaumāra, Pāṇinīya, Śakaṭāyana, Śabdānuśāsana, and other grammars.

'[it is] the place for writing commentaries on the Nyāya, Vaiśeṣika, Mīmāṁsā, Sāṅkhya, Bauddha and the six Darśanas;

'[it is] the place for [expounding] commentaries on the Lakuḷasiddhānata, the Patāñajala and other Yogaśāstras;

'[it is] the place for the [discussion of] eighteen purāṇas, the dharmmaśāstras, all poems, dramas, comedies, and every branch of learning;

'[it is] the place where food is freely distributed to the poor, the destitute, the lame, the blind, the deaf, story-tellers, singers, drummers, flute-players, dancers, eulogists, the naked, the wounded, the kṣpaṇakas, ekadaṇḍins, tridaṇḍins, haṁsa, paramhaṁsa and other beggars from all countries;

'[it is] the place for the treatment of the diseases, of destitute, and sick persons;

'[it is] the place of security from fear for all living things'.

After this, the poet describes, how the Southern Kedāra and its maṭha supported the whole world like Kamaṭha (tortoise), how it was known for acts of charity (comparable to that of Hiraṇyakaśyapa) and how it shone like Kurukṣetra and Khacaraloka with the learned, etc. He concludes his petition with the suggestion 'that if the Deva [the king] were to perform in this maṭha some work of merit, it would endure as long as sun and moon'.

Impressed by the greatness of the maṭha and the attainment of its preceptors, king Bijjaḷa not only made a generous grant of villages in seven different administrative divisions, but also conferred on Vāmaśakti the position of *rājaguru*. He also extended grants to the Kāḷāmukha establishments at Ablūr which was also under this preceptor.[111] Between 1168 and 1193, nearly in about five major records (found so far), Vāmaśakti is addressed as *rājaguru*, and, with the exception of the last record of Hoysaḷa Vīra Ballāḷa II,[112] all these were issued during the time of Kaḷachūryas. It is obvious that it was Bijjaḷa's generous endowments that elevated Koḍiyamaṭha above all other monasteries at Baḷḷigāve, in about AD 1162.

In 1164, when Bijjaḷa's feudatory built a temple for [Ma]llapeśvara, Kedāraśakti and Koḍiyamaṭha are named for the last time in the recorded history of Baḷḷigāve.[113] Though Śaktiparise had lost its hold on, and even disappeared from, Baḷḷigāve, the Mūvarukoṇeyasantati, somehow, survived till 1164, with or without the memory of Kedāraśakti and disassociating itself from the Parvvatāvaḷi.[114] Distancing itself both from Śaktiparise and Mūvarukoṇeyasantati, the Parvvatāvaḷi survived till 1193, never to make its appearance again in Baḷḷigāve.[115] All this proves that the Kāḷāmukha order underwent fast changes after about 1160, before it became a historical debris between 1164 and 1193. The leadership of Vāmaśakti is the most noticeable feature of this period for he is acknowledged as the *Lakuḷīśvarayati*, head of Koḍiyamaṭha and a Kāḷāmukha.[116] What went wrong in this order during the time of Gautamārya and what were the forces which were prompting Vāmaśakti to be somewhat indifferent to Śaktiparise, Mūvarukoṇeyasantati of Parvvatāvaḷi, and on the whole, to the Kāḷāmukha order itself, cannot be divined.

IV. Cracks in Communal Harmony

Kāḷāmukha Extremists: At Ablūr another temple town of the Banavase – 12000 province, the Kāḷāmukhas were also breaking away from the Śaktiparise between 1104 and 1144,[117] and delinking themselves from all Kāḷāmukha establishments after 1150. During the time of Kaḷachūrya Bijjaḷa, a militant Śaiva named Ekānatada Rāmayya (Rāmayya, the Loner) was waging a single-handed, but vigorous battle, against Jains, until he successfully exterminated them at Ablūr. His aggressive campaign against Jains was within the knowledge of Kaḷachūrya king, but it seems to have had no explicit sanction from the Kāḷāmukhas of the Banavāse region. Nonetheless, the anti-Jaina movement of Rāmayya could not be either disowned or condemned by the Kāḷāmukhas, who were themselves at the crossroads of their history in the latter half of the twelfth century.

The rabid militarism advocated by Kāḷāmukha Rāmayya at Ablūr had nothing in common with the contents of the neo-Śaivism, sponsored by Basava and his colleagues at Kalyāṇa, later known as Vīraśaivas. The *vīra* (heroic) suffix to the Śaiva movement of Basava is of a much later origin, and even if some of Basava's contemporary followers were men of heroic temperament, they directed it only against the social evils rooted in Vedic fundamentalism. However, it cannot be denied that just as the declining Kāḷāmukhas had to bear the splinter extremist groups, the neo-Śaivas

(Vīraśaivas) also had to bear them at the early stages of their history, for alienation of such strong men as Ekāntada Rāmayya and his ilk would have gone against the interest of this infant reformist movement. Whether the militant (Kāḷāmukha) Śaivas who aimed at the dismemberment of rival orders and desecration of their establishments were already in the fold of Vīraśaivism, tired of the reconciliatory policies of Lakuḷa-Kāḷāmukhas, cannot be clearly made out. As all this happened during the latter half of the twelfth century, we may assume that they were parallel events to begin with. With the decline of the Kāḷāmukhas, the extremists seem to have crossed over to the reformist group of Śaivas, and made it also somewhat militant.[118] That the neo-Śaivas at Kalyāṇa maintained a kind of nexus with the Kāḷāmukhas in the twelfth century is revealed by a variety of evidence. Like the Vīraśaivas, the Kāḷāmukha preceptors at Hombaḷ, Gadag and such other centres were addressed as *jangamas*, and as early as AD 1159, muni Vāmaśaktipaṇḍitadeva and, sometime later, his disciple Jñanaśaktideva were also addressed as *ārādhyas*.[119] The *jaṅgamas* and *ārādhyas* enjoyed a high status in the Vīraśaiva hierarchy, and later played a vital role in strengthening the neo-Śaivism through their monasteries. To begin with, the Vīraśaivas were neither interested in building or maintaining temples, nor giving or receiving grants: as such, they had no occasion to issue *dāna-śāsanas* like the Kāḷāmukhas. This has denied us access to the details of their early activities. But the Vīraśaiva tradition confirms the association of several of its founder-fathers with Baḷḷigāve, and through this centre, with the Kāḷāmukhas. Among the most notable ones were Prabhudeva and Akkamāhādevī, two of the great leading lights of the Vīraśaiva movement. Whether the early Vīraśaiva saints lived in Baḷḷigāve or not, there is little doubt that all the religious establishments of Kāḷāmukhas were taken over, early or late, by them. Besides the Prabhudeva temple, and the 'tomb' of Prabhudeva in the Viraktamaṭha, which have survived to the day, the Vīraśaivas established afresh, or took over, at least, six *maṭhas* of Kāḷāmukhas at Baḷḷigāve. Assuming new names, such as Hosamaṭha (New Monastery), Kallumaṭha (Stone Monastery), Kāsīmaṭha (Monastery of Kāsī), Viraktamaṭha (Monastery of Celibates), Āridremaṭha (Monastery of Āridre month) and Samayācāramaṭha (Monastery of Vīraśaiva Congregation), all these have survived to this day, though they were not named in records.[120]

The Chālukyas and Kaḷachūryas of Kalyāṇa, either by turning their nelson's eye or by viewing indifferently the fundamentalists amidst them, allowed them to grow so strong as to throw challenge to their own political sovereignty. Kaḷachūrya Bijjaḷa, in particular, had to pay a heavy price for this. He lost his head in his own court hall to the same Kāḷāmukha extremists who had, by then, carved out a niche in the neo-Śaivism. What a State – and the head of the State – which fails to recognize and does not promptly deal with the fundamentalist movements has to pay, is well borne out by the Kaḷachūryas in the twelfth century. This needs to be briefly summarised here.

(1) The extremist elements in the Kāḷāmukha order were thirsting to attack and decimate their rivals, of whom Jains were the most influential, affluent and, powerful minority in the Chāḷukya-Kaḷachūrya kingdoms. Initially, this section of Kālāmukhas was content with imposing its symbolic authority on Jinālayas. For examples, the Jinālayas at Arasīkere (1068), Kuppaṭūr, (1075), etc. were made to name themselves as *Ekkoṭi-Jinālayas* (perhaps after *the ekkoṭi lingas*) and house two Śaiva symbols – *nandi* pole and *jogavaṭṭige* or box of *Śivayogi*. Further, it was insisted that their affiliation to the Kāḷāmukha order was to be expressly declared and acknowledged: the Sahasrakūṭa Jinālaya at Arasīkere complied with this by declaring its affiliation to the Kāḷāmukhas (*kāḷāmukha-pratibaddha*); elsewhere, the affiliation – accepting subservience – was made to local Śaiva temple. During the eleventh-twelfth centuries, these practices gained currency all over the Chāḷukya-Kaḷachūrya kingdoms.[121]

(2) Where the encounter between Śaivas and Jains led to a showdown, it was concluded either with the conversion of the defeated and humiliated ones to the sect of the victors or with the desecration of their establishments. The Kāḷāmukhas established their supremacy and desecrated several 'hundreds' of basadis after defeating the Jains in debates; of these, the ones led by Devara Dāsimayya at Kalyāṇa in about 1015–1040 and Ekāntada Rāmayya at Ablūr, instanced earlier, are celebrated. The latter episode is borne out not only by epigraphical records but also by vividly depicted relief-sculptures on the walls of the Someśvara temple that have survived to the present day. This is perhaps one of the rarest instances where contemporary historical event is chosen as the theme and content of the relief work on a temple wall.[122]

(3) Sometimes the movement became violent, aggressive and ruthless, involving innocent masses. Such mass movements were spread over a wide area. A record issued in 1184 at Tāḷikoṭe, recalls the extremists among Kāḷāmukhas who identified themselves as '*jina-samaya-vana dahana-dāvālanarum*' and desecrated temples of rival orders, mostly Jains, at Pariyaḷige, Aṇilevāḍa, Uṇakal, Saṁpagāve, Abbalūru, Māruḍige, Āṇampura, Karahāḍ, Keṁbāvi, Bommakūru, etc., all of which can be identified now. This is another unique list of desecrated monuments – an event of near contemporary period – preserved in the Chālukyan records.[123]

Kalachūrya Bijjaḷa perhaps did not realize the implications of the incident which took place at Ablūr under Ekāntada Rāmayya, though he was approached for justice and protection by the Jains. He let the Śaivas have their way. But this leverage seems to have emboldened the Kāḷāmukha extremists to intensify their campaign not only against the rival religious groups, but against all those who stood in their way. They moved away from their Kāḷāmukha roots as they achieved more and more successes under individual leaders like Dāsimayya and Rāmayya and gradually located themselves in the Vīraśaiva order, into which fold they were invited with considerable respect and admiration. It was perhaps this section that ultimately challenged Bijjaḷa and claimed his head when he tried to defend the Vedic orthodoxy which was opposed by Basava, the founder of Vīraśaiva reformist movement.

Notes and References

1. *Archaeologinal Survey of Mysore, Annual Report (ASMAR)* 1941, 38: *Epigraphia Carnatica (EC.,)* VII, Shikaripura (Sk.) 131 of AD 1104; 99 of 1113 and 92 of 1168 respectively.
2. Sk. 100 of 1129.
3. Sk. 120 of 1048.
4. Sk. 100 of 1129.
5. *Ibid.*
6. *ASMAR* 1929, 62; *ASMAR* 1911, p. 46.
7. Sk. 154 of AD *c.* 685.
8. During the last century, B.L. Rice salvaged and published about eighty-five records. In the early decades of the twentieth century, about thirty-one more records were noticed, but only thirteen of these were published until 1941. Including eight noticed as early as 1911, a total number of twenty-nine records were brought to light in 1970. Stray records have been noticed occasionally, but they are only few in number. All these total up to about one hundred and thirty. Perhpas more records may be found if the accumulated debris is removed and a more thorough search of Baḷḷigāve is undertaken. Nonetheless, we may assume that the records discovered so far constitute the most important body of sources for the study of this centre, and future discoveries may only help substantiate or marginally alter some of the present conclusions (Rice, B.L., *Mysore: A Gazetteer Compiled for Government*, vol. II (Rev. Ed), Westminster, 1899, p. 448. See *EC VII*, Sk. 87–170 and 323 for the texts of eighty-five records. For subsequent notices, see Settar, S., (ed.) *ASMAR – A Study*, vol. III, 1910–11, (Dharwad, 1976), pp. 111–16, and also *ASMAR* 1931, pp. 58–65, 1941, pp. 78–84. For the remaining twenty-nine records (including eight noticed in 1911 and twenty-one subsequently discovered) see, *EC VII & VIII (S)* (Supplementary Inscriptions). For stray records, vide *Quarterly Journal of Mythic Society (QJMS)*, LXVIII, 3–4 (Jan-Dec. 1977), pp. 24–28; *Art and Architecture in Karnataka* (ed.) Devaraj, D.V. and Patil, C.S., (Mysore 1996), pp. 208–11.
9. Sk. 120 of 1048, 134 of 1075, 136 of 1068, 123 of 1075 respectively.
10. Sk. 106 of 1098; Sk. 130 of 1075, Sk. 153 of 1039; Sk. 94 of 1094.
11. A careful study of published records reveals names of about thirty-five hamlets which were given as grants to temples during the eleveth-twelfth centuries. Many of these hamlets lay in the vicinity of Baḷḷigāve, but some are at some distance away from it. It may be of interest to note their area-wise and temple-wise distribution, as

such an impressive list of hamlets and villages given as grant is not easy to come by in records:

The largest number of hamlets (about 22) were granted to the Kedāreśvara temple, followed by three to the Narasimha, two to the Keśava, two to the Bheruṇḍeśvara, two each to the Buddha Vihāra and the Tārā Bhagavatī temple, one each to the Sarvveśvara, Mallikārjuna Hariharāditya and Jinālaya (of Pārśvanātha). The majority of these thirty-four hamlets were, in turn, attached to various administrative divisions. They are as follows (those within brackets indicate names of temples and the date on which grants were made):

A. *Jaḍḍuḷige Dv.:* (1) Harvagabūru (Bheruṇḍeśvara: 1047); (2) Harige and Mandase (Buddha Vihāra: 1065); (3) Bidiringere (Hariharāditya: 1071); (4) Manevaṇe (Jinālaya: 1077); (5) Hiravūr (Mallikārjuna 1078); (6) Beḷvaṇihaḷḷi (Keśava: 1159); (7) Bekkale (Kedāra: 1162); (8) Kirubaḷḷigāve (Kedāra: 1162); and Sirivoḷala (Kedāra: 1186).

B. *Nāgarakhaṇḍa Dv.:* (1) Harvadevappa (Sarvveśvara: 1090); (2) Pokkale (Narasimha: 1104); Tattavanale-Hakkalehola (Kedāra:?); (4) Karinele (Keśava: 1159); 5–9) Javaḷi, Karinele, Maruvāse, Mutiganahaḷḷi and Kundaṇgi (Kedāra: 1162); and Mittase (?) (Narasimha: 1075).

C. *Mugunda-12 Dv.* Kundavige (Narasimha: 1071).

D. *Sāntaḷige Dv.:* (1) Salivūru (Kedāra: 1193).

E. *Kalnandi-96 Dv.:* (1) Koṇeneralige (Kedāra: 1162).

F. *Kodanāḍu-30 Dv.:* (1–2) Abbase and Hosahaḷḷi (Kedāra: 1149).

G. *Raṭṭihaḷḷi Dv.:* (1) Tiregañchhi (Bheruṇḍeśvara: 1047).

H. *Sattaḷige Dv.:* (1) Sidiyanūru-Divige (Kedāra: 1162).

I. *Maduvoḷalu Dv.:* (1) Govindanahaḷḷi (Kedāra: 1149).

J. *Bhāgūru Dv.:* (1–2) Changūru and Mattiyahaḷḷi (Kedāra: 1162).

K. *Pāṇḍyarājya Dv.:* (1) Chittūru (Kedāra: 1162).

L. *Hānungal Dv.:* (1) Chikka-Kaṇṇugi (Kedāra: 1162).

M. *Nūrambāḍa Dv.:* (1) Kirugeri (Kedāra: 1162).

N. *Mangutoḷalu Dv.:* (1) Ayiraṇe (Kedāra: 1162).

12. Sk. 164 of 1149, Sk. 123 of 119.
13. Sk. 125, 126; *ASMAR* 1941, 38; *EC* VII & VII (S), 345.
14. Sk. 100 of 1129, 133 of 1131.
15. Sk. 94, 103. In fact, the name Baḷḷigāve (Creeper Village) was derived from the name of the local goddess, Bhagavatī Baḷḷiyabbe, in whose name a temple had existed for sometime and which was renovated in AD 1046, Sk. 323.
16. Sk. 123 of 1159.
17. Sk. 100 of 1129.
18. Sk. 92 of 1168.
19. Sk. 100, 119 and 138.
20. Sk. 123 of 1159.
21. Sk. 102 of 1162.
22. *ASMAR* 1929, 63; Sk. 101 of 1181.
23. Sk. 136.
24. Sk. 98, of 1103; 99 of 1113.
25. Sk. 105 of 1193, 124 of 1077, 129 of 1071, 146 of 1160, 169 of 1067 respectively.
26. Sk. 133 of 1131; *QJMS* LXVIII, 3–4, (July-Dec. 1977), pp. 24–28.
27. *EC VII & VIII* (S), 61.
28. Sk. 112.

29. Sk. 133.
30. *ASMAR* 1929, 60.
31. Sk. 118.
32. *EC VII & VIII* (S), No. 334.
33. Sk. 105, 150, 169; EC VII & VIII, Sk. 341–342, 351; Sk. 97.
34. Settar, S., *The Hoysaḷa Temples* (Bangalore-Dharwad, 1992), Vol. I, pp. 98–99.
35. The Dharmeśvara at Baḷḷigāve appears to be a very important temple, for, not only sculptor Dāsoja (*EC* IX (1990), B1.6), but also queen Śāntalā as well as her father Mārasingamayya acknowledged that they were the devotees of this god. In fact, Śāntaḷā and Mārasingamayya built another temple of this very name, after establishing Śāntigrāma in 1116–1117. I have inadvertently identified Dharmeśvara of this record with a temple at Baḷḷigāve, but, in fact, it does not exist now. (*Ibid.*, p. 59).
36. Sk. 169.
37. Sk. 148 and 113 respectively.
38. Sk. 111.
39. Sk. 94.
40. Sk. 94 of 1094.
41. Sk. 94 of 1094.
42. Sk. 118 of 1054, 99 of 1113, 133 of 1131, 1118 of 1150, 168 of 1182, 148 of 1186 and 61 of 1289 respectively.
43. Sk. 94 of 1094, 112 of 1139 and *EC VII & VIII* (S), 334 of 1143.
44. Sk. 99 of 1113.
45. Sk. 112 of 1139.
46. Sk. 118 of 1150, 118 of 1054 and 94 of 1094 respectively.
47. See the temple list, below.
48. *ASMAR* 1941, 38.
49. *ASMAR* 1929, 60; Sk. 140 of 1284.
50. Sk. 110 of 1129.
51. They traditionally possessed rods in their hands, white umbrella as canopy, kettle-drum, and elephant; they were endowed with moat, hand-guards, standard bearers, treasures, belt-tassel, dagger, etc. – Sk. 118 of 1150.
52. We are not sure whether they maintained their guild, or lived in the world of a phantom-guild. They were trading, no doubt, in the kingdom of the south but whether they traded, as they claim, in all the following countries is doubtful: Cera, Coḷa, Pāṇḍya, Maleya, Koysala, Saurāṣṭra, Dhanuṣṭra, Kurumbha, Kāmboja, Gauḷa, Lāḷa, Barvvara, Pārasa, Nepāḷa, Ekapāda, Laṁbukarṇna, Strīrājaya and Goḷamukha. They are also stated to have traversed in routes penetrating all the six continents by land and water. Their presence in some of these kingdoms is attested by records, in others it is not. It may be possible that the extensive contact which they maintained during the early phase of their trade, lingered on in their memory even after their trade activities had been considerably curtailed in about the twelfth century.
53. *Ibid.*
54. *Ibid.*
55. Sk. 118 of 1150.
56. *EC VII & VIII* (S), 334 of 1143.
57. Sk. 143; Sk. 140.
58. Sk. 118.
59. *ASMAR* 1929, 57.

60. Sk. 119 of 1181.
61. Sk. 323 of 1046, Sk. 131 of 1072; *ASMAR* 1941, 38 of 1103; Sk. 137 of 1114 and 165 of 1149, Sk. 111 of 1118, Sk. 123 of 1159, Sk. 138 of 1194 respectively.
62. Sk. 125, 118 and Sk. 106 and 99 respectively.
63. Sk. 119 and 168 respectively.
64. Sk. 106.
65. Sk. 118 and 1123.
66. It is not clear to me whether this term indicates a single institution (*pañcamaṭha*) or a cluster of five separate institutions (*pañcamaṭhas*) as the records often seem to use it to indicate both, but I have preferred to take it to mean a cluster of five.
67. Sk. 169.
68. Sk. 132 of 1072; *ASMAR* 1941, 38 of 1103; Sk. 99 of 1113.
69. Sk. 131, 169, 132, etc.
70. *EC* VIII, Sb. 277.
71. This appears to have been based on the statement occuring in one of the records on the five sects and on five maṭhas 'which shone like the five arrows in the world'.
72. Lorenzen, *op. cit.,* p. 124.
73. Sk. 106.
74. Sk. 106; also *see* (Sk. 99 of 1113) and Sk. 123.
75. Sk. 169.
76. Sk. 132.
77. *ASMAR* 1941, 38; Sk. 131, 99; *EC* VII & VIII (S); Sk. 334.
78. Sk. 106 of 1098; Sk. 99 of 1113.
79. Sk. 123.
80. Sk. 168 of 1182.
81. Sk. 112.
82. Sk. 123.
83. Sk. 102 and 108 and *EC VII & VIII* (S), 370.
84. These are Sanskrit-Kannada terms. Here '*parise*' = '*pariṣad*' means 'assembly or council; *āvaḷi* means 'line' or 'dynasty'; *āmnaya* stands for sacred tradition and *santati* means lineage. *Śaktiparise* means an 'assembly of the (devotees of) Śakti or Devi; *Parvvatāvaḷi* means mountain-lineage (of Śrīparvata or Śriśaila in Karnool Dt.,) – see Lorenzen, D.N., *The Kāpālikas and Kāḷāmukhas: Two lost Śaivaite sects*, (New Delhi, 1982), pp. 98–99.
85. *ASMAR* 1926, 65.
86. Sk. 126 of 1046.
87. Sk. 151 of 1047.
88. Sk. 114 of 1096; 118 of 1054, *EC VII & VIII* (S), Sk. 335 of 1062, Sk. 114 and 342 *ASMAR* 1929, 63, respectively.
89. *Progress Report of Kannada Research Institute for 1953–57*, (Dharwad, 1958), no. 13. I am obliged to Ms. Varija Bolar of the Dept. of History and Archaeology, Karnataka University, for drawing my attention to this reference. The earliest references to the Kāḷāmukhas in Karnataka are made in the Nandi Plates of Rāṣṭrakūṭa Govinda III, dated in December 807, and Chikka-Baḷḷāpur Plates, dated in AD 810 – *Report of Archaeological Department for 1913–14*. Attention to these has been already drawn by Venkata Subbaiah, A., – see *QJMA VII*, (Apr. 1917), no. 3, p. 177.
90. Sk. 94.
91. Sk. 111 of 11080; *ASMAR* 1929, 65.

92. Sk. 114.
93. Sk. 106.
94. Sk. 110.
95. See above note 11. The earliest village grant was received by the Kedāreśvara in 1129 (Sk. 100), followed by grants in 1149 (Sk. 103), 1164, (Sk. 108), 1179 (Sk. 350), 1186 (Sk. 97) and 1193 (Sk. 105). The first two (1129 and 1149) comprised two hamlets each, the third (1162) as many as fourteen, and the rest one hamlet each. The largest number of villages – about fourteen – were granted by Kalachūrya Bijjaḷa in 1162 to this temple. It received very little land measures, cash grants and tax releases.
96. *Epigraphia Indica* (*EI*)V, A–B; *EI* XV, No. F-1.
97. Sk. 94 and 99.
98. If Kedāreśvara temple had been built in 1078 as assumed by scholars so far, absence of references to it in records issued before 1103 cannot be explained. Also it would be difficult to explain why either the direct disciple of Kedāraśakti or his disciple's disciple, were not associated with this temple though they served as priests of other Śiva temples at Baḷḷigāve.
99. Sk. 99.
100. Sk. 94.
101. Sk. 98.
102. Sk. 104, 100.
103. Sk. 100.
104. Sk. 100 and Sk. 103.
105. Sk. 112.
106. Sk. 103 of 1149.
107. Sk. 104.
108. Sk. 104 and 105. Only once does he recall the line of the preceptors of Kedāraśakti, Śrīkaṇṭha, Someśvara and Vidyābharaṇa.
109. Sk. 104 and Sk. 123.
110. Sk. 102.
111. *Ibid.*
112. Sk. 102.
113. Sk. 108.
114. Sk. 104 and 108.
115. Sk. 105.
116. Sk. 92 of 1168, Sk. 123 of 1159 and 109 of 1162, Sk. 108 of 1164 respectively.
117. *EI* V, pp. 213 ff, 232 ff.
118. For the recorded evidence, see Tāḷikoṭe (*South Indian Inscriptions (SII)*, XV, 66 of 1184) and Ablūr (above cited) inscriptions.
119. 123, *SII XV*, 73, 1159, Sk. 123; *EI XVIII*, no. J.
120. Rao, Hayavadana, *Mysore Gazetteer*, V. (N.E), (Bangalore), 1930, p. 1283.
121. *EC V*, Ak. 77 and *EC VIII*, Sb. 262.
122. *Op. cit.* The reliefs are found on the outer face of the railing of the Someśvara temple at Ablūr.
123. *SII* XV, 56.

FIVE

❖ Pan-Indian Outlook of the Neo-Vaishnavites of Assam

S. L. BARUAH

THE COMMON BELIEF held even in some scholarly circles till recently was that Assam remained excluded from the mainstream of Indian culture up to the country's struggle for Independence. Perhaps because of such an unconscious assumption, the history of Assam, particularly of ancient and medieval times, was more or less neglected in the works of Indian historians. Inhabited, by and large, by the Kirata or Mongoloid people and located in the extreme eastern frontier of India, touching the boundaries of Burma, China and Tibet, Assam had been considered by most historians as a *Pandava-varjita* land, meaning a country untouched by the civilizing influence of the Aryans.

However, a deep study of the problem of Assam's link with India shows that Brahmanic religion penetrated into Assam as early as the later Vedic period and all the kings of Assam, beginning with Pushyavarmana (*c.* 350–80), the founder of the historic lines of the kings of Kamarupa or ancient Assam, had links with Indian sovereign powers like the Guptas and patronized the expansion of Aryan culture in their kingdom. Two kings, Bhaskaravarmana (*c.* 594–650) and Harshadeva (*c.* 725–50), took part in pan-Indian politics and attempted to claim suzerain power against other Indian rulers. Bhaskaravarmana established friendship with Harshavardhana (*c.* 606–48), the king of northern India, and led a campaign in person against Sasanka (*c.* 605–19), the powerful king of Gauda, who was a common enemy of both the rulers. Unable to resist the two-fold attack, one from the east by the king of Kamarupa and the other from the west by Devagupta of Malwa, Sasanka retreated towards the south. Bhaskaravarmana occupied Karnasuvarna, the capital of Gauda, and thus became one of the most trustworthy friends of Harshavardhana. As a mark of this, Bhaskaravarmana was given special honour in the assemblies organized by Harshavardhana at

Prayag and Kanauj in honour of the Chinese pilgrim Hiuen-Tsang, who had also visited the court of Bhaskaravarmana in AD 642.[1] Harshadeva of ancient Assam married his daughter Rajyamati to the Nepal Licchavi king Jayadeva II, with whose help he conquered Gauda, Odra, Kalinga and Kosala.[2] Some other kings of ancient Assam also established marriage relations with the royal families of Kashmir, Gauda and Dravida. Thus the Kamarupi princess Amritaprabha was married to king Meghavahana of Kashmir[3] and Indrapala (1040–65), a Kamarupa king, married a Rashtrakuta princess.[4]

Religion was the main basis of culture in ancient and medieval times, and it transcended the geographical boundaries of the country. Long before the dawn of her historic period, *i.e.* the fourth century AD, Assam, inspite of its geographical isolation and independent political existence, cultivated a feeling of togetherness with the rest of India through the bonds of Hinduism. Such relations with other kingdoms of India cleared the way for the entry into Assam of various elements of pan-Indian culture, some of which got transformed in the local setting and assumed distinct forms. This cultural affinity received strong stimulants from the Neo-Vaishnavite or Bhakti movement sponsored in Assam by Sankaradeva (1449–1568) and his apostle Madhavdeva (1489–1596), which was only a response to the Indian Bhakti movement, first started by Ramanuja in the eleventh century in the south.

Sankaradeva was a versatile genius, who combined in himself the qualities of a religious preceptor, a social reformer, an artist of high rank and a literateur of distinction. The religious bent of his mind got an opportunity to develop after the death of his first wife. At about the age of thirty-five, along with seventeen companions, he went out on a long pilgrimage of twelve years' duration in course of which he visited places like Puri, Gaya, Prayag, Vrindaban, Mathura, Kurukshetra, Badarikasram, and Rameswara Setubandha.[5] During this period he came in contact with many saints and scholars and gathered much first-hand knowledge of India and Indian life. He stayed at Puri for more than a year and it was in the holy Jagannath-kshetra that he received *jnanabhakti* (knowledge of *bhakti* or devotion) and *ajna* (orders) to propagate *bhakti-dharma* in his own country.[6] He must have been deeply impressed by the nature and working of the Bhakti movement as carried on, in different parts of the country, by the sects of Ramanuja, Madhavacharya, Nimbark and Ramananda.[7] In his celebrated work, the *Kirtana*, Sankaradeva refers to the popularity of Kabir's songs in places like Varanasi and Oresha (Puri).[8] During the period of his stay in Badarikasram, he found the place so appealing that he composed a *bargit* or devotional song expressing his keen desire 'to rest on the feet of Rama'.[9] Returning from the pilgrimage, he composed that part of the *Kirtana* called *Oresha-Varnana*, where the mythological origin of the Jagannath shrine is described.[10]

Sankaradeva's pan-Indian outlook and his outside contacts led his biographers to assume that he had disciples outside Assam. They even furnish the names of a few like Kavi Gopinath, Radha Sannyasi, Rupa, Sanatana, Vrindavanadasa and Ramakanta Kshatriya, the first of whom was initiated by him at Pushkaratirtha, the second at Gokula, the third, fourth and fifth at the Kaliya lake and the last at Upadvaraka. But as M. Neog points out, it is difficult to trust these accounts.[11] Be that as it may, it points to the fact that Sankaradeva had admirers in different parts of India and his biographers had also a pan-Indian outlook.

It is also said that Sankaradeva started propagating the new creed only after he received from Puri, through the courtsey of one Jagadish Mishra of Tirhut, a copy of the original *Bhagavata Purana* furnished with Sridhara Swami's commentary. Jagadish Mishra came to Sankaradeva's place at Bardowa in Assam and recited the entire *Bhagavata* and explained its meaning to him. A few months after this, Jagadish Mishra died.[12] This holy book helped Sankaradeva to get a clear idea of the philosophy of the *Bhakti-dharma.* In the words of one of his biographers, Ramananda Dvija, 'From that day (the day on which the *Bhagavata* was first recited by Jagadish Mishra), the *Bhagavata* came to get currency and devotees began to listen to its composition with unflinching faith.'[13]

Sankaradeva's pan-Indian contact resulting from his long pilgrimage widened his mental horizon, and his empirical knowledge of the working and implications of the Bhakti movement in other parts of India inspired him to reorganize his own society at the grass-root level using the movement as an effective weapon. Unlike most other parts of India, however, Islam did not provide an impetus to the movement in Assam, nor was Sankaradeva an apostle of any Indian Vaishnava saint. But there were in Assam perversions and debaucheries in the name of religion, and religion, instead of being a bond of social unity and a dynamic force in life, was acting as an obstacle to progress and enlightment. Sankaradeva realized that the principles of *Bhakti-dharma* with Vishnu or Krishna as the only god and *nama* or *kirtana* (devotional recital) as the only mode of worship would wipe away all socio-religious differences among the people and unite them all – Hindus or non-Hindus, tribals or non-tribals on the platform of the new creed. While applying the movement to the situation of his own country, Sankaradeva borrowed elements from both its northern and southern counterparts but more from the latter. Of all the Indian Vaishnava saints, Kabir was held by Sankaradeva in highest esteem.[14] This may have been due to Kabir's strong opposition to ritualism of both Hinduism and Islam and his endeavours to wipe out all differences between the Hindus and the Muslims by minimizing the value of both mosques and temples. Sankaradeva, however, did not lead any crusade against caste distinction but treated the devotees of diverse castes and communities as equals on the spiritual plane. There was among his converts a Muslim tailor, Chandsai, who was raised by him to the status of an *Ata* (comparable to the Buddhist Arhat).[15]

Such catholicity of Sankaradeva inspired the later Neo-Vaishnava reformers to initiate Muslims and place them on an equal footing with other disciples. Thus Aniruddhadeva (1553–1626), the founder of the Mayamara Satra in upper Assam, initiated another Muslim tailor, Dheli Darji, christened him as Dhyanapati,[16] and issued instructions that any one refusing to eat food cooked by him in his residence would be excommunicated from the order. That in other parts of India, Bhakti reformers were creating conditions for the Hindus and the Muslims to live together, on the platform of the new religion, was known well to the Neo-Vaishnavites of Assam. Therefore, in spite of Islam not being a threat to the existence of Hinduism in Assam, as the Muslim population in the state at that time was very small, the Neo-Vaishnavite reformers responded to the social implications of the movements in the Indian scene and attempted to achieve social integration.

Sankaradeva made a second pilgrimage in his old age in or about 1553, accompanied by 120 devotees. This time his itinerary was limited to Puri. In the account narrated by his biographers, it is mentioned that during this pilgrimage, Sankaradeva met Chaityanadeva of Bengal either at his native place at Navadvipa or at Puri[17] and on his way to Puri via Gaya, he visited Kabir's *math* or *than* (abode), where he met Kabir's grand-daughter. But Sankaradeva cannot have met Chaityanadeva, since the latter passed away in 1533; also there is much difference of opinion in accepting Kamali as Kabir's daughter by a woman named Loi. Be that as it may, these references bear testimony to Sankaradeva's reverence for both Chaityanadeva and Kabir, as he must have expressed it before his devotees. The biographers also record that Sankaradeva met two mendicants after he left Puri. These mendicants introduced themsleves as Rup and Sanatan's nephews (sister's sons) and disciples and they stated that they were sent out by their maternal uncles 'to see how Sankaradeva's order was thriving'.[18] The account may be surcharged with a great amount of imagination, but it can be easily accepted as a fact that all the 120 disciples except Madhavdeva, as stated in all the biographies, were eager to visit Vrindaban to see how Rup and Sanatan's order was functioning there; they also wanted to find out the points of affinities between their order and that of Sankaradeva's.[19]

It is also on record that a copy of Vishnupuri Sannyasi's *Bhakti Ratnavali* was received by Sankaradeva through Kanthabhusan, the son-in-law of his disciple Ramaram and the family priest of the Koch king Naranarayana (1540–1587). According to Daityari Thakur[20], Kanthabhusan bought this copy at Varanasi and presented it to Sannkaradeva. The other biographers, on the other hand, state that Kanthabhusan, while studying at Varanasi under Brahmananda, reported to him about Sankaradeva's activities in Assam.

Brahmananda was greatly impressed and sent the book through Kanthabhusana to Sankaradeva as a friendly gesture. Sankaradeva received the book very cordially and instructed Madhavdeva to make an Assamese rendering of it. It should be noted that several yeas before receiving this book, Sankaradeva had compiled a similar work, *Bhakti Ratnakara*, in Sanskrit, collecting materials on the essentials of Bhakti from diverse sources.

Sankaradeva's pan-Indian outlook inspired his apostle Madhavdeva and the Neo-Vaishnavites of the subsequent period to follow his line. Although only a few Vaishnava preceptors after him took on organized pilgrimages to different places of India, the Indianness instilled into the minds of the devotees through their works continues to pervade till today. The Neo-Vaishnavites felt proud if they could associate their works with Jagannath kshetra or Vrindaban. Thus Madhavdeva, as already mentioned, prepared an Assamese version of Vishnupuri Sannyasi's *Bhakti Ratnavali*; he also translated into Assamee the *Nama-Mallika* by the Orissan king Purusottam Gajapati. Madhavdeva's monumental work, *Nama-Ghosa*, based mainly on the *Bhagavata Purana*, also contains Assamese rendering of many *slokas* from the *Bhagavata Gita*, different *Puranas* like the *Brihanaradiya, Padma, Skanda, Vishnu*, and *Vamana* and Vishnupuri's *Bhakti-Ratnavali* and Sankaracharayya's *Moha-Mudgar*.[21]

The biographers of the Vaishnava saints, who also had the vision of an immortal India, wrote not only about Assam Vaishnavism and Assamese preceptors but also, at relevant places in their respective works, gave glimpses of the religious history of other faiths, such as Saktism, Tantricism and Buddhism, that prevailed in the country during the period.[22] They made the names of the contemporary Vaishnava saints of India, such as, Vishnupuri Sannyasi, Harivyas, Chaityanadeva, Kabir, Rupa, Sanatan and other, familar to the masses in Assam.[23] While giving detailed accounts of Sankaradeva's pilgrimage, they provide description of all the holy places of India, of the mode of worship in different Vaishnava temples, of people they came across, of their experiences of shopping in places like Cuttuck, Mahananda and Jahadpur and of the system of transport and communication that then existed.[24] Such descriptions of India and of the lives of Indian saints strengthened the feeling of togetherness and prompted the growth of pan-Indian culture.

Since it had been a matter of great pride to have contacts with prominent Vaishnava centres like Vrindaban and Jagannath, the patron kings and certain *Satradhikars*, while installing images of god Vishnu or Krishna in the *Satra* temple, tried their utmost to get one from these places. Thus Jayadhvaj Singha (1648–63), the first Ahom king to formally accept Vaishnavism, got the image of Vamshivadan (Krishna) from Jagannath for the *Satra* at Garamur.[25] Likewise, the head of the Dakhinpat *Satra* got the image of Jadav Rai

(Vishnu) purchased at the same place.[26] Even earlier, a peace mission sent by the Ahom king Suhungmung (1497–1539) to the Orissan ruler Vikramasena, usually identified with Pratap Rudra (1497–1540), offered worship to the Jagannath temple and excavated a tank nearby.[27]

The culture of Assam Vaishnavism was moulded by elements that prevailed in other parts of India. The institution of *Satra*, particularly that of monastic order, where celibacy is strictly followed, bears close resemblance to Buddhist *viharas* of ancient times and mathas of the medieval period. Like *prabbajja* and *upasampada* of Buddhist monasticism, there are also two stages of devotional hiearchy, *sarana* and *bhajana*, in Assam Vaishnavism.[28] Like the Sikhs, the Dadu-panthis, the Jainas and the Pranamis, the Neo-Vaishnavites of Assam also worshipped the sacred scriptures, the *Bhagavata* or the *Kirtana* and the *Namghosa* installing them on an alter. This practice continues till date in the village *Namghars* or prayer halls and is strictly followed in the *Satras* of Kala-Samhati order.[29] The Vaishnava rites and practices, the festivals, drama and music in Assam were profoundly influenced by elements in other parts of India. In the process of fusion, a distinct type of one act play, called *Ankia Nat*, and a distinct school of classical music and dance, which can be called Kamrupi, were evolved by Sankaradeva.

Their pan-Indian outlook made the Neo-Vaishnavites of Assam liberal enough to accept certain elements of Mughal music as *Nagera* and some items of Mughal dress as *chapkan, jama* and *pag* to their *Satriya* culture.[30] In his own writings Sankaradeva freely used Arabic words, such as *forman, duniya, wasil* and *haramhi khor*. In a very popular *bargit*, the first couplet of which runs as follows – *Govinda dina dayala swami / Tuhu meri sayeb, chakara hami* – he addresses God as *Sayeb* or Lord and identifies himself as His *chakara* or servant. Madhavdeva, in his *bargits* used Arabic terms like *omrao, dukani*; such words are found also in the compositions of Aniruddhadeva. Sankaradeva's *Kirtana* and Madhavdev's *Namghosa* so appealed to people of all stocks and religious shades that Hajrat Ajan Peer, alias Shah Milan, who came to Assam from Ajmere, his fore-fathers having hailed from Baghdad, to reform the practice of Islam there composed devotional songs called *Zikirs* in imitation of them.[31]

The Neo-Vaishnavite movement in Assam led to the creation of a huge mass of religious literature known as Vaishnava literature, a discussion on which is beyond the scope of this paper. The language used by the Vaishnava reformers for their religious compositions was Brajabuli, an admixture of Maithili and Assamese. One of the reasons for their using this language was the immense popularity of the songs and dramas composed by Vidyapati and others of Mithila who preceded Sankaradeva in eastern India, including Assam. The language could be easily understood by the Assamese audience.[32]

In a like manner, Assamese manuscript painting developed in the Ahom court and the *Satras* show a blending of the local elements with those from outside. Painting for religious purpose was first used by Sankaradeva as part of his first dramatic performance, *Chihna-Yatra*, organized at Bordowa when Jagannath Mishra was also present there. Of the illustrated religious manuscripts, the most noted is the *Chitra Bhagavata.* According to S.K. Chatterjee, Assamese painting, whether cultivated in the court or in the *Satras*, shows a happy blending of eastern Indian style of religious miniatures with more sophisticated Mughal and Rajasthani paintings and possibly also of the Kangra art.[33]

The response of the Neo-Vaishnavites of Assam to the Indian Bhakti movement and their earnest desire to mingle with the mainstream of Indian culture was not a one-way process. It is a fact that many youths of Assam from the aristocratic circle went to Kasi (Benaras), Vardhaman and Navadvip to have their education there. Thus the Koch princes, Narnarayan and Chilarai were educated at Benaras under Brahmananda Sannyasi.[34] And the Ahom kings, particularly Rudra Singha (1696–1714) sent youths to Bengal for pursuit of education and learning there. The *Katha-guru-charita* also records many instances of Assamese scholars going to Benaras, Mithila and Nadiya for higher studies. At the same time, scholars from these places, particularly from Santipur in West Bengal came to Assam to hold scholarly discussions with their counterparts.[35] In the above work there is reference to one such scholar named Kavichandra, who came to Narnarayan's capital with one hundred students in search of a rival disputant.[36] The *Bardowa Gurucharit* makes mention of one Asurari Bhattacharyya, who came from Varanasi to have discourses with the scholars of Kamarupa.[37] It is held that the Sikh Guru Nanak also came to Assam[38] sometime between 1517 and 1526, possibly to see the prospect of propagating his religion here. His period of stay, however, was very short and possibly he did not advance beyond the Kapili valley.

Assam as a land of Vaishnavite devotees earned reputation as far as Rajputana, so that Ram Singha, the General of Emperor Aurangzeb (1658–1707), was dissuaded from leading an expedition to Assam (1669) by his widowed mother and wife in the following words: '. . . we are told that there is universal *nama-kirtana* in that country and that Vaishnavas, Brahmanas and cows are living there in peace and happiness. By invading it, oh, how long could Mir Jumla thrive? So, take heed and do so you think proper.'[39] Ram Singha was accompanied by the ninth Sikh Guru Teg Bahadur, who came up to Dhubri, which had been visited by Guru Nanak also. The soldiers of Ram Singha, at the instance of Guru Teg Bahadur, raised a mound on the top of a hillock on the bank of the Brahmaputra, each man putting five shieldfuls of earth. On this site, was built the famous Gurudwara of Dumdume. Knowing that Guru Teg Bahadur was a successor of Guru Nanak, crowds from long distances came to have his *darshan* and obtain blessings. It is said that a local chieftain named Raja Ram had a son born to him through the blessings of the Guru. While at Dhubri, Guru Teg Bahadur received the news of the birth of his son Gobinda at Patna, who after the execution of his father by Emperor Aurangzeb in 1675, was to become the tenth Guru of the Sikhs.[40] *Gurubad* or unstinted devotion to the Guru by the Sikhs influenced a section of Neo-Vaishnavites of Assam, namely, the disciples of the *Satra* of the *Kala-Samhati* order and more particularly those of the Mayamara Satra, who organized the first popular rebellion against the Ahom monarchy in 1769, resolving to take vengeance for the persecutions heaped upon their *Gurus* by the Ahom government.[41]

Thus it was mainly through the Neo-Vaishnavites that India and Indian culture were introduced to the illiterate masses of Assam, who, like their counterparts elsewhere in the country, knew only their local identity and were vague about regional identity. Sankaradeva's *Kirtana*, in particular, is flooded with graphic descriptions of the cities of Dvaraka, Mathura, Vrindaban, Orissa (Puri), Kundila, etc., in a language that people readily understood, and the epic characters associated with these places, centering round Lord Krishna are presented in his works in so lively a manner that all the characters and places became familiar to them. The *bhaonas* or dramatic performances based on Vaishnava religious themes gave the audience a feeling as if the epic characters were physically present among them. They saw the Ganges and the Yamuna flowing in the waters of the Brahmaputra, and in the neighbouring hills, they found the presence of the Trikuta and the Govardhana. It was not Assam or Cooch-Behar, which always glistened before their eyes but a far greater and beautiful land called Bharatavarsha, of which their own country was an integral part. This feeling of Indianness was ingrained into the people's hearts and they thought themselves as Indians.

In numerous passages of his works, Sankaradeva glorifies Bharata or Bharatavarsha. In the *Anadi Patan*, for instance, he says that Bharata is the best and the holiest country of the world and even the gods aspire to have their births here. To be born in India is like acquiring *nava-nidhi* (nine jewels). He therefore, would forsake heaven to be born in India.[42] In the *Ajamil Upakhyan*, he explains the reason why it is a great fortune to be born in India. Ajamil, the hero of the book, scared at the approach of the messenger of *Yama*, the god of death, shouted at his son Narayana. But since Narayana is the name of God, the agent of God immediately appeared before him at this crucial moment, rescued him from the jaws of death and took him to heaven. *Mukti* (salvation), or *Baikuntha* (heaven) can be so easily attainable only in Bharata.[43] The substance of this eulogy of Bharata, as found in numerous passage of his works, is that this is the best country in the entire *Jambudvipa*. Whereas other parts of the world are fit for the enjoyment of sensual pleasure it is only in India that one can attain spiritual enlightment by serving *Hari* (God). There is no *Karma-bhumi* superior to this country, where one can serve according to one's needs. To be born as a human being is itself a great fortune because only human beings can serve God; and to be born in India is a far greater fortune because this can happen only when God is pleased. Even after acquiring this fortune, if some one does not worship God, he or she is destined to go to hell.

Madhavdeva in his *bargits* compares Bharata or Bharatavarsha with a treasure land and Vaishnava devotees as traders looking for jewels.[44] In another *bargit*, citing the example of Ajamil, he says *dhanya dhanya kali kal / dhanya nara tanu bhal / dhanya dhanya Bharatvarish*, meaning that when in *Kali Yuga* people recite the name of Hari, the human life and the country of Bharatvarsha are all blessed, because all these three are complimentary to one another. In yet another *bargit*, Madhavdeva called upon the Vaishnava devotees to trade in the Indian market before it was too late.[45]

Thus the two leading Neo-Vaishnavite preceptors of Assam, while organizing the Bhakti movement in accordance with the local needs of their land, so oriented its ideals and reality that it led forth the people from the narrow orbit of localism to the vast meeting ground of all Indians.[46] People of different castes and communities joined their hands together to sing the praises of God, forgetting their local identities and mingled with the inhabitants of Dvaraka, Brajadham or Gokulban. It is because of this pan-Indianness ingrained in the hearts of the people of Assam that they could play a remarkable role in India's struggle for Independence.

This also shows that Indian unity is not a gift or product of British rule. The very name Bharat or Bharatvarsha symbolized a fundamental unity of the people, who lived in the vast country north of the ocean and south of the snow-clad mountains. This sense of unity was imparted to the people by the saints, the theologians and the scholars throughout the ages and more effectively by the propagators of the Bhakti movement. It is the cultural unity, based upon spiritualism or philosophy of life and literary ideas which transcends geographical or linguistic barriers, that brings Indians of all parts of the sub-continent to the mighty bosom of Indianness and inspires them to strive together for peace, harmony and progress in a free India.

Notes and References

1. For details see, P.C. Choudhury, *History of Civilization of Assam to the Twelfth Century* AD, 2nd edn, Guwahati, 1966, pp. 167–84; S. Beal (tr.) *Life of Hiuen Tsang*, London, 1914, pp. 177f.
2. P.C. Choudhury, *op. cit.*, pp. 198–207; K.L. Barua, *Early History of Kamarupa*, Guwahati, 1966, pp. 71–73.

3. Stein (trans.), *Rajatarangini*, BK II, London, 1900, pp. 147ff.
4. M.M. Sharma (ed)., *Inscriptions of Ancient Assam*, Gauhati University, 1978, p. 215.
5. U.C. Lekharu (ed.), *Katha-guru-charita*, Nalbari, 1951, pp. 29ff.
6. Aniruddha Kayastha (trans.) *Bhagavata*, Bk.V.; H.N. Dutta-Barua (ed.) Bhagavata, *v. 4391.*
7. S.N. Sarma, *The Neo-Vaisnavite Movement and the Satra Institution of Assam*, Gauhati University, 1966, p. 10.
8. M. Neog (ed.), *Kirtana-Ghosa Aru Nama-Ghosa*, Guwahati, 1967, p. 28.
9. cf. M. Neog, *Sankardeva and His Times*, Gauhati University, 1965, p. 109.
10. M. Neog (ed.), *Kirtana-Ghosa Aru Nama-Ghosa*, pp. 558–615.
11. M. Neog, *Sankaradeva and His Times*, p. 105.
12. Ramananda Dvija, *Guru-charita*, p. 156, v. 670; Daityari Thakur, *Sankardeva-Madhavdeva Charita,* (ed.) H. Gupta, Tejpur, 1900, p. 25; S.N. Sarma, *op. cit.*, p. 12.
13. Ramananda Dvija, *op. cit.*, p. 156, v.670.
14. M. Neog, *Sri Sri Sankardeva*, Dibrugarh / Guwahati, 1987, p. 97.
15. Among his other disciples, there were Govinda, a Garo; Paramananda, a Miri; Jayananda, a Bhutiya; Narahari, an Ahom; Sriram, a Kaivarta; Madhava of Jayantiya, a potter, and Damodara, a baniya or trader.
16. C. Goswami, *Sri Sri Aniruddhadevar Charit aru Mayamara Satrar Gosain Sakalar Vamsavali*, Tinsukia, 1933, v. 20.
17. Daityari Thakur, *op. cit.,* vv. 577f.; M. Neog (ed.), *Bardowa Guru-Charit*, Guwahati, 1980, chap. 26; *Katha-guru-charit*, p. 152.
18. *Bardowa Guru-Charit*, pp. 141ff.; *Katha-guru-charit*, pp. 154(*a*) and (*b*). For details see, M. Neog, *Sankardeva and His times*.
19. *Katha-guru-charit*, p. 154(b).
20. Daityari Thakur, *op. cit.*, vv. 700ff.
21 M.Neog (ed.), *Kirtana-Ghosa and Nama-Ghosa*, preface, p. 45.
22 B.K. Kakati and B.K. Barua, Forword to the *Katha-guru-charit*, pp. iv–v.
23. *Ibid.*, p. 19f.
24. *Ibid.*, p. 29ff.
25. M. Neog (ed.), *Pabitra Asam*, Jorhat, 1960, p. 63.
26. *Ibid.*, p. 66.
27. S.K. Bhuyan (ed.), *Asam Buranji* (obtained from the family of Sukumar Mahanta), Guwahati, 1960, pp. 20ff.
28. S.N. Sarma, *op. cit.*, p.120.
29. After the death of Sankaradeva, Assam Vaishnava school got divided into four *Samhatis* or orders, such as, *Purusha, Brahma, Nika* and *Kala. Kala Samhati* was so called because its founder, Gopaldeva, had his headquarters at Kaljhar near Bhavanipur in Cooch Behar.
30. A. Bhagawati, 'Satriya Nach', *Ramdhenu*, vol. xvii, no. 2; cited in A. Sattar, *Sangmrishanat Asamiya Sanskriti*, Jorhat, 1972, p. 21.
31. For details, see S.A. Malik, *Asamiya Zikir aru Zari*, Guwahati, 1958.
32. S.N. Sarma, *op. cit.*, p. 164.
33. *Place of Assam in the History and Civilization of India*, Gauhati University, 1970, p. 58.
34. N.C. Sharma (ed.), *Darrang Raj Vamsavali*, Pathsala, 1973, vv. 265f.
35. *Katha-guru charita*, pp. iv, 10, 194, 357.

36. *Ibid.*, p. 193.
37. M. Neog (ed.) *Bardowa Gurucharit*, Guwahati, 1980, pp. 190f.
38. M. Neog (ed.), *Banikanta Rachanavali*, Guwahati, 1991, pp. 204ff. During the period of his stay in Assam, Guru Nanak is said to have converted a queen named Nur Shah, who was ruling in Kamrup, *i.e.* lower Brahmaputra valley. Failing to cast spells on the Guru and lure him by the offer of precious jewels, she, along with her attendants, laid prostrate at the feet of the Guru and became his disciple. The actual name of Nur Shah might have been different. Since she is described as the queen of a matriarchal state, she might have ruled somewhere at the foot of the Garo hills, or in the plains area of the Jayantiya kingdom, both being parts of the state of Meghalaya at present, as the Garos and so also the Khasis and the Jayantiyas are still matriarchal. It is also possible that she ruled in the western part of the Kapili valley, where the Lalungs or Tiwas had the same system in the past.
39. S.K. Bhuyan (ed.), *Asam Buranji*, p. 121; H.C. Goswami (ed.), *Purani Asam Buranji*, Guwahati, 1922, p. 147; S.K. Bhuyan, *Studies in the History of Assam*, Guwahati, 1965, p. 87.
40. S.K. Bhuyan, *Lachit Barphukan and His Times*, Guwahati, 1947, pp. 115f.; M.A. Macauliff, *The Sikh Religion*, vol. IV, Oxford, 1909, pp. 352–98.
41. The war cry of the rebels was *Maari jaon, Mari jaon / Gurur wrin suji jaon*, meaning 'I will kill or get myself killed, but I will repay my debt to my *Guru* – S.K. Bhuyan (ed.), *Tungkhungia Buranji*, Guwahati, 1932, p. 29; For details on the Moamariya rebellion, see, S.L. Baruah, *Last Days of Ahom Monarchy*, New Delhi, 1993, chap. 2.
42. K.D. Goswami (ed.), *Srimad Bhagavata*, Dibrugarh, 1993, p. 54, vv. 105–19.
43. M. Neog (ed.), *Kirtana Ghosa aru Nama-Ghosa*, pp. 46–64.
44. H.N. Dutta Barua (ed.), *Bargit aru Bhattima – Gunamala*, by Sankaradeva and Madhavdeva, Nalbari, 1958, p. 14.
45. *Besayu Bharaste hat, aur beli nate* – H.N. Dutta Barua, *op. cit.*, p. 153.
46. A.C. Goswami, *Sankar Kahatu Upay*, Guwahati, 1985, p. 28.

SIX ❖ # How the Chinese saw the different Communities in India?

HARAPRASAD RAY

INDIA IS INDEED A great sea of humanity, into which have flowed different races with their cultures. Some came looking for a safe haven driven by their enemies; others came as settlers but later turned into conquerors. Tagore looked at it as *Bharatatirtha* – Bharata the Land of Pilgrimage, and invoked the cause of national unity:

> Aryans and non-Aryans, Dravidians and Chinese, Scythians, Huns, Pathans and Moghuls, all have merged and lost themselves in one body.[1]

This may seem to be a poet's romantic view of the history after all the political vicissitudes and social upheavals that have taken place in this subcontinent during the five decades or so after 1947. However, history does stand testimony to the fact that different communities in India have lived in harmony and amity most of the time.

In this context it may be interesting to delve into the ancient records and writings of foreigners to find out what impressions they had of the local people who were divided into different sects and religious groups.

During the early Christian era, a large part of Chinese population embraced Buddhism. In consequence, innumerable Chinese monks came to India to study Buddhism to be able to translate various Buddhist scriptures into Chinese after their return to China. They knew Sanskrit and maybe also Pali and some other local languages. It was therefore possible for them to understand the relations between the Buddhists, the Jains and the followers of Brahmanic cult whom the Chinese called the 'worshippers of the Devas' (various Hindu Gods).

I

When Faxian came to India through the central Asian route, the entire central Asia, the north-west India (present-day Afganisthan, Iran and Pakistan) and northern India abounded in Buddhist temples alongside the roads together with Deva temples. We know this first from his first-hand account of India. Faxian was in India for six years from around AD 405 to 411. During his passage he found a large number of Sangharamas; on both sides of the Yamuna in Mathura, he counted twenty of them with nearly 3000 priests. Brahmins and even the followers of Devadatta and other Deva-worshippers were also there. After visiting Kanauj, Koshala, Sravasti and Jetavana viharas and other holy places, he had a good grasp of the social structure of India which enabled him to remark:

In this country of Mid-India there are ninety-six heretical sects, all of whom allow the reality of wordly phenomenon. Each sect has its disciples, who beg their food but do not carry alms-dishes. They also piously build hospices by the side of solitary roads for the shelter of travellers, where they may rest, sleep, eat and drink, and are supplied with all necessaries. The followers of Buddha also, as they pass to and fro, are entertained by them, only different arrangements are made for their convenience. Devadatta also has a body of disciples still existing; they pay religious reverence to the three past Buddhas, but not to Sakyamuni Buddha.[2]

This unambiguouns statement and many other instances like the Brahmana Radha-svami of Pataliputra, who extended the influence of Buddhism and neutralized the impact of other schools (termed heretics by Faxian), take us into a world very different from ours of today, a world where diverse faiths contended with each other, tolerated each other and co-existed with each other.[3]

By the time Xuanzang (Hiuen Tsang) came to live in India between AD 629 and 645, different Buddhist schools had sprung up: these sects were constantly at variance with, and criticized each other, yet these partisans of the Great (*Maha*) and Little (*Hina*) Vehicle (*Yana*) were content to dwell apart.[4] We have the well-known case of King Sasanka who is said to have tried unsuccessfully to banish Buddhism from Bengal.[5] But Sasanka's case is symptomatic of the revival of Brahmanism which was still about three centuries away in the womb of future. As a matter of fact, both Faxian and Xuanzang cite many instances where disputes, mainly ideological, were settled through open polemics in the assembly of the well-acknowledged and respected scholars from opposite camps, and in most cases the defeated individual would accept the tenets of the victor as in the case of Madhava (*Muo-da-bo*) who was worsted by Gunamati followed by the defeat of six Brahmans by his servant.[6]

Apart from this we do not find any other kind of 'Holy War' followed by homicidal religious inquisition for suppression of herersy. Everywhere, from Mathura to Kamarupa, we find rows of Buddhist viharas and temples in existence by the side of the Deva (*i.e.* Hindu and other) temples, and sometimes overlapping.[7]

Xuanzang described Sasanka as the wicked king of Karnasuvarna who oppressed the Buddhists[6] and even cut the Bodhi Tree. But this remark is not borne out by the presence of Raktamrittika Vihara near Sasanka's capital, Karnasuvarna, which was visited by the Chinese pilgrim who spoke in glowing terms about the proper condition of the monastery, the ruins of which have now been excavated near Chiruti, about ten kilometers from Murshidabad town of West Bengal. Probably the pilgrim was influenced by Harsa's rivalry with Sasanka who had also engineered the murder of Harsa's elder brother and brother-in-law. The liberal policy followed by most Indian rulers must have been a part of the state policy. But in actual public life and religious writings there were sectarian forces at work. A spirit of animosity is found in the epics and Puranas towards the heterodox systems. A lot of passages may be cited from the epics and the Puranas which speak contemptuously of other systems. Tensions existed not only between the adherents of different religions or sects, but sometimes even between two groups belonging to the same sects as it appears from the Paschimbhag copper plate inscriptions of Sricandra, a king of the tenth century AD in eastern Bengal.[8]

It appears from all available sources that sectarian or communal hostilities in the ancient period of Indian history were due to a kind of sectarian chauvinism, a perverted glorification of one's own sect or creed, by criticizing other sects. Apart from this, it had no ulterior motive to achieve any political or other specific goal, unlike the modern forms of sectarianism or communalism. Use of invectives in polemics is a universal practice even today, not only in the field of religion but also in that of race, language and culture. The Mimangsakas were severe critics of Buddhism, but they did not fail to appreciate many of the Buddhist fundamentals. Buddhist scholars and logicians in their turn were not lagging behind in refuting many aspects of the Sānkhya, Vedānta, Nyāya-Vaiṣeśika, Mimāngsā, Yoga and Jainism. But they reciprocated the spirit of tolerance and appreciation of the views of their opponents and enriched their own doctrinal viewpoints by assimilating and accepting many of their concepts. This phenomenon is reflected in the travelogues of Faxian, Xuanzang, Dao Shi, Hui Li and others.

II

Similarly, in the South, the multicoloured Kerala society has been created over centuries with Hindu, Jaina, Buddhist, Jewish, Christian and Islamic elements coexisting without losing their identity or even their contrast in character. Each religion brought not only a creed but also a specific way of life. The majority community was much influenced by these cultural contacts: they received several non-Indian strains of plants like tapioca, papaya, cashew and tobacco from the West, Chinese pottery, gun powder and chillies from China, and best imported Arab horses, and Persian scents and Greek wine. Through these contacts the people of Kerala acquired a high level of temperamental adjustability and open-mindedness. Minority groups were Indianized, Hinduized and also Keralized. It is worth noting that the Jainas were almost completely absorbed in the Nayar community and the Buddhists in the Ilava community, both typical of Kerala.[9]

There is a whole community of Malayalam-speaking Black Jews in Kerala in spite of the fact that the Jews are known for their exclusiveness and racial arrogance. What is more, the Christians adopted Hindu names, ritual of worship (like *nila-vilakku*), and customs like the wearing of *tali* by the bride. The Muslims constructed temple-like mosques, adopted matriliny in certain areas, and cultivated a new dialect of Arab-Malayalam with its own folk literature.

It is a fact that early Jews and Christians came to this undeveloped Dravidian society with shiploads of gold and the promise of trade. The interest of trade induced harmony in spite of religious and racial differences. The Christian church established by *Mar Sapir Iso* in the ninth century, and the wealth of Joseph Rabbon, the Jew, who flourished at the beginning of the eleventh century AD, came under the protection of the state.[10]

The Brahmin-Kshatriya prejudice against trade and navigation induced them to leave such mundane affairs in the hands of the foreigners. This made it easy for the Jews, the Christians, the Muslims the Chettys and the Europeans at a later stage, to gain entry into the society of Kerala. Even the advent of Islam at the close of the Cera period in the twelfth century did not materially alter the framework of society in Kerala. While the Muslims entered north India as invaders and fanatical iconoclasts, they came to the west coast as friendly merchants and ambassadors of Arab culture. They were well received in Kerala by the rulers who found in them a substitute for the Syrian Christians and Jews whose international standing was on the wane.

Under the conquering impulse of Islam, the Arabs seized the countries lying on the Indo-Syrian route (AD 632–51). Being both a trading and fighting race, they realized the commercial importance of this route, and soon both Busserah and Baghdad under the Caliphs became the opulent headquarters of Indian trade. There was a prosperous Arab trading community settled at Canton (*Khanfu*) during the seventh century, and it is believed that four disciples of the prophet Muhammad were in the coastal towns of Canton (Guangzhou), Yangzhou and Quanzhou (Zaytun).[11] The tombs of two of these holy men can be seen in Quanzhou. These were repaired by the great eunuch Zheng He in the early fifteenth century.

Muslim influence penetrated into the Hindu society in northern and eastern India through the preachings of Fakirs, who were known as Pirs (mostly Sufis from Iran). There were innumerable Pirs and Gazis in Bengal. They exerted religious as well as administrative authority, and were popular both among the Hindus and the Muslims. Many songs were composed in praise of the Pirs and Gazis. It is interesting that most of these songs were influenced by the *Padavali Kirtan* of the Vaishnavas. Such admixture of two religious tenets not only produced good feelings between the two communities but also had some other good results. Many Muslim rulers patronized Hindu poets, encouraged the study of Hindu religious texts and appointed scholars to translate the Ramayana and the Mahābhārata from Sanskrit into Bengali.[12]

By the end of the fourteenth century, the Sultans of Bengal had already established their power over every nook and corner of Bengal as they had no rival to challenge their supremacy. But in Kerala, particularly in Calicut (Kozhikode), the Hindu Samuttiris (Zamorin) had the political power firmly in their hands: for their material prosperity, however, they depended safely on their Arab allies, so that new Muslim settlements developed in all the coastal towns. With their help the Samuttiris extended their sphere of influence. As a reward for their help the Kozhikkottu Koya (the Qazi) was given a place on the right side of the Samuttiri during the ceremonial function of the *Mamaka* or *mahamagha*. The Shah Bandar or the Port Commissioner of Calicut was a Muslim. The Chinese noted his presence without mentioning his name. The Samuttiri patronized the Muslims to such an extent that in the West, he was known as a Moorish Chieftain. The trade interests of Kozhikode made the Zamorin a vital link in the chain of Moorish powers from Cordoba in west Europe to Malacca in east Asia.[13]

In northern and eastern India, many among the populace embraced Islam either being attracted by the piety or the miracles of the Muslim saints or under coercion. Political power was shared between the local kings and the invading power. The armies of the Turkish and Khalji emperors as well as those of the Sultans of Bengal were composed of Hindus and Musalmans. The general of the Bengal Sultan Jalaluddin was a Hindu named Rājyadhara.[14] In Bengal many Islamic folk compositions, based on ancient tradition, began to appear, some of which are, *Sunya Purāna, Dharma Purāna*,[15] and *Satya Pirer Pānchāli*. The Hindus visited the *Pir dargah* (cemetery), and the Muslims would attend the Hindu pujas and often they would fix the date of a marriage after consultation with a Hindu astrologer.[16]

The religious fervour accompanying the introduction of Buddhism slowed down in 907 after the downfall of the Tang dynasty. It continued in an indifferent manner following the decay of Buddhism in India. By the tenth century AD it was only a rare phenomenon.

In the meantime, in the Coromandal (Cholamandala) coast in the peninsular India, rose a strong naval power, called the Cholas (*cola*), who resurrected the old bond with China. The Sundara Pandyas came as their rivals in the Madura region (called Mabar by the Arabs). The Arabs and the Persian traders came into close contact with these rulers and served as their envoys to the Chinese Court. One such confirmed case known from Chinese historical writings is that of Fakhruddin (*Bo-ha-li* in Chinese) who died on the way while returning from China to the Malabar in 1305.[17]

At the turn of the twelfth century, we find frequent mention of foreigners from central Asia. The Arabs had already become a force to reckon with in the sub-continent. They were known as *Turki* or *Turaska*, which indicated that they were Muslims from Iran, Afghanistan or the Arabian countries. The Chinese also used the same term in its Sinified form, *i.e.*, *Dashi*, meaning the Taziks. Zhao Rugua (Chau Jukua), writing in 1225 or 1226, uses twelfth-century information to describe Indian states like the Chola, Gujarat, Malwa, Bengal, Malabar, etc. In the course of his narration he mentions a state called *Nan-ni-hua-luo*, *i.e.,* South Nihualo, as a habitat of orthodox Hindus who lived separately from the Arab settlers and 'when Arab (*Dashi*) foreigners came to this place they gave them seats outside the doors and lodged them in separate houses supplied with bedding and household utensils.'[18] At first it gives the impression that the foreign Muslims were treated in this way either through caste prejudice or to show them special honour. Wang Dayuan presumably speaks about the same area when he says about Huoluo in 1350 that 'when neighbours come, they may not enter each other's houses unless they are of the same class'.[19] Here class may also mean caste as well as religion and race.[20] It means that these people lived in exclusion. Probably Wang Dayan visited a Brahmin village while Zhao Rugua's statement, as is well-known, came from the Arab traders. The place may be South Honovar or Honnore in both cases, since the description of the people and their habits and customs are similar and they resemble the Malayali people in the south.[21]

However, none of the authors or their informants give any indication of caste or religious disharmony in any place in India at a time when Islam was well entrenched in almost all the parts of India except perhaps Assam. The author whom we have already quoted above is quite reliable, since he had travelled widely along the Gulf area and collected detailed information not only of these places but also regarding the countries he had heard about.

Moreover, in his detailed description of the then Orissa (called Udra, and changed into *Wudie* in Chinese) he notes that, 'they [the people of Orissa] do not (even) pick up things (dropped) on the highways. All the villages live on terms of amity, and their gentry esteem right doing . . .'[22] this is a reliable testimony to show that religion and creed did not mar mutual relations in our society.

The Chinese frequented the coastal towns like Chittagong, Quilon, Cain

Kollam (Cranganore), Cochin and Calicut, and the capitals of Bengal, Pandua, and the Tughlaq Court at Delhi where population was probably divided into two groups, Muslims and Hindus (*Yindu*). Customs of the two groups were different but in dress they bore similarity. This led to the wrong conclusion by the interpreter Ma Huan, who was a Chinese Muslim, that the inhabitants of Pandua as well as of the port town of Calicut (today known as the Nagaram quarter) were all Muslims.[23] However, this misconception was removed by the observation of other contemporary travellers like Fei Xin who visited the Indian states on several occasions with the imperial fleet between AD 1407 and 1433.[24] The confusion was created by the dress put on by the men in Bengal, which was 'white cotton turban and a long white cotton shirt',[25] which have been clearly noted as 'Muslim style clothing'[26].

The most remarkable point worth noting about the Sultans and their officials who had migrated to Bengal around late thirteenth or fourteenth century is the fact that by early fifteenth century these royal personages had already adopted Bengali as their mother tongue, a fact that did not escape the notice of the Chinese interpreters who knew Persian (and probably Bengali also). They do, of course, mention that the courtiers knew Persian as well.[27]

Fei Xin has an interesting observation to make about the Hindus:

> There is a class of people called Hindu (*Yindu*) who do not eat beef, and the men and women do not eat in the same place; when the husband dies, the wife does not marry again, nor does the husband marry again when the wife dies. If there are any very poor among them without any (means of) support, the various families of the village will, in turn, support them; but they are not allowed to seek their food in other villages. So this broad mindedness (of the people) is lauded.[28]

It is apparent, the informer of the Chinese official was a Bengali Hindu eager to show off male chastity. Otherwise the statement is eloquent testimony to a self-sufficient society eager to preserve its traditional social fabric.

The Chinese writings on India are all the more interesting because of the fact that those were the days when the Europeans were not heard of in India, and the central Asian Muslims as a whole were partners (somewhere major partners as in Bengal and elsewhere equal as in Kerala) in trade, but formed only a small minority in the social life of the common people. Yet we find them an integral part of the society.

Thus, when the Chinese travellers describe the people of Kerala from Cochin up to Calicut, they include the Muslims among the five classes of people, the four others being: *Namphi* (Namboodiris – a general term presumably including the Nairs also, if this class was in existence in early fifteenth century), the Chettys, the Klings and the Mukuvas. Ma Huan does not stop there; he further adds in his discription of Calicut: 'The kings of the country and the people, all refrain from eating beef. The great chiefs who are Muslims (on their part) refrain from eating the flesh of pig. A former king (of

Calicut) made a sworn compact with the Muslim people that, "you do not eat beef, I do not eat pork; we will mutually respect the taboo." This (compact) has been honoured right down to the present day.'[29]

On the social customs, the same author adds: 'As to the popular customs and the marriage and funeral rites, the Soli (Chola, a generic term used for all Hindus belonging to the south Indian stock) people and the Muslim people each follow the ritual forms of their own class, and these are different.[30]

The Hindu and Muslim usages differ in many respects. The rulers in the south were Hindu, while in the north, the rulers, in the main, were Muslim settlers, except the local chiefs who were the hereditary Hindu nobles. But, on the whole, the entire country was a Hindu country, and it had the tradition of treating all foreigners as guests, and after they were absorbed into the society, they were left to themselves so that they could follow their vocation and religious practices without interference from any quarter. Although the Hindus discriminated against the low caste Mukuvas, etc., they meant no disrespect to foreigners.[31] This characteristic of the Indians was to be their undoing as well.

A Resume

The picture of the medieval Indian society that emerges from the description given by the Chinese is one of a mixed kind. People lived separately but dressed in a way that might lead one to make the mistake of assuming a Hindu aristocrat to be a Muslim. The Muslim head-dress, the turban, had been so popular that even the great poet Krittibasa Ojha, the author of Bengali Ramayana, had included it as the head-dress of Rama and Laksmana during their marriage.[32]

New cults transcending religious barriers developed during the medieval period. This was the natural outcome of a common village life shared by Hindu and Muslim peasants. Marco Polo and Ibn Baṭṭuṭā and the Chinese saw Buddhists, Muslims and Christians pay homage to a relic on Adam's peak in Sri Lanka. In Assam and Bengal, this took the form of joint pilgrimages for some deity or deified human as a saintly *pir*. The most remarkable of this was *Satya Pir*, which probably later spread all over India in the guise of *Satya-narayana* the true Narayana, a popular Hindu observance without any past religious sanction. We may recall that the teachings of Guru Nanak [1469–1538] attracted both the Muslims and the Hindus, as did the simple poetry of the almost contemporary Muslim weaver Kabir [1455–1517].[33]

From what we learn from the Chinese writings which are confirmed by other sources, the economic life of the people flowed uninterrupted along the same course as in the past. The cultivator, the oil-presser, the brewer, the weaver and the mason earned their livelihood through the pursuit of their ancestral callings. In the towns and the neighbourhood, one could see the prevalence of a few of the new crafts and techniques brought over from Persia or central Asia. Among the textiles one finds some new fabrics of fine variety like *bafta, sahnbaft, sakelat, saf* (scarlet or broadcloth and woollens respectively) and *makhmal*, along with local products like *pachari* (pitchery of later period), *jhamartali*, and white, smooth and glossy-like-deer-skin mulberry-made paper, were probably perfected through introduction of new artisans and new methods. Precious stones, and different kinds of aromatics like frankincense, metal engravings and the like, which were originally from central Asia, were also being manufactured and / or processed in India for export abroad.[34]

Capital towns like Pandua, Gaur and Delhi had beautiful buildings and mosques. It is definite that there were many Hindu craftsmen of the old regimes; for example, Iltutmish engaged Hindu craftsmen for building a mosque in Ajmere at the foot of the Taragarh hills in the thirteenth century. There is also historical proof that Mahmud of Ghazni and Timur forcibly carried away stone workers from Afghanistan and central Asia. While effects of external pressures on traditional arrangements are evident, we may take it that these arrangements remained more or less unbroken. Productive arrangements in the country remained more or less unaltered during the period preceding the British rule.[35]

There are ups and downs in all aspects of life in the history of a country, and India is not an exception. In times of crucial moments it is indeed the balancing efforts of those who are concerned with the fate of the nation that have, in the past, ushered in harmony among the people of different faiths and beliefs in India. And in our age, Tagore invokes the cause of national unity:

> 'come, one and all, to the Mother's crowning, come, fill the sacred bowl and let all unite and consecrate the waters on the shores of vast humanity that is India'[36]
>
> (*Bharatatirtha*)

Notes and References

1. Rabindranath Thakur, *Rabindra Rachanabali* (complete Works of Rabindranath Tagore), centenary edn. (Government of West Bengal Calcutta, 1961) (in Bengali), vol. IV, p. 195).
2. See Samuel Beal, *Si-yu-ki: Buddhist Records of the Western World*, translated from the Chinese of Hiuen Tsang (AD 629,) (reprinted, Delhi, 1969), p. XVIII.
3. *Ibid.*, p. VI.
4. *Ibid.*, vol. I, p. 80. For some cases of conflict, see, vol. II, p. 8.
5. For Sasanka, see *ibid.*, vol. II, p. 42.
6. The text says Madhava died out of fear for defeat, ibid., pp. 104–10, 121–22. Hui Li in his life of Xuanzang titled *Dazi En Si Sanzang Fashi Zhuan* (The Tripitaka Master

of the great Zi En Monastery), (Peking, 1959), also gives a few instances, pp. 156–57, 174–75 (here we find the solitary case of an attempt on the life of Xuanzang).

7. See, for instance, Beal, *op. cit.*, vol. I, pp. 179–80, 187, 190, 198, 202, 207, 230; vol. II, pp. 2, 14, 44, 66, 81–82, 186, 200–1, 206, 208 and so on.
8. See N.N. Bhattacharya, 'Communalism, Integration and Allied Problems: Ancient Indian Perspective', *Presidential Address*, Ancient Indian History Section, Indian History Congress. 52nd Session, Delhi, 21–23 February, 1992, p. 12.
9. M.G.S. Narayanan, *Cultural Symbiosis in Kerala,* (Trivandrum: Kerala Historical Society, 1972), p. IX.
10. *Ibid.*, p. 5.
11. F. Hirth and W.W. Rockhill, tr., *Chau Jukua, His work on the Chinese and Arab Trade in the Twelfth and Thirteenth Centuries, entitled Chu-fan-chih* (St. Petersburg, 1911, Paragon Reprint, New York, 1966), pp. 14–15.
12. Aparna Bhattacharya, 'Worship of Satyapir, example of Hindu-Muslim Rapprochement in Bengal', *Proceedings of Indian History Congress, 32nd Session*, 1970, pp. 204–5.
13. Naranayanan, *op. cit.,* (no. 9 above), p. 6.
14. Haraprasad Ray, *Trade and Diplomacy in India-China Relations: A Study of Bengal during the 15th Century*, (New Delhi: Radiant, 1993), p. 102.
15. Abdul Karim, *Social History of the Muslims in Bengal (Down to AD 1538)* (Dacca, 1959), pp. 142–44.
16. Aparna Bhattacharya, *op. cit.*, p. 206.
17. See, Haraprasad Ray, 'Identity of the fugitive king of South India who sought China's help during late 13th century AD', *Proceedings of the Indian History Congress, 56th session*, (R.B. University, Calcutta, 1995), pp. 165–71.
18. Hirth and Rockhill, *op. cit.*, (no. 11 above), p. 97.
19. Su Jiqing, (ed.), *Daoyi Zhilue Jiaoshi, Wang Dayuan Zhu* (Wang Dayuan's Records of the Foreign Islands Annotated) (1350), (1968, reprinted, Beijing, 1981), p. 292.
20. Rockhill translates the term *lei* as caste: see *idem*. 'Notes on the Relations and Trade of China with the Eastern Archipelago and the coast of the Indian Ocean during the 14th century,' *Toung pao*, vol. XVI, 1915, p. 466.
21. Su Jiqing, (ed.), *op. cit.,* (no. 19 above), pp. 292–93.
22. *Ibid.*, p. 375.
23. Feng Chengjun, (ed.), *Yingyai Shenglan Jiaozhu* (Ma Huan's Overall Survey of the Ocean's Shores Annotated), (1934, reprinted, Taipei, 1970), pp. 44 (Calicut), 59 (Bengal).
24. *Idem*, (ed.), *Xingcha Shenglan Jiaozhu* (Feixin's Overall Survey in the Starry Raft Annotated), (1936, reprinted, Taipei, 1970), pp. 31–32, 39–40.
25. *Ibid.*, p. 40.
26. Feng, (ed.), *Yingyai Shenglan, op. cit.*, (no. 23 above) p. 59.
27. *Ibid.*, Ma Huan remarks that 'Bengali is a distinct family of language'. This is confirmed by other writers also. See Haraprasad Ray, *Trade and Diplomacy in India-China Relations, op. cit.*, 1993, p. 102, for dresses, see, pp. 103–4.
28. Feng, (ed.), *Xingcha Sehnglan, loc. cit.* (no. 24 above)
29. Feng, (ed.), *Yingyal Shenglan, op. cit.* (no. 23 above), p. 43. Feng quotes a different version in his note which runs: as 'you do not eat pork, I do not eat beef,' which seems to be reasonable, and hence preferable.
30. *Ibid.*, pp. 48–49.

31. The Chinese interpreter (Ma Huan) has noticed that the Mukuvas were not allowed to wear clothing beyond the navel on the upper part of the body, and beyond the knee at the bottom, and, when they went out on to the road, if they met a man of the Namboodiri or Chetty class, they prostrated themselves on the ground, and waited in that posture till the former passed by; ibid., p. 39.
32. For this and other aspects of fifteenth century Bengali society, see, Haraprasad Ray, *op. cit.*, (no. 14 above), pp. 102–5.
33. D.D. Kosambi, *An Introduction to the Study of Indian History*, (Bombay: Popular Prakashan, 2nd edn., 1975), p. 389.
34. See for details, Haraprasad Ray, *op. cit.*, (no. 14 above) pp. 83–93, 114.
35. See, Nirmal Kumar Bose, *The Structure of Hindu Society*, tr. by Andre Beteille, (revised edn., New Delhi: Orient Longman, 1975), pp. 131–32.
36. Rabindra Nath Thakur, *loc. cit.*

SEVEN ❖ # Social Relations in Medieval Maharashtra: Experiments in Living Together

A. R. KULKARNI

MEDIEVAL PERIOD WAS A period of confrontations in the history of Deccan in general and of Maharashtra in particular. The Maratha society, particularly during the seventeenth century, was experiencing the interaction among the three political powers: Bahamani kingdom and later on its offshoots, the Mughals, and the Marathas. Religion-wise the Maratha society was broadly divided into two major groups: the Hindus and the Muslims. The Portuguese who occupied Goa in the early sixteenth century were slowly infiltrating in the Konkan, a natural division of the Maratha country on the west-coast, and converting the Hindus to Christianity on a mass scale. With the consolidation of Maratha power in the seventeenth century, a remarkable change was introduced in the social, political, and economic life in the Maratha country where the political supremacy of the Marathas was directly or indirectly accepted. It is, therefore, worthwhile to know how the indigenous society reacted to these changes in political life, and how, in spite of the differences in social, political, and religious practices of the three religious communities, the Hindus, the Muslims, and the Christians lived together as integral parts of the village communities in the past, and continue to do so today. A history of social relations is essentially a history of living together; it is an analysis of the tendencies and efforts of individuals, social groups, and the State, which made it possible for peaceful co-existence of all the social groups of a particular region.

The political history of the Maratha country created a complex social structure which necessitated the promotion of cordial social relations, peaceful co-existence and integration. The rulers of the Maratha country, both Hindus and Muslims, therefore were following the policy of toleration, particularly in religious matters.

The Muslims who came to India in the early medieval period had political motives behind their activities rather than religious. They were in search of a permanent home, and they found some place for settlement in the north Konkan. They were called *navayats* meaning thereby newly arrived. They were Sunnis from Persia who had been persecuted and expelled in the eighth century.

These *navayats* later on mixed with the Hindus of Konkan and in the course of time entered into matrimonial alliances with the local people. The Muslim community that emerged out of this mixture of the Hindus and Musalmans came to be known as Konkani Muslims. The Konkani Muslims are of two types – *Jamatis i.e.,* pure Muslims, and *Daldis*, the converted Hindus, probably from the *Koli* community of the west-coast. The *Daldis* were essentially fishermen, and were associated with maritime activities or professions connected with the sea.

Colonization of villages was a continuous process in the medieval period. Whenever the settlement of a new village was under consideration a layout was prepared and different parts of the village were assigned first to the families of the pioneers of the village, and then to different groups whose services were essential to the village, and thus a community was created. In such proposed villages a place was also reserved for the Muslims. V.N. Mandlik gives an account of the colonization of Murud, a village in the Konkan, based on a Marathi document in which it is mentioned that quarters for the *yavanas* (*i.e.* Muslims) were provided on the outskirts of the village, including a piece of land for building a mosque called *shunyalaya*, *i.e.* abode of nothing.[1]

The mutual respect for each other was revealed in the activities of both the communities in their day-to-day life, political, social or otherwise.

The official documents of the Muslim rulers in the medieval period were generally bilingual, *i.e.,* Persian and Marathi (in the *modi* script), and sometimes they begin with an invocation to a Hindu goddess in the form *aja puja Saraswati.*[2] The Adilshah of Bijapur has been referred to by the Hindus as *Jagatguru.*[3] Persons serving Muslim governments particularly were expected to know Persian; therefore, we find a class of scribes called *parasnavis* or *parasnis* emerging in the Maratha country in the medieval period. Many Persian words infiltrated into Marathi language and even the format of correspondence was influenced. A Marathi document in modi script of the year 1570 has only 150 words, of which only seven were Marathi.[4] According to the Maratha historian V.K. Rajwade, there were only 14.4 per cent Marathi words in a Marathi letter of 1628 and the rest were Persian. The situation improved after the establishment of Maratha sovereignty, and the ratio of Marathi words in a document of 1677 was 62.2 per cent and in 1728 it was 93.7 per cent.[5] We find many Persian terms being used in Maratha administration, such as the *Peshwa*, the *daftardar*, the *hukumatpanhah*, the *mukadam*, the *mirasdar*, and so on. Hindus had adopted Muslim names such as Shahaji,

Sharifji, Piraji, Sultanji, Subhanji, Sahebrao, and even some forts, villages and hills assumed Muslim names like Malang-gad, Mangrula Pirache, Shaikh Sallah Dongar (hill) and many others. The French traveller Bornier had aptly remarked: 'the Hindus from the sixteenth century took so zealously to Persian education that before another century had elapsed, they had fully come up to the Muhammadans, in the point of literary acquirements'.[6] A brahman family of Wai (Pune district), which had adopted sultana as its family name under the Muslim rule, later on changed it to *suratrana*, a corrupt form of *sultana*., The Arabic word *sultan* has been written in a corrupt form as *Suritrana, Suritan*, etc. in the *devanagari* script.[7]

The assimilation of these two religious communities is reflected even in the pledges or oaths, mentioned in inscriptions, mahajars, sanads, and other agreements. In an inscription of the sixteenth century (1579 AD), recently discovered at Kunkali (Goa), on a slab of a phallus, it is announced that, if a Muslim breaks it, he will be equated with breaking his pledge with the supreme being, and if a Maratha (Hindu) breaks it, he will be regarded as a sinner, as a killer of a brahman. Similarly, if a Muslim restores it, he will earn the credit of visiting Mecca,[8] and if a Maratha helps in restoring it, he will get the credit of visiting Varanasi.

The works of the numerous saint-poets of Maharashtra promoted the Bhakti cult – the worship of one god – Vitthal of Pandharpur, which in the subsequent years developed into a sect called *varkari panth*. This Bhakti movement is often compared with the Sufi movement of Islam. It may be noted here that both the movements emphasized reforms in socio-religious life of their respective communities. Muslims studied Sanskrit and the sacred works of the Hindus, particularly the contribution of the saint-poets; they also contributed richly to the Bhakti literature of Maharashtra. It would therefore be interesting to study the activities of the Muslim literati, who promoted a healthy society devoid of communal conflicts.

When two religions with different ideologies meet, conflicts are inevitable. How the protagonists of the religions were attacking each other and how, when their emotions and prejudices subsided, they came to a better understanding of each other, has been vividly depicted in the poetry of Eknath, a medieval Marathi saint-poet of the sixteenth century. In his '*gatha*' (collection of verses) there is a famous chapter called *Hindu Turk Samvad* (A dialogue between a Hindu and a Turk (Muslim)), in which Hindu and Muslim leaders at first attack each other, but ultimately they come to an agreement and accept that 'Hindus and Muslims, O brother, are the creations of Khuda'. Eknath concludes that it was because of this exchange of arguments that all the doubts in their minds were cleared, friendship developed and both enjoyed the ecstasy.

Eknath (1533–99), a great saint-poet after Jnyaneshwar (thirteenth century), was well known for social justice. He was closer to the Sufi cult through his 'guru' Janardana Swami (1504–75), an officer of the Nizamshahi of Ahmednagar. Janardana Swami was influenced by a contemporary Sufi saint, Chand Bodhale of Kadari sect.[9]

Shaikh Muhammad, a Muslim saint-poet and a contemporary of Janardana Swami, contributed richly to Marathi literature. His famous Marathi work is *Yoga Samgram* (1645). He was a contemporary of Sant Tukaram of the seventeenth century. He preached unity of both the religious communities. He was regarded by the contemporary literati as the incarnation of Kabir.[10]

We know very little about the life of this great Marathi Muslim saint-poet who virulently attacked superstitions, hypocrisy, multiplicity of gods, atrocities, and so on, practised by both the religions. He was born about 1565 at Dharur (Marathwada), where his father, Sayyed Raje Muhammad, was serving the Nizamshahi of Ahmednagar, and who was the first Sufi of the Kadari tradition. When Maloji Bhonsale, the grandfather of Shivaji, shifted to the Nizamshahi, he brought Shaikh Muhammad also along with him, whom he considered as his guru.[11]

Chand Bodhale, who was initiated to Sufism by his father Raje Muham mad, was his guru.[12a]

Shaikh Muhammad was proud of the Marathi language and his famous works, *Yogasamgram, Nishkalanka Prabodh, Pavan Vijaya* and about three hundred *abhangas* (verses), are in Marathi. He died at a ripe age of 95 in the year 1660.[12b] He says at one place, 'I am born in a *yavan* family, and started talking about *Quran* and *Puran*'.[13] He resented the traditional Muslim practice of breaking idols and temples of the Hindus. He was initiated into the Bhakti cult by a Hindu guru but that did not affect his faith in Islam. His discourses in Marathi were attended by many people irrespective of their caste, creed or social status.[14]

He did not believe in the religious controversies between the Hindus and the Muslims. He emphasized what was common in both the religions and suggested that the *Sachcha Pir* of Muslims and the *Sadguru* of Marathas are the same, if we keep our minds open.[15] A happy blending of Islam and Hinduism is found in his famous *Maha Āaratī* (Grand Prayer), in which more than hundred saints, both Hindu and Muslim, for whom he had high regards, have been skillfully knitted together.[16]

Ramdas, a saint-poet of the seventeenth century, a great critic of the Muslim rule, however, was full of praise for Shaikh Muhammad, whom he had immortalized in a poem composed in his honour. He says: 'This body which is a borrowed thing from the elements, essentially exists due to your grace and I would sacrifice it for your sake. I do not know what is *bhava* (emotion) or *bhakti* (devotion), but only this, that we have been reared by the saints. Ramdas is, in fact, the dust at the feet of the great saints like you.'[17]

Another Muslim saint of the seventeenth century, Shah Muntoji Bahmani, also known as *Mrutyunjaya* (conqueror of death), who belonged to the royal family of Bidar, an offshoot of Bahamani Kingdom, was initiated into the cult of Bhakti by a Hindu saint, Sahajanand Swami of Kalyani (Bijapur). He became a devotee of Vitthal of Pandharpur. His famous work, *Panchikarana*, written in Dakhani Hindi, emphasizes that the fundamental ideas are common in both Hindu and Muslim scriptures. His Lingayat followers called him *Jnansagrayya.*' He preached all that was good in Hinduism without losing his faith in Islam. There are some ten poetical works, known so far, written in Marathi and Dakhani, that are attributed to him.

Husain Ambarkhan of this period, a devotee of Lord Ganesh, wrote a commentary on Bhagvatgita in Marathi. Shah Muni, another medieval saint sees the origin of Islam in the Hindu god Vishnu, and laments for the unnecessary enmity between the two religions which was due to lack of proper understanding of the teaching of their respective faiths. He writes, 'The Muslims misunderstand the practices of Maharashtra Dharma and these people consider the practices of the Muslims as something strange or abnormal.'[18]

The Muslims must have taken lessons in Hindu scriptures from brahman pandits right from the thirteenth century onwards, the period of emergence of Sufism. Saraswati Gangadhar, the celebrated author of *Gurucharitra*, a poetic work of the fourteenth century, complained that the brahmanas had fallen from their assigned duty and had started teaching vedanta to the Muslims.[19] It appears from the *Gurucharitra* that Alauddin II (1435) of the Bahamani dynasty was a tolerant king and held Narsimha Saraswati, the hero of *Gurucharitra*, in high esteem. This policy of appeasement on the part of the king was resented by the kazis and they tried to change his sympathetic attitude towards the gods of the Hindus and the brahmans, as that was unbecoming of a Muslim, according to them. It was argued that the 'Brahmans who find the god in cow, fire, sun, water, and so on, and regard what is intangible as tangible are ignorant people and therefore the Muslims who worship them go to the hell.'[20]

However, the king set aside the advice of the kazis and pointed out to them the futility of condemning other religion with a view to establishing one's own creed.[21]

During the medieval period, Christianity was striking its roots particularly on the west-coast of India. The Jesuits were producing literature in Marathi from the sixteenth century onwards. But there was a difference between the attitudes of the Muslims and the Christian Marathi literati. The contribution of the Muslims in Marathi, briefly stated above, shows that they used the vehicle of Marathi not for preaching Islam or translating the tenets of Quran in Marathi, but for their own understanding of the Hindu scriptures, philosophy, mythology, and so on. The Christian saints produced a vast amount of literature in Marathi for spreading their own religion and condemning the Hindu mythology. Father Thomas Stephens (1549–1619), a British Jesuit who came to Goa in 1579, wrote his *Christ Purana* in 1616, a poetic work, bigger in size than the well-known Marathi work *Jnānēshwarī* of the fourteenth century. Stephens wrote this in the same style as *Jnānēshwarī* (a commentry on the Gita) only with a view to spreading Christianity and providing the text of the Bible to the Marathi-speaking converts of the Portuguese State.

Father Etienne de La Croix (1579–1643), who came to India in 1602, wrote a book entitled *Dissertation*, on the life of the apostle St. Peter, in which St. Peter has been depicted as persuading the 'gentiles' (Hindus) of Western India to abandon their false gods. He ridicules Ganesh and Parvati in such terms as: 'Parvati has not produced your Lord Ganesh, but was created by her hands out of the dust of her body'.[22] Professor A.K. Priyolkar writes about this book, 'it refutes Hindu belief with great vehemence and pours ridicule on Hindu deities like Vishnu, Mahesh, Ganesh and Tulsi, and the stories connected with their deities'.[23]

The Portuguese, in the wake of their religious fanaticism, pulled down temples, burnt or confiscated books in vernacular languages and thus created a vaccum in the spiritual life of the community. The Jesuits thought it desirable to write in Marathi for the benefit of the natives and thus they produced a number of books on Christian religion in Marathi in the seventeenth and eighteenth centuries. Priyolkar says that though the literature aimed at popular presentation of Christianity, actually it aimed at weaning away the converts from their old faith by attacking and ridiculing forcefully the tenets of Hindu religion and the gods of Hindu Pantheon.[24]

Thus it is clear that the Muslims used the medium of Marathi to promote for the Hindus devotion and social solidarity, whereas the Christian literature in Marathi aimed at inducing the Hindus to embrace Christianity, and at breaking the Hindu society.

The appeal of the Muslim saints for social harmony does not appear to have gone unheeded, as we find many Hindus worshipping the Muslim *Pirs* and participating in the *Urs* and Muharram celebrations. We come across a number of grants given by Hindu rulers to Muslim *Pirs* and *dargahs* or (khanqahs). Maloji Bhonsale gave 12 bigha land to Shaikh Muhammad and got constructed a *math* (hermitage) for him at Shrigonde.[25] His wife Umabai had taken a vow to Shah Sharif of Ahmednagar for a son, and due to his blessings, perhaps, she gave birth to two sons, who were named after him as Shahaji and Sharifji.[26] The *dargah* of Shah Sharif at Ahmednagar enjoyed two villages – Eklare and Konosi (Ahmednagar) – from the Marathas.[27] Mir Sayyid Sadi of Nasik and the Mulla Husaini Mosque of Rannebennur (Dharwad) received *inam* lands from Shahaji.[28] Shivaji respected Baba

Yakut of Utambar village near Kelashi (Ratnagiri) and it is learnt that Sambhaji had undertaken the task of constructing his *dargah* which could not be completed, due perhaps to political disturbances in the Maratha country during that period.[29] Many holy men of the Muslim community received allowances for maintenance, illumination and upkeep of the mosques from Shivaji.[30] He had issued orders to the officers of Poona region that the Pir of Sayyid Sadat Hazrat and other mosques should get the usual oil for illumination from the villages under their charge.[31]

The Kazi of Indapur had received three *chavar* (20 bighas) of land and some allowance.[32] The *khidmatgar* of the Bhambavade mosque received similar benefits from the Maratha king.[33] It was believed that Sambhaji could register victory against the Portuguese due to the blessings of Pir Abdullah Khan and so Kavi Kalash, the Prime Minister, was pleased to grant to the Pir an annual allowance of 50 hons for the payment of two Mujawars and for flowers, lamp, franckincense and the Urs celebrations.[34] During the course of a raid, a village Sakase (Thana) was plundered and the Mujawar's house was also washed out. As the villagers wanted the Mujawar to continue serving the Dargah Pir, the village council compensated for the loss and reinstated him.[35] Some of the grants to Brahmanas given by the Muslim rulers were discontinued during Shivaji's period, but when the aggrieved parties appealed to Rajaram, he took a sympathetic view and the Adilshahi grants were restored to them.[36]

The Muslim saint Sayyid Ata-ullah Shakarkoti of Loni (Poona) received the entire village in grant from Shahu. Ajam Sayyid Qutb-uddin Pirzade of Kalyan, Bhivandi and the Dargah of Pir Malik Husain Qadri were enjoying cash allowances from various villages from the days of Malik Ambar, which were continued under the Mughals, and as this territory of Swaraj was transferred to Shahu by the Emperor, the privileges enjoyed before were continued under the new government.[37] The two Pirs – Sayyid Sadat and Shaikh Salah – received a grant of Rs 1400 from the Peshwas for construction purposes.[38] Shaikh Salah Dargah and the Takiya of Angad Shah of Poona were considered as holy places and therefore one *sher* rice and one paisa for franckincense were to be given daily to them from the Royal palace.[39] Even the dispute over precedence in the procession of the Muharram between Sayyid Sadat and Shaikh Salah was settled by the Peshwas.[40]

The Muslim rulers also had reciprocated in the same manner. The Mahanbhav Matha of Otur (Poona), which was established by Keshava Chaitanya, received land grant from the Nizam Shahi rulers and confirmed by the subsequent rulers. It was for a short period confiscated but Chandbibi renewed it in 1599 with the note that the officers should respect all such grants to Hindus and Brahmanas.[41] The priest of Pedgaon (Ahmednagar) received land grant from Malik Ambar.[42]

One interesting incident from medieval history may be cited in connection with the co-existence of the two communities. It was but natural for a Muslim ruler to hesitate in putting a Hindu person at the head of a military command. Being dissatisfied with the inactivity of his Muslim commander in an expedition against the Shirkes, one Maratha captain, Janoji Pisla of Bidar, out of sheer disgust, killed his master and then to avert the wrath of the king embraced Islam and requested him to put him in charge of the expedition. He further requested the king that he should issue a *mahajar* in his favour stating that if he dies in this conflict, he should be regarded as Pir and the lands which the king bestows upon him should be transferred to the Jagadale of Masur, who was related to him through his wife's side, and when a monument is erected, the Muslims should assemble to its left side and prepare 'Kanduri'[43] for distribution among the devotees, and the Hindus should gather to the right flank of the monument for preparing and distributing the 'Khairat'[44] so that he would be regarded as 'Pir' by the Muslims and 'Vir' (a hero) by the Hindus."

The fight with the Shirkes proved to be fatal and Janoji Pisla preferred death to defeat. He invited Jagadale, handed over the *mahajar* as well as his head which he himself severed from his body with a request to establish a 'ghumat' (a *dargah*) at Masur in his honour.

Thus Janoji became Jalaluddin Pir of Masur, and Jagadale carried out his instructions by appointing Mujawars to look after the 'ghumat'.

A critical study of folklores in Kannad Taluka (Aurangabad) based on field-studies shows many elements of cultural fusion between the two communities, which has survived. This survey shows how the Hindus have traditionally worshipped the Pirs, participating in the Muharam festival, Urs, praying and vowing for something, offering eatables to the Pirs, fasting for the Pir, etc. The Pirs of that region, like Ramlal, Fakirbaba, Shaikh Marubaba, and Bhikanshah Baba, have been immortalized by womenfolk in their songs, passed on from generation to generation by oral tradition, and even now these songs are sung by women in many homes in the villages of Marathwada while they perform their domestic duties.[45]

The conflicts among the Marathas and other sects like the Jains and Lingayats were amicably settled by the Muslim rulers. They respected the authority of village councils or other local bodies in resolving religious disputes, as it was necessary for the smooth functioning of the village communities and for fostering better social relations.

The next problem arising out of this is to know what the position of the Muslims was in the village councils (*gotsabha*) that decided cases that affected the society as a whole? The *gotsabha* enjoyed supreme position in the society as well as in the state. It was equated with God or parents, and people were regarded as the offspring of the *gota*.[46] The avowed policy of the *gota* was to bring about a compromise between any two contending parties.[47]

The Kazi and the Maulana had seats on the *gotsabha*. The number of Muslims on a *Got* was usually in proportion to the population of Muslims in the concerned village. The Maulana was a *balutedar*[48] and the *mulansara*, a cess originally introduced by the Muslims for the maintenance of the Mulana, continued under the Marathas without any difficulty.[49]

Both the Muslims and the Hindus sat together, preferably in a temple in the village, and settled the disputes referred to them irrespective of caste and creed. Disputes regarding the privileges of brahmanas or *mahars* (untouchables) were decided in a *majalas* attended by both the communities.[50] A Maratha and a Muslim contended over the *naikwadi* watan of Parner[51] (Ahmednagar). The Muslim claimed that he was the rightful successor to the watan which was first granted to his ancestors by Malik Ambar, and later confirmed by the Mughals. The case was argued in 1644 in a council of 41 members, all of whom were Hindus, but the decision was given in favour of the Muslim contender. The watan of Patil of Wai was enjoyed by a Muslim for a long time under the Marathas, but it was confiscated in 1697, the most critical period in the Maratha history, when it was discovered that the Patil had become disloyal and joined the Mughals. It was then conferred on the Dabhades.[52] The Patil of Katraj (Poona) was a Muslim. Whenever such village hereditary offices were held by Muslims, they were entitled to all the privileges and perquisites due to those offices.[53]

The Muslim rulers did not usually overlook the traditions of village communities. The right of precedence was a matter of prestige among the village communities. A Muslim officer of Chaul punished a brahmana astrologer who refused to read the almanac to him on the new year day before visiting the houses of watandars for that purpose. The brahmana lodged a complaint against the officer with the higher Muslim authorities stating that the tradition which he followed was an ancient one, and neither the Nizamshahi, nor the Marathas disturbed it. The case was decided by the Mughal Government in favour of the brahmana; the fine inflicted on him was withdrawn and the officer concerned received a warning for violating the custom of the village.[54]

As regards the Muslim practice of idol-breaking, or destroying temples and constructing mosques on their ruins, though they were not absolutely unknown in the Maratha country, they were not pursued, it seems, with the same vigour as in the North. The Muslim rulers in the Deccan were more concerned with colonization, bringing more land under cultivation, rather than scaring away people from their lands. The policies of Malik Ambar can be cited in this behalf. When Chaul, an important post on the Western coast in the seventeenth century, went under the Adilshahi kingdom after the death of Malik Ambar, the people requested the new government to follow the policy of tolerance initiated by Malik Ambar. It was stated in the petition that the Hindus had settled down at several places in that region, and were working for the prosperity of the region. It was, therefore, requested that neither their religious practices nor their temples be disturbed.[55]

The problem of proselytization both by Muslims and Christians often created friction in the society. From the instances of conversions recorded in Marathi documents, it appears that the converts mostly accepted the Islamic faith for their personal gains but sometimes through intimidation. Such considerations as watan, an office, some high military position had attracted a few person towards the religion of the ruling class of Muslims. However, the real problem was of reconversion from the point of view of social relations. Since the Hindu society is somewhat closed and rigid, unconditional readmission into its fold was not quite smooth. Nevertheless, we find that some adjustments were made generally through the agency of *gotsabha* or state government with a view to fostering harmony and a spirit of fellow-feeling and love in the society.

Traditions die hard. We find that, even after conversion, people scarcely forgot their family traditions. This was perhaps to win the sympathies of the community which would accept them if they went back, or perhaps to avert the wrath of gods of the former religion.

A brahman called Vitthal Jagadevrao turned Muslim, became Haibatkhan, and assumed the office of havaldar at Wai. But he could not give up the practice of worshipping his former family deities. He therefore engaged the services of a brahmana for this purpose.[56] The Muslim government did not object to this to avoid any friction in society. One branch of a brahman Deshpande family of Nilanga (Marathwaḍa) was converted to Islam during the regime of Adilshahi of Bijapur and both branches of the family – the Hindu and the Muslim Deshpandes – lived as neighbours for many generations. The Muslim brothers, it is reported, attended all the religious functions performed in their brahman brothers' house.

The rise and spread of Christanity in Maharashtra made the problem of social relations much more complicated. Prior to the advent of the Portuguese, Goa was under Adilshahi rule. When the Portuguese occupied it in 1510, a general crusade was led against Islam, 'an act of defiance of Europe against the Muslim menace' according to Dr Maraes.[57] During the early period of the conquest, conversions to Christianity were few and far between. Albuquerque, the first Portuguese Governor, experimented with mixed racial marriages by converting good-looking Muslim women and offering them with a dowry to eligible bridegrooms. The efforts of the friars and the experiment of racial marriages bore results in the course of time, and by 1520, most residents of a village in the Goa island were converted to Christiamity, and a Church was built, there; by 1626 the number of converts rose sufficiently.[58] According to Dr Pissurlencar, the noted historian of Goa, the Portuguese had by 1667 converted the entire population of Sashti (Salset) and about 4000 out of 7000 Hindus from Bardesh to their faith.[59]

The methods of proselytization of the Muslims were different. The Muslims induced only those people who were of much significance to them politically. But we hardly come across in the Deccan any instance of an entire village being converted to Islam. Maratha families were so scared of forcible religious conversion that, when threatened with that prospect, they would rather desert their native places and seek asylum in some neighbouring states.[60] The government of the day had issued orders that no new temples or mosques were to be constructed by the people in the Portuguese territories.[61]

The methods adopted by the Portuguese missionaries were quite interesting. After sufficient brain-washing, if a Hindu was somewhat inclined to get converted, first his *shendi* (hair tuft) would be cut, and then he was made to eat some food prepared by the Christians – thus making it impossible for him to change his mind. At times he was given wine without his knowledge, and his sacred thread was broken. All this was calculated to make him lose his caste.

Dr Pissurlencar has produced statistical information based on original documents concerning the destruction of temples and conversions of persons by the Portuguese in the sixteenth century in Goa, Bardesh and Sashti. According to him, temples in 131 villages were pulled down and a number of persons from 110 villages were converted in the later half of the sixteenth century.[62]

The Inquisition, also known as the Holy office, was an ecclesiastical tribunal for the suppression of heresy and punishment to the heretics. But in the course of time, Hindus and other non-Christians were also accused of obstructing conversion or infringing some of the laws directed against their religion and were punished by the Inquisition.[63]

Thus, it seems that at least in the seventeenth century, the relations between the Christians and others in the Portuguese territory do not seem to have been cordial. But the gradual suspension and final abolition of the Inquisition in the eighteenth century, the existence of a large number of Hindus in the Goa region, and the continuance of a number of holy places of Hindus in Goa indicate that the rulers must have realized that a ruthless policy of conversion embittering the social relations would not help them in justifying their rule in Goa.

Lastly, two more problems that disturbed the social relations, namely the *jiziya* and the cow-slaughter, may be considered. Akbar had abolished this humiliating tax on the Hindus in 1564 but it was revived by Aurangzeb after a lapse of more than a hundred years in 1679. There is enough documentary evidence to show the imposition of this tax on parts of the Maratha country which were under the Mughals.[64] It was strongly protested by Shivaji, most probably immediately after its imposition. It seems that the tax was extended to the Maratha country only after the death of Shivaji in 1680, as the documents, which are available on this subject, all belong to the period between 1684 and 1706. This was a critical period in the history of the Marathas, as the Emperor had personally descended on this country with a view to eradicating the Maratha power, and so the unsettled state of affairs in this region must have adversely affected the collection of *jiziya*. We hardly find any references to its continuance after the death of Aurangzeb in 1707.[65]

The Portuguese were not lagging behind in imposing a similar humiliating tax on the Hindus. They levied as late as the eighteenth and nineteenth centuries, a capitation tax upon the Hindus called *Pensao do Shendy*. In this respect Dr deSouza remarks: 'It was the last flicker of the flame of proselytism which burnt high in the previous centuries, and a symptom of the rapid decay of the Portuguese power.'[66]

The second problem that created some occasional tension in the medieval Maratha society was cow-slaughter. Cow was a sacred animal to the Hindus and the Muslim practice of killing cows and eating the beef, particularly during the festival of *Bakrid*, irritated the Hindus. However, during the seventeenth century, we do not come across any legal prohibitions imposed by the Marathas on cow-slaughter. It was only during the Peshwa period that cow-slaughter was considered as a cognizable offence, and those who were guilty of it, whether Hindus or Muslims, were punished according to the practices of those days.[67] An imperial *farman* prohibiting cow-slaughter was issued in 1789.[68]

Thus, the two dominating communities of the medieval period – Hindus and Muslims – were making experiments in living together in this country, as both of them considered India their Home Land.

Notes and References

1. N.V. Mandlik (ed.), *Writings and Speeches of the late Hon. Rao Saheb Vishwanath Narayan Mandlik*, Bombay, 1896, pp. 201–34.
2. *Shivacharitra Sahitya*, vol. II. 94, (Hitherto referred to as S.C.S. – publication of Bharat Itihas Samshodhak mandal, Pune, vol. no. and document no. There are 14 vols. published so far under this title).
3. S.C.S. 2: 243.
4. V.K. Rajwade (ed.), *Marathyanchya Itihasachi Sadhane* (MIS), vol. 8, Kolhapur, 1908 – see Introduction.
5. G.H. Khare (ed.), *Aitihasik Farsi Sahitya*, vol. II, 18, p. 22 (BISM publication) Pune.
6. Bernier Francois, *Travels in the Mughal Empire*, London, 1914, p. 131 (fn. i).
7. G.H. Khare, *Dnyanprakash*, a Marathi daily of Pune, 28 August, 1946.
8. "हे स्थानक मुसलमा होऊन तोडी तै तालाची सव म-हाटा होऊन तोडी त-ही त्या ब्रह्महत्येचे पातक,

मोडले करी तै मुसलमानासी मके गेली याचे फळ म-हाटा होऊन कासी यात्रेचे फल" See also Vad, Mawaji, Parasnis, (eds.), *Sanada Patre*, Poona, 1913, p. 25.

9. G.B. Sardar (ed.), *Eknath Darshan*, Pune, 1978, Introduction p. 30. Chand Bodhale, it is said, was originally a brahman called Chandra Bhat, and being influenced by the first Kadari Sayyed Muhammad Gausa converted to sufi sect.
10. शेख महंमद पीर। कबिराचा अवतार। For a detail account of the works of Muslim Saints, see R.C. Dhere, *Musalman Marathi Sant Kavi*, Pune, 1967.
11. A place in Ahmednagar district, the Watan land of Mahadji Shinde, the Maratha Sardar of the eighteenth century.
12. For details of Shaikh Muhammad's life, see V.S. Bendre (ed.), *Shaik Mahamadbaba Shrigondekar Krita Yogasamgram*, Bombay, 1959, and *Shaik Mahamadbaba Yancha kavita Samgraha*, Bombay, 1961.
13. अविंध यातीस निपजलो। कुराण पुराण बोलो लागलो।।
14. यवन देवतास करिती मार। हे तव चालीले अपटपार।।
 . . . शेख महंमद अविंध। त्याचे हृदयीं गोविंद।।
 . . . याति मुसलमान। म-हाष्ट्री वचन। ऐकती आवडीने। विप्र शूद्र।
15. सच्या पीरे कहे मुसलमान। म-हाटे म्हणती सद्गुरु पूर्ण। परी दोन्हीत नाही भिन्न पण। आंखे खोल देखो भाई।।
16. BISM Shaka 1838 (AD 1916).
17. देह जरी वोवाळू, उसने पांचांचे। जीव शिव वोवळू, तरी देणे तुमचे।। भाव भक्ति नेणे, पोसणे संतांचे। रामीरादास चरण रज संतांचे।।
18. महाराष्ट्र धर्माची राहाटी। अविंध मानिती उफराटी।। आणि यवन लोकांची राहाटी। विपरित वाटे या लोका।।
19. कर्मभ्रष्ट झाले द्विज। म्लेंच्छा सांगती वेदांत बीज।
20. धनूसी म्हणती देव। म्हणती देव अग्नि सूर्य। समस्त देव म्हणती देखा। ऐसे विप्र मंदमती निराकारा साकार म्हणती। त्यांते म्लेंच्छे जे भजती। अधोगति पावती ते।।
21. प्रतिष्ठावया आपुल्या मता। द्वेष आम्ही का करावा।।
22. तुमचा गणेसु येणे रिती। नुपजला तरी पार्वतिए पोटी। पण देह मळिता तियेच्या हस्ती। उपजला जरी।। 101।। Quoted in A.K. Priyolkar's, *French Kavine Lihileli Marathi Purana* (ed.), Bombay, 1965, p. 29.
23. A.K. Priyolkar, *Goa Rediscovered*, Bombay, 1961, p. 85.
24. *Ibid.*, p. 78.
25. R.C. Dhere, *op. cit.*, p. 60.
26. Wakaskar V.K. (ed.), *91 Qalmi Bakhar*, Baroda, 1930, Article 2.
27. V.S. Bendre (Ed.), *Maharashtretihasachi Sadhane*, vols. 1–3 (Hitherto referred to as *MS,* vol. & letter No.) vol II: 314, 315.
28. *Shivakalin Patrasar Samgraha,* vols. 1–3, *BISM* Publication, Pune (Hitherto referred to as *SP* vol. & letter No.).
29. *Aitihasik Samkeerna Sahitya*, BISM Publication, Pune, vol. 8, Introduction by D.V. Potdar (ASS Vol.).
30. S.C.S. 7: 55, *Peshwa Daftar* (PD), vol. 31: 18; Vad, Mawaji & Parasnis (ed.) *Sanda Patre,* (SP) Bombay 1913, pp. 102–3.
31. SP, pp. 121–22.
32. S.C.S.: 3: 663.

33. PD: 31: 18.
34. S.C.S.: 8, p. 51.
35. ASS: 6: 9.
36. MS 11, p. 223.
37. D.B. Parasnis (ed.), *Peshwe Daftaratil Sanadpatratil Mahiti*, Bombay, 1917, pp. 10, 240, 248.
38. PD 22: 200.
39. ASS 1: 113.
40. PD 43: 33.
41. SP, p. 94.
42. *Ibid.*, p. 10.
43. MIS 15: 2.
    Kanduri a feast held by Musalmans in honour of Fatima, the daughter of Muhammad.
44. *Khairat* – charitable distribution of alms.
45. P.B. Mande, *A critical study of Folk Lore in Kannad Taluka*, unpublished thesis, Marathwada University, Aurangabad, 1967.
46. MIS 15, p. 25.
47. S.C.S. 2: 98.
48. S.C.S. 3: 427.
49. MIS 20: 58.
50. BISM Quarterly, year 8, p. 159; MIS 20: 186.
51. PD 31: 17.
52. S.N. Joshi (ed.), *Dabhade Daftar*, BISM, 1951, Part I, p. 9.
53. MIS 18: 9.
54. S.V. Avalskar (ed.), *Angrekalin Patravyavahar*, Pune, 1948, Letter 16, p. 21.
55. S.C.S. 9: 34.
56. S.C.S. 6, p. 65.
57. G.M. Moraes, *A History of Christianity in India AD 52–1542*, Bombay, 1964, p. 154.
58. *Ibid.*, p. 162.
59. P. S. Pissurlencar, *Portugese Marathe Sambandh*, Pune, 1967, p. 58.
60. Avalskar, *op. cit.*, p. 42.
61. *Ibid.*, pp. 15–16.
62. A.K. Priyolkar, *The Goa Inquisition*, Bombay, 1961, pp. 69–70 & 79–84.
    Boletim Do Instituto Vasco Da Gama No. 68:1952.
63. Priyolkar, *op. cit.*, p. 42.
64. S.C.S. 4: 694, 704; S.C.S. 5, pp. 7–8; ASS 1: 3, 9, 13.
65. A.R. Kulkarni, *Medieval Maharashtra*, New Delhi, 1996, see chapter IV Jiziya in the Maratha Country, pp. 176–208.
66. T.R. De Souza, *Goa to Me*, New Delhi, 1994, p. 106.
67. PD 43: 144.
68. G.S. Sardesai, *Musalmani Riyasat* Part II, 4th edn., 1959, pp. 431–32.

EIGHT

Contribution of Sant Prannath to the Composite Culture of India

P. S. MUKHARYA

If we survey Indian history from the Ancient to the Modern times, we find that 'Unity in Diversity' is the underlying current running throughout its course. This is a very distinct and unique feature of the Indian history. The fusion of different races, religions, arts and cultures constitute its composite culture. The historians have written volumes on this theme. The different perspectives of this culture have been studied by the eminent historians but the contribution of *Sant* (Saint) Prannath to the composite culture of India has been consistently neglected by them mainly because its original sources are in Hindi or Hindustani written in the *Devnagari* script.

Sant Prannath was perhaps the last in the glorious tradition of those saint-poets of Medieval India who worked for Hindu-Muslim unity. Besides, he also laid a solid foundation for the synthesis of all religions for the first time in India. While saint-poets like Kabir, Nanak, Raidas, Dadu etc. have received full attention of the historians, the historicity and the contribution of Prannath remains comparatively an unexplored field.

Nature and Extent of the Source-material

The primary and original sources of *Sant* Prannath are vast. There is a vast literature behind him in the form of the *Bani Sahitya* and the *Bitak Sahitya.* The *Banis* or teachings of Prannath are collected in the *Kulzamswarup* or *Tartamya Sagar* which means a vast ocean of knowledge. It is in fourteen volumes or *granthas* with more than eighteen thousand verses. The *Bitak Sahitya* contains his biographies (written in verse-form), running into hundreds of verses, by his learned disciples. There are seven *Bitaks* about him. These *granthas* are as follows:

Bani Sahitya: Sant Prannath's *Banis* or teachings are collected in the *Kulzamswarup* or *Tartamya Sagar*. It was published in 1965 for the first time. It is a collection of fourteen books as follows:

	Name	Language
1	Raas	Gujarati
2	Prakash	Gujarati / Hindi
3	Shadritu	Gujarati
4	Kalash	Gujarati / Hindi
5–11	Sanandh, Kirantan, Khulasa, Khilwat, Parikrama, Sagar and Singaar	Hindi
12	Sindhi Bani	Sindhi
13–14	Marfat Sagar and Kayamatnama	Hindi

Bitak-Sahitya: There are seven *Bitaks* or biographies written in Hindi by his learned disciples as follows:

1. Laldas, *Bitak*, 1982.
2. Navrang or Mukunddas, *Bitak* (Manuscript hereafter Ms.).
3. Brij Bhushan, *Vratant Muktavali*, 1978.
4. Hansraj, *Mehraj Charitra* (Ms.)
5. Karuna Sakhi, *Tartam Sagar* (Ms.)
6. Lallu Bhatt, *Vartman Deepak* (Ms.)
7. Sneh Sakhi, *Leelaras Sagar*, 1993.

Although Prannath's mother-tongue was Gujarati, he was well-acquainted with Persian, Arabic, Sanskrit, Sindhi, Rajasthani, Hindi etc. His *Kulzamswarup* is a collection of fourteen *granthas* of which four are in Gujarati, one in Sindhi and the rest in Hindi or Hindustani. After his tour of northern and central India, he was convinced that Hindustani or Hindi was understood by a vast majority of people. He then began to write in Hindustani. In Medieval India he was the first Hindi poet to use the word *Hindavi* (Hindustani) and considered it as the national as well as a link language. This was not merely a theory. He practised it and his *Banis* or teachings in other languages were written in the *Devnagari* script during his lifetime. All the *Pranami* literature is in Hindustani or Hindi written in the *Devnagari* script.[1]

It is not possible to analyze this vast material in this paper as it is a separate subject for research. In this paper a brief but connected account of the life and times of *Sant* Prannath based on the secondary sources has been developed. At the same time the original sources have been tapped while dwelling on the contribution of Prannath to the composite culture of India.

Devchand: The Preceptor and Guru of Prannath

Devchand, the preceptor and *guru* of *Sant* Prannath, was the founder of the *Nijanand* (seeking pleasure of one's self) sect in Gujarat in the seventeenth century. It was further expanded in the northern and central India by Prannath as the *Pranami* sect with its centres at Jamnagar and Surat (Gujarat) and Panna (Madhya Pradesh).

Devchand was born at Amarkot in Sind on 11 October 1581. He belonged to a rich Kayasth family. At the age of thirteen he went to Kutch alongwith his father on a business tour. At Bhojnagar he met Haridas Gusain of the *Radhavallabh* sect and became his disciple. For three years he studied religious scriptures and many questions cropped up in his mind. This study made him uneasy and at the age of sixteen he left his home for Kutch which was famous for religious studies. He met there various *pundits* and *maulvis* and studied their scriptures but his religious curiosity was not satisfied.

Through a comparative study of various religions, he noticed their underlying unity but could not decide his course of action. He went again to Haridas Gusain at Bhojnagar and began to live with him as he had a vast following and a great influence in Kutch. The followers of the *Radhavallabh* sect worshipped Lord Krishna in the form of a child as Balkrishna or Balmukund. They gave importance to his *Brajalila* and worshipped him in the *Sakhi bhava* or in the spirit of a lady friend. They studied the *Bhagavat Puran* as a religious scripture.

As Devchand had been away from his home for more than four years, his parents searched him and found him with Haridas Gusain. After a great persuasion they got him married so that he might lead a worldly life. It was a vain effort, for, after eight years with Haridas Gusain, at the age of twenty-five he went to Jamnagar, where a learned Brahmin, Kanhji Bhatt, used to discourse upon the *Bhagavat* in those days daily. His discourses were very impressive. Devchand, impressed by them, listened to *Bhagavat* daily for fourteen years. According to the *Pranami* scriptures, Devchand obtained *jnana* or knowledge at Jamnagar at the age of forty. It was based on the *Bhagavat Puran*. For the propagation of his doctrines he used to narrate the *Bhagavat* in a very. impressive manner Very soon he attracted a large following.[2]

Early Life of Sant Prannath

Sant Prannath was the second *guru* of this sect. He was born at Jamnagar in Gujarat on 6 September 1618 in a Kshatriya family. His birth-name was Mihraj. His father was Keshav Thakur, a *Diwan* of the Jamnagar state. His mother's name was Dhanbai. His elder brother, Govardhan, was a great devotee of Devchand. When he was twelve years of age, Govardhan took him to Devchand. Both of them were attracted towards each other and this mutual attraction resulted in teacher-and-pupil relationship. He listened to his teachings and studied Vedas and *Puranas* under his direction. In the meantime he was married to Baiji who always accompanied him on his voyages.[3]

As desired by his *guru*, Mihraj travelled widely in the neighbouring regions and undertook voyages to the ports of the Persian Gulf. He is said to have stayed in the Arab countries for about five years (from AD 1646 to 1651) in order to settle the business of one Khetaji, who was the brother of a disciple of Devchand. In this connection he went to Baghdad and met Sultan Imam in person. Here he also met some learned religious Muslims. It resulted in a fair exchange of views. He then began to understand the finer aspects of the Islamic theology. He returned to India in 1651.

On his return he worked as a *Diwan* of Jamnagar after his father's death. In August 1655 when Devchand realised that his end was approaching, he sent for Prannath. Devchand impressed upon him the essential unity of all religions and the need of proper synthesis between the teachings of different faiths. It was the need of the hour. He gave him the name Prannath and asked his followers to call Mihraj as Prannath. He wanted Prannath to carry his message to everybody irrespective of caste, community, nation or faith to which he belonged. Devchand died in September 1655. On his death Prannath decided to devote his life to the propagation of the teachings of his *guru* and resigned his post.

The presence of Portuguese and British traders in Kathiawad led to the Anglo-Portuguese influence over him in the study of the Christian scriptures. This also broadened his mental horizon. After propagating the teachings of this sect for some time, he left Jamnagar in 1665 for further propagating it in Kathiawad, Kutch and Sind. He toured along the western coast for three years visiting places such as Diu, Navi, Porbander, Kapiabandar, Lathibandar etc. Everywhere he attracted a large number of followers who were initiated into his fold known as *Sundersath*.[4] While preaching he used to invite religious discussions and satisfy the curiosities of the listeners. Several times he had to face the challenges of the various learned *pundits* and *maulvis*, Kabirpanthis, Nanakpanthis and others. Many were impressed and became his followers.[5]

In 1668, he sailed again for the Arab countries for its further propagation. He stayed at port-towns of Muscat, Koga, Abbas etc. for a period of four years. After enlightening many in the Arab countries, he returned to Gujarat in 1672. After a dispute over the religious preachings of Devchand with Bihariji, the son of Devchand, he left Jamnagar and established a new *gaddi* (seat) at Surat. It was at Surat that this sect assumed its widest form as some five hundred *Sundersath* disciples dedicated themselves to the cause of this sect and worked tirelessly for its propagation.[6]

Aurangzeb's Religious Bigotry

During this time Aurangzeb was ruling India. He was a zealous and fanatic Muslim; hence he turned the territory under him into a veritable hell of persecution for the non-Muslims. In 1669 by a *firman* he ordered the demolition of the Hindu temples and schools and reimposed the *jaziya* on the Hindus in 1679 which Akbar had wisely abolished. The wanton destruction of temples took place accompanied by acts of desecration, such as slaughtering of cows and getting the idols trodden down in public places without the least care for the feelings of the Hindus.

The Hindus were highly agitated over the religious bigotry of Aurangzeb. The Sikhs of Punjab under Guru Govind Singh, Satnami Jats in the region between Delhi and Agra under Gokla Jat, Rajputs in Rajputana under Durgadas Rathore, the Bundelas in Bundelkhand under Chhatrasal and the Marathas in Deccan under Shivaji had risen in arms. In Deccan Shivaji had successfully opposed this policy to a certain extent. Its echo was heard everywhere. This anti-Aurangzeb wave had also touched Prannath. In his preachings he vehemently opposed the religious bigotry of Aurangzeb. He made up his mind to convince the fanatic Aurangzeb about his erroneous ways. With this object in view he left Surat with a large number of his devoted followers.[7]

Towards Delhi: Failure in Meeting Aurangzeb

After visiting Ahmadabad, Broach, Palanpur (Gujarat), Merta (Rajasthan), Agra etc. he reached Delhi. An attempt to convince Aurangzeb was a very risky one but Prannath was determined to win over his hate and anger by love and affection. At first it was decided to convey his message to the Emperor, not directly but through the five royal courtiers close to him. They were Kazi Sheikh Islam, Rizvi Khan, Amir Auquil Khan, Sheikh Nizam and the Kotwal Siddi Faulad. The draft message contained in it an appeal to the Emperor which brought out the similarity of approach in the scriptures of Hindus as well as of Muslims. The *Quran* and several Hindu scriptures were extensively quoted in testimony but the courtiers paid no attention to it.

Hence, it was decided to carry the message to the Emperor in person in spite of all the difficulties in meeting him. Aurangzeb used to visit the Jama Masjid on every Friday when he stayed in Delhi. On the following Friday Prannath's twelve disciples met him through the Imam of the mosque who was very much impressed by their scholarship. Aurangzeb was amazed to find that Hindus, as most of them appeared to be, had a remarkable scholarship of the Islamic scriptures. They appealed to him to give up his misguided policy of persecution of the non-Muslims, but their mission failed as Aurangzeb had a suspicious nature and his counsellors kept on poisoning his ears. Moreover, he was in a hurry to go to the south to deal with his enemies. Thus, Prannath could not meet Aurangzeb personally even after sixteen months of stay at Delhi and his attempt to convert Aurangzeb not on political lines but like a humble and courageous student of comparative religion failed miserably.[8]

Towards Panna: Meeting with Chhatrasal

Prannath was now in search of a bold and warlike prince who could oppose Aurangzeb. After leaving Delhi, he visited important places like Anupshahar (Uttar Pradesh), Amer, Sanganer, Udaipur (Rajasthan), Mandasaur, Ujjain (Malwa), Burhanpur, Aurangabad (Khandesh), Deogarh, Ramnagar (Madhya Pradesh) etc. for the spread of the *Pranami* message. Unmindful of the inclemency of weather and the rigours of travel of those days, he moved about northern and central India and thousands of men became his followers.

About this time in Bundelkhand Chhatrasal had revolted against Aurangzeb. He had neither the resources nor the strength of an army to offer resistance. Moreover, Bundelas were yet to be united for the common cause but Chhatrasal had a strong determination to free Bundelkhand from the persecution of Aurangzeb. The meeting of Chhatrasal with Prannath came about suddenly at Mau (near Chhatarpur in Madhya Pradesh) in 1683. According to Chhatrasal's letter to his son, Jagatraj, they met in a jungle near Mau where he had gone for hunting. At this time Chhatrasal was thirty-four and Prannath was sixty-five years of age. At the request of Chhatrasal Prannath decided to stay in Bundelkhand permanently. He spent about eleven years in Bundelkhand moving from place to place, spreading his message with Panna as headquarters. He died at Panna on 29 June 1694.[9]

Relation of Chhatrasal and Prannath

The relationship of Chhatrasal and Prannath was like that of Shivaji and Samarth Guru Ramdas. Prannath not only provided for the moral and spiritual needs of Chhatrasal in Bundelkhand he also made him aware of the importance of his political aims. On Shivaji, the influence of Ramdas was spiritual rather than political but Prannath was politically more helpful to Chhatrasal. In Bundelkhand he created a strong public opinion in Chhatrasal's favour by strongly criticising the reactionary policy of Aurangzeb. He successfully encouraged the public to co-operate with Chhatrasal.

His personality and emphasis on non-secretarian and classless society attracted many followers. Many of them were recruited in Chhatrasal's army. Prannath also used to accompany him in his army campaigns to encourage the soldiers. He also made his financial position strong and sound by giving him the knowledge of diamond mines near about Panna. On the advice of Prannath, Chhatrasal made Panna his capital. He conferred the choicest title of *Maharaja* on Chhatrasal and coronated him for enhancing his prestige in Bundelkhand. He was thus the source of inspiration and strength to Chhatrasal and was the friend, philosopher and guide to him.[10]

The Pranami Sect

Although the *Pranami* sect was founded by Devchand, it was organised into a definite order by Prannath. According to the *Pranami* scriptures the philosophy of this sect was revealed to Devchand by Lord Krishna himself while he was reciting *Srimadbhagavat.* According to this sect the world is divided into two parts, *kshara* (perishable) and *akshara* (imperishable) but superior to these two parts is one Supreme God, *i.e.*, *Aksharatita.* It emphasises the worship of *Aksharatita* and prescribes meditation as the best form of worship. The unity of God and the theory of *Karma* has been propounded and idolatory discouraged. In fact, it was a liberal reform movement in the Hindu religion.[11]

Fifth Synthetic Current of The Medieval Bhakti Literature

Dr Matabadal Jayaswal, who has done a pioneer research-work in the *Pranami* literature, is of the opinion[12] that this literature formed the fifth synthetic current of the medieval *bhakti* literature in Hindi. Between AD 1400 and 1600 the following four currents had flowed: (1) *Sant* poetry (Kabir, Nanak, Raidas, Dadu etc.), (2) *Sufi* poetry (Jayasi, Manjhan, Kutban etc.), (3) *Ramabhakti* (Tulsidas etc.), and (4) *Krishnabhakti* (Surdas, Nanddas, Mira etc.) In the seventeenth century all these currents had become weak and a new current flowed in the form of the *Pranami* literature. For the first time in India this new current emphasized the integration of India and Indian society through the proper synthesis of all the religious scriptures.

Sarva-Dharma Samanvaya: Synthesis of All the Religions

Prannath was well-versed in the Hindu scriptures like the Vedas, Upanishads, Geeta and Bhagavat and the *Quran* and was well-acquainted with the

Christian scriptures. He knew well that without the proper synthesis of all these scriptures, the call of the unity amongst the different communities would become an empty slogan. He, therefore, based his philosophical teachings on the solid foundation of the synthesis of all these religious scriptures.[13]

As *Sant* Prannath was an erudite scholar and a linguist, he studied various religious scriptures of the prevalent religions of India and found that their basic tenets were the same. It can be gleaned from the study of his *Kulzamswarup*. His first book, *Raas* (which means the love-play of Lord Krishna with his divine *Gopi*-souls) was also named as the *Anjeel* or Bible which gave the message of love to the world. It deals with that part of the Bible which gave a detailed account of the Garden where Noah's Ark had landed. That garden was Madhuvan (Madhu-forest) of Vrindavan of the *Bhagavat* where the God-loving souls took delight in the infinity of the divine-bliss. His second book, *Prakash* (which means light) abounded in the soul's yearnings and wailings for God, and was considered to be a further revealation of the songs of David (Psalms) of the Old Testament. It was named as *Zaboor* of Daud *Paigambar*. His fourth book, *Kalash* (which means a pot symbolic of one's pot of mind to the Supreme for His wisdom to pour in), highlighted the summum bonum of the religious knowledge as unifying the under-currents of all religions. It was named as *Taurait* (Torah-Old Testament of Moses) to signify the historical episode of Moses' rescue operation of the people from the land of Egypt to Jerusalem. His other books like, *Sanandh, Khulasa, Marfat-Sagar* and *Kayamatnama* reflected the true religion of Muslims based on the *Quran*. By laying stress on the comparative study of the Holy books of all the religions, he explained to the people that the fitting reply to the bigotry and religious fanaticism was the proper understanding of the religion and not the religious wars.[14]

He advised followers of different religions 'who sing praises of God under different names and put on different garbs not to quarrel amongst themselves as their God is one.' He embraced Him in a 'Universal Being' as in this verse:[15]

> *Jude jude nam gavahin, jude jude bhekh anek.*
> *Jin koyi jhagdo aap main, dhani sabon ka ek.*

He defined a *sadguru* (true teacher) as one who embraces all religions. He was firmly convinced that all of them talked about the same thing. The ignorant alone sees the difference. He observed:[16]

> *Sastra le chale satguru soyi, bani sakal ko ek arth hoyi,*
> *Sab sayano ki ek mat payi, par ajaan dekhen re judai.*

One more verse[17] in the same vein which is particularly significant and claims attention:

Ek sristi dhani bhajan ekai, ek gaan ek aahar,
Chhod ke bair milen sab pyar so, bhaya sakal main jai jai kar.

He advised all the contending religious groups to forget their petty differences and radiate an atmosphere of love and mutual understanding since they stand on a common ground with one order of creation, one all-pervading God, one hymn, one note and common food. This done, they are bound to be hailed in the world.

Hindu-Muslim Unity

During this period the Indian society was torn mainly by the differences between the Hindus and Muslims. As the Christians had just entered India, their entry was not of much consequence. In the reign of Emperor Aurangzeb, the religious persecution of the non-Muslims was the order of the day. Prannath had opposed this policy as he deemed the Hindu and Muslim communalism to be the bane of Indian society as it is even now in the present century. He tried to inculcate a spirit of tolerance and unity among them.

In *Kulzamswarup* he attacked the superstitions and the fanaticism of both the Hindus and Muslims and tried to remove their contradictions. He attempted to reconcile their controversies and pointed out repeatedly that both the Vedas and the *Quran* laid stress on the allegiance to the one Supreme God. In these verses,[18] he observes that 'the Quran and the Vedas emphasise the same. Both Hindus and Muslims are the disciples of the same Lord. It is the difference in languages, names and customs that created illusions. I will undo their disillusionment by elucidating various names and signs of the existence of the common God to all of them.'

Jo kuchh kahya kateb ne, soyi kahya Ved.
Dou bande ek sahab ke, par ladat bina paye bhed.
Boli sabon juda pari, nam jude dhare saban.
Chalan juda kar diya, taathen samajh na pari kin.
Taathen huyi badi urjhan, so surjhaun doy.
Nam nisan jaher karun, jyon samjhen sab koy.

In the following lines[19] he stressed the unity of God and said that "there is only the difference of names and rituals. All consist of the 'soul' and the 'universe'. In fact Khuda and Brahma are the same."

Nam saron juda dhare, layi sabon judi rasam.
Sab main ummat aur duniya, soyi khuda soyi brahm.

Several verses can be quoted which teach Hindus and Muslims to have amiable feelings for each other and tolerance. His noble mission was to unify the Hindus and Muslims as he understood their deceptions and would impart them right knowledge as in this verse:[20]

Karna sara ek ras, Hindu Musalman.
Dhokha sabka bhan ke, sabka kahungi jnan.

In fact he emphasized the equality of mankind and propagated religious toleration. He was not against any religion but he did not tolerate the religious persecution and considered its opposition the primary duty of all. For this reason he did not oppose Islam as a religion but he did not lag behind in encouraging and organising Hindus against the religious persecution of Aurangzeb. He inspired the Hindu kings of his times against this policy:[21] 'O the Rajas, the Ranas and Raots, the religion is in danger. Run to its rescue. You warriors rise from the accursed sleep and be on your feet. The sword of the Kshatriyas seems to be broken. Religion of the Hindus is endangered. You followers of the true religion, do not abandon it. The Turks are gaining the upper hand. In the three *lokas* (worlds) the land of *Bharat* is most glorious and in it Hinduism is the best of all religions. The crowned heads of the land are down with shame. The *asuras* (demons) have imposed *jaziya* on the Hindus. They are not even getting food and water. The poor who are unable to pay *jaziya* are forcibly being made Muslims. Lo! The Bundela Chhatrasal has heard the appeal. He has come forward with the sword in hand and has taken this service upon his head. The God has marked him to be the general and the leader.'

Raja ne malo re ranan ray tanon, dharm jata re koi daudo.
Jago ne jodhare uth khade raho, neend nigodi re chhodo.
Chhutat hai re khadag kshatriyo se, dharam jaat hinduan.
Sat na chhodo re satvadiyo, jor badhyo turkan.
Traloki main uttam khand bharat ko, taa main uttam hindu dharm.
yaki chhatrapatiyo ke sir, aayi rahi it saram.
Asure lagaya re hinduyo par jejiya, bako mile nahin khan pan.
Jo garib na de saken jejiya, taye mar karen musalman.
Baat ne suni re bunndele Chatrasal ne aage aaye khada le talwar.
Lai seva re sari sir kheinch ke saaiyen kiya senyapati sirdar.

In the *Pranami* sect, Chhatrasal is deemed to be the incarnation of God alongwith Devchand and Prannath. In Bundelkhand, this couplet[22] is often heard: 'one who worships these five personages Krishna, Muhammad, Devchand, Prannath and Chhatrasal, his sorrows vanish immediately'. The couplet runs as follows:

'Krishna, Muhammad, Devchand, Prannath, Chhatrasal,
In panchan ko jo bhaje, dukh hare tatkal.'

This couplet speaks volumes for the Hindu-Muslim unity.

It is a noteworthy fact that some 300 years ago during the reign of *Maharaja* Chhatrasal, the followers of the *Pranami* sect used to read the *Bhagavat Puran* and *Quran* together. An Englishman who visited the temple of Prannath at Panna in 1764 had recorded,[23] 'I saw in it a small bed with a turban on it, called Sri Prannath's seat. On each side of it was a stool. On one of these was a copy of the *Quran* and on the other a copy of the *Puran*, with the learned men of both religions in attendance, ready to give profitable answers to all enquiries. Most of the replies made to them involved unity of God.'

As in his congregations, the *Bhagavat Puran* and *Quran* were read together, it was the only example of its kind in the Medieval India. In the twentieth century we find the same ideal during the prayer – meetings of Mahatma Gandhi where *Geeta, Quran* and Bible were read together. In a way we can say that Prannath was a forerunner of Gandhi in the present century as Kabir was his forerunner in the Medieval times.

Conclusion

As we have seen Prannath was well-acquainted with the political conditions of his times. He wished to pave the way for political, social, religious and linguistic integration of India through synthesis of various religions. In India of the seventeenth century this experiment was unique. It was a significant contribution of Prannath to the emotional integration of Indian society. It was really unfortunate that he was not understood by the orthodox Hindus, fanatic Muslims and the followers of the other religions of his times. Perhaps he was ahead of his times.

Although the *Pranami* sect is not widespread in India and the number of its followers is not very large either, yet its importance cannot be underrated under the existing conditions of India. Under the present circumstances of India, the relevance and importance of *Sant* Prannath in the cause of Hindu-Muslim unity and synthesis of all religions is to be properly evaluated. Considering the communal harmony, secularism and national integration of India which are the prime needs of the time, the contribution of *Sant* Prannath to the composite culture of India is self-evident and can be considered seminal.

Notes and References

1. Dr Matabadal Jayaswal, *Rashtriya Ekta aur Dharmik Samanvay main Mahamati Prannath ka Yogdan* (in Hindi), Souvenir on *Sant* Prannath (Prannath Mission, Delhi, 1974), f.n.23, pp. 25–26.
2. Dr B.D. Gupta, *Maharaja Chhatrasal Bundela* (in Hindi), (Agra, 1958), pp. 102–4.
3. *Ibid.,* p. 104.
4. P. Krishnamurty Iyer, *Lord Prannath* (Panna, 1965), pp. 5–7.
5. Gupta, *op. cit.,* pp. 104–5.

6. Iyer, *op. cit.,* pp. 7–9.
7. Gupta, *op. cit.,* p. 105.
8. Iyer, *op. cit.,* pp. 12–16.
9. *Ibid.*, pp. 16–20.
10. Gupta, *op. cit.*, pp. 106–7.
11. *Ibid.,* pp. 107–8.
12. Dr Matabadal Jayaswal, *Pranami Sahitya: Madhayakalin Bhakti Sahitya ki Panchvi Samanvayi Dhara* (in Hindi), Research Seminar on *Sant* Prannath (Prannath Mission, 1978), p. 5.
13. *Ibid.*, pp. 9–11.
14. Dr B.P. Bajpai, *Mahamati: The Supreme Wisdom*, (Prannath Mission, Delhi, 1981), pp. 33, 54, 71, 87.
15. *Kulzamswarup, Sanandh*, Canto 41, Couplet 72.
16. *Ibid., Kirantan*, Canto 4, Couplet 4.
17. *Ibid.*, Canto 54, Couplet 12.
18. *Ibid.*, *Khulasa*, Canto 12, Couplets 42–4.
19. *Ibid.*, Couplet 38.
20. *Ibid.*, *Sanandh*, Canto 3, Couplet 3.
21. *Ibid.*, *Kirantan*, Canto 58, Couplets 1, 2, 4, 16 and 20.
22. Gupta, *op. cit.,* f.n. 22, p. 146.
23. G.A. Grierson in Hastings *ed., Encyclopaedia of Religion and Ethics,* vol. X, pp. 150–51, quoted in Pyareal, *Mahatma Gandhi*, vol. 1, p. 214.

NINE

❖ Cultural Transformation, Transmission and Coexistence

J. S. GREWAL

HISTORIANS OF MEDIEVAL INDIA have talked of 'Islamization' of India due to a number of factors involving forced and voluntary conversion as well as immigration of Muslims from outside the Indian subcontinent. They have also talked of the influence of Islam on Indian culture in the spheres of religion, art and literature as well as in terms of political and social institutions. There is also an awareness of a kind of 'Indianization' of Islam. These approaches leave out the phenomenon of cultural transformation and its transmission through an altogether new medium.

We propose to take up the case of a mystic who used the spoken language of the people of the Punjab as the medium of expression and communication. His feelings, moods and attitudes are difficult to define as either Hindu or Muslim. He addressed himself to all men and women irrespective of their caste or creed. Though occupied primarily with the relationship of human beings with God, he had an implicit social message for his listeners. This message has come down to the present century not only through the written record of his compositions but also through their recitation by popular singers for the last four hundred years. This mystic was Shah Husain, a contemporary of the Mughal emperor Akbar. By the early nineteenth century his *mazār* at Lahore had become the venue of a popular fair attended by Hindus, Muslims and Sikhs and patronized by Maharaja Ranjit Singh.

In the first section of this paper we deliberately dwell on some of those compositions of Shah Husain which are popular with the folk-singers of the Punjab. In the second section, we analyse his compositions in detail to identify his basic ideas and attitudes, which reinforce what we find in the popular transmission. In the third section of the paper we try to reconstruct Shah Husain's world to show how it gets completely indigenized so that the reader or the listener also feels that it is his or her world. This reconstruction enables us to see where Shah Husain himself stands in this world.

I

Shah Husain is still popular among the singers of Punjabi poetry. We may turn to some of his popular verses in search of his ideas, moods and feelings.

There is no room for uttering a word, O Friend. When the same One Lord is within and without, to whom does one speak? The same Beloved is within everyone; there is no other anywhere.[1]

This verse underlines the immanence of God. Shah Husain emphasizes this idea in another verse:

You know my state, O Lord. You are within and you are without; you are in each and every hair of my body. You are the warp and the woof; you are my all.[2]

God within man remains concealed, leading to the painful feeling of separation:

To whom should I go, my mother, to talk of the pangs of separation? The hearth of my *murshid* is smouldering, and when I poke it I find it red hot. I have been demented by the thorns of separation; it refuses to leave me. Sorrows are my bread and pangs my *sālan*, cooked on the fire of sighs. In search, I wander in the wilderness and in thickets, but I have not yet found the Beloved.[3]

There is another verse which expresses the same mood and alludes to Rānjhā.[4] Separation and union are the reverse and the obverse of the coin of love. Shah Husain sings of love with full-throated ease:

My heart is set on the One-without-cares, the Master of the spiritual and the temporal world. The *qāzi* and the *mullā* give me advice, showing their way of piety and wisdom. What has love to do with their path? The abode of Ranjhan is across the stream, and I have promises to keep; I implore the boatman to ferry me across.[5]

Shah Husain appears to have been fascinated by the tale of Hīr and Rānjhā who serve as the symbols of love between man and God. Shah Husain was the first Punjabi poet to make frequent use of these symbols. Rānjhā stands for God:

I have to go to the abode of Rānjhan: I wish someone could go with me. I implore everyone and fall at their feet, but I have to go alone.[6]

The longing for a meeting, the difficulties involved, the pangs of separation, and the hope of grace are acutely felt in this verse. In another, anything other than God is rejected:

Do not talk to me of the Kheṛās, O my mother, I belong to Rānjhā and he belongs to me; the Kheṛās have a false expectation.[7]

The relationship of love between Hīr and Rānjhā, between man and God, is eternal. Union is foreordained:

Change if you can, O my mother, the writing of the pen on the tablet. I have no power to resist the Kheṛās who are forcing me into the bridal litter to take me away. But the hook of Rānjhan's love has sunk deep into my heart. I wriggle like the fish; the string is in the hands of the Omnipotent Lord.[8]

Nothing short of the sight of Rānjhā can console Hīr:

My heart yearns to meet Rānjhan. In his search I wander in the wilderness, and he is with me.[9]

Finally, the difference between Hīr and Rānjhā is obliterated:

Crying 'māhī-māhī' I have myself become Rānjhan. All should call me Rānjhan and none should call me Hīr. I have found the spouse I was searching for.[10]

The path of love is not an easy path:

You would take to the path of love only if you are a true lover. The path of love is narrow like the eye of the needle; you can pass through it only if you become a thread.[11]

Love demands constant devotion:

Stick to the Friend, always. Bear with hundreds of taunts and thousands of slanders. Do not divulge His secret even if your head is cut off from your body.[12]

Only they can be martyrs, says Husain, who lay down their life for the Friend.[13]

Love is antagonistic to the things of this world:

They who love do not spin. Why should they? Prudence ends where love begins. Companions are forgotten. Wounded by love and attracted towards the Friends, the maiden wanders crazily; she has no time for the spinning wheel.[14]

Love is intoxicating:

My arms are around the neck of my Friend, how can I say 'leave it now'? I have found the source of intoxication, like poppy-husk by the addict.[15]

The things of this world do not count for Shah Husain:

Your life here is of a few days; you can see the time passing before your own eyes. No one takes with him the treasured riches of this world. Mother, father, brother, son and wife do not go with you.[16]

What lasts for ever is the name of the Lord:

Mīrs, Maliks and Sultāns have been seen going the same way. The Lord Himself gives life and takes it away; the mediacy of Azrāīl is a contrivance.[17]

In the face of the futility of worldly possessions, man should think of the eternal God:

Whose are the horses, elephants and palaces, and whose are the riches? Where have gone the learned *mullās* and *qāzīs*, and where have gone the serried ranks? This world lasts but for a few days, my dear; stick to the Lord's name.[18]

What is important is to acquire merit:

A man is judged by his deeds, whether an addict or an abstainer.[19]

It is important to place trust in God, and to invoke His mercy rather than His justice:

Ignore my demerits O Lord. I am devoid of all merit, and there is evil in every hair of my body. Keep me as you wish; I am lying at your door. Show me your mercy and not your justice, says Husain, the humble *faqīr*.[20]

Shah Husain prefers to associate with persons who practice loving devotion in detachment:

Fortunate are they who have *faqīrī* as their lot. With the needle of consciousness and the thread of love, they darn the holes in association with holy men.[21]

In another verse, Shah Husain identifies himself with the lowest of the low:

I am the sweeper-woman at the Lord's court. With the tray of meditation and the broom of knowledge, I dust anger and lust every day. The *qāzī* knows and the *hākim* knows that I am exempt from forced labour. The *mall* knows and the *mehtā* knows that I serve the *sarkār*.[22]

II

Shah Husain uses a number of epithets for God: Rabb, Maulā, Sāhib, Sāīn, Prabhū, Thākur, Har, Rām, Sāwal, Mahbūb, Dilbar, Sajjan, Mittar, Mīt, Piāra, Rānjhā, Rānjhan, Māhī, Dhol, Shauh, Kant, for example. They all refer to the same entity. Shah Husain is quite explicit on the unity of God and underlines this unity in his verses: 'I know only you and no other'. 'The same thread is in the woof and the warp; I know no other'. What He decrees comes to pass. He gives life and takes it away. Even mountains tremble due to His fear. He can destroy Pātshāhs, Princes, Mīrs and Maliks in a trice; He does not allow anyone to live in tall mansions for long. Everyone leaves the world in accordance with His decree; His *bhāṇā* cannot be evaded. He determines the number of days for one's life on earth. No amount of wailing can change what is 'inscribed' for him. God created man for worship. He is the master and man is the slave. He takes account of everything that man does. They who have little to their credit have to weep and wail when account is taken. God is just. Everyone is treated strictly in accordance with his good or bad deeds. God is merciful too. He is all-knowing and all-wise; He is the strength of the weak; and He alone is everlasting. By contrast, everything other than God is subject to annihilation; it is 'false'.[23]

Shah Husain underlines the transitory character of human life on earth. This world is like the pearly drops of dew on a leaf. It is the *sarāi* where the way-farer can spend only a night. You cannot be sure of the next breath: the soul may leave the body never to come back, like the leaf fallen from a tree. This world is like the father's house for a girl who has to go sooner than later to her in-laws, the next world. The lanes of her native village soon become a dream. The soul leaves the body just as the bumble-bee leaves the flower. Even when you are alive, your body goes on declining imperceptibly like the shadow. The youth and beauty of which you are proud will turn into ashes at the end. Youth, beauty and riches are dupes.[24]

Shah Husain frequently dwells on death. Departure from this world is inevitable; none can stay here long for death is preparing its ropes to gather in the harvest. The fish in deep waters is caught unaware in the net; the sparrow is constantly watched by the fowler. Death knows no distinction: It takes away Khāns and Sultāns.

'Why do you stray into alien patches, for all that you own in the end is three and a half cubits of land?'

'Be not proud, says Husain, the humble *faqīr*, you will mingle with the dust at last'.[25]

Death inevitably leads to the grave. The corpse is covered in a cloak and taken to its destination. 'Four persons bear you on their shoulders and leave you in the wilderness'. The grave calls you to come home. 'Remember the grave which is your home of old'. You cannot carry anything to the grave. 'They who were *shiqdārs* of forts are nowhere to be seen now'. The Pātshāhs, princes, Maliks and Mīrs who used sweet-smelling scents and remained intoxicated with pleasures have been seen departing in their bare feet. The millionaires leave all their wealth behind; it does not go with them.[26]

What goes with man to the grave is the record of his deeds to serve as the basis of justice. 'Without good deeds, O my friends, there is nothing but humiliation and misery, says Husain.' You will reap what you have sown. When we go to the Master's court He questions everyone regarding his deeds on the earth. He who is without good deeds to his credit suffers humiliation and punishment. Human life, therefore, should be treated as an opportunity for earning merit: 'There are two angels over your shoulders who record everything to your credit or discredit. If you do not take this chance, O girl, you will suffer'. Your time for 'the shuttlecock' is passing. We come into this world only once; the gourd does not flower all the time; the rain is celebrated only in the month of Sāwan. Life is a sport in which one should earn distinction. Regard each breath as your last; much of your life is already wasted, and only a little more is left; the trader who gave the goods on loan is knocking at your door.[27]

Human beings do not realize their intrinsic interest because of the lure of sensual pleasures which result in spiritual death. Sensual pleasures are like holes in a vessel, emptying it of its water; they are the thieves who steal everything and leave nothing with the wayfarer. The choicest fruit that you enjoy here becomes the bitter *tummā* for the life hereafter. The bridal bed becomes the cremation ground. The five senses are the 'the black buck' which eats up the crop. They are hungry like hens and attractive like peacocks. They are the five streams which engulf the boat. 'If one is hungry, another is thirsty; if one is asleep, another is awake; they go on making noises.' Shah Husain advises young maidens to turn inwards and look within.[28]

Detachment is the antidote prescribed by Shah Husain for the poison of sensual pleasures. 'Wherever you look there is deceit; there is no comfort anywhere; leave this deceitful world for a quiet corner, O Husain'. Shah Husain is happy that 'flies have eaten all the jaggery'; he does not have to buzz around. He is happy that the 'old pond' has been licked by dogs; he can wash himself in the pool of love. Men of the world pursue self-interest when they meet one another, when they give away dresses and food in charity, and even when they worship *gurūs* and pīrs. He who discards self-interest is the king of kings.[29]

Among the adversaries of man, there is yet another: *gumān, mān, takabbar* or *khudī*. The antidote to this moral flaw is modesty and humility (*halīmī*). 'There are flowers of rare variety in the garden but you are merely a *gandhuli*' (which does not have even an edible root). Shah Husain explicitly advises men to discard pride and to adopt humility. Fear the Lord, give up bitterness, and appropriate humility. Tear out the chapter of power from your book, discard pride, and adopt sweetness and humility. Some go on weeping and wailing, but others laugh and laugh, and score the goal. 'Discard pride, and adopt humility, for you gain nothing from pride and self-centredness'. 'You will see the Lord if you bend lower and lower'.[30]

It is incumbent on man to remember God. 'May you never forget God, is the prayer of the *faqīrs*. May you forget everything but not God.' The time spent in the remembrance of God is the time that counts. 'Get up and meditate on Rām; this is the time to remember Him. You will regret when the time is past'. Only the name of God is everlasting; stability is acquired only by appropriating His name. 'My desire is for the name of the Lord'. Desirous of God's name, Shah Husain lies at His door. The name of the Lord is the cow that yields milk readily. Stick to God's name all the time; this is your only chance, the only way.[31]

Complete trust in God and steadfast devotion to Him set man on the right path. 'I am the kite of the Friend with its string in his hands.' There is no one else to depend upon. Shah Husain's only hope is God who can save whomsoever he wishes to save. Shah Husain advises men to bear with the reproofs and rebukes of the Friend for their defaults; they should accept whatever comes from God. Men should beg from God who alone is the bestower of gifts. Shah Husain advises men to devote themselves to God, leaving everything and everyone else. 'I shall please my Spouse on my own, without an elaborate ritual. Says Husain, the *faqīr* of the Lord: May I become the dust at His door'. The woman who dances in His court with abandon becomes a *sohāgan.*[32]

When God is pleased, He shows His grace. When Rānjhan felt the spark of love in his heart, he left Takht Hazara to seek the beloved, Hīr. God Himself brings about the meeting. It is only through His grace that the devotee can see God. 'I am a sacrifice to you, O my Master. You know my state, O my Friend, show me your face, once my dear'. Shah Husain implores God to show His grace. Meeting God and seeing Him face to face is the purpose of Shah Husain's life. They who have the Lord on their side have nothing to worry; His beautiful face fills their eyes; He fills their inside, and never leaves them even for a moment.[33]

For Shah Husain, the essential relationship between man and God is that of love. No one is acceptable to God without love. Some smear their bodies with ashes and sit in meditation; others wander naked in the wilderness; there is no yearning for the Lord in their hearts. Some keep awake at night and perform *zikr*; others go about fasting; they find no place. Some read the words of the Qur'ān; others debate abstruse matters; but this is not a laughing matter. If you go to the door of the Perfect One to beg, ask for love as the alms, so that you may come to know the place. Love to the *faqīrs* is like the walking stick to the blind; it enables them to negotiate the unseen; 'my loving desire is to see you, and I meditate on you all the time.'[34]

Seeing God, meeting Him and uniting with Him is made possible by love. The night is dark and cloudy and it is raining: the Friend has called Shah Husain, and he has to go; only they can appreciate his plight who have experienced love. He has to see God face to face, with his eyes sunk into His eyes. 'Open your book O Brahman, and tell me when my dear Friend would meet me face to face'. Shah Husain has thrown away the 'basket' with all its contents; his desire now is to see the Lord. The image of the beloved Friend remains impregnated on his heart day and night. 'The mad world looks upon me as crazy, but I am dyed in the Master's hue.' 'You may congratulate me now that my beloved Friend has come home. I have found now the Friend I was searching. My courtyard has become beautiful and my forehead shines with bliss.'[35]

Separation is the reverse of union. The night becomes long, too long, without the Friend. 'Love is hard to conceal when the tent of separation is pitched tight over my head'. No one regards Shah Husain of any consideration when his Friend turns away from him. The syndrome of longing, union and separation occurs frequently in the compositions of Shah Husain. The path of love is not easy. The lover has to incur ignominy, to hold live fire, to weep and wail, and to die before death. Your feet are nailed by thorns when you ascend the high hill. You have to entertain the Friend with your blood. Difficult is the terrain, heavy the tread, and long is the way. The lover of God has to be ready to sacrifice his life; he has to choose between the Beloved and his head. If his love is genuine he kisses the cross. He does not care for his life; he places the truth above self. To cross the river of love, Mansur accepted the gibbet. Shah Husain is neither a worldly man who is proud of his possessions, nor a renunciant who is proud of his renunciation; he has become a *faqīr* because of the spark of love. And love demands sacrifice. Life without love is death. But only a few receive the boon of the Spouse's embrace.[36]

Shah Husain identifies himself with the *faqīrs* who dedicate themselves to God in loving devotion. The whole world is false except the *faqīrs* of God who are under His care; they see all that is manifest and hidden; all their problems are solved; joy and sorrow do not enter their hearts; they remain intoxicated all the time. 'Throw your white sheet in the oven; it is far better to put on the rough woollen blanket of the *faqīrs*'. They who live with these holy men, their wisdom is strengthened. The *faqīrs* belong to the same 'village' as Shah Husain. The whole world begs from God, and Shah Husain prays for three things for all: *giān, dhiān* and *sādhū-sang*.[37]

More than half of the *kāfīs* of Shah Husain are either addressed to women or they are in female voice. There is a wide range of metaphors related to women. It is possible to form a fair idea of Shah Husain's attitude towards them. There is the woman with merit (*guṇwantī*), and the woman without merit (*awguṇiārī*). There are some who enjoy their union with the spouse (*shauh, kant*); they are *sohāgans*. There are others who fail to please the spouse and remain strangers to the bliss of union; they are *dohāgans*. However, there are still others who have not yet met the spouse but yearn for such a meeting; they are *jogins* or *bairāgans*. Then there is Hīr, who is devoted to Rānjhan but whom the Kheṛās also claim. There is no misogyny in Shah Husain's verses. It must be added that Shah Husain's metaphors invoke a structure which is partiarchal. Normatively, a woman is a devoted wife. Thus, it is within the partiarchal framework that Shah Husain creates space for women in relation to God.

III

Shah Husain uses similes and metaphors from the familiar world around, creating his own 'world' in the process. There are metaphors for the morning, the evening and the night. The difficulties of the spiritual path remind him of the steep hillock, or the deep stream. The five senses become 'the five rivers'. The human soul is represented by the bumble-bee (*bhaur*). The bitch at the door of its master symbolizes humility and self-effacement. The men of the world who pursue earthly purposes to the exclusion of spirituality are the flies which stick to jaggery, the dog which licks the dirty pond, the crow or the hog which eats dirt. The black buck symbolizes the lure of *māyā*.[38]

Shah Husain chooses to refer to the moonlit night and the dark night, the clouds and the rain, the breeze and the dust storm, the dew and the snow, the fire and its sparks. The passing days bring in the concept of time which is counted in moments, days, months and years. The fast lengthening shadows indicate the passage of time. Then there are the mountains and steep hills, the sea and the river, the whirlpools and rapid streams, the islands of sand and shallow beds for easy crossing. There are pools and ponds, mud and dry dust, ordinary earth and the saline soil. Not all, but most of these phenomena fell under Shah Husain's directed observation in the Punjab.[39]

The vegetation that covers the earth in Shah Husain's world, whether natural or cultivated, is the vegetation of the plains. There are jungles, forests, thickets and woods in the river valleys. There is wilderness or wasteland, and there are fields and gardens. There are green pastures for the cattle to graze. There are trees with their branches and flowers. There are fruit trees and flower plants. There is fire-wood and there are sharp splinters and thorns. There is poppy with its intoxicating seeds and gourd with its flowers in bloom. There is the *babūl* tree in the wilderness and the *pīpal* tree close to human habitations. In the gardens there are trees laden with sweet fruit and in the fields there is the bitter *tummā* which springs up as a part of the natural vegetation. Shah Husain mentions one tree which was not there in the plains of the Punjab: the *chandan*. But the metaphor made sense because the fragrant sandal wood was within the range of observation.[40]

The one winged creature which could not be within the range of Shah Husain's observation was the swan (*hans*), unless we take it to represent the white goose. But the other birds were quite familiar to the people: the heron, the crow, and the sparrow. A little less familiar was the moth that burnt itself on the flame; much more familiar was the common fly. Then there was the *bulbul* (commonly referred to as the nightingale) which was expected to be found in the gardens. There are hens in the homes and peacocks outside the human habitations. The only creature in the water is the fish. Among the domesticated animals are the cattle, the cow and the buffalo, the goat and the lamb, the dog and the bitch, horses and elephants. There are worms which eat up the wollens. There are harmless ants. Then there are deadly cobras and frightening lions in the wilderness. Roaming in the fields and eating the crops is the black buck. The bumble-bee (*bhaur*) flies from flower to flower in search of juice.[41]

The flora and fauna as well as the physical phenomena are a part of Shah Husain's universe (*jahān*), or his world (*duniā*). The other synonyms used are *'ālam* and *jagg*. In this world there is one's own country (*des*) and there are alien lands (*pardes*). There are villages and towns in each country. Just, as there are frontiers between different countries, so there are boundaries between different villages and towns. There are lanes and *bāzārs* in villages and towns, and there are houses with their large and small rooms and their courtyards. Not all the houses have a second storey. There are doors and windows and niches, and there are attics and balconies. There is a reference to the five rivers, which may remind the reader of the Punjab. But the places specifically mentioned by Shah Husain are Kashmir, Multan, Gujrat, Jhang and Takht Hazara. In Shah Husain's universe of 'thousand worlds', there are people (*khalqat, lok*) in lacs. A few belong to your own village. If you go to another village, you are a stranger or a guest. Only two clans are specifically mentioned: the Siāls and the Kheṛās. This too because they were linked with Hīr. The entire world for Shah Husain is a sport (*khel, bāzī*); it is the kind of sport displayed by the master of a trained monkey.[42]

Nonetheless, the world of Shah Husain is inhabited by the mighty and the rich. His Pātshāhs and Sultāns can do what they will. They have their thrones[5], their treasury and their serried ranks. They have huge palaces. There are princes, *rājās* and *runks*; there are *khāns* and *maliks*; and there are the *'umarā*. There are *hākims, shiqdārs* and *qāzīs*; there are 'wrestlers' and 'foot-soldiers'. Justice is performed; orders are passed; grants are given; and sometimes the criminals are executed. Wealth is not confined to the rulers and the ruling class. There are magnates who are millionaires. They lend money and make collections. They have their agents. The wealth of the rich is reflected in gold and silver, pearls and diamonds, tall mansions, golden walls and balconies, spears and trumpets, the game of *chaugān*, bejewelled couches, sweet scents and female slaves.[43]

There are cultivators of land in the world of Shah Husain. They sow and reap. The crops mentioned are sugarcane. cotton and inferior grain. There are wells dug for irrigation, and the Persian wheel for drawing water. The harvest is carried on pack-animals. Jaggery is made from sugarcane, and oil is extracted from *til*. The fields are clearly demarcated. Some colour is added by the mustard and the gourd in bloom. Shah Husain dwells more on manufactures, particularly textiles in cotton, wool and silk. The cotton is picked, ginned and carded before it is spun on the wheel. The thread is dyed, if necessary, before it is used as warp and woof. The handloom is worked by the weaver. Sometimes the cloth is dyed after it is woven. In the whole process of cloth manufacture, women do a good deal of work, especially in spinning and preparing the warp. The *sarrāf* who advances money collects the goods prepared and settles his account with the weaver, man or woman. Several varieties of cloth are manufactured, and dresses of different colours are stitched by the tailor working with scissors, the needle and the thread. The *gaz* is used for measurement. The colours mentioned are red, crimson, green and black. There are references to *bhūrī, loī, bhochhan, chīr, chunnī* and *sālū*. There are references to trade and the merchant, the *bāzār* and the shops, the goods and the customers, the capital and the interest, the loans and their return, the efficient magnate and the indifferent shop-keeper. Occasionally, we come upon a hawker with a shallow basket of goods over his or her head. For the merchants travelling over long distances there are *sarāis* enroute.[44]

There were many other categories of people in the world of Shah Husain. For the domesticated elephant, there is the elephant-driver (*mahāwat*). For sailing in seas and rivers, there are sailors and boatmen (*mallāh, muhāṇā, pātaṇī*) who ply their ships and boats and rafts (*beṛā, beṛī, tullā, mūṛhā*). The fisherman and the angler are there to catch the fish. There is the fowler to catch birds. The cattle are looked after by the cattle-herd (*mahīnwāl*). If he serves without wages he is a *chāk*. Then there is the *nāi* who serves as a hair-dresser, a manicure and a surgeon. His women folk dress the hair of ladies, forming partings and plaits. Medicines are administered by *vaids* and *tabībs*. There are professional 'representatives' (*vakīls*) to represent illiterate persons and ladies in the court, or to act as envoys. There is the sweeper-woman with her broom and basket. There is the brahman-astrologer with his book (*pothī*). There are beggars and paupers, thieves, thugs, gamblers, addicts and lustful men in the world of Shah Husain, as in the world around him.[45]

There are yet other human situations and activities in the relatively crowded world of Shah Husain. There are masters and slaves outside the ruling class circles. Friendship is a value, and a guest is shown consideration. The way-farer travels with a bundle of his wherewithal. The blind man needs a stick to feel his way. There are persons who carry burden for others on payment of wages. There are persons whose profession is to read and write. Some use caps as their head-dress. Soap is used for washing clothes. There are public and private ovens for cooking. Some ladies go about with veils on their faces. Strings and ropes are used for various purposes. The elephant driver uses the *ankush*; the fisherman uses a net. The bow and the arrow are used as a weapon. There are sports and playing fields; and people come first and second or last in competitive games. There is *chaupaṛ* with its eighty-four 'houses' which reminds one of the belief in eighty-four lac lives. There is kite-flying; there is dance, especially *luddī* and *jhūmar*; there are stringed instruments for music. Foods of various kinds are mentioned; *rotī* and some *lāwan* or *sālan* to go with it, stale bread, *rotī* kneaded in milk, *ghī* and sugar; there are hemp, poppy and pepper. There are pots and pans and there are mugs and trays. Some made a bowl of their palms to drink water. Some pray in humility; some offer 'sacrifices' for the protection of their dear ones; some distribute sweets when their prayers are answered; others illuminate their homes as a mark of rejoicing. Most people observe social conventions and customs.[46]

Shah Husain dwells long on the young maiden who leaves her childhood behind and is at the threshold of marriage. She has friends with whom she spins and plays in the courtyard of her father's house; she sings and dances and enjoys the swing; she wears rings on her fingers, red shoes on her feet, and golden pendants in her ears. She plays with the ball, and she sits on a colourful *pihṛā* or *panghūṛā*. Her work consists of *kashīdah*, sweeping the house clean and cleaning the utensils in which the family members have eaten. With her friends she goes out to fetch water for the home in pitchers of different kinds and colours. Her father and mother, brothers and sisters are in the home. She is expected to cherish the honour of the family and not to do anything that infringes social norms. Her father looks for a suitable match for her, either directly or through an intermediary. When the day of her marriage is fixed, messages are sent to relatives. The bride uses *mehndī* on her hands and feet, puts on a large coloured-bangle on her priest, and wears a *sālū*. Her dowry has been prepared. The bridegroom comes with a marriage party. The ceremony of marriage is performed through *lāvān* (not *nikāh*). The parents bid farewell to their newly-wed daughter; she sits in a planquin to be taken away to her in-laws. There she is received by her mother-in-law. The wedding couch is decorated for the first meeting with her spouse. She is expected to observe norms of her new home and remain veiled. Otherwise, she would be called 'the unveiled one' (*ghūngat-khullī*).[47]

There is not much of the unseen or the metaphysical in Shah Husain's universe. By far the most important entity is God. Then there is the angel of death, Azrāīl, who is also referred to as *jam* or *jangā*. There are two angels who remain un-named, but there is absolutely no doubt that they are Munkar and Nakīr who sit on the shoulders of men and keep account of all their good and bad deeds. Ultimately, an account of good and bad deeds is taken by God, but there is no mention of paradise in Shah Husain's compositions. There are references to prophets, *walīs, pīrs, murshids* and *murīds*; there are references also to the fire kept burning (*dhuān*) by the *murshid*, and the patched frock of the *faqīr*. Shah Husain refers directly to the '*ulamā* and the Qur'ān but only metaphorically to *hajj*. There are ascetics in Shah Husains's world who remain naked or smear their bodies with ashes and sit in meditation. He refers specifically to *jogīs*. There are *jogins* and *bairāgans* too in his world. He talks of the tenth door (*daswān duār*), revealing his familiarity with the *jogīs*. He brackets *gurū* and *pīr*, and he talks of the *sādh-sangat*. His sant is the *tabīb* who prescribes the medicine for liberation. All misgivings are removed when you meet the *sādhs*. Shah Husain would rather be a slave of the *sādhs*.[48]

It is possible now to appreciate the multiplicity of epithets used by Shah

Husain for God. Some of these come straight from the Islamic tradition, like Allah, Maulā, Rabb, Kāmil, Qādir and Sattār. The conception of God as the master of the universe is reflected also in the epithets like Sāhib, Sāīn, Shāh, Sultān and Sarkār. He is also *beparwāh* or self-sufficient. Some of the epithets come from the Indian tradition like Prabhā, Thākur and Har. A few of them come specifically from the Vaishnava *bhaktī*, like Rām, Shām, Sāwal and Lāl. Characteristically *sant* epithets used by Shah Husain are Satgur, Shauh and Kant. Then there are epithets coming from the popular tradition, like Yār, Yār-Piāra, Yār-Sipāhī, Mīt, Mittar, Mittar-Piārā, Sājan, Sajjan, Dilbar, Dhol, Māhī, Rānjhā and Rānjhan. It may be obvious that the multiplicity of epithets used for God does not infringe His unity; it widens the range of Shah Husain's audience and suggests a large measure of indigenization. We cannot look upon Shah Husain as just a representative of Islam.

Shah Husain's stratified social world is crowded by powerful potentates and penniless paupers, with traders, merchants, shopkeepers, street-hawkers, cultivators, artisans, daily wage-earners and slaves. He refers to himself as a weaver (*julāhā*). But he does not talk of high and low castes in the traditional formulation. He is aware of the great differences in the economic means and resources of the various categories of people: some long for a quarter of a bread while others can give away the whole many times over. He does not like to be with the rich, the millionaires: let their 'white sheet' be thrown in the fire; far better is the rough blanket of the *faqīrs*. He does not claim to be a Shaikh; he is happy to remain a begging *faqīr*. All the castes are higher than the caste of the *faqīrs* who have no caste. Shah Husain identifies himself with the *faqīrs*. They belong to his own village. They have nothing to worry about because the Lord is with them. They are protected by God and loved by Him; their outer and their inner life is the same; all their difficulties are resolved; indifferent to happiness and sorrow, they subsist in a state of intoxication; they alone are the true ones, and the rest of the world is false. Shah Husain is neither with the rich nor with the renunciant. The former are proud of their earthly possessions and the latter are proud of their poverty. 'I am neither the one nor the other, and all and sundry laugh at me'. He has left the world, with its poverty as well as its riches, for the love of God, and this is known to the Master.[49]

Obviously, the *sādhs* and *faqīrs* of Shah Husain were not *mullās* or *qāzīs*. They were not *jogīs* or *saniyāsīs* either. He does not use the word Hindu or Muslim anywhere in his compositions. We get the impression that his *sādhs* and *faqīrs* are a category apart. They know the truth, they have experienced love, and they are one with God. They are the men and women who follow the path of love in complete dedication to God. Irrespective of their social background or formal affiliation to a particular system.

IV

In retrospect we can see that Shah Husain's conception of God and the epithets he uses for Him tend to take God out of all sectarian contexts. He does not discriminate between one human being and another except in terms of devotion to God and love for Him. He talks of the deeds of men and women but not on the basis of any external rituals prescribed by an institutionalized religion. Importance of the distinctions of birth, social position and political power is sought to be minimized. There is no hatred for any class, community or gender. All men and women who love God and love one another belong to 'the village' of Shah Husain. The moods and feelings he expresses are devoid of ill will. The attitudes he suggestively approves of are conducive to social tolerance and cultural coexistence. Shah Husain has told millions of people over the centuries how to live together.

Notes and References

1. Harjinder Singh Dhillon (ed), *Sufi Kavi Shah Husain* (Amritsar: Waris Shah Foundation, 1992), Kāfi 139. All the *kāfis* in this volume are numbered and *the reference here, as elsewhere, is to the number of the relevant kāfi* (*stanza*)
2. *Ibid.*, 1.
3. *Ibid.*, 105.
4. *Ibid.*, 145.
5. *Ibid.*, 119.
6. *Ibid.*, 73.
7. *Ibid.*, 74.
8. *Ibid.*, 78.
9. *Ibid.*, 124.
10. *Ibid.*, 132.
11. *Ibid.*, 11.
12. *Ibid.*, 25.
13. *Ibid.*, 19.
14. *Ibid.*, 95.
15. *Ibid.*, 144.
16. *Ibid.*, 36.
17. *Ibid.*, 15.
18. *Ibid.*, 55.
19. *Ibid.*, 59.
20. *Ibid.*, 38.
21. *Ibid.*, 67.
22. *Ibid.*, 90.
23. *Ibid.*, 15, 22, 27, 33, 43–44, 51, 76–77, 85–86, 98, 114, 129, 140–41, 151, 153, 158.
24. *Ibid.*, 6, 9, 21, 28, 48, 54, 72, 84, 121.
25. *Ibid.*, 49, 54, 71–72, 85, 128, 142.
26. *Ibid.*, 14, 22, 53–54, 62, 79, 129, 151.

27. *Ibid.*, 12, 32, 41, 79, 83, 92, 113, 128, 134–35, 140.
28. *Ibid.*, 50, 57, 62, 81, 91, 99, 114, 127, 156.
29. *Ibid.*, 20, 46, 60.
30. *Ibid.*, 37, 54, 101–2, 131, 154.
31. *Ibid.*, 2, 7, 9, 24, 42, 48, 53, 131.
32. *Ibid.*, 3, 23, 45, 88, 111, 147, 161, 164.
33. *Ibid.*, 23, 35, 76, 100, 116.
34. *Ibid.*, 67, 87, 117.
35. *Ibid.*, 13, 64, 88, 118, 122, 142.
36. *Ibid.*, 16, 37, 43, 63, 66, 73, 87, 93, 102, 107, 133, 155, 164.
37. *Ibid.*, 4, 24, 126, 160.
38. *Ibid.*, 5–6, 9–10, 21, 34, 42, 44, 73, 99, 110, 141.
39. *Ibid.*, 18, 20–23, 26–27, 29, 36–37, 44, 46, 50–51, 54, 58, 73, 76–77, 79–80, 99, 104–5, 114, 121, 123, 130, 134, 136, 140, 143, 153, 164.
40. *Ibid.*, 22, 25, 29, 32, 37, 62–63, 66, 71, 80, 84, 88–89, 103, 105, 118, 124, 144, 148, 152, 154.
41. *Ibid.*, 20–21, 33, 48, 50, 55, 57, 73, 78, 87, 92, 104, 106, 110, 121, 123–24, 130–31, 136, 141, 148.
42. *Ibid.*, 2–5, 9, 15, 19, 22, 24, 28–29, 34, 44, 46, 48–50, 58, 63–64, 68, 71, 73– 74, 85, 92, 109, 114, 119, 122, 124, 129–30, 162.
43. *Ibid.*, 4, 9, 15, 18, 31, 36–38, 45, 52, 54–55, 64, 66, 69, 75–76, 79, 90, 92, 94, 107, 109, 113, 119, 123, 128, 136, 142, 151, 155–56.
44. *Ibid.*, 1–2, 4, 6–8, 11–15, 19–20, 26, 29–30, 37, 40–42, 47, 50–51, 61, 63, 76, 82–84, 89, 106, 111, 115, 117, 123, 125, 127–28, 134, 136, 141–42, 147.
45. *Ibid.*, 1–2, 9, 13, 19, 25, 27, 34, 41, 45–46, 51–52, 59, 62, 73–76, 81, 87, 90, 97–99, 102–3, 106, 112–13, 118, 121, 127, 130, 133, 140, 142, 144–45.
46. *Ibid.*, 3, 5, 18, 23, 26, 29, 39, 43–44, 48–49, 55, 58, 65–66, 70, 72, 75–78, 83, 85, 87, 97–98, 100, 102–3, 111, 117, 127, 131, 137, 141, 143, 145, 151, 160.
47. *Ibid.*, 3, 9, 19, 22, 26–30, 33, 36, 39, 44, 48, 56–58, 61, 63–64, 66, 69–70, 73, 75, 81, 91, 95, 98–99, 106, 110–11, 117, 123, 129–30, 136–38, 143, 146, 150, 153, 157.
48. *Ibid.*, 4, 10, 11, 60, 62–63, 66–67, 93, 105, 112, 117, 122, 124, 130, 144, 153, 160.
49. *Ibid.*, 4, 8, 9, 11, 16, 24, 34, 117.

TEN

Contribution of Mystics to Amity and Harmony in Indian Society

K. A. NIZAMI

HAVING SURVEYED THE MARCH of civilizations in world history, Arnold Toynbee came to the conclusion: 'The missions of the higher religions are not competitive; they are complimentary'. This higher religious ethos is represented by the mystics who, as Tagore puts it, 'set at naught all differences of men, by the overflow of their consciousness of God'. The faith of the mystics was the outcome of the love in their hearts rather than the conclusion of their logic. For them God was neither a theological myth nor a logical abstraction of Unity, but an all-embracing Reality present in ethical, intellectual and aesthetic experience. They furnished the inspiration for creating an ideal realm of values – the kingdom of Heaven – in a distressed and struggling world.

Robert Vaughan traced 'the unconscious unity of mystical temperaments in every communion'. Indeed it is right to say that mysticism has no genealogy. It is the eternal and earnest quest of Man to have direct experience of the Ultimate Reality. The mystics used the elan that this quest released for establishing a healthy relationship between God, Man and the Universe.

In India, the Sufi and the Bhakti saints incessantly struggled to bring about amity and harmony in the diverse components of society. The essence of their teachings is neatly epitomized in the following verse:

یگانه بودن و یکتا شرن ز چشم آموز
که هر دو چشم جدا و جدا نمی نگرند

Learn from the eyes the way to develop unity and harmony;
The two eyes appear different but their vision is one.

This cosmopolitan approach emanated from their faith in the following principles which constituted the basis of the structure of their thought, emotions and behaviour:

1. All men are the children of God on earth, and are made of the selfsame clay.
2. The Ultimate Reality – by whatever name one calls Him – is One, Omnipotent and Indivisible.
3. Man should learn from God the basic principles on which his relationship with fellow human beings should be adjusted. God treats all human beings equally and does not discriminate between one individual and the other.
4. Nothing brings higher spiritual reward to Man than service of Mankind.
5. All religions are different ways to reach the same goal. There is essential unity in all religions.
6. Religious scriptures of all faiths should be respected.
7. The reward for doing good to human beings is higher than that for the performance of ritualistic practices of faith.
8. Emphasis on denominational classification which accentuates differences in society should be avoided.
9. Non-violence should be developed in relationships with all living beings.
10. Revenge and retaliation form part of the law of the jungle. One should return evil with good.

It is around these ten cardinal principles that the life and approach of Muslim, Hindu and Sikh saints was nurtured. During the medieval period these principles determined the ethos of the Indian society.

The Sufis emphasized through word and deed their faith in:

الخلق عيال الله

(All people are the children of God).

They cited a tradition of the Prophet quoted in *Sunnan-i Abu Da'ud* that the Prophet used to pray at night: 'O God! I bear witness that all Thy Creatures are brothers.' اناشهدأن العباد كلهم اخوة Sa'di compared people of diverse backgrounds to the limbs in the human body which function only if the different parts cooperate. Developing further the concept of oneness of human society and the 'unity of human origin' he remarked:

بنی آدم اعضاے یک دیگر اند
کہ از آفرینش زیک جوہر اند

All human beings are like limbs of a body,
For in their origin they are from the same substance.

The Sufi saints advised their followers to 'adopt the ways of God' (تخلقوا باخلاق الله). It was a pithy and profound advice. Man was expected to imitate the ways of God in his dealings with other human beings: God did not discriminate between rich and poor, high and low, believer and non-believer, man and woman, emperor and humble shepherd. When clouds appeared on the horizon, they poured water on the palace and the hut alike. When the sun shone, it did not discriminate between the rich and the poor. The earth opened its bosom for the believer and the non-believer alike. Khwaja Mu'in-ud-din, Chishti of Ajmer, the distinguished founder of the Chishti order in India, advised his followers to develop river-like generosity, sun-like affection and earth-like hospitality. Discussing this principle of Divine Providence, Maulana Abul Kalam Azad writes:

> The phenomenal activities of the Sun, the cycle of the seasons in all their moods, the forces of the earth, and the interaction of elements seem intent on seeing when the egg of an ant delivers its offspring and the peasant's bag drops its grain.

It is also stated:

> And He hath subjected to you all that there is in the heavens and all that there is in the earth; all is from Him. Verily, herein are signs for those who reflect. (*Qur'an*, 45:13).

The strangest thing about this scheme of Providence, is the uniformity and harmony underlying it. The method and manner of providing sustenance for every living object are the same everywhere. The Sufis of the medieval period saw these principles as operative forces in human life.

Muslim mystics built their hospices outside the caste-cities in the midst of the non-caste people. Historical records reveal that many of the earliest Indian entrants to the mystic fold belonged to the *Antyaja* group – basket-makers, sellers of curd, rope-makers, etc.

The *khanqahs, derahs* and *jama'at khanahs* kept their kitchens open for all. *Fawa'id-ul-Fu'ad*, records an exhortation of Shaikh Nizam-u'd-din Auliya (ob. 1325) that discrimination in providing food and shelter is against the true spirit of religion. He told his audience that once Prophet Abraham was reluctant to ask a non-believer to partake food with him. God admonished him thus: 'Oh Abraham! We can give life to this man but you cannot give him bread.' Even Chengiz Khan's practice of giving food to all irrespective of caste, colour or creed was praised by Saikh Nizam-u'd-din Auliya.

Dara Shukoh, a famous student of comparative religious thought in India, once asked Shah Muhibbullah of Allahabad, an advocate of Ibn Arabi's pantheistic philosophy, if discrimination between Hindus and Muslims was justifiable from the religious point of view. The saint firmly rejected such an approach and said that the Prophet Muhammad was sent as 'Mercy for all worlds' (رحمة اللعالمين) and not for Muslims alone. Hence any approach which discriminated between human beings is against the spirit of Islam and the teachings of the Prophet.

The Sufi saints firmly believed in the principles of their faith and maintained their religious identity, but did not approve of unnecessary harping on differences of faith. Shaikh Hamid-u'd-din Sufi of Nagaur, a distinguished disciple and *khalifah* of Khawaja Mu'in-u'd-din Chishti of Ajmer, reprimanded a disciple who had referred to a Hindu as a *kafir*. 'You do not know the inner life of this man', he said. Shaikh Abdul Quddus of Gangoh (*ob*. 1537) firmly cautioned his disciples thus:

Why this meaningless talk about the believer, the kafir, the obedient, the sinner, the rightly guided, the misdirected, the Muslim, the pious, the infidel, the fire worshipper. All are like beads in a rosary. Another distinguished saint of the century, Shah Niaz Ahmad of Bareilly, wrote:

یہ سب ادیان وملل ہیں شاخ ہائے یک درخت
اک جڑ سے ہیں نکلی ڈالیاں سب پھوٹ پھوٹ

All these religions and faiths are branches of the same tree,
They have sprouted from one and the same root.

This catholic and cosmopolitan spirit opened avenues of social and ideological contact between people of different faiths and created an atmosphere of religious large-heartedness and tolerance.

The spirit of toleration which inspired this attitude of mind needs clear analysis. The spirit of toleration, as Gibbon has remarked and Dr M. Iqbal has approvingly quoted, springs from very different attitudes of the mind of man. There is the toleration of the philosopher to whom all religions are equally true; of the historian to whom all are equally false; and of the politician to whom all are equally useful. There is the toleration of the man who tolerates other modes of thought and behaviour because he has himself grown absolutely indifferent to all modes of thought and behaviour. There is the toleration of the weak man who, on account of sheer weakness, pockets all kinds of insults heaped on things or persons whom he holds dear. It is obvious that these types of tolerance have no ethical value. On the other hand, they unmistakably reveal the spiritual impoverishment of the man who practises them. True tolerance is begotten of intellectual breadth and spiritual expansion. Iqbal considered the following verse of Amir Khusrau as the best illustration of religious toleration:

اے کہ زبت طعنہ بہ ہندو بری
ہم زوے آموز پرستش گری

O you! who sneer at the idolatry of the Hindu,
Learn also from him how worship is done.

No mystic experience was possible without faith in the unity of Godhead. The Hindus believed in one Universal Spirit or Eternal Essence, without beginning or end, called *Brahman* which means the World-Soul. The *Upanishads* contained the earliest exposition of pantheistic thought. However, when it came to the level of common man, gods and goddesses were introduced. Dr Radhakrishnan says: 'The *Upanishads*, no doubt, shattered the authority of these gods in the world of thought, but did not disturb their sway in the world of practice. Mystical thought could not reconcile itself to any polytheistic concepts. A Hindu, Hirday Ram, wrote to Shaikh Ahmad Sirhindi Mujaddid-i-Alf-i-Sani that *Ram* and *Rahman* were the same. The Shaikh firmly rebutted his opinion and said that *Ram* was a human being while *Rahman* was the All-powerful God.

Bhakti saints also did not lag behind in rejecting polytheistic ideas. Kabir told his devotees that God is not *Hari* or *Ram* or *Krishna*. He transcends all conception. 'I cannot bend my head', firmly declared Kabir, 'before one (*Rama*) who took birth and died.

In this connection I may reproduce here the remarks I made while inaugurating the Noruz Lecture series at Washington University:

If the course of different streams of thought in Iran is closely followed, it would appear that there has been considerable cycling and recycling of ideas between Iran and India. India is the cradle of pantheistic philosophy and the *Upanishads* contain the earliest exposition of these ideas. When Islam reached Khurasan and Transoxiana the religious atmosphere was saturated with Buddhist and Hindu ideas. The temples of Bamyan, Balkh and Marv were centers of Buddhist tradition. It was but inevitable that some of their concepts influenced the Iranian mind. The *Upanishads* proclaim *Tattvam asi* (Thou art that), and the idea finds its echo in Bayazid. The *Karramiyan* cult was a halfway house between Islam and Buddhism. Hujwiri has given an account of twelve schools of mystic thought which flourished during the eleventh century of the Christian era. An analysis of the thought contents of these *garuhs*, as he calls them, reveals the impact of Indian ideas. Concepts like *fanaṅ, baqa, hulul*, etc. are inexplicable except in the context of Hindu and Buddhist religious traditions. Thus some of the Iranian mystical ideas that reached India during the medieval period had in fact originated in India and were cycled back to India under Islamic rubrics. Indian fables (like *Panchatantra*), lexical and phonological traditions, mathematical theories and astronomical concepts reached Iran and influenced Iranian thought.

The mystics considered service of mankind to be the real aim and ideal of religious devotion. Shaikh Nizam-u'd-din Auliya considered devotion to God (*Ta'at*) to be of two kinds *ta'at-i-lazmi* (intransitive) and *ta'at-i-mut'addi* (transitive). In *lazmi* devotion the benefit that accrues is confined to the devotee alone. This kind of devotion includes prayer, fasting, pilgrimage to

Mecca, recitation of religious formulae, turning the beads of rosary, etc. On the other hand *muta'ddi* devotion brought advantage and comfort to others. It consisted of serving other human beings in their need and performing acts to reduce their misery. He told his devotees that serving human beings brought greater divine reward than the other kind of devotion. Sa'di declared:

طریقت بجز و خدمت خلق نیست
به تسبیح و سجاده و دلق نیست

> *Higher spiritual life is nothing but service of humanity,*
> *It is not (chanting) rosary, remaining on the prayer carpet or (wearing) the coarse garments.*

The mystic teachers therefore advised their followers:

دل بدست آور که حج اکبر است
از هزاران کعبه یک دل بهتر است

> *Bringing solace to human heart is like Hajj-i-Akbar,*
> *One heart is better than a thousand Ka'bas.*

Man attained gnosis by helping his fellow human beings. Bibi Fatimah Sam, a highly respected woman mystic of Delhi whom Shaikh Nizam-u'd-din Auliya deeply venerated, used to say that giving a loaf of bread and a glass of water to the hungry brought greater reward to a person than countless prayers and endless fasts. The following *Hadis-i-Qudsi* which appears in *Sahih Muslim*, was cited to bring home to the devotees the spiritual value of saving people from hunger and misery:

> On the day of Judgement, God will address a particular individual: 'O Son of Adam! I fell ill but you did not attend on me.' Bewildered this individual will say: 'How is that possible? Thou art the Creator and sustainer of all the worlds.' God will reply: 'Doesn't thou know that such and such a creature of mine living near thee fell ill, but you did not turn to him in sympathy. If you had but gone near him you would have found Me by his side? In like manner, God would address another individual: 'O Son of Adam! I had asked of you a piece of bread but you did not give it to me! The individual will submit: 'How could this happen? Thou doesn't stand in need of anything.' And God will reply: 'Don't you remember that so and so among the hungry creatures of Mine had asked you for food and did you not refuse to give it to him. If you had fed him, you would have found Me by his side.'

In his *Gifford Lectures* Toynboee dwelt upon the significance of the emphasis on service of humanity in different religious:

> All the living religions are going to be put to a searching practical test. 'By their fruits

ye shall know them' (Math. VII. 20). The practical test of a religion, always and everywhere, is its success or failure in helping human souls to respond to the challenges of suffering and sin.

The Sufi and the Bhakti saints created an environment of amicable co-existence between communities and cults. Their respect for the sanctity of all Revealed Books led them to their faith in the Unity of Divine Revelation. Explaining this concept in the light of the *Qur'an*, Maulana Azad remarks:

The *Qur'an* points out that the tragedy of man has lain in his effort to make distinction between the prophets or in his accepting some and rejecting others. Its attitude is summed up in the following verse:

Say: We make no difference between them (Prophets of God) and we are Muslims resigned to God (3:78).

Amir Khusrau made an intensive study of Hindu religious literature and declared:

نیست ہنود ارچہ کہ دین دار چوما
ہست بسے جائے باقرار چوما

Though Hindus do not believe in the religion in which we do,
Yet in many matters they and we believe in the same thing.

Mirza Mazhar Jan-i-Janan believed in the divine character of the Vedas. Works like the *Bahr-ul Hayat, Jawahir-i-Khamsa, Majma-ul-Bahrain*, etc. could never have come into existence without being inspired by this basic ideological position. The *Upanishads,* which contain the earliest exposition of pantheistic thought, inspired Muslim mystic thought in many ways.

The Sufi hospices were the meeting ground of Hindu and Muslim religious thought. In the *khangahs* of Shaikh Farid Ganj-i-Shakar of Pakpattan, Shaikh Nizam-u'd-din Auliya of Delhi, Syed Muhammad Gisu Daraz of Gulbarga, Shaikh Ahmad Khattu of Ahmedabad, Rishi Nuruddin of Kashmir and a number of other distinguished saints of the medieval period we find frequent exchange of religious views between Sadhus, Yogis, Sufis and others.

Some Sufi saints like Shaikh Hamid-ud-din Suwali of Nagaur and the Nur Bakhshis of Kashmir adopted vegetarian habits.

All important Sufis advised their disciples to return evil with good and to avoid use of force. Shaikh Nizam-u'd-din Auliya used to recite the following verses of Shaikh Abu Sa'id Abul Khair

ہر کہ مارا یار نبود ایزد اورا یار باد
و آں کہ مارا رنجہ دارد راحتش بسیار باد

هر کہ او در راہ ما خارے نہد از دشمنی
هر گُلے کز باغ عمرش بشگفد بے خار باد

He who is not my friend - may God be his friend,
And he who bears ill-will against me may his joys (in life) increase,
He who puts thorns in my way on account of enmity
May every flower that blossoms in the garden of his life be without thorns.

A comparative study of the works of Muslim Sufis – particularly their *malfuzat* and *maktubat* – and the poetic compositions of the Bhakti saints like Kabir, Nanak, Dadu, Pipa, Sena, and Chaitanya reveals the extent to which the two mystical traditions had come together and responded to each other.

The Muslim saints recited the following verses of the Qur'an in their prayers:

Say: He is God
The One and the Only
God, the Eternal, Absolute
He begotten not,
Nor is He begotten;
And there is none
Like unto Him (S.C. XII).

The Bhakti saints recited the following Vedic hymn in their prayers:

Of Him there is not any master in the world, nor is there any ruler to rule Him, nor is there any sign of Him. He is the cause of all and is the Lord of the sense-deities. Of Him there is neither progenitor nor Lord.

(*Shwetashwatara Upanishad*, Ch. 6.9.)

In the sayings of Guru Nanak one finds that the ideas of Attar, Shaikh Ganj-i-Shakar, Farid and Sa'di echoed with great felicity and wisdom.

The mystics rejected linguistic chauvinism and communicated in the language of the people. It is for this reason that the Sufis and the Bhakti saints are credited with having developed regional languages. The Urdu language – and its earliest form known as Hindivi – was born in the *khanqahs* of Sufi saints.

The role of the Sufi and Bhakti saints in creating amity and harmony in Indian society cannot be overestimated. Their belief in Divine Presence inculcated in them a sense of social awareness and responsibility and they looked upon human beings as the children of God on earth.

ELEVEN ❖ Syrian Catholics in India

K. S. MATHEW

SINCE THE DAWN OF the sixteenth century, the society, economy and culture of the Afro-Asian and Latin American countries had been greatly affected by the colonial power. The extent of the transformation affected through the interaction between the western and the eastern worlds can be perceived in its fullness against the backdrop of the conversion of the so-called 'first world countries' into the 'third world countries' and vice-versa through the 'strenuous efforts' made by those committed to the 'missio civiliatrix' or 'civilising mission' or by those who happily carried the 'whiteman's burden' on their shoulders. The 'development of underdevelopment' in these countries, initiated by the European powers, was chiefly responsible for such a turn of events. The barbaric and atrocious fights put up by the present 'first world countries' to obtain a foothold in the Afro-Asian and Latin American countries bear out the fact that they crossed swords on the high seas not for a share in the misery of the 'third world countries' and to lighten the burden, but, rather, for a lion's share in the wealth and prosperity of the countries that were considered to be forming a part of the 'first world' at that time.

Cultures, communities and liturgies fell a prey to the onslaught of the colonizing powers which, in their eagerness to establish their sway in all the realms of life, crushed several institutions that did not conform to their monolithic culture. They smothered several active forms of culture in these countries and did not pay any heed to the fact that unity was different from uniformity and that unity could survive in diversity. The Syrian Catholic community, the seed of which was sown as early as the first century after Christ by St. Thomas, the apostle, flourished in the Indian social milieu against several odds for centuries together keeping its individuality intact. It was closely connected with the East Syrian Church or Chaldean Church as far as liturgy and liturgial language were concerned. But it grew up in Malabar, evincing the characteristic features of an India institution. A particular Church of this nature was not spared by the colonizers who went on trying to dominate it against constant resistance on the part of the local people and even against the recommendations of the Pope, the Supreme Pontiff. Some of the bishops, sent from Catholic hierarchies in the Middle East for the Church in Malabar, were kept behind bars for their unwillingness to be subservient to the colonizing powers. But the unquenchable desire to remain independent could not be totally wiped out through the colonial domination that lasted for a couple of centuries.

In the wake of decolonization, the voice for restoring the Syrian Catholic Church to its pristine purity reverberated at various levels. The decrees promulgated by the Ecumenical Council of Vatican II insisted on unity in diversity, independence and equal dignity of the oriental churches in general and of individual Church in particular. The guidelines and recommendations furnished by the Conciliar decrees were interpreted succinctly, elucidated and clarified by one of the participants of the Council, an Indian sage, who witnessed the ravages of colonialism and imperialism in India. It was none other than the 'light from the Orient', His Eminence Cardinal Simon Loudursamy, who worked as the Cardinal Prefect of the Oriental Churches from 30 October 1985. His clarifications of, and the conclusions from, the Conciliar decrees, given vent to at the Synod of the bishops on 28 November 1985,[1] found clear expression in the historic letter of Pope John Paul II written to the bishops of India on 28 May 1987.

The vicissitudes of the Syrian Catholic Church in her history forms an important chapter in the history of the Catholic Church in general. We will try to trace in this paper an outline of its origin, development and struggles against the colonial powers to maintain its individuality and finally its attempts to restore its originality in the post-colonial period.

The history of the past can be reconstructed from several sources, such as the existence of a particular community, a living tradition, archaeological evidence, numismatical facts, parallel evidences corroborating a living tradition, and literary sources, besides, of course, written histories. Fully conscious of the validity of the plurality of sources, Pope John Paul II, after his historic visit in 1986 to various parts of India, wrote in the subsequent year:

> Since very ancient times a considerable community of Christians known as the 'St. Thomas Christians' has existed in Southern India. Indeed there is a very strong tradition that St. Thomas himself visited and laboured in India, both in the extreme south and in what is known today as Madras-Mylapore area. There is even a tomb in Mylapore which is venerated as his resting place. Later at on various times, the Church in India was strengthened by other groups of Christians from the Middle East who became assimilated into the Church already there.[2]

According to the ancient tradition corroborated by the existence of a community called St. Thomas Christians, literary evidences of the last quarter of the second century[3] and archaeological sources, St. Thomas, the apostle, preached the Gospel in India when the Parthian King Guduphara, or Gundaphares, ruled Afghanistan and Punjab in the first century AD. The name of the ruler is historical and it has been found on coins and on an inscription of Gandhara.[4] The *Veeradian pattu*, the song of Rabban Thomas and the *Margamkali pattu* point to the South Indian apostolate of St. Thomas.[5] It is argued by Cardinal Tisserant that Acts of the Judas-Thomas written in Mesopotamia support the general conviction of the contemporaries in the second century in Mesopotamia that the apostolate of St. Thomas was in South India. Similarly, Eusebius writes about Alexandrine Pantaenus who found Christians in India reading the Gospel of St. Mathew probably in Aramaic or Syriac at the end of the second century.[6]

The fathers of the Church like St. Ephrem, St. Gregory Nazianzus, St. Ambrose, Gaudentius, St. Jerome, Paulinus of Nola, ecclesiatical calendars, and martyrologies relate St. Thomas with India.[7] St. Ephrem (+373) testifies that the body of St. Thomas was shifted from India to Edessa. An ancient Syrian calendar has reference to July 3, as the day on which St. Thomas was pierced through by a lance in India and that his body was taken to Edessa by a certain merchant called Khaban. The Divine office of the East Syrians influenced by the Acts of Judas Thomas often refers to India as the field of activity of St. Thomas who,according to the same office, died in India. These East Syrians believed that the mortal remains of St. Thomas were taken from India to Edessa. Adai and Mari, who preached the Gospel to the East Syrians, were the disciples of St. Thomas and so they had great devotion to the Apostle. *Chronicum Edessenum* (XXXVII) makes mention of the solemn deposit of the relics of St. Thomas in the Church dedicated to the Apostle in Edessa in AD 393 or in 705 of the Greek Era.[8]

The fact that St. Thomas, the Apostle, preached the Gospel and converted a number of Indians to Christ is testified by several writers like Marco Polo, the Venetian who visited the tomb of St. Thomas at Mylapore in 1295 and speaks of the large number of pilgrims coming to the tomb at Mylapore.[9] Similarly Blessed Oderick, the Italian Franciscan wrote in 1324 about the holy remains of St. Thomas, the Apostle in Ma'bar and of a Church of St. Thomas.[10] Marignoli, the Papal legate to China in 1394 refers to the Church of St. Thomas and the province of India.[11] Nicholas de Conti, an Italian merchant (1425–1430), makes mention of 'Malepor', the tomb of St. Thomas and the Church of St. Thomas.[12]

The Portuguese on their arrival were informed of the tomb of St. Thomas at Mylapore and they conducted serious researches and were convinced of the St. Thomas apostolate in South India. They issued coins in the name of the apostle, built a ship in his name and held firm to the tradition.[13]

The bricks of the tomb of St. Thomas at Mylapore measuring 15×8" and 2'9" thick are of the same period as those found in Arikamedu in the vicinity of Pondicherry about 150 kilometers south of Mylapore which flourished as a Roman settlement from the first Century BC to the third century AD. This archaeological evidence about the tomb of St. Thomas, just as the tomb of St. Peter under the St. Peter's Basilica, is a solid proof for the origin of the St. Thomas Catholics and their connections with St. Thomas, the Apostle. There are no rival traditions nor rival tombs nor rival St. Thomas Christians in the whole world.[14]

A few persecutions on the Coromandel coast drove the Christians to Thiruvancode. The seduction, attributed to a Hindu conjuror Manikavachakar made a number of Christians leave Christianity and embrace Hinduism. Some of those who wanted to remain in the Catholic faith fled to places like Quilon on the Malabar coast.[15] The Hindu revival movement coupled with the Muhammedan inroads into the South also could be instrumental in destroying Christianity in the Coromandel region especially around San Thome-Mylapore. But the tomb continued to be there.

It is quite natural that the European missionaries who came to India to preach the Gospel of Christ and convert people to Christianity wanted to show that they got the faith earlier than the people of the country which they were trying to convert. Consequently for a long time these missionaries and their converts were not willing to accept the evidences regarding the Indian apostolate of St. Thomas. Now, on account of the availability of various sources confirming the fact of the origin of St. Thomas Christians especially in the light of the scientific studies conducted by Mgr. A.E. Medlycott[16] and a good number of others, the doubt about the origin of the St. Thomas Christians are satisfactorily cleared. The Euro-centered considerations of the missionaries and their converts are now left without any support and they are bound to accept the historical facts. Even those who used to raise doubt whether India was known to outsiders in the early centuries of Christianity came to know about the contacts of Rome with India through West Asia even before the dawn of Christian era such as the commercial contacts with Korkai. Arikamedu, Dharanikotta, Nagarjunakonda, Cranganore, Broach and so on. Kaveri-poompattinum or Poompuhar had even a separate section of the town occupied by the foreigners.

Some of the important families in Malabar, such as Pakalomattam. Sankarapuri, Kalli, Kalikavu, Koyakkam, Madeipur, Muttodal, Nedumpally, Panakkamattam and Kottakkali, were held in great esteem by the St. Thomas Christians, since priesthood and prelacy for several centuries were confined to these families. Some of them trace their origin to those converted by St. Thomas.

New groups that came to Malabar at different times after the arrival of St. Thomas were added to the members of the St. Thomas Christians. Approximately 400 Syrian migrants under Thomas of Cana, a merchant of

Jerusalem, including bishops, priests and deacons came to India in AD 345.[17] There were two more migrations of Christians from Syria in AD 825 under a certain bishop called Thomas Cana[18] and later under two bishops, Mar Sabarisho and Mar Peroz, who settled down in Quilon confirming the local Christians in their faith.[19] Thus the community of Christians that existed at the time of the arrival of the Portuguese consisted of the St. Thomas Christians.

They followed the East Syrian language and Liturgy, and so they were called otherwise Syro-Malabar Christians who were liturgically connected with the East Syrian rite and had an independent existence in Malabar on account of the local traditions and practices kept intact by them. The Church is generally known as Syro-Malabar Church, distinguishing it from the Syro-Malankara Church which follows West Syrian language and liturgy and came into existence from the section of the followers of those who were converted to Christianity by St. Thomas and who left the Catholic faith in 1653 after the oath of *koonamkurisu*. It could be defined as the 'community of Christians in India some of whom trace back their origin in faith to St. Thomas the Apostle, and others to Thomas of Cana or to other Syrian immigrants and who were once hierarchically connected with the Chaldean Church of Mesopotamia and Persia'.[20] Hence the Syro-Malabar Church as it exists at present comprises two different sections known as the Nordhists and the Sudhists (*vadakkumbhagar* and the *Thekkumbhangar*), the former claiming their ancestry to those brought to faith in Jesus Christ by St. Thomas, the apostle in the first century after Christ and the latter to the migrants.

Syro-Malabar Church and the Church of Seleucia-Ctesiphon

The Indian Christians of St. Thomas came into close association with Edessa certainly before the end of the second century as is evident from the composition of the Acts of Judas-Thomas.[21] The East Syrian rite had its origin in Edessa and developed in the Seleucian Church, together with the development of that Church. Seleucian Church had always the East Syrian liturgy and this was bequeathed to the Christians in India. The Syrian Christians of Kerala were connected with the Church of Seleucia-Ctesiphon, now represented by the Catholic Chaldean and the dissident Nestorian churches. The name Seleucia-Ctesiphon took its origin from the twin cities of Seleucia and Ctesiphon situated on either side of the river Tigris. This Church is also known by two other names, The Church of the East, and The Babylonian Church, because it flourished in the Persian (Sassanian) empire.[22] A certain bishop, David was reported in Chronicle of Seert to be leaving the see of Basrah in AD 295 to take up missionary activities in India.[23]

The Syro-Malabar Church in India was directly under the jurisdiction of the Persian Ecclesiastical provinces. Therefore, we find a certain John, 'the Persian Bishop of all Persia and greater India' as a signatory of the decrees of the first Ecumenical Council of Nicea in AD 325.[24] The Bishop of Selecucia-Ctesiphon tried to bring the bishops of Persia under his subjection in the fourth century. With the approval of the Western Fathers Seleucia was created as a Metropolitan See and all the bishops who resisted the attempts of the bishop of Seleucia-Ctesiphon submitted themselves to Mar Issac at the Synod he convened in AD 410. He was thus recognized as the head of all the bishops of the country. Mar Dadjesus proclaimed in AD 424 at the Synod his own independence from the Patriarch of Antioch. Thus the Catholicos of Seleucia began to be called Patriarch.[25] The Seleucian Church which had broken away from the Patriarch of Antioch favoured Nestorian views. But there were many bishops in Persia and Seleucia who depended on the Catholic Antiochian See. Even when the Seleucian Church brought the Church of Persia under its jurisdiction, the latter continued to exercise its right to send bishops to India. Cosmas Indicopleustes during his travels between 520 and 525, came across Christians in Socotra and in Ceylon who were under the Persian clergy. He also makes mention of Christians in Quilon and Male, the last being interpreted as Malabar coast.[26] Isho-Yahb, the Patriarch of Seleucia (650–660), in his correspondence with Simeon, the Metropolitan of Riwardashir in Persia, made mention of this right.[27] In the face of resistance from the Persian bishops, who used to send bishops to India, the Seleucian Patriarch Saliba-Za-Kha (714–728) raised the Church of India to the dignity of a Metropolitan See.

Patriarch Timothy I of Seleucia (780–823) speaks about many Persian monks who voyaged across the seas towards India and China. Later he constituted the Church of India independent of the Metropolitan of Persia and gave it a Metropolitan of its own. During this period the usage of the term 'Christians of St. Thomas', indicating the Christians in Malabar, came into existence for the first time.[28] The East Syrian Patriarch of Mesopotamia used to send bishops regularly to Malabar. Christianized Hindu customs were also practised by the Church in Malabar, on account of which it had a separate identity and differed from the churches in Persia and Mesopotamia.[29]

There is no evidence to show that the bishops sent from Persia to India were from the Nestorian Church in Persia. It is possible that bishops were sent from the Catholic See of Antioch as well as Seleucia during the period from 800 to 1200.[30] The Antiochian Church fell into the Greek Schism in the eleventh century and the Persian Church was destroyed by the Mongolians in the thirteenth century. Hence, from the thirteenth century Seleucian Church alone had jurisdiction over the Church in India and especially Malabar. Patriarch Jabballa III of Seleucia (1281–1317) had an Indian Metropolitan under him.[31]

Mar John made Cranganore the centre of his Metropolitan See in 1129.[32] The Dependence of the Church in Malabar on Seleucian Church for jurisdiction is clear from the Syriac Manuscript written in 1301 at Cranganore by Mar Jacob, the Metropolitan Bishop of the See of Divus Thomas and all the Church of Christians in India. This manuscript is preserved in the Vatican Library. Mar Jabbalaha was the Patriarch of all the oriental Churches when this manuscript was written.[33]

A letter written by the bishops of Malabar to the Patriarch of Bagdad in 1504 speaks of the consecration of two monks from the coenobium of St. Eugenius under the names of Mar Thomas and Mar John at the request made by three illustrious men from India who came to the Patriarch in 1490. This was done during the Patriarchate of Mar Simon. After a year Mar Thomas went from India to the Patriarch and reported about the Malabar Christians and Mar John continued to be in Malabar. Mar Thomas came back to Malabar in 1503 along with three other bishops consecrated by Mar Elias, the Patriarch of that time. These three bishops were Mar Jabbalaha, Mar Denha and Mar Jacob.[34] Thus there were five bishops in Malabar in 1503. Of them Mar Jacob alone lived until 1552 looking after the administration of the Church in Malabar. St. Francis Xavier was a great friend and admirer of Mar Jacob and so he wrote to the King of Portugal for Mar Jacob about the way in which the bishop was maltreated and misunderstood by the Portuguese in Malabar.[35] The report of St. Francis Xavier is a clear indication that Mar. Jacob followed the Catholic faith in Malabar and was not a Nestorian.

This relation with the Church of Persia lasted till the end of the sixteenth century when the Syro-Malabar Church was brought under the Portuguese Padroado after Mar Abraham (1568–97).

The Portuguese, who were interested in firmly establishing their *Padroado,* found the presence of Chaldean bishops a great hindrance. So they took all measures not to allow any more Chaldean bishops to come to Malabar after the death of Mar Jacob. As a result, Mar Joseph, the brother of John Sulaka, the Chaldean Patriarch who made his profession of faith before Pope Jullius III, was detained in Portuguese Bassein in 1556.[36] This proves that the chief factor that played an important role in the conflict between the Portuguese and the Syro-Malabar Church was not concerned with matters of faith but with the eagerness to assert the rights of *padroado*. One could recall the constant fights picked up by the Portuguese and the Congregation of the *propaganda fide* in a later period. The existence of two churches one belonging to the Padroado and the other belonging to the Propaganda, both of which were under Latin rite, on the eastern coast of India can substantiate this view. Moreover, the lack of familiarity with a Church other than the Latin Church coupled with the inordinate passion to keep off the influence of Protestant revolution striking roots in Europe in the first half of the sixteenth century must also have prompted them to assume a hostile attitude towards the Syro-Malabar Church and its bishops. The Portuguese claimed that they had jurisdiction over the Syro-Malabar Church and so they retained Mar Joseph and the two Dominicans for eighteen months in Bassein.

When the Portuguese found that Mar Joseph was properly trained in Latin practices, they sent him to Malabar. But on reaching Malabar he turned out to be totally against the latinizing spirit of the Portuguese and refused to ordain clerics not instructed in Syriac language. On account of his opposition to the latinization initiated by the Portuguese, he was accused of Nestorian tendencies. He went to Rome and Portugal in 1557 where he explained his position. His innocence was proved and he was proposed to be a cardinal. This would not have been sensible if he had belonged to a heretic or schismatic Church. On the eve of his nomination however, he died in 1569 at Rome.[37]

In the meantime, the Chaldean Patriarch sent Mar Abraham to Malabar. He too was detained by the Portuguese and was deported to Portugal. But he escaped from the Portuguese on reaching Mozambique and went to his Patriach who sent him to the Pope with letters of recommendation. The Pope sent him back to Malabar recommending him to the Portugese. The Portuguese detained him in prison in Goa from where he escaped and reached Malabar. Mar Abraham was given the title of Angamalee by the East Syrian Patriarch at the recommendation of the Pope.[38] The people received him with great happiness.[39] He was also 'The Gate of all India' and the superior of all the bishops and Archbishops of his rite. Like his colleague Mar Joseph, he too was accused of heresy. By an apostolic Brief dated 27 December 1595 it was decided that the successor of Mar Abraham was to by nominated not by the East Syrian Patriarch, but by Rome directly.[40] Mar Abraham continued to look after the Church in Malabar till his death in 1597. He was asked by the Pope to attend the third Provincial Council of Goa in 1585 and had to sign a number of decrees of the former councils too.

Based on the Brief of 27 December 1595 and another of 21 January 1597,[41] Dom Menezes, the Portuguese Latin Archbishop of Goa, entered Malabar and exercised jurisdiction over the Malabar Church. Archbishop Menezes, intent on reducing the Syro-Malabar Church to the Portuguese *Padroado* jurisdiction, convoked the synod of Diamper in 1599. Archdeacon George, administrator of Angamalee and of the St. Thomas Christians, opposed this move. But they were threatened with excommunication and were asked to condemn their legitimate head, the Patriarch of Babylon. The liturgical books of the Syrians were burned. Thus the Syro-Malabar Church was brought under the jurisdiction of the Portuguese *Padroado*.[42]

The bishops of Syro-Malabar rite had their headquarters at Cranganore from the fourth to the sixteenth century, and in the sixteenth it was shifted to Angamalee. After the death of Mar Abraham the Syrian bishop, the Syrians were, for three centuries entrusted to the care of the Latin bishops. Till 1597 they had their bishops from the Middle East till the death of Mar Abraham, the last bishop from the Middle East as mentioned above.

Roz S.J. a Latin priest was nominated as the successor of Mar Abraham on 5 November 1599 to Angamalee which was reduced by Menezes to a mere diocese on 20 December, 1599 as suffragan to the Portuguese Latin Diocese of Goa.[43] Thus the primatial see of the St. Thomas Christians was reduced to the status of the suffragan of Goa. The *padroado* of the Portuguese king was extended over Angamalee on 4 August 1600. Latinization of the liturgy was initiated. Many of the existing items of the liturgy were substituted with Syriac translation of the Latin (Roman) liturgy. In view of the requests of the people and of Bishop Roz, Archbishopric of Angamalee was restored in 1608. But its title and headquarters were transferred to Cranganore. It remained under the *padroado* though not as a suffragan of Goa. In 1610 when Roz was the Archbishop of Cranganore, ecclesiastical territory in India was divided among the Padroado prelates of Goa. Cranganore, Cochin and Mylapore[44] and the people of the Syro-Malabar Church were divided between Cranganore and Cochin.

Though the Syrians of Malabar, being obedient to the Pope, accepted the Latin prelate as their ecclesiastical superior, they did not cease from demanding a bishop of their own. This eagerness prompted them to welcome a certain Ahathalla, as impostor, as their bishop. As the Portuguese refused to release him at Cochin, the Malabar Christians took an oath before the Coonan Cross at Mattancherry on 3 January 1653 refusing to obey the Portuguese Jesuits represented by Archbishop Garcia S.J.[45] Those who took this oath met at Alengadu and witnessed the consecration of a pseudo-Bishop Thomas by twelve priests paving the way for a schism and the acceptance of Jacobitism with West Syriac liturgy.[46]

Subsequent to the revolt of 1653, the Latin *Propaganda* jurisdiction was also introduced into Malabar. The Syrian Catholics, who remained loyal to the cathoic faith even after the revolt of 1653, were thus divided between the *Propaganda* and *padroado* jurisdictions. The propaganda prelates were called generally Vicars Apostolic. From 1700 to 1787 all of them were foreign Latin Carmelites. Still the St. Thomas Christians continued to fight for their independence from the Latin domination. There were some conflicts led by Bishop Gabriel in 1715, Bishop Pandari in 1799, Bishop Roccos in 1861 and by Bishop Mellus in 1874. Pandari was a native of Malabar consecrated in Mesopotamia while the others were Mesopotamians. Those who followed Mellus became 'Nestorians' in 1908. Thus the Church in Malabar lost a number of Catholics to the schismatic Church in its fight for the liberation from the Latin domination.

The *Padroado* jurisdiction over the Syro-Malabar Church was totally supressed in 1886 and a ritual separation was made in the following year between the St. Thomas Catholics and the Latins. The members of the Syro-Malabar Church were put under two Latin *Propaganda* Vicars apostolic who were not Carmelites as their predecessors. Thus in 1887 the vicariate apostolic of Kottayam and Trichur were created for the Syrian Catholics separating them from the archdiocese of Cranganore and the vicariate apostolic of Verapoly. Archdiocese of Cranganore was abolished in 1887. The craving for independence continued and in 1896 these vicariates were reorganized. Three *propaganda* vicariates were constituted under Trichur, Ernakulam and Changanacherry with prelates from the St. Thomas Catholics. Rt. Rev. Aloysius Pazheparambil was appointed the first vicar apostolic of Ernakulam in 1896. The vicariate apostolic of Kottayam, exclusively for the Sudhists, was established in 1911. Mgr. Pazheparambil was succeeded by Mar Augustine Kandathil in 1919. The Syro-Malabarians were brought from the *Propaganda* to the Sacred Oriental Congregation in 1917 and the Malabar hierachy was restored in 1923 with Ernakulam as the Metropolis and Changanacherry, Kottayam and Trichur as suffragans and Mar Augustine Kandathil was appointed the first Archbishop. In 1923 itself Kottayam was erected exclusively for the sudhists. The diocese of Changanacherry was bifurcated in 1950 and Palai was created. Tellicherry diocese was created in 1953 for those who migrated to the Malabar regions from Travancore. Changanacherry was raised to the Archbishopric in 1956 with Palai and Kottayam as suffragans. The diocese of Kothamangalam was erected in 1956. The diocese of Tellicherry was bifurcated and a new dioceses by name Manthawady was erected in 1973 with Mar Jacob Thoomkuzhy as its first bishop. Similarly the Diocese of Trichur was divided and Palaghat was erected as a new diocese in 1974. Diocese of Kanjirapally took its origin from the Archdiocese of Changanacherry in 1977. As the Trichur diocese was still bigger, it was divided once again and the diocese of Irinjalakuda came into being in 1978. The division of Tellicherry was further done and a new diocese called Thamarassery was established in 1986 with Mar Sebastian Mankuzhikkary as its first bishop. Diocese of Kanjirappally was created in 1977 from Changanacherry and Mar Joseph Powathi L was consecrated as its first bishop.[47] A major Archbishopric, in tune with the traditions of the Oriental Churches, was created with the titles of Angammelee and Ernakulam on 29 January 1993. Cardinal Padiyara was appointed as the first Major Archbishop. The Archdioceses of Tellicherry and Trichur were established in 1995. Thus there is a Major Archbishopric with archdioceses like Changanacherries, Ernakulam, Trichur and Tellicherry at present for the Syrian Catholics living in Kerala. The dioceses of Kanjirapally, Kottayam, and Palai form the suffragan dioceses under the Archdiocese of Changanacherry. The other divisions like Irijalakunda, and Palaghat come under the archdiocese of Trichur, while the archdiocese of Ernalulam has Kothamangalam as its suffragan. Dioceses of Manathawady and Thamarassery are placed under the Archdiocese of Tellicherry. It is worth noting that the Diocese of Kottayam has personal jurisdiction over the members of the sudhist community all over India, or rather all over the world. A bifurcation of Changanacherry for the Syrian Catholics in the areas of Trivandrum and further south was a long-felt need which was also fulfilled in 1996. The restoration of the dioceses of Cranganore and Angamalee is also a historical desideratum. The ever growing Church of St. Thomas needs more ecclesiastical provinces to cater to the needs of the Catholics. Here one can appreciate the growth of the Church of the Syrian Catholics *rite* after a chequered career under the colonial oppression and suppression.

SYRO-MALABAR CHURCH OUTSIDE KERALA

In the wake of independence from the English and the establishment of the Indian republic, the mobility of catholics from the Syrian Christians of Malabar became easier. Though there were missionaries, namely priests, brothers and sisters from the Syro-Malabar Church working in various parts of British India under several religious congregations and dioceses administered by Latin hierarchy, they had to conform themselves to the Latin Church and Latin rite. They were bound to give up their original rite and adopt a new rite. The candidates, trained for priesthood or life in the convents who left their native place and original rite at the tender age, were not taught sufficiently about the existence of other rites let alone Syro-Malabar rite even as part of their general formation and general knowledge. This sort of colonial mentality cherished by the Church in India with the tacit approval of the authorities in Rome prevented the Syro-Malabar church from expanding its activities outside Kerala. The Universal Church realizing this mistake initiated the establishment of eparchies outside Kerala to be administered by the Syrian Catholics of Kerala. Taking into account the role played by the Syro-Malabar Church in the evangelization of India the Holy See erected a Syro-Malabar diocese in Chanda in 1962. Mar Vijayanand Medumpuram C.M.I is the current Bishop.

The Holy See took serious measures to put into effect the ideas contained in number 4 of the Conciliar Decree *Orientalium Ecclesiarum* which was brought out by Cardinal Lourdusamy at the synod of the Bishops on 28 November 1985. 'Let provision be made therefore all over the world for the safeguarding and growth of all the particular churches, and hence let parishes and own hierarchies be established where the spiritual good of the faithful demands.' With a view to doing reparations for the centuries of the suppression of the Syro-Malabar Church, and to effect what is decided in the Second

Vatican Council, the Holy See created a few exarchates for the activities of the Syro-Malabar Church and entrusted them to the prelates of the Syro-Malabar rite. Sagar, Satna and Ujjain were founded on 28 July 1968 as exarchates under Mar Clemens Thottungal, Mar A.D. Mattam and Mar John Perumattam respectively. All these three exarchates were raised to the status of diocese in 1977. Jagadalpur in Madhya Pradesh became an exarchate in 1972 and a diocese in 1977. The Present bishop is Mar Simon Stock Palathra C.M.I. Mar Joseph Pastor Neelankavil C.M.I. is currently the bishop of Sagar. Thus, four Syro-Malabar dioceses were established in Madhya Pradesh during the past 15 years which speaks volumes for the importance of the Syro-Malabar Church in the evanglization of India and the recognition on the part of Rome. This is clear from the establishment of other dioceses like Rajkot in Gujrat in 1977 and Bijnor in 1977, both of which are under the prelates of the Congregation of Mary Immaculate, Mar Gratian Mundaden and Mar Gregoy Karotemprel. Kalyan was erected as a diocese for the Syro-Malabar Church with Paul Chittilapilly as its first bishop in 1988.

The contribution of the Syro-Malabar Church can be further assessed by having a glance at the number of Bishops from Kerala working in various Latin Dioceses outside Kerala. To give their names, Rt. Rev. Dr Thomas Thiurthalil C.M. in Balasore, Archbishop. Most Rev. Dr Raphael Cheenath S.V.D. in Cuttak-Bhuvanswar, Rt. Rev. Dr Thomas Katturkudil in Diphu, Mar. Dominic Kokkat C.S.T. in Gorakhpur, Rt. Rev. Dr Thomas Menamparabil S.D.B. in Guwahati. Rt. Rev. Dr. Joseph Mittathany in Imphal, Rt. Rev. Dr George M. Anathil S.V.D. in Indore, Rt. Rev. Dr Symphorian T. Keeprath O.F.M. Cap. in Jalandhar, Rt. Rev. Hippolytus Kunnunkal O.F.M. Cap in Jammu-Kashmir, Rt. Rev. Abraham Viruthukulangara in Khandwa. Rt. Rev. Joseph Mukhak S.D.B. in Kohima, Rt. Rev. Joseph Augustine Charanakunnel in Raipur, Rt. Rev. George Mamalassery in Tura, Rt. Rev, and Joseph Pathalil in Udaipur.[48]

A number of members from the Syro-Malabar Church in Kerala are scattered in various parts of the subcontinent on account of the positions occupied by them in the Republic of India. They, in the so-called 'diaspora', require pastoral care and that too within their own liturgy. Since the Universal Church is no more interested in the continuation of the colonial hegemony of the Latin hierarchy and, on the contrary, is bound by the decisions taken in the Councils and Synods, and makes provision for them. His Eminence Cardinal Lourdusamy, the Prefect of the Oriental Congregation, declared in 1985 'Regarding the oriental faithful, especially in the *diaspora*, this congregation has not ceased insisting that Latin Bishops observe carefully the norms contained in number 23 of the conciliar decree *Christus Dominus* on the pastoral offices of Bishops in the Church about the care of the faithful of different rites. Where there are faithful of other rites, the diocesan Bishop should provide for their spiritual needs, either through priests of parishes of the same rite, or through an Episcopal Vicar, given the necessary faculties and if the case demands even endowed with an episcopal character.'[49]

The tenor of this passage is understood by several Archbishops and Bishops who made necessary arrangements for fostering the patrimony of the oriental churches. The Holy See has already erected oriental territories for different Churches like the territories for Ukranians in Argentina, for Maronites and Ukranians in Australia, for Maronites and Greek Melchite Catholics in Brazil, for Ukranians, Maronites, Greek Melchite Catholics and Slovaks in Canada, for Ukranians, Maronites, Greek Melchite Catholics, Ruthenians, Rumanians and Chaldeans in the United States. Apostolic Exarchates are created by Rome for exarchates Americans in Latin America, and North America.

Catholic hierarchy in the United States has made provisions for the Syro-Malabar Church by appointing priests from the Malabar Church to look after the well-being of the faithful, in places like Detroit, Chicago, Texas, New York and New Jersey. Some of the ecclesiatical authorities in India too have begun to realize the importance of the above-referred Proclamations of the Prefect of the Oriental Congregation and made arrangements for the pastoral care of the members of the Syro-Malabar Church in Delhi, Madras and so on. The visit of Pope John Paul II to India in 1986 was an eye-opener to the Holy See and it gave an opportunity to have first-hand information about the Syro-Malabar Church and the necessity of preserving its individuality.

Pope John Paul II constituted a Pontifical Commission under the chairmanship of the Cardinal Secretary of the State, composed of the cardinal prefects of the two Roman congregations directly concerned in this matter, the Apostolic Pro-Nuncio in India, Archibishops representing the three Rites in India and others. On 28 May 1987 the Pope, in view of the recommendations of this commission, wrote to the Bishops of India. 'In this process of evangelization, there has always existed a generous collaboration on the part of priests, religious and laity baptized in the Syro-Malabar rite, and in recent years also on the part of the Syro-Malabar Church itself in certain areas of the north. This collaboration should not be forgotten, for it points to a willingness, on the part of all concerned, to accept the age-old adage *salus animarum suprema lex*.[50]

The Pope adds: 'Since the celebration of the Second Vatican Council, the Catholic Eastern Churches have manifested an ever greater desire to undertake, wherever possible, the pastoral care of the Eastern Rite faithful in accordance with their ecclesial traditions and heritage. In India this desire has intensified in recent years in the face of the ever increasing phenomenon of the migration of Eastern Rite Catholics to areas covered by Latin Rite dioceses in the northern part of the country, such that at times they form a considerable number of the faithful of these ecclesiastical territories, as for example in the areas of Bombay-Pune.[51]

He notes: 'The Second Vatican Council, in speaking of the pastoral duties of the Bishops, declared that where there are faithful of a different rite, the diocesan Bishop should provide for their spiritual needs, either through the priests or parishes of that rite, or through Episcopal vicars endowed with the necessary faculties.'[52]

The successor of St. Peter writes to the Bishops of India further: 'Attention should everywhere be given to the preservation and growth of each individual Church. For this purpose, parishes and a special hierarchy should be established for each where the spiritual good of the faithful demands. All Eastern Rite members should know and be convinced that they can and should always preserve their lawful liturgical rites and their established ways of life.'[53]

As there are many members of oriental Churches living among the members of Latin rite, the Pope clarifies the point that unity is not uniformity and that unity can be achieved even in diversity. He alludes to the Mystical Body of Christ and the different roles to be played by different parts in the body. 'This need to be faithful to the traditions and heritage of one's own. Rite can in no way be considered as interfering with the task of the Church to 'gather into one all the children of God who are scattered abroad' (John 11:52), or with the mission of the church to bring about the communion of all persons with the Redeemer. For as the same Decree rightly remarks: 'That church, holy and Catholic, which is the mystical body of Christ, is made up of the faithful who are organically united in the Holy Spirit through the same faith, the same sacraments and the same government and who, combining into various groups held together by a hierarchy, for separate Churches or Rites. Between these there flourishes such an admirable brotherhood that this variety within the church in no way harms her unity, but rather manifests it.' (Orientalium Ecclesiarum. 2)[54]

The Pope emphasizes the duty of the pastors of the areas where persons belonging to other rites live. 'Regarding the pastoral care of the faithful of the Eastern Rites who are living in Latin Rite dioceses, in accordance with the spirit and letter of the Conciliar Decrees *Christus Dominus* 23.3 and *Orientalium Ecclesiarum* 4, the Latin Ordinaries of such dioceses are to provide as soon as possible for an adequate pastoral care of the faithful of these Eastern Rites, through the ministry of the priests, or through parishes of the Rite, where this would be indicated, or through an Episcopal Vicar endowed with the necessary faculties, where circumstances would indicate' (*Christus Dominus*, 23, 3, *Code of Canon Laws*, Canon 383).[55]

The history and the present position of the Syro-Malabar Church, thus, convincingly prove that the Church in Malabar was founded by the Apostle,

St. Thomas. A number of sources like archaeological, numismatic, oral tradition, the writings of the Fathers of the Church, liturgical and above all the existence of a catholic community by name St. Thomas point to the apostolic origin of the Church in Malabar. When we try to take a look at the history of a church existing in the early centuries of the Christian era, we should be careful not to project our ideas about the set-up of a church in our own times so that we are not blamed for anachronism in historical researches. We should try to understand the colonial mentality which cast its shadows even on ecclesiastical matters. The socio-political movements in the Coromandel regions did not permit Christianity to flourish in that region though the tomb of St. Thomas was located there. Similarly, the rise of Islam in West Asia must have seriously affected the growth of the Syro-Malabar Church closely connected with the Church of Persia. Those who look for close and constant contact with the Church in Rome have to understand the dynamics of the oriental church and also the problems in West Asia which did not permit such a close contact. The supression of the Syro-Malabar Church right from the sixteenth century by the colonial powers and the attitude of the Ecclesiastical authorities not to permit the St. Thomas Catholics to extend their activities under the banner of the Syro-Malabar Church outside Kerala may explain why the Apostolic church could not and did not develop. The sudden change of attitude on the part of the authorities in the wake of decolonization and the new trends set by the Fathers of the Second Vatican Council, coupled with the appointment of an Indian Cardinal as the Perfect of the Oriental Congregation as well as the visit of Pope John Paul II, gave a fillip to the growth of the Syro-Malabar Church. Just as the Republic of India continues to labour under the hangover of its colonial past, the Syro-Malabar Church also has to fight against a host of fissiparous tendencies. If the church founded by the apostle could survive the ravages of colonial powers, it will continue to remain active and united amidst divisive forces at work.

Notes and References

1. The Examiner Bombay, 28 December 1985.
2. Pope John Paul II wrote on 28 May 1987 to the Bishops of India. Quoted by P.P. Xavier, *A Light from the East: Cardinal Loudusamy*. A Biography (hereafter *Biography*, Pondicherry, 1987), p. 230.
3. Acts of Judas Thomas originated in a milieu of Upper-Mesopatamia, perhaps in Edessa. It may be dated back either to the last quarter of the second century AD or to the first years of the third century.
4. Eugene Cardinal Tisserant, *Eastern Christianity in India, A History of the Syro-Malabar Church from the earliest time to the present Day*. (Bombay, 1957), pp. 2–3.
5. P.J. Podipara, *The Thomas Christians* (Bombay: St. Paul Publications, 1970), pp. 18–19.

6. Tisserant, *op. cit.*, pp. 6–7.
7. Podipara, *op. cit.*, pp. 17–18.
8. Podipara, *op. cit.*, p. 25.
9. Colonel Yule, *The Book of Marco Polo*, 2nd edn., vol. 1, (London, 1875), pp. 21–22.
10. A.E. Medlycott, *India and the Apostile St. Thomas* (London, 1905), pp. 90–92.
11. A.E. Medlycott, *op. cit.*, pp. 93–94.
12. 'Proceeding onwards the said Nicolo arrived at a maritime city which is named Maleput, situated in the Second Gulf beyond Indus-Bay of Bengal. Here the body of Saint Thomas lies honourably buried in a very large and beautiful Church., – R.H. Major, *India in the Fifteenth Century – being a collection of Narratives of Voyages to India* (Delhi: Deep Publications, 1974), p. 8.
13. K.S. Mathew, 'The South Indian Apostolate of St. Thomas and the Portuguese in the Sixteenth Century', *Christian Orient*, Kottayam, vol. VI, no. 1, pp. 5–12.
14. Podipara, *op. cit.*, p. 28.
15. Podipara, *op. cit.*, p. 29.
16. A.E. Medlycott, *India and the Apostle Thomas: An Inquiry with a Critical Analysis of the Acta Thoma* (London, 1905), S. J. Dahlmann S.J. Die Thomas-Legende und die aelten historischen Beziehungen des Chris tentums zum fernen Osten, Frieburg, I.B. 1912, J.N. Fraquhar, 'The Apostile Thomas in South India, in B.J.R.L. 11, 1927, pp. 20–50, Tisserant, *op. cit.*, Podipara, *op. cit.*
17. Medlycott, 'St. Thomas Christians' in *The Catholic Encylopedia* (New York, vol. XIV), p. 680.
18. J.S. Assemani, *Bibliotheca Orientalis*, vol. III, p. 441.
19. E. Tisserant, *op. cit.*, p. 15.
20. Thomas Puthiakunnel, *Syro-Malabar Clergy and their General Obligations* (Ernakulam, 1964), p. 1.
21. Cardinal Tisserant, *op. cit.*, p. 10.
22. Podipara, *op. cit.*, p. 26.
23. Chronique de Seert, *Histoire Nestorienne inedite*, ed. Mar Addai Scher, in P.O.4. p. 236.
24. Labbeus, 'Sacrosancta Concilla', tom. III, 1728, col. 304, C. viii.
25. Le Quiesn, O.P., *Oriens Christianus in Quatuor Patriachatibus digestus Paris*. 1704, 1858, vol. II, col. 1086–1088.
26. E.O. Windstedt, *The Christian Topography of Cosmas Indicopleustes* (Cambridge, 1909), pp. 321, 332, 344, 346; McCrindle, *The Christian Topography of Cosmos* (London, 1897), pp. 118–19.
27. J.S. Assemani, *Bibliotheca Orientalis*, vol. III, part 2, p. 438.
28. Tisserant, *op. cit.*, pp. 14–15: A Forescur, *The Lesser Eastern Churches* (London, 1913), p. 350.
29. Georg Schurhammer, *The Malabar Church and Rome during the early Portuguese period and before Trichinopoly*, 1934, pp. 29ff.
30. Assemani, *op. cit.*, vol. III, part 2, p. 616.
31. Adrian Forescue, *op. cit.*, pp. 96–98.
32. J.S. Assemani, *Bibliotheca Apostolica Varticana Codicum manuscriptorum Catalogus*, vol. III, p. 599.
33. *Ibid.*, pp. 117–88.
34. *Ibid.*, pp. 589 ff.
35. Puthiakunnel, *op. cit.*, p. 9.

36. G. Beltrami, *La Chiesa Caldea nel Secclo dell'Unione* (Roma, 1933), p. 38.
37. J.C. Panjikaran, *The Syrian Church in Malabar* (Trichinopoly, 1914), p. 45.
38. For the decree of the Patriarch-ref Beltrami, *op. cit.*, pp. 95–96.
39. F. Raulin, *Historia Ecclesiae Malabaricae cum Diamperitano Synodo* (Roma, 1745), pp. 13–15.
40. Beltrami, *op. cit.,* pp. 248–49.
41. *Ibid.*, pp. 248–49.
42. Goa was erected as an independent bishopric in 1534 and an archbishopric in 1558. Cochin was constituted as a diocese in 1558. Both of these were under the Portuguest Padroado.
43. Beltrami, *op. cit.,* p. 133.
44. Mylapore was erected as a diocese in 1608.
45. Bernard, O.C.D., *A Brief Sketch of the History of St. Thomas Christians* (Trichinopoly, 1925), p. 61.
46. This separated section was in due course of time split into various denominations and a part of it came back to the Catholic faith and formed the Syro-Malankara Church in 1930. The Marthomite church was formed from the Jacobites around 1875.
47. For up-to-date information on the Church in India, ref. Augustine Kanjamalaed., *Integral Mission Dynamics: An Interdisciplinary Study of the Catholic Church in India* (New Delhi: Intercultural Publications, 1995).
48. *Ibid.*
49. *Biography*, pp. 223–24.
50. *Biography*, p. 230.
51. *Biography*, pp. 230–31.
52. *Biography*, p. 231.
53. *Orientalium Ecclesiarum* 4 & 5 quoted by the Pope. Ref. *Biography*, p. 231.
54. *Biography*, p. 232.
55. *Biography*, p. 233.

TWELVE ❖ # Communal Relations in Pre-Modern India: Some Observations

EUGENIA VANINA

ANALYZING COMMUNAL RELATIONS IN pre-colonial India, modern historians find themselves divied into two camps, opposing each other in sometimes rather harsh polemics. Some insist that the relations between Muslims and Hindus (the latter category may include all followers of the indigenous religions of India) have been throughout the Middle Ages nothing but an endless chain of mutual animosity, oppression and bloody conflicts.[1] Others argue that pre-colonial India has been an abode of tolerance and secularism, that such have been the policies of most Indian rulers including even Aurangzeb, who, despite the alleged Muslim bigotry, offered donations to some Hindu temples and promoted non-Muslims to the high administrative positions.[2] All Hindu-Muslim clashes of colonial era and the tragic events of 1847–48 are thus viewed as a result of the British provocations.

In both cases the scholars aptly quote from original sources to corroborate their positions and, explicitly or implicity, they have in mind the communal relations of nowadays and their understanding by different socio-political forces. It is but natural to look at history for the sake of finding the roots of modern problems, but such an aspiration should hardly result in 'pulling' suitable facts out of the wide historical context and neglecting the events which may not agree with the already constructed scheme. Historical reality has always been complicated and contradictory; it has had a place for different, sometimes polar, tendencies. Perhaps some observations by a researcher bound by no communal or political affiliations in India, except the feeling of affection and gratitude its people as a whole, may be of some interest to the readers.

The very course of medieval history posed a serious challenge to the integrity of Indian civilization, to its capacity to accommodate different religious communities. It is well known that the Hindus began to realize themselves as a community only with the advent of Islam. Prior to that it would hardly have occurred to anyone to view a twice-born and a *shudra* as brethren in the same religion. Polemics between the Hindus, the Buddhists and the Jains, as well as rivalry and even struggle between them, had a bearing on competing theologians or political elite only; it was even more so since the lay Buddhists and Jains in their lifestyles differed little from the Hindus. It was only with the coming of Islam that the notions of 'Hindu' and 'Turk' acquired a special sense each which allowed one to delimit the two communities and to neglect, to a certain extent, all caste, ethnic and social distinctions within each.[3] Many medieval sources testify to the fact that lifestyle, traditions, moral norms and behaviour of one community were viewed by another as strange, alien, ugly and unreasonable, for, in the words of the great Maithili poet Vidyapati Thakur, 'what was *dharma* for one was a mockery for the other'.[4] The very character of relations between the victors and the vanquished was in no way conducive to mutual understanding. These historical facts and many others allied to them constituted a background which was anything but beneficial for communal harmony and coexistence, and we have to bear this in mind to realize how difficult it was for the Hindus and Muslims of India to learn the art of *living together*.

Throughout the whole of medieval period two tendencies existed and collided, both being the premises for modern developments. One of them we are tempted to describe as a predecessor of what is now known as communalism if by it one understands not a concrete socio-political phenomenon, but a complex of ideas insisting upon the superiority of a certain religious community over all others and projecting the state as the defender and advocate of those who profess the 'true' religion. Such an approach in its non-extremist form (and it has been such in a majority of cases) was compatible with a tolerant attitude towards the followers of 'false' religions who, in case they were obedient to the laws of the 'true believers', submissive and serviceable, could hope for relatively good treatment and some autonomy of belief and social life. Such was the policy of the Hindu rajas towards the non-Hindu minorities (first Jains and Buddhists, then Muslims residing in the Hindu principalities), such was also the attitude of the majority of Muslim kings. Moreover, similar approach was dominant in medieval Europe also towards the non-Catholic clusters of population (like Jews, Muslims in some places, or Russian Orthodox Christians in Poland or Venice).

The attempt of the orthodox ulema to make the Delhi Sultan Shamsuddin Iltutmish offer his Hindu subjects the 'death or Islam' choice miscarried and throughout the whole of medieval period such an appeal was never taken seriously even by the most bigoted Muslim rulers. Likewise the extremities of anti-Mughal struggle never made the Sikhs, the Marathas and the Rajputs enemies of Islam as a faith and Muslims, a community,[5] still all of them projected their 'svarajyas' as the states expressing the interests of the followers of the 'true religion'. Thus, the domination of one community over the others, of the 'rightful pathway to God' over 'wrong ones' did not necessarily imply fanaticism and was able to co-exist with the tolerant attitude towards the 'alien.'

In this connection, we have to be more careful and selective while praising all Sufi and Bhakti saints as the 'great integrators' and advocates of Hindu-Muslim amity. While some of them are, no doubt, to be described as such, there are others among them who cannot be so described. For many Sufis as well as for the Satpanthis with their syncretism, the interest in the Hindu religion, philosophy, literature and culture was dictated by the aspiration to convert as many 'infidels' to Islam, as possible; kindness, compassion and tolerance were viewed as much more effective weapons of conversion than violence.[6] Preaching in vernacular language authorship of the poems like 'Chandayan' by Mulla Daud, use of the Hindu religious categories, literary images or folklore, even the aspiration to find analogies between the holy texts of the Hindus and Muslims never diminished the proselytizing zeal of the Sufis and their firm belief in the superiority of their religion. For the Satpanthis also the Quran was the last Veda; they instructed their followers that 'Brahma has passed away and the Imam has succeeded him'.[7] Abdul Quddus Gangohi who in his famous 'Rushd Namah' treatise had studied the similarities between Hindu and Islamic mystical categories, saw nothing illogical in appealing to Humayun and beseeching him to stop the Hindu' promotion to state posts.[8] The stories of the Sufi saints' victories over brahmans, reciprocated, for instance, by the legends of Surdas, Nabhadas and other members of the Pushti Marga set meeting Akbar and triumphing over the Muslim emperor are evidence of the process which Muzaffar Alam has rightfully denoted as 'competitive spirituality'.[9]

This model of communal relations as described above was able to a certain degree to ensure peaceful co-existence of the followers of different religions, especially on man-to-man level. Even under the most bigoted kings pre-modern India never experienced anything comparable to the massacre and banishment of Jews and Muslims as in the late fifteenth to early eighteenth century Spain. But in relation to the state policies this 'proto-communalist' approach was fraught with danger, since it was always, especially in times of crisis, tempting for the ruling elite to solve the problems at the expense of a subordinate community thus taking full advantage of the state as the representative and defender of the followers of the 'true' religion. The present author has no intention to join Professor Satish Chandra's efforts to vindicate Aurangzeb[10] or to engage in polemics with him, but his aspiration to overcome the simplified attitude to this ruler and to discuss Aurangzeb's policies in connection with the real developments in the crisis-ridden Mughal empire are commendable. Aurangzeb seems to be a clear example that shows how problems like economy or state crisis, centrifugal tendencies, rivalry of different elite groups, social conflicts, etc. could be solved within the framework of the above-described model.

Of much greater significance, in the context of both Indian and world history, was the second approach to communal relations which may be described as a predecessor of what in modern India is known as secularism. It implies the view of all religions as equally valid and rightful paths to God and the state as the defender and representative of all people irrespective of their faith; the laws governing social life and state policies are in this case to be determined not by the dogmas of the 'true' religion, but by the requirements of reason, commonwealth or the will of the absolute Supreme Being, worshipped by all religions under different names. Among the societal developments which facilitated the evolution of secularist tendencies in socio-political life and though of pre-modern India, the following may be discussed.

I. Socio-cultural

It seems that to a considerable extent the 'proto-secularist' approach owed its existence to urban life in medieval India. While the pre-modern cities of Europe were homogeneous as concerned religious affiliation of the residents with relatively small clusters of non-Catholics, in India the majority of cities exhibited a rainbow of faiths. Apart from Hindus and Muslims (the latter remained a minority throughout the whole of the period, but their share in urban population was significant), there were Jains, Parsis, and since the fifteenth century Sikhs. If we take into consideration the fact that for many parts of India a city with a population of one lakh was viewed as a medium-sized one, while some metropolitan cities like Agra, Delhi or Lahore had by the seventeenth century more than half a million population each,[11] the picture will be peculiar to itself.

In medieval European cities, the non-Catholics usually lived in isolated blocks. The sinister word 'ghetto' originated from Italian 'geto' (foundry), a place where a special Jewish quarter was established in Venice in 1516.[12] It was thus easy to isolate the 'unbelievers' and to restrict their contacts with the majority to business only. In India there were Hindu and Muslim *mohallas*, but no ghetto-type isolated minority quarters, for in the context of big cities in India a 'minority cluster' might have had a population of tens of thousands or even lakhs. Thus, we see as an important factor the concentration of huge masses of people belonging to different religions in the relatively small areas of medieval Indian cities. This had had a direct bearing on everyday life of crowded cities where the followers of different religions were destined to live, work, suffer and rejoice together, rubbing shoulders in the narrow streets and noisy bazaars.

Many descriptions of medieval Indian cities stressed this peculiarity of urban life. For example, Vidyapati's *Kirtilata* has a colourful picture of Jaunpur: Here Muslims say 'bismillah' and slaughter cattle, there Hindus worship gods; here they perform namaz, there they offer puja; here dwell the Ojhas, there reside the Khwajas."[13] In *Chandimangol*, the sixteenth century Bengali poem by Mukundaram Chakrabarti, the hero, blessed by the goddess Chandi, builds and populates an ideal city which is finally described as inhabited by Hindus and Muslims of all professions who live together happily like good friends.[14] Here we see not only a real description, but a reflection of social ideal.

It is a well-known fact that in India the Muslims have entered the sophisticated system of the Hindu caste society and established their own hierarchy of castes, clans, lineages. As a result many professions and social grades, especially in the urban environment, were represented by a parallel structure of Hindu and Muslim castes or other social divisions. This may be described as a negative phenomenon, leading to communal clashes and social discord,[15] but there is a different interpretation also.

This parallel structure of Hindu and Muslim caste divisions made it possible for a majority of professions and social groups, from nobles to craftsmen, to have counterparts belonging to other religious communities. Thus the followers of so different faiths as Hinduism and Islam were able to feel the similarity of their lifestyles, joys and sorrows. No doubt, every one considered his religion to be the best, but in the city bazaar a Hindu weaver and his Muslim counterpart (julaha) had their shops side by side; both equally suffered from poverty and oppression. Difference in religion was no obstacle to business and intellectual contacts, as well as friendship and other kinds of human relationship; in social conflicts Hindus and Muslims defended their rights shoulder to shoulder.[16]

Parallel structure of this kind was to a considerable extent an urban peculiarity: in the villages where concentration of people belonging to different communities was relatively small and a different type of social hierarchy existed, the situation was different, although in the villages with mixed population some norms of living together were also worked out.

This process as described above was facilitated by the fact that many Muslims were converted Hindus who preserved many traditions and practices of their pre-Islamic ancestors. The result was a unique feeling of oneness which made a Hindu and a Muslim, bound together by the same profession and caste status, view themselves as more close to each other than to their respective co-believers of a higher or lower social position. Thus the values and lifestyle of a Hindu trader or a craftsman were much closer to those of his Muslim counterparts, than to, say, a Hindu noble's, who, in his turn, shared the attitudes and social habits with Muslim nobles, who served in many cases Muslim kings and sometimes fought under their banner against Hindu co-believers.[17]

II. Ethnic

Both the great communities were heterogeneous as regards ethnic and regional affiliations as well as their languages. Thus for Raja Jai Singh, a noble Rajput, his Maratha co-religionists were 'foreign', while many Maharashtrian Muslims, including some celebrated Sufis, were proud of their Marathi identity and language[18] and actively supported the anti-Mughal movement. In fact, when the Mughals invaded Maharashtra they were resisted by the local people not so much as Muslims, but as invaders representing a strange culture, language and military ethics, while the Deccani Muslims and states ruled by them were viewed more positively as representatives of the same or allied regional identity.[19]

This regionalism is often deplored, and rightfully so, as an obstacle to the integrity of India and one of the main reasons of its incapability to withstand the menace of colonial invasion. But the development of regional cultures was a process to which all communities contributed; perhaps it was on this level first that what is now known as composite culture has emerged. Suffice it to remember the role played by Dawlat Qazi and Sayad Alaol in Bengal, Bulhe Shah in the Punjab, Shah Abdul Latif in Sindh and many other Muslims who, shoulder to shoulder with their Hindu brethren, created the regional languages, literatures and cultures. As for the region known now as the 'Hindi belt', we may recall not only the well-known Sufi Hindi poets like Jayasi, Usman and some others: the penetration of Abdur Rahim Khan Khanan and Alam into the Hindi language, religion and culture of the north Indian Hindus was so deep that reading their compositions one really does not feel that the authors belonged to some religion other than Hinduism.

In this sense India differed much from other countries with ruling elites professing a creed different from the majority of population, like, for instance, the Christian domains of the Turkish empire where the Muslims were a consolidated dominant group opposed to the mass of 'infidels'. In India ethnic cultures and regional identities were instrumental in bringing together people of different communities; no doubt similar processes developed on the all-Indian level also, but it was realized much later.

III. Spiritual and Intellectual

There was a conscious quest for the common basics of all religions spread in India, first and foremost of Hinduism and Islam. This extremely important phenomenon had two levels, two fields of evolution – from the 'bottom' and from the 'top'. 'From the bottom' of social pyramids there were popular saints of both religious affiliations whose devotion meant the predominance of inner forms of worship over the outward and formal ones, all that 'trumpery' as Kabir had put it.[20] Their mystical union with God required no canonical language, holy books, priesthood or formal rituals; to quote from Kabir once more:

> The abode of Hari is in the East, Allah's abode is in the West. But in your heart, in your heart do you search, there you will obtain Karim and Rama.[21]

The most radical Bhakti and Sufi saints, who themselves belonged to the lower strata of the society, lived and preached in the midst of common people, made a really herculean effort to overcome the centuries-old prejudices and realize Hari, Rama and Allah as different names of the same absolute God, whom, for example, Punjabi Sufi poet Bullhe Shah addressed as follows: 'In Brindaban you grazed the cattle, invading Lanka you made the sound of victory, you again come as the pilgrim to Mecca.'[22] Garibdas, the successor and perhaps the son of the celebrated Dadu Dayal, in his small work *Anabhay Prabodha* (I608) listed all Hindu and Muslim epithets of God as identical and summed it up: 'Innumerable are God's names, but the Creator of Hindus and Muslims is the same.'[23]

It was indeed a great social contribution of the Bhakti and Sufi saints as well as of the Sikh gurus to work out new criteria of holiness, piety and purity. According to them, it was not by the profession of the true faith or noble origin but by kindness, mercy and truthfulness that one could attain purity and bliss. In Dadu's opinion, a kafir was not the follower of a different religion, but one who lied and had his heart impure.[24] For Malukdas, the seventeenth century follower of Kabir, all holy places, Hindu or Muslim, were false if there was no mercy.[25] His pathway to God was simple and impressive:

> One who gives water to the thirsty is a true slave of the Prophet.
> One who feeds the hungry will obtain God at once.[26]

The saints spared no bitter words to condemn religious strife which, according to them, concerned not God, but the 'trumpery' of formal cult. 'Hindu-Turk Samvad', a *bharuda* (dramatized poem) by the famous Marathi saint poet Eknath depicts a quarrel between a Hindu and a Muslim, who sneer at each other's religion, holy book, rituals and practices, but come to friendly terms and even embrace each other like brothers the moment it comes to them that

> As a matter of fact you and I are one.
> The controversy grew over caste and dharma.
> When we go to God, there is no such things.[27]

Kabir castigated the hypocrisy of the professional priesthood of all religions and insisted that religious strife and fanaticism were due to the fact that neither Hindus nor Muslims knew 'God's secret'.[28] Guru Gobind Singh, under whom the Sikh community became radical and militant to the utmost, stated: 'One is a Hindu, another a Sunni or Shia Muslim, but all of them belong to one caste, the caste of men'. He also authored a beautiful hymn in which the Absolute God was equally praised and worshipped by Hindus, Muslims and other people of the globe including English and French.[29] Perhaps this attitude by the Guru explains why after the defeat he was saved and given shelter by Muslims. The seventeenth century Sufi poet Barkatullah (note his Bhakti-style pen name Pemi) was bold enough to condemn Aurangzeb's bigotry and to state that:

> Hindus and Muslims alike possess all the virtues.
> The same light illumines both the temple and the mosque.[30]

Such was the position of the radical Bhaktas and Sufis who lived among the people (mostly in the cities) and reflected the feeling of oneness based upon the social and ethnocultural developments as described above. This ideology, penetrating from the 'bottom' to all spheres of society, met with the attitudes of a part of the educated elite 'at the top'.

The development of secularist thought in medieval India owes much to the intellectual efforts of rationalists and free-thinkers like Abu-l Fazl, some other 'enlightened philosophers' of Akbar's court, Dara Shukoh and others. Their inquiring mind brought them to the conclusions similar to those achieved by the mystical practices of the saints. They made it their purpose to analyze and compare the dogmas and practices of Hinduism and Islam and to form an independent and objective opinion of them. In the preface to his celebrated work *Sirr ul-akbar* Dara Shukoh praised 'those who in our age acquire knowledge independently and get attached to monotheism notwithstanding all scandals, insults and accusations of heresy'.[31]

The result was a rationalistic and pragmatic evaluation of both religions and a firm belief that, firstly, they had much in common and, secondly, none was free from obsolete practices and unreasonable dogmas; thus no religion was to claim superiority over all others and none was to be dismissed as false.[32] Freedom from all prejudices, fanaticism and bigotry, equally respectful attitude to all creeds, 'so that after your death Muslims may wash your body in Zamzam and Hindus may cremate it' in the words of Urfi Shirazi,[33] – such was their social ideal, and all efforts were made with this very purpose in mind, be it translations of the Sanskrit and Hindi literature into Persian or objective, respectful, scholarly description of the Hindu beliefs, philosophy and practices. This aim was clearly stated by Abu-l Fazl whose encyclopaedic work in the third volume of the *Ain-i Akbari* was dictated by sincere love of India and the aspiration to reach a stage 'that hostility towards this race (the

Hindus) might abate and the temporal sword be stayed a while from the shedding of blood, that dissension within and without be turned to peace and the thornbrake of strife and enmity bloom into a garden of concord.'[34] No doubt, these ideas were a great inspiration for Akbar's policies of *sulhe-kul*. Akbar himself was a rationalist and a free-thinker. Enough research work has been done to successfully prove that his *din-i-illahi* was not at all a new religion[35], but something like a combination of a spiritual order and a club of enlightened intellectuals. If we look at the *din-i illahi* regulations,[36] we may evaluate them as a moral code and rules of conduct of a free-thinking, secular-minded person of whatever community; these norms are to a certain extent relevant even to modern days.

IV. POLITICAL

Objective socio-economic and ethno-cultural processes led the evolution of the Mughal state towards the more advanced centralized forms. By the latter we mean not just an empire, but an integrated state with a well-structured hierarchy of estates and social groups, unified administrative system and the royal power gradually assuming more command than the traditional institutes like guilds or communities or local potentates. This necessity was realized by the forward-looking thinkers in India also. Not satisfied with the traditionally existing concepts of 'Hindu state' and 'Muslim state' they tried to work out a rationalist and secularist theory of state which was to be sanctified by the absolute Supreme Being, common to all religions. Such a state was to represent not a community of the king's co-believers, but the people as a whole; it had to be governed by the principles of reason and universal well-being. It logically required a consolidated elite, bound together by the loyalty to the motherland, common for all communities, and obedience to the king.[37] No doubt the greatest step in this direction were Akbar's reforms.

The fact that the state theory put forward by Akbar and his associates failed due to a number of objective reasons to prevail and to dominate over Indian socio-political scene should in no way diminish the significance of this noble effort. Despite all failures a great impetus was given which has been felt for decades and even centuries of further development. It has already been mentioned that none of the anti-Mughal wars were fought by the Marathas, the Sikhs, the Rajputs, etc. against the Muslim religion and its followers; quite a number of them actively supported the 'rebels'.

The tragic and turbulent eighteenth century was also an epoch of critical re-assessment of the Mughal legacy, especially after the collapse of the empire. In this connection, it seems important to stress that no eighteenth-century Indian state, including the small replicas of the Mughal empires like Hyderabad or Awadh, had inherited the religious policies of Aurangzeb.

Though no post-Mughal state reached the heights of Akbar's epoch, still it was a normal practice for the Hyderabad court to celebrate Hindu religious festivals and for the Peshwa to donate richly to the Muslim hospices and shrines.[38] Many eighteenth century saints and free-thinking intellectuals continued their efforts to advocate equal validity of all religions and to refute communal discord.[39] No doubt, the turbulent atmosphere of the eighteenth century, the rivalry of the successor states were a tempting circumstance to use religion for political means, but still it was nothing illogical for, say, Tipu Sultan to style the rulers of Hyderabad as 'infidels' and at the same time to allow free worship to his Hindu subjects, to appoint some of them to the highest positions and to offer all assistance to the Swami of the Sringeri Matha, pillaged by the pindaris.[40] The architecture styles of the post-Mughal states, the eighteenth-century literature and arts – all bear the stamp of composite culture and the secularist tendencies in Indian thought and social life.

This 'proto-secularism' of late medieval and early modern times, given all its weaknesses and failures, was nevertheless a phenomenon of universal significance, perhaps India's choicest contribution to world civilization, more important than even the invention of decimal numeration and other achievements of the Indian genius. To realize this the reader is invited to compare, for instance, the ideas and practices of Akbar and his associates with the developments in late medieval and early modern Europe.

Around time when Akbar was the Mughal emperor in India there were bloody religious wars in France: their culmination was the horrible Night of St. Bartolomew in Paris (24 August 1572) and similar events in nearly every city of the country, when tens of thousands of innocent men, women and children were massacred for the only crime of worshipping Christ in a slightly modified way. In Spain the dilemma 'death or conversion' was placed before Muslims and Jews; even those who accepted Christianity were later on accused of clandestinely following their original faith and slaughtered or banished. In the Netherlands, the then domain of the Spanish kings, the notorious Duke of Alba used fire and sword to teach 'the true religion' to the protestants.

How different the perceptions of the Indians and the Europeans at that time were one may judge by the documents relating to the Jesuit missions at the court of Akbar. The holy fathers were surprised to find among the nobles and common people a genuine respect for the teachings of Christ as well as sincere interest in this religion and full freedom of worship and preaching. This attitude demonstrated that for Akbar and many of his subjects, Hindus and Muslims, Christianity was nothing but one more pathway to God, as valid and rightful, as all others. On the Jesuit side, however, the opposite was the case: for them only one religion was of God, all others were of Satan. Learned as they were, the missionaries proved unable, and never even bothered, to understand the soul and spirit of India: they just abused both Hinduism and Islam as paganism and a 'mixture of lies and errors'.[41]

Moreover, one has to bear in mind that the bigoted attitude of the then Catholicism to other creeds was fully shared by the Protestant Reformation.[42] Even the celebrated thinkers of the Renaissance were not ready to acknowledge the right of the non-Christians to follow their ancestral religions. Tolerance and freedom of worship, advocated by the reformers and humanists of pre-modern Europe, concerned Christians only; all others were at best pitied as the poor souls ignorant of the only true faith. For example, Erasmus of Rotterdam, the great humanist and pacifist, condemned wars, especially those fought under the banner of religion, but, according to him, if war was such an unavoidable malady of human nature, this evil should have been used against the Turks though it would have been better to convert them to the true faith by kindness and benevolence.[43] The art of living together with 'other worshippers of God', to use Abu-l Fazl's words, was not known to pre-modern Europeans despite all their achievements in other arts.

No doubt, medieval India had enough fanatics to match Torquemada or Mary Tudor. The evolution of secularist ideas has been anything but a march of triumph. The scholars who, with a noble purpose in mind, prefer to paint a rosy picture of communal harmony and secularism ruling supreme in pre-modern India, may come to quite unexpected results. Firstly, they leave the 'unsuitable' facts to be interpreted by their opponents in a particular way and suffer themselves to be accused of distorting historical facts. Secondly, they unintentionally play down the courage of secularist forces, since there is nothing heroic in being non-communal in the realm of amity and tolerance. Orthodox reaction and fanatical 'plunderers of caravans on the way to God', as Faizi called them, were always powerful to allow the 'heretics' to spread their views. How strong this conflict of ideas was, when even co-believers, friends and relatives became sworn enemies, we may discover from innumerable sources analysed by S.A.A. Rizvi in his celebrated books.[44]

Nearly all hagiographic life-stories of saints, especially of the most liberal Bhaktas and Sufis, include episodes of their persecution by the bigoted qazis and brahmans. Sometimes the orthodox forces of both communities joined hands, as we see from the episodes of the Navadvipa orthodox pandits complaining about Chaitanya to the Muslim judge or Hindu and Muslim bigots jointly persecuting Dadu.[45] Even the persons of the rank of Abu-l Fazl or Dara Shukoh were not spared: they had to pay the greatest price for the right to think independently and to evaluate all religions as equally rightful. India has every right to be proud of the daring minds and vision of Kabir, Dadu, Nanak, Guru Gobind, Akbar, Abu-l Fazl, Dara Shukoh and many others; it can also be proud of millions of common people of all creeds, who have for many centuries shared a number of holy places, participated in each other's festivals, lived together through good and bad times, created a composite culture. All these facts were of special value against the background of medieval obscurantism, communal and caste self-identification of people, rivalry of elites and the overwhelming tendency of socio-political conflicts to acquire religious and quasi-religious forms. Similar background was there in other countries of pre-modern and even modern world, but in its secularist experience, imperfect and non-absolute as it has been, India stays unique.

It would be out of place here to discuss the development of communal relations during the colonial era. Two short observations are, however to be made on this subject. Firstly, these tendencies – communalist and secularist – continued to exist and oppose each other. No doubt, the former one was suitable for the British, who not only provoked tensions, but took full advantage of the really existing conflicts. Secondly, those who wanted India to be free, notwithstanding all differences in approaches, in a majority of cases were secular-minded: even the call of jihad made by the anti-British insurgents of the early nineteenth century and the Great People's War of 1857–59 went hand in hand with the appeals for communal amity.[46]

Many social reformers, freedom fighters and builders of modern India mentioned medieval saints and free-thinkers as their spiritual precursors.[47] Those who advocated opposite views were also able to find in history quite a lot of material to support their positions. It has been an important phenomenon of India's socio-political life that the legacy of pre-colonial epoch, especially in the sphere of communal relations, has been and still is being discussed, so that even the actions of modern governments and politicians are compared with the policies of Akbar.[48] This legacy is being extensively appealed to and used by various political forces as an inseparable part of the people's historical memory, culture and outlook.

Lastly, while analyzing the role of traditions in different spheres of life of the present-day India, we have to bear in mind that tradition itself is heterogeneous and contradictory and may support the opposite tendencies of modern life. If we take communal relations, what is a tradition and who is a traditionalist in India now? There has been a tradition which evolved through the whole of Indian history: it insisted upon only one religion to be true and the community of its followers to dominate and to rule according to its own laws; quite a number of political forces in modern India may subscribe to this approach now in the name of this or that creed. There is nothing unusual in such a position, for it has been common, as we have seen, for so many societies. In the Indian milieu it has not necessarily led to conflicts, but has always been fraught with them.

What seems more important is the fact that the attitude to all creeds as equally rightful and to all communities as equal co-sharers of the Indian identity has been deeply rooted as a tradition in India. Secularism has never been an artificial creation or an imported slogan; neither has it been confined to some narrow elitist circles: on the contrary, it is a natural result of the centuries-old practice of living together, established firmly both in the intellectual findings of the enlightened minds and in the everyday life of common people. Hence it appears to have a future in India despite all obstacles on its way.

Maybe some readers would not agree with this author's views or some would not like a foreigner to touch upon so sensitive a topic. But the history, culture and civilization of India do not belong exclusively to its people. They are an inseparable part of the world history and culture and as such deserve to be studied outside India, especially as they concern the unique experience of secularism and living together which has been India's unique legacy and will, no doubt, contribute to its progress in future.

Notes and References

1. Vide, for example, K.M. Panikkar, *A Survey of Indian History* (Bombay, 1954), p. 129; K.P. Bahadur, *A History of Indian Civilization*, vol. X pt. 2, (Delhi, 1980), pp. 202–8.
2. Vide, for example, F. Mujtabai, *Hindu-Muslim Cultural Relations* (Delhi, 1970 XXX), pp. 104, 130–32; M. Athar Ali, *Encounter and Efflorescence: Genesis of the Medieval Civilization*, Address of the General President to the Golden Jubilee Session of the Indian History Congress, Proceeding Indian History Congress, 50th Session (Gorakhpur, 1989–1990), pp. 1–15.
3. Interestingly, Chand Bardai in his 'Prithviraj Raso' freely uses both terms (*i.e.* 'hindu' and 'turk'), (ed.) Kavirao Mohan Singh (Udaipur 1955) vol. I, pp. 219, 242.
4. Vidyapati Thakur, *Kirtilata*, (ed.) V.S. Agraval (Jhansi, 1962), p. 111.
5. Eugenia Vanina, *Ideas and Society in India: from the Sixteenth to the Eighteenth Centuries* (Delhi, 1996), pp. 74–77.
6. A. Nizami, *The Life and Times of Shaikh Farid ud-din Ganj-i Shakar* (Aligarh, 1955), pp. 106–7.
7. Some Specimens of Satpanthi Literature, tr., by V.M.N. Hood – Collectanen Geiden, 1948), vol. I, p. 75.
8. Muzaffar Alam, *Indo-Islamic Interaction in Medieval North India Itineraction*, 1989, vol. XIII, pt. I, pp. 46–47.
9. *Ibid.*, pp. 41–44.
10. S. Chandra, *Reassessing Aurangzeb – Historiography, Religion and State in Madieval India* (Delhi, 1996), pp. 153–62.
11. I. Habib, 'Population' in Tapan Raychaudhuri and Irfan Habib (ed.), *The Cambridge Economic History of India*, vol. I, (Cambridge, 1981), p. 179.
12. L.W. Spitz, *The Protestant Reformation 1517–1559*, (New York, 1985), p. 356.
13. Vidyapati Thakur, *Kirtilata*, pp. 111–14.

14. I have used the Russian translation of Mukundoram's poem by I.A. Tovstykh (Moscow, 1980), pp. 150–51.
15. A.L. Srivastava, *Akbar the Great* (Agra, 1973), vol. III, p. 56.
16. M.P. Singh, *Town, Market, Mint and Port in the Mughal Empire, 1556–1707* (Delhi, 1985), p. 274; B. Ambastha, *Non-Persian Sources of Indian Medieval History* (Delhi, 1983), p. 22.
17. The way the Hindu and the Muslim nobles shared common political interests has been profoundly studied by Satish Chandra, *Parties and Politics at the Mughal Court* (Delhi, 1972), pp. 257–58.
18. A.R. Kulkarni, *Social Relations in the Maratha Country (Medieval Period)* – Presidential Address, 'Medieval India Section,' 32nd Session of the Indian History Congress (Jabalpur, 1970), pp. 7–31 (Reprint).
19. Gordon Stewart, *The Marathas 1600–1818* (The New Cambridge History of India, 1993), pp. 42–51, 79.
20. H. Dvivedi (ed.), *Kabir* (Bombay, 1960), p. 262.
21. *Ibid.*, p. 273.
22. Lajwanti Rama Krishna, *Punjabi Sufi Poets* (Delhi, 1973), p. 78.
23. W. Callewaert (ed. & tr.), '*The Anabhay Prabodha of Dadupanthi Garibadas, Orientalia Lovaniensia Periodica,* 1974, vol. V, p. 123.
24. W. Callewaert (ed. & tr.), *The Hindi Biography of Dadu Dayal* (Delhi, 1988), p. 38.
25. *Malukdasji ki Vani* (Allahabad, 1946), pp. 36–37.
26. *Ibid.*, p. 22.
27. E. Zelliot, *A Medieval Encounter between Hindu and Muslim: Eknath Drama Poem: Hindu-Turk Samvad*, F. Clothey (ed.), Images of Man, Religion and Historical Process in South Asia (Madras, 1982), p. 187.
28. H. Dvivedi (ed.), *Kabir*, p. 326.
29. *Hindi Kavya Pravah* (Allahabad, 1964), p. 689; M.A. MaCauliffe, *The Sikh Religion* (Oxford, 1909), vol. V–VI, p. 275.
30. P. Chaturvedi (ed.), *Sufi Kavya Sangrah* (Allahabad, 1967), p. 235.
31. Dara Shukoh, *Sirr al-akbar* (Tehran, n. d.), p. 6.
32. Discussed in more detail by the present author in *Ideas and Society*, pp. 62–72, 77–82.
33. Quoted by Mujtabai, p. 125.
34. Abu-l Fazl Allami, *Ain-i Akbari*, Tr. by H.S. Jarrett, vol. III (Delhi, 1978), p. 2.
35. M.P. Srivastava, *Policies of the Great Mughals* (Allahabad, 1987), p. 90; S.A.A. Rizvi, *Religious and Intellectual History of the Muslims in Akbar's Reign, With Special Reference to Abu-l Fazl* (Delhi, 1971), p. 391.
36. Abu-l Fazl Allami, *Ain-i Akbari*, Tr. by H. Blochmann, vol. I (Delhi, 1977), pp. 170–76: *The Dabistan or a School of Manners*. Tr. by D. Shea and A. Troyer (Paris, 1843), vol. II, p. 140f.
37. Discussed in more detail by the present author in *Ideas and Society*, pp. 32–43.
38. *The Chronology of Modern Hyderabad – From 1720 to 1890 AC* (Hyderabad, 1954) pp. 80–81, 87; A.R. Kulkarni, *Marathas and the Maratha Country* (Delhi, 1996), vol. II, pp. 124–25.
39. Z.U. Malik, *The Core and the Periphery – A Contribution to the Debate on the Eighteenth Century* – Proceedings, Indian History Congress, 51st Session (Calcutta, 1990), pp. 185–91.

40. B.A. Saletore, *Tipu Sultan as a Defender of Hindu Dharma* – Medieval India Quarterly (Aligarh, 1950), vol. I, pt. 2, pp. 46–53; M. Hasan Khan, *History of Tipu Sultan* (Calcutta, 1951), pp. 375f.
41. J. Correa-Affonso, *Letters from the Mughal Court* (Bombay, 1989) p. 22–23; Jarric S.J., *Akbar and the Jesuits* (London, 1926), pp. 29, 67–68.
42. L. Spitz, *The Protestant Reformation*, p. 368; S.E. Ozment, *Mysticism and Dissent: Religious Ideology and Social Protest in the Sixteenth Century* (New Haven & London, 1973), p. 50.
43. I have used the Russian translation of Erasmus' works in *Erasmus of Rotterdam and His Times* (Moscow, 1990), pp. 244–75; vide also D. Webster and Louis Green (eds.), *Documents on Renaissance and Reformation History* (Stanmore, 1969), pp. 114–15.
44. S.A.A. Rizvi, *Muslim Revivalist Movements in Northern India in the Sixteenth and Seventeenth Centuries* (Agra, 1965), pp. 167, 207–54; also by the same author, *Religious and Intellectual History*, p. 427.
45. K.K. Das Gupta, *Sri Chaitanya and the Gaudia Vaishnava Movement* – S.P. Sen (ed.), *Social Contents of Indian Reform Movements* (Calcutta, 1978, p. 63; W. Callewaert (ed. & tr.), *Hindi Biography*, p. 38.
46. Vide, for instance, Iqbal Hussain, *Elements of the Ideological Background to the Rebellion of 1857* – Proceedings, Indian History Congress, Golden Jubilee Session (Gorakhpur, 1989–90), pp. 424–33.
47. *The Complete Works of Swami Vivekananda* (Calcutta, 1989), vol. III pp. 219, 379; in his paper 'The Role of Sufism in Building the Values of the Composite Culture of India', read at the International Seminar on Sufism (ICCR, Delhi, 1991), the late Professor Rasheeduddin Khan presented a chain of secularist tradition from the early sages, Bhakti and Sufi saints, free-thinkers of the Middel Ages, modern reformers and freedom fighters up to Nehru, Gandhiji, Azad and Ambedkar; *Contemporary Relevance of Sufism*, (ed.) Syeda Saitidain Hameed. (Delhi, 1993), pp. 235–37.
48. Vide, for instance, the remarks by Satish Chandra, J.S. Grewal and especially Irfan Habib at the symposium 'Akbar and His Age' (Delhi University, 17 October 1992), published in *Social Scientist* (September-October 1992), vol. XX, no. 9–10, pp. 61–72.

THIRTEEN ❖

Agrarian Systems in the Southern Maratha Country: Maratha and Early British Period

K. N. CHITNIS

THE REGION OF THE Southern Maratha Country formed an important geopolitical division and offered a fertile ground for the co-existence and integration of different types of traditions and ideas. Roughly this was the region bounded by the Krishna in the north and Tungabhadra in the south. The Marathas called it 'Doab' or 'Prant Karnatak'. However, its extent was not clearly defined. In the north some portions of the erstwhile Kolhapur State, the Kaladgi sub-division of the Bijapur district, and the princely states such as Mudhol and Jamkhandi, and parts of princely states such as Sangli, Miraj and Kurundwad, were included. The southern boundary was, of course, marked by the Tungabhadra. Under the Kolhapur state were Raibag and Kadkol. The Patwardhans of Jamkhandi, Miraj with all its branches, Sangli and Kurundwad had their jagirs or mahals here. The Rastes had their jagirs in Badami, Bagalkot and Hungund talukas of the Bijapur district. Besides these states and jagirs, Nargund, Ramdurg, Shedbad, Nippani and Chinchni were other independent Maratha principalities in the Southern Maratha Country. In addition, the region included some native princely states like Kittur and Savanur. This was loosely described by Munro in one of his despatches by saying that 'the District known politically as the Southern Maratha Country corresponds nearly with the Maratha geographical division of the 'Carnatic', or country situated between the rivers Krishna and Tongbuddra.'[1] However, Edward West modifies this description and explains the term by giving more details, an explanation with which the meaning of the region given in the beginning largely agrees.[2] This region had the advantage of passing under many rulers, Hindu, Muslim and British, and hence it absorbed a number of features from the agrarian administration of these potentates. The very nomenclature of many terms and also the different practices and traditions of the agrarian system all existing together were acceptable to the people, and there seems to have been no complaints against such a state of affairs. On the other hand, some new and improved methods were gladly welcomed, although the old practices were not given up wherever they were convenient and less expensive.

Geographically this area could be broadly divided into three types, *malenad, gadinad* and *belavalanad.** The malenad was the hilly region and received heavy rains ranging approximately from 1270 mm to 2540 mm. Hence it was fit for growing crops which depended on heavy rains such as rice, bananas, etc. This strip of territory ran from north-west to south-east roughly along Khanapur taluka in the Belgaum district, and Kalghatgi, Shiggaon, Hangal as well as Hirekerur talukas in the Dharwad district. The gadinad, which received rains ranging almost from 635 mm to 1270 mm, ran roughly along Chikkodi, Hukkeri, Belgaum and Sampgaon talukas in the Belgaum district, Mudhol, Bilgi, Badami and Bagalkot talukas in the Bijapur district, and Dharwad, Kundgol, Shirahatti, Karjagi and Ranebennur talukas in the Dharwad district. The belavalanad received rainfall ranging from about 381 mm to 635 mm and ran along Athani, Raibag, Gokak, Parasgad and Ramdurg talukas in the Belgaum district, and Nargund, Ron, Gadag and Mundargi talukas in the Dharwad district.

Types of Lands

The lands were generally classified into *gadde, beddalu* and *tota* on the basis of the availability of water supply, and as *yeri, masab, masari, gonikal*, etc. on the basis of the quality of the soil. For the common soils there were some other terms in other languages used generally by the common people. *Jirayit*, originally an Arabic word and *bagayit*, originally a Persian word, were used for dry (beddalu) and wet (gadde) lands respectively. Similarly, *tari* and *khushki*, a set of two Persian terms, were used for the dry and wet lands respectively. These terms were very common in Maharashtra where the Marathas had adopted them from Arabic or Persian, and as the Peshwas ruled over the Southern Maratha Country these terms became well known to the people of this area also. The tota was a garden land, where fruits and nuts were grown. It required water supply all the year round. The term 'bagayit' was used for both wet and garden lands. If the mango plantation was done in the garden it was known as '*amrayi*' in Marathi and '*mavina-tophu*' in Kannada. In the Southern Maratha Country, however, the term 'amrayi' was more popular and the word 'mavina-tophu' was rarely used. Although the classification of soils here was not so scientific and accurate as under the Company Government later, yet one finds a sincere attempt being made at the classification of the soils on different principles like the fertility of the soil, colour of the soil, availability of water supply, etc. There were many varieties of black soil. *Yeri, regad, masab, karl, hakkal* and *kumri* may be given as examples.[3] Yeri was rich black soil. Regad was rich black loam or mould. Many times these two terms were interchangeable. Masab also was a black soil, but of a slightly lesser quality. Karl was gravelly black soil. Hakkal was high ground where, as in gadde, rice cultivation was done, but where rain water was the only source of water, and kumri which was also high ground like hakkal, but cultivation could be done only after clearing the ground of woods. In these last two types the yield was not much expected because of the meagre supply of water. In malenad black regad was classified under 7 heads and masab under 14 and 9, applying two different principles.[4] If the lands did not get sufficient water supply from the rains, they were provided with water supply from other sources, such as wells, tanks and irrigation works. In this area it had been an age-old practice to dig tanks and wells for irrigating lands. This the people used to do for earning religious merit. The rulers in this area either dug new tanks, wells and canals or repaired the old ones with this religious objective in view. That is how we find a number of totas or gardens and amrayis or mango plantations in this area. In the Marathi-dominated areas there were actually two specific terms for the well-watered land and the canal-watered land, viz., *motsthal* and *patsthal* respectively. In P/Mishrikiti [P = Pargana], which was later under the Patwardhans, both Kannada and Marathi (originally Persian) terms were used so that both Kannada and Marathi people would know the meaning well. For dry land the double term '*kadarambha jirayit*' and for wet land '*nirarambha bagayit*' were used.[5] Here kadarambha means jirayit and nirarambha means bagayit. It is like *kunabini-vokkalagitti* (maid servant) which was used in the early days of the Maratha occupation of this region when the local people were rather new to such terms, but later they came to understand the meaning of such terms . In fact they were assimilated in the day-to-day language of the people.

Measurement of Lands

There were various land measures in this region as there was no uniformity in the measurement of lands. Some were inherited from Vijayanagara and Bijapur, some introduced by the Peshwas and some by the British, while a few were indigenous. Until the lands were actually measured with a measuring rod corresponding to that prevalent under the Marathas, there were indigenous methods in this region employed for land measures, especially in the southern portion of the Southern Maratha Country. The more prevalent among these were the *bijawari* method and the plough method.

In the bijawari method the extent of arable land was expressed in terms of a certain quantity of seeds. Each type of land would yield the maximum produce only if the required amount of seeds were sown. The yield would be less if the seeds sown were either more or less than the required quantity. Good and fertile lands required more seeds, and ordinary lands required less seeds for the same extent of land. Hence in those days when no other methods of measurement were possible in some areas, the bijawari or the sowing capacity method came in handy. Here the extent of land was expressed in terms of grain measures such as *khandugas* (*khandis*) and *kudos*. The quantity of these land measures was not the same everywhere. There were some minor variations in certain areas. A khanduga was generally equal to 20 maunds and a maund equal to 40 sers. In some areas a maund was equal to 12 *payalis*, a payali consisting of 4 sers, in other words, the maund was equal to 48 sers. In some other areas a khandi was equal to 20 *kudos*, a kudo consisting of 10 payalis, and a payali being made up of 8 *kachcha* (as against *pakka*) bijawari sers.[6] In all the three cases a khandi was equal to 20 next smaller measures only, be they maunds or kudos. Here the maund and kudo were supposed to be equal in their measures. However, in the next smaller measures, such as the sers of the maund and the payalis as well as the kachcha bijawari sers of the kudo, there were some minor variations.

The next method employed for determining the extent of the land was the plough method. The *kurgi*, another native land measure, was determined by this method. H.H. Wilson gives the meaning of the term 'kurgi' as 'a measure of land, as much as may be ploughed and sown in one day with a pair of bullocks and a drill plough.'[7] However, the literal meaning of the term 'kurgi' is the seed-drill. Here it is actually the plough method that determines the extent irrespective of the amount of seeds required, and not the bijawari method, and the extent is expressed not in terms of land measures but by a specific term 'kurgi'. The land here is not only ploughed but also sown. This extent of land is better expressed by the term '*gale*', which actually means a ploughshare, and which also was in vogue. The extent of the kurgi varied from about 2 to 8 acres, the average being about 5 acres. These variations were caused by the nature of the land in different places and the capacity of the peasant and also of the bullocks to plough the land. Here the average was generally accepted to be roughly 4 acres, especially after the middle of the nineteenth century. Yet the local variations were always there, which could not be ignored.

The basic measures of land that came down to the Southern Maratha Country from Vijayanagara through the Adil Shahs of Bijapur was the *rayarekhe mar*. The mar also, like the kurgi, was fixed by the plough method. But here instead of one day a week or so was taken for ploughing the land, and the extent ploughed during this period was styled a 'mar'. Again, as in the case of the kurgi, the extent of the mar would vary depending upon the hardness or otherwise of the land, the quality of the ploughshare, the capacity of the peasant and of the bullocks to plough the fields, etc. Consequently, the mar varied from 4 to 20 kurgis. Generally in this region a mar consisted of 8 kurgis, a kurgi being 4 acres in extent. In the documents the term '*bele*' is often used as a land measure.[8] The bele was one-eighth of a *hana*, which was replaced by the term 'mar' in land measures. Hence a mar in this area consisted of 8 kurgis. A mar was equal to 36 bighas,[9] and a kurgi equal to 4.5 bighas. However, there were two types of mars here, the rayarekhe mar and the Viththalapanti mar. As the latter mar was popularized in this area, especially in the southern portion, by one Viththalpant, who was the governor of Karnataka under Vijayanagara, it was called the Viththalapanti mar. The Viththalapanti mar was bigger in extent and was approximately equal to three rayarekhe mars. There were some other land measures such as the *patti* and the *chigar*. It is difficult to ascertain any fixed ratio between these measures and the mar. The *kulavan* was another land measure in the southern part of the Southern Maratha Country whose extent was much varying, but which was about half a kurgi in some places, it being the extent of land ploughed by a peasant with two ploughs in one day.

In the northern portion there was more Maratha-Mughal influence. The Maratha princely states and the Maratha jagirs were mostly situated there. Hence in the agrarian matters there was more of Maratha influence than of Vijayanagara. Here the chawar was often used as the unit of land measure. The chawar had come down to this region through the Bijapur administration also. A Modi document in this area clearly mentions 'Idulshahi chawar'.[10] The basic measuring rod called a *kathi* was 5 cubits and 5 fists in length, 20 sq. kathis made one pand, 20 pands constituted one bigha and 120 bighas were equal to one chawar. This method was originally based on the Muslim system and was applied in the Deccan after suitable modifications.[11] It was also prevalent in the northern part of the Southern Maratha Country, as in P/Bilgi and Prant Raibag.[12]

There was thus a medley of confusing land measures with variations depending upon the location of the lands, upon the local traditions and upon rulers under whom these lands passed in the past. Yet among the local people there were no conflicts about these land measures. The mar existed as much with the patti in the south as with the chawar in the north. The rayarekhe mar mingled freely with the Viththalapanti mar. The kurgi and the bigha co-existed merrily. The kulavan and the acre had no quarrel with each other. The traditions of Vijayanagara were no less accepted than the customs of the Marathas welcomed.

LAND TENURES

Land tenures were closely related to the distribution of lands in a village. The lands were parcelled out among the people by different tenures. Out of the total lands in a village or, for that matter, a samat or a pargana, some were held by religious tenure, some by service tenure, some by umbali tenure and some by raitwari tenure. Of the remaining lands some were fallow lands and some border lands. This was the usual division of lands in a village. Among the lands held by religious tenure, there were three types: *brahmadaya, devadaya* and *mathadaya*. Brahmadaya lands were granted to Brahmins for religious purposes, the devadaya lands were grants to the temples for services in the temples and the mathadaya lands were granted for services in the mathas. The service tenure lands were granted to the individuals for their services in the government and the state. The ministers, the military officers, the feudal administrators such as the Sardesai, Desai, Nadgauda and Nadkarni, the village officers such as the gauda (patil) and senabova (kulkarni), some of the *ayagars* (*barabalute*) such as the Mahar and Talawar and finally the local militia (*setasanadi*) received lands from the rulers or held them traditionally for their services to the state.[13] The lands held under religious tenure were, as a rule, totally exempted from the land tax (*sarvamanya*) and the lands held by service tenure were usually subject to some quit-rent (*judimanya*). The lands held by *umbali* tenure were granted to the individuals for their subsistence or in recognition of some past achievement of theirs. They were mainly subsistence grants. Finally the lands held by the raiyatwari tenure were called the *khalsat* lands or government lands in contrast to the inam lands. The holders of these lands had proprietary rights in these lands, but the government levied full tax on them as against the inam lands. However, they could not hold them unless they paid the tax to the government. Here is a clash between two opposite ideas, the ownership of the land and the compulsion to pay the tax. In theory the agriculturist could be dispossessed of his land for his failure to pay the tax. But in practice he never lost it, unless he sold it. Since he was the proprietor of the land, he had the right to sell it, to mortgage it and to transfer it.[14] Like the religious tenure, there were three sub-tenures of the raiyatwari tenure also, *viz*., *chali, khandgutga* and *khandmakta*. sometimes a fourth one, *kaul*, was also found. In the chali tenure the holders of the lands were the original settlers of the villages. In the khandgutga tenure the land was held by some contract, with an agreement to pay a fixed land revenue. The khandmakta was similar to khandgutga, but of a lower type. The kaul was also a contract given for a fixed period of time, say, of 2 or 5 or 7 years. The contract was usually given in the case of lands of very low productivity. In 1818 in some parts of Prant Raibag, as in M/Bhiradi [M=Mauza], the lands were divided into three groups, the best, the middling and the worst, the first two containing the chali, khand and kaul lands, and the third only the khand and kaul lands.[15] Generally, but not always, the lands held by religious tenure were more than the lands held by all other tenures put together or at least held by the raiyatwari tenure. The former paid either no tax or paid some quit-rent and got all the revenue for themselves while the latter paid full tax to the government and held comparatively less lands. For example, in Q/Murgod [Q = Qasba] of Taluka Manoli there were 62 chigars of lands in 1777. The distribution of these lands was as follows:

Chigars	:	*Particulars of Lands*
21.47	:	Streams, hilly areas, waste land, etc.
49.41	:	Dharmadav lands, Inam lands, *Baje* (miscellaneous) Inamdars' lands and setsanadi lands
11.12	:	Khalsat lands[16]

According to the distribution of lands in Q/Guttal in Taluka Savanur in 1791, the Inamdars' lands were 127.13 mars while the khalsat lands were just 77.75 mars out of a total of 232.38 mars. From the remaining lands, 6.13 were with local militia and the fort and 21.38 were fallow lands.[17]

This naturally divided the population of a village mainly into two classes, the class getting almost all the revenue, but rendering no tangible services to the state, and the class toiling all the while in contrast to the first, and getting very little revenue. As a rule, the holders of inam lands leased out their lands for brief periods to the tenants-at-will, grabbing a major portion of the yield for themselves leaving to the tenants what was just necessary for their subsistence. Even among the khalsat land-holders, some were rich peasants who were mainly the chalidars but who also held lands by other tenures. Such peasants also generally leased out some of their lands seizing the lion's share from the yield of the leased lands. In the division of the society the holders of judi-inam lands like Desais, Sardesais, Patils and Kulkarnis also joined hands with the class of sarvamanya lands. In some places the Patils and Kulkarnis were empowered to collect the transit duties or muhtarfa for the government mostly on the agricultural products in transit, themselves being exempted from the payment of such dues. They owned a number of houses from which they got handsome amounts by way of rent. In Ranebennur, for example, in 1840 there were four Patils and two Kulkarnis owning 59 and 77 houses respectively; the Kulkarnis had more houses than the Patils, from which they got considerable house rent. They came to enjoy certain perquisites at the cost of small craftsmen who worked with agriculturists, such as oil-pressers and weavers. In his report, dated 31 January 1840 to L.R. Reid Esq., Acting Chief Secretary to Government of Bombay, on the situation in the Konkan and the Southern Maratha Country Longford said that although these industrious classes were in many cases 'apparently overassessed', yet "they do not complain but appear, as remarked by Mr Simson, 'a contented and happy people'."[18] Among the barabalute, some had no lands, but received only the *aya* or traditional allowance from the raiyats. In addition to them, there were many landless labourers. All these people formed the second class which was oppressed and exploited by the first, supported by the government. A situation such as this further divided the population into the 'haves' and 'have-nots'. Although there were thus forces of antagonism in the village, the people quietly accepted the existing position, as they were not aware of their rights as citizens, an idea which reached them very late.

Land Assessment

The land assessment rates varied with the type of land and with the type of tenure. As we have seen, the land measures were not the same everywhere in the Southern Maratha Country – the mar, the patti and the chigar were not exactly the same in all areas. In some cases a distinction was made even between the Viththalapanti mar and the regular Vijayanagara mar, as already pointed out. Although the mar and patti are said to have been more or less equal to each other in general, yet there were some differences between them in some places. In M/Siddapur of P/Rayara Hubli, for example, a patti of land was equal to two mars.[19] Although the number of kurgis in a mar is found to have been on an average 8 in this region, there were local variations which should not be ignored, if possible, while making revenue calculations. Likewise the extent of the chigar was confusing. Therefore, an ascertainment of uniform rates of assessment for various types of lands in different parts of the Southern Maratha Country is next to impossible. Yet in the following paragraphs of this section, an attempt is being made to find out some order in this maze of revenue rates.

The assessment rate was known by different names in different parts of this region. The Vijayanagara, Bijapur, Savanur and Maratha terms and traditions were all mixed up. In Vijayanagara the standard assessment was known by the term 'rayarekha' or 'rayarekhe'. This rayarekhe with all its attendant imposts and cesses was consolidated into a new standard rate of assessment during the Adilshahi period and was called '*asl*' or'*raqm*'and rarely '*tankha*.' In course of time many pattis or cesses came to be added to this Bijapuri rate, and hence Ali Khan, the Diwan of the Savanur Nawab, Abdul Rauf Khan, again revised the assessment rate along with its additional pattis or extra levies, consolidating all of them into a new standard rate styled '*ainati*'. The ainati became the basic assessment rate when this area passed under the Peshwas. In a number of Modi documents of the Peshwa and Post-Peshwa times the original assessment or ainati was given first, and then the revenue to be levied was calculated on its basis.

A taleband of M/Konnur in P/Gokak in 1795 gives the following rates per chigar (calculated from the revenue figures given in the document itself) for various type of lands: 20, 19, 13 and 2.5 hons for types I, II, III and IV respectively. These were the rates for the khalsat lands. Here only the types are given. But the same rates were found for different classes of soils when they were specifically mentioned, for sarvamanya and judimanya lands and even for the waste lands freshly brought under cultivation. The rates of assessment in hons per chigar for sarvamanya lands were 20 for *nadgada* land, 19 for *nadisete*, 13 for *melgai* land, 2.5 for masar land, 6 per *thikan* of *bag* land and 2 per *thikan* of amrayi land. For judimanya lands the rates in hons per chigar were 19 for type II and 13 for type III, 2.5 for masar and 6 per *thikan* for *bag* lands. The rates for different soils were 19 for regad, 13 for melgai, 2.5 for masar and 6 per thikan for *bag* lands.[20] The first two types of land had the best type of soil besides being either on the river bank or watered by the rivers. Here the first type was usually yeri, the second type regad, the third melgai and the fourth masar which was very much inferior to the above three. Accordingly they were taxed in a descending order. In 1795 the tax rates were the same as in 1758 in M/Konnur, with no changes in between.[21]

In 1730 the assessment rates in M/Kundgol were 32 hons per mar of chali land, 24 hons per mar of khandgutga land and a little below 10 hons per mar of khandmakta land.[22] Here only the tenure under which the lands were held seems to have been taken into consideration, and not the type of land and other factors, or at least the latter are not mentioned in the document. In 1784 in M/Sul the assessment rate seems to have been 6 hons per mar. No specifications about the types of lands are given.[23] In 1785 the rate for the chali lands in Q/Konnur of Mamla Torgal in Taluka Nargund varied from 7 hons to 20.79 hons, for the katgutta lands from 2.92 hons to 9.80 hons and for the makta lands from 6.84 hons to 8.75 hons.[24] In M/Hiremaralihalli Budrukh of P/Karadgi the rates for regad and masab lands in 1791 were 36 hons and 1.13 hons per mar respectively.[25] In Peth Haveri the *sist* or land tax paid in 1795 was at the rate of 3 'hons' per mar in most of the cases. Although the unit of coinage is called 'hon' here, it is really the varaha as can be made out from the way in which the figures are given. As there were two hons in a varaha the rate was actually 6 hons per mar. Here both the Vijayanagara and Bijapur traditions are mixed up. The local people understood both the traditions well and accepted them without a murmur.[26] In M/Chikkop under the Ramdurg state the tax rates in 1810 for the chali, Khandugutga, maktagutga and *natttkaula* lands were 10.5, 2.5, 1.5 and 1 hons per mar respectively. The rate for the makta land in the village varied from 1.5 to 0.75 hons per mar.[27] In 1825 the tax rates for the lands held under chali, katguta, khandmakta, kaul and kor tenures were 21.13, 5.43, 5.52, 1.17 and 16.8 hons per mar respectively in Q/Gadag where a mar consisted of 6 kurgis, and not 8 kurgis as usual.[28] For a mar of 8 kurgis the rates would be 28.17, 7.24, 7.36, 1.56 and 22.4 hons respectively. In case of the above examples, full information about the types of lands, the crops grown on them, their nearness to the market or otherwise and other related information is not available. Yet an attempt can be made to deduce certain conclusions on the basis of whatever information is available. The rates for the chali lands varied from 32 hons to 10.5 hons per mar. The highest rate was 36 hons per mar for the regad land in M/Hiremaralihalli Budrukh, but here we do not know under which tenure the land was held. The rates for the khandgutga lands varied from 24 to 2.5 hons per mar, and for the khandmakta lands from 10.00 to about 0.75 hons per mar. Here it is quite obvious that the rates varied in each case according to the kind of the soil, the location of the land, the type of crops grown on the land and other similar factors.

According to an undated Modi yadi of the lands of Havanur Desai in P/Kupelur[29], the following were the rates of assessment per patti of land: 23 hons for yeri, 15 hons for *kengal* and 12 hons for masab. Other details about the land are not found here. In 1770 the rates of assessment for the sarvamanya, judimanya and khalsat lands are given in a taleband of Samat Kalghatgi.[30] The rate in all the three cases is 10 hons per patti. For judimanya land the rate is given by the document itself, and for the other two types of lands the rates are calculated on the basis of the figures given in the document. Here only in the last case full tax must have been levied. Except the tenures no other details about the lands are given. A Modi document dated in 1792 gives the tax rate for the bagayit land in Q/Kalghatgi as 10 hons per patti, the rate for the *koradavahu* (dry) land being 12 hons per patti. The rates for the bagayit and koradavahu lands in M/Madki Honnihalli of Samat Kalghatgi in 1792 are given by the document as 24 and 36 hons per patti respectively.[31] The dry land was, as a rule, taxed less than the wet or bagayit land, but here there is no means of knowing why the koradavahu land was taxed more than the bagayit land. There might have been some specific local reasons for this kind of phenomenon. In 1813 the rates in the village of Badni of P/Lakshmeshwar are given in rupees, and when converted into hons the rates for the chali, khandgutga and kaul lands were 52.90, 11.36 and 5.65 hons per patti respectively.[32] The tax on the chali land was 4.5 times more than that on the khandgutga land, and the khandgutga tax was double the tax on kaul lands. It is clear that the tax per patti ranged from 52.90 hons for the chali land to 5.65 hons for the kaul land in 1813 in M/Badni. In other cases the highest and lowest rates were 23 for yeri and 12 for masab, 36 for koradvahu and 10 for bagayit lands.

Mode of Collection of Land Revenue

The land revenue was usually collected every year either in cash or in kind. The heads of various princely states sent their revenue officers to collect the land revenue. The Peshwa had appointed special officers called Kamavisdars for this purpose. If there were any epidemics or damages caused by wars or some other calamities, the land revenue was remitted, and if possible, it was recovered the next year. When the waste lands were brought under cultivation, they were, as a rule, given to the raiyats under a *kaul*, a contract, of five or seven or ten years. The payment of land revenue in the kaul system was made possible by assisting the raiyat to pay it gradually step by step. Sometimes the revenue for the first year or for the first two years was remitted, and from the third year onwards it was gradually raised until the full revenue was paid in the last year. For example, in a 7-year kaul the raiyat did not have to pay any land revenue for the first two years. He had to pay one-fifth of the full land tax in the third year, one-third in the fourth year, three-fifths in the fifth, three-fourths in the sixth and the full amount in the last and seventh year of the kaul.[33]

The land revenue was paid mostly in hons in the early years of the eighteenth century, but in the nineteenth century it gradually came to be paid in rupees, and under the British it was definitely paid in rupees. To properly understand the unit of coinage and its denominations in which the land revenue was paid, it is necessary to know its difference from the Vijanagara varaha. The varaha was the unit of coinage under Vijayanagara. Under the Adil Shahs the land revenue came to be paid either in hons or in rupees. In the Bijapur documents relating to this region the revenue amounts have been written in terms of hons. The hon was actually a half-varaha. Under Bijapur although the varaha was called a hon, yet the payment was made in varahas, because in the revenue documents all the impartant denominations of the varaha were used. But only the following terms, hana, bele, *visa* and *arevisa* were popular. The varaha was divided into two hons, a hon into five *hanas*, a hana into four *hagas*, a haga into two beles and a bele into two visas. But later, retaining this Vijayanagara tradition, they made changes in the denominations. Dropping the higher denominations above the hana, they made the hana itself the unit of coinage but called it the *honnu* or hon. And this hana, now called a hon, became the unit of coinage. From the hon (former hana) down to the visa (the sixteenth part of a hana), the immediately higher denomination was equal to two immediately lower denominations. Thus there came to be an exact ratio between the immediately higher and immediately lower denominations, the ratio being 1:2. Thus each hon (former hana) was equal to 2 *addas*, each adda equal to 2 hagas, each haga equal 2 beles and each bele equal to 2 visas. Amongst these the words 'adda' and 'haga' were not used in the Bijapur tradition. The term 'bele' was regularly used, and 'visa' sometimes, the haga being expressed as 2 beles and the adda as 4 beles.* Thus they adopted the Vijayanagara coinage frame, but fitted it into another system retaining only a few terms of the earlier frame. Later under the British the same table was continued replacing only the nomenclature. The hon became the rupee, the haga a 4-anna piece, the bele a 2-anna piece and the visa an anna. In many parts of the Southern Maratha Country there were specific terms for the 4-anna and 2-anna pieces called *pawli* and *chawli* respectively. The rupee had come from the Delhi Sultans through the Mughals, and now it took the place of the hon. While going through the Modi and Kannada documents relating to this period and this area we find that in some places the old Vijayanagara system was followed with vertical and horizontal strokes for all the lower denominations except the hana for which the figures were used, while in the new Bijapuri system only the strokes were used without the figures. A document of 1827 mentions two types of money, calling them 'new money' (*nave rokka*) and 'old money' (*june rokka*).[34] This reformed table was very useful. It was even employed for land measures, the hon and the later rupee taking the place of the mar, the bele that of the Kurgi and the arevisa that of the acre. Under the Company, Davidson used this table (except the arevisa) for indicating the varying fertility of the soil and the varying degree of the produce of the soil. The people welcomed them and lived with them. It was not much difficult for them to understand this change which was quite necessary.

Improvements under the British

When the British conquered this area, they could not understand these local variations and were baffled by them. The land revenue accounts were in a deplorable condition. The British found that the assessment was made up of (1) the raqm or ainati, (2) the customary cesses or dues called 'mamul patti' and the extra dues or imposts called 'jasti patti' which were added to the first two amounts so as to meet the latest assessment demand determined by the Mamledar for a given year.[35] The farming system of Bajirao II became rampant, and the raiyats were in great disress. Elphinstone in his *Report* has given a graphic description of this system, wherein he says that 'a man's means of payment, not the land he occupied, were the scale on which he was assessed.'[36] The British took some immediate steps such as grants of remissions to relieve the misery of the peasants, but to no avail. The Company officers found it extremely difficult to make a reasonable demand of revenue on the basis of the revenue accounts of the Kulkarnis, because under the farming system the earlier system had fallen into disuse and great confusion had prevailed in the revenue administration. About this situation Chaplin stated in his revenue report of 1818–19 that 'authentic accounts of the real collections of villages in detail are scarcely anywhere procurable.' Many of the accounts were entirely fictitious. He speaks of 'the absence of authentic accounts by which to fix the assessment of a village upon data that may be relied on.' 'Accounts are,' he adds, 'everywhere mutilated or interpolated, and whole sets for whole districts are sometimes fabricated for our inspection.'[37]

Finally in 1827, Pringle, the Assistant Collector of Poona, was appointed to study the existing conditions and suggest some concrete measures for reforming the revenue system. First he was to suggest these measures for Poona and the neighbouring districts, and they were then to be applied in other parts including the Southern Maratha Country. Briefly the main features of Pringle's settlement were (1) the measurement of lands with the chain and cross-staff, (2) the division of lands into acres, (3) the classification of lands on the 'net produce' scale, and (4) the collection of land revenue at the rate of 1st class assessment. Pringle's system of survey and settlement failed to achieve its objects mainly for the following reasons: (1) The actual 'net produce' could not be ascertained as the Kulkarnis' books were mostly unreliable, (2) the methods employed to find out the 'net produce' were complicated and faulty, (3) the earlier heavy assessment rate was not lightened, and (4) the introduction of this settlement was followed by famines with the result that it could not be given a fair trial.[38]

After the failure of Pringle's settlement, the Company Government appoined Goldsmid and Wingate in 1836 for making a new settlement. They started their work in the talukas of Mohol and Madha, which are at present in the Solapur district. Lands were measured and the soil was classified into nine types. These classes were fitted into the rupee scale, a scale which the local people could easily understand. The soil was assigned to a particular class on the basis of its fertility, its depth and the nature of deteriorating ingredients.[39]

For determining the average assessment rate of a given field, sample soils were selected in different parts of the field. They were then classified on the twin principles of quality and depth of the soil. The assessment rates of these sample classes were averaged and then applied to the whole field. The new system became quite successful, and the factors responsible for its success were (1) moderation in demand, (2) 30 years' guarantee, (3) a comparatively clear and simple method, (4) concurrent settlement of rights in land, (5) strict supervision by the Europeans, and (6) the settlement of field boundaries.

In 1847 the *Joint Report* of Goldsmid, Wingate and Davidson was issued. The Report mainly dealt with the unit of assessment, the assessment of the unit and the settlement based on them. Its two main features were the principle of grouping and the system of survey numbers. The grouping was based on permanent features like climate, markets, communications, standard of husbandry and past revenue history.[40]

In 1843–44 and onwards the original Revenue Survey Settlement was introduced in the Southern Maratha Country. In all the talukas situated in the Southern Maratha Country the lands were broadly divided into three types, viz., dry-crop, rice and garden lands. The dry-crop lands were divided into groups and then the maximum rates were determined for them. For rice and garden lands also the assessment rates were fixed, and finally the average rates were calculated for all these lands. The maximum rates per acre for dry-crop lands in this whole area in the early years of the British period varied from Rs 2.25 to Re.0.66. The average dry-crop land rates varied from Re.1.56 to Re. 0.31. As against this, the old rates varied from Rs 11.89 to Re. 0.17. For rice lands the maximum was Rs 5.00 per acre and the minimum Re. 1.50. The average rate per acre ranged from Rs 2.50 to Rs 2.00. In the old system the variation was not marked, the highest rate being Rs 3.54 and the lowest Rs 3.11. In garden lands there were wide variations, the rates per acre ranging from Rs 40.00 to about Re. 1.28. In the average rates, the highest was Rs 18.94 and the lowest Rs 5.00, the rates in the old system varying from 8.58 to Rs 8.00. In all these cases the rates under the old system, when the farming system was in vogue, had been, by and large, with one or two exceptions, heavier than those under the new system.[41]

The grouping system followed in the British Survey Settlements had existed, though in a crude form, in the pre-British period too. The grouping of lands into 4 types in M/Konnur of P/Gokak was similar, though in a very crude form, to the grouping followed later under the British. Gokak is on the banks of the Ghataprabha, which flows through that taluka. To its north lies the Raibag taluka and to its south the Parasgad taluka. There were only 2 groups of dry-crop lands in Gokak there maximum rates being Rs 2 and Re. 1.25 respectively. In Raibag there were 4 such groups, and the maximum rates for these groups were Rs 2.50, 1.75, 1.50 and 1.25 respectively. In Parasgad the lands were grouped into 5 classes, and the maximum rates for lands in these groups were Rs. 1.56, 1.38, 1.25, 1.13 and 1.00 per acre respectively. These rates could be compared with the Gokak rates of the pre-British times. The hons per chigar in old Gokak have been converted into rupees at the rate of Rs. 3.75 per hon prevalent in those days, and then reduced to the assessment rates per acre. The rates per acre for these 4 classes of lands in the Gokak taluka would be Rs 2.34, 2.23, 1.52 and 0.29 respectively. Presumably these rates, not necessarily the highest but the standard ones, were for both dry and wet-crop lands, because the rates for garden lands and mango plantations immediately follow. These rates were constant for a number of years, at least from 1858 to1895. Here it may be noted that the 3rd group rate of Raibag, the 2nd group rate of Gokak (under the British) and the 1st group rate of Parasgad were more or less equal to the 3rd group rate of pre-British Gokak. In Raibag the 1st group rate was slightly higher than that of old Gokak, the second was less and the fourth was considerably more than those of old Gokak. In Parasgad the 1st, 2nd and 3rd group rates were certainly, and the first two considerably, lower than the corresponding rates in old Gokak while the rates of the last two groups in

Parasgad were much higher than the rate of the 4th group of old Gokak. Thus we see that not all the group rates of either Raibag or Parasgad talukas are either higher or lower than the corresponding group rates of pre-British Gokak *mahal*. Again the higher rates are not even twice as much as the Gokak rates. All this shows that the rates of Raibag, Parasgad and old (and also new) Gokak are not much different from one another, given the gap of time and also the lands being both dry and wet in old Gokak.

To conclude, it is obvious that except for the period of Bajirao II when the farming system was at its height, the rates during the early Maratha and Savanur periods, *i.e.*, during the pre-British period and those under the first Survey Settlement in the Southern Maratha Country do not show, when compared, highly marked fluctuations. However, the old methods were rough and crude while the British methods were scientific and accurate based on many experiments. The system of grouping, the method of determining assessment rates, the various tenures, etc. during the pre-British period were in fact inherited from early times. They were not devised by the Peshwas. The Peshwas only continued the earlier tradition even keeping the earlier assessment rates, but fixing the revenue amount equal to many times more than the original standard rate called *rayarekhe*, or *asl*, or *raqm* or *ainati* or by some other term.[42] Thus we find the mingling of many traditions and ideas in the use of revenue terms, in making land measurements, in determining revenue rates, in following the several modes of payment of revenue and in adopting the different types of coinage existing side by side at different times in this region. In fact, a number of different and even conflicting elements in the agrarian system had become integrated. The people accepted the British improvements in the agrarian field as willingly as they had lived with the pre-British system. Whether under the Marathas or under the Company Government or under the local potentates, the people in the Southern Maratha Country had learnt through experience to live together with various traditions and practices, with various customs and systems.

Notes and References

1. Edward West, *A Memoir of the States of the Sourthern Maratha Country* (Bombay, 1869), Introduction, p. v.
2. Ibid. *(1) The non-English words are italicized when they are introduced for the first time in this paper. Thereafter, they are used without italics like all other English words. (2) The non-English words that have become very common like chawar, bigha, ser (seer) and jagir are also not italicized. (3) Some words, of course, are italicized for the sake of emphasis, or for some other specific reasons, as in the case of bag which here means a garden.
3. Pune Archives, Karnatak Jamav, Bundle No. 246, Sr. No. 1538; from the same bundle, Rumal No. 232, Sr. No. 643. In the Pune Archives, the Karnatak Jamav is a

big division where the Modi documents relating to this area are kept. The documents are kept in various bundles known as Rumals. Each bundle contains varying numbers of documents depending on the size of the documents. Some of the documents run into more than 100 pages. The above reference is here abbreviated as KJ: 246: 1538, 232: 643.

4. *Sannika*: 54: 608. '*San-ni-ka*' is an abbreviation of the Marathi expression '*Sanshodhanasathi nivadalele kagad*' meaning 'Papers selected for research.' These Modi documents were selected by G.S. Sardesai for further research and some of them contain very valuable documents throwing light on the agrarian system in the Southern Maratha Country.
5. KJ: 84: 1324.
6. KJ: 1938: 1543.
7. *Glossary*, p. 303.
8. Bharat Itihasa Samshodhaka Mandal Archives (BISMA henceforth): Lakshmeshwar Desai Daftar (LDD henceforth): 1630.
9. Nargund Pujari Daftar: 1042.
10. KJ: 1095: 296.
11. Sannika: 54: 608; See also William Chaplin, *A Report exhibiting a View of the Fiscal and Judicial System of Administration introduced into the Conquered Territory above the Ghauts under the Authority of the Commission in the Dekhan*. (Bombay, 1877), p. 21. According to another view, the pand was made up of 20 kathis in length and 1 kathi in breadth. See the *Bijapur District Gazeteer* (Bangalore, 1966), p. 321.
12. KJ: 405: 1184, 268: 627. For other examples, see KJ: 268 : 614–17, 620–22.
13. Kolhapur Archives (Kol. Arc. henceforth), Diwan O.A. Rumal No. 273/1310.
14. BISMA: LDD: 1632–35, 1637.
15. Kol. Arc., Torgal Daftar, Lavani Akar of M/Bhiradi, Prant Raibag.
16. KJ: 364: 467.
17. KJ: 246: 1538.
18. Bombay Archives, Revenue Department, 97 1181 of 1840, 16th para.
19. KJ: 64: 801.
20. KJ: 531: 96.
21. KJ: 531: 68.
22. KJ: 77: 1323.
23. KJ: 77: 1319.
24. KJ: 239: 276.
25. KJ: 174: 900.
26. KJ: 177: 348.
27. KJ: 241 : 353
28. KJ: 177 : 602
29. KJ: 212 : 1550
30. KJ: 80 : 1477
31. KJ: 79 : 1437
32. KJ: 554 : 523
33. Sannika: 54 : 608

* *Vijayanagara tradition*

Varaha = 2 hons
Hon = 5 hanas
Hana = 2 addas

Bijapur tradition

Hon = 8 beles
Bele = 2 visas

Adda = 2 hagas
Haga = 2 beles
Bele = 2 visas

34. Karnatak Archives (Kar. Arc. henceforth), Sheshadri Papers, No. 30.
35. *Selections from the Records of the Bombay Government* (SRBG henceforth): XII: Wingate's *Reports on the Revenue Survey Settlements of the Hubli, Navalgund, Kod and Dharwad Talukas of the Dharwad Collectorate*, 25th para.
36. Mountstuart Elphinstone, *Report on the Territories conquered from the Paishwa, submitted to the Supreme Government of British India* (Bombay, 1872), pp. 27–28.
37. Quotations given in SRBG: XII, 35th para.
38. R.G. Gordon, *The Bombay Survey and Settlement Manual*, Vol. I (Bombay, 1917), pp. 28–31; See also A. Rogers, *Land Revenue of Bombay*, Vol. II (Delhi, First published 1892, Reprint 1993), p. 102.
39. SRBG: XII. The best soil which was assigned to the 1st class was valued as 16 annas and the worst soil which was assigned to the 9th class was valued as 1.5 anna. The classes in between were valued according to their grades and assigned to their proper places between 16 annas and 1.5 anna.
40. For details of the 1836 Settlement and of the 1847 *Joint Report*, see Gordon, *op. cit.*, pp. 34–66 and 67–83 respectively.
41. SRBG: CLV-New Series: No. 15 of 1848, para 16; Rogers, *op. cit.*, pp. 364, 371–74, 377–78.
42. Kar. Arc., Sheshadri Papers, Bundle No. 3., According to this document, the patti or extra levy for the chali lands was 11 times more than the original standard assessment called here 'ainat'. Although the document is dated in 1821, *i.e.*, just three years after the fall of the Marathas, obviously the patti rate was fixed under the farming system.

FOURTEEN ❖ # Assimilation of Cultures: The Kerala Experience

K. K. N. KURUP

SINCE THE FORMATION OF Kerala society, there had existed different religious communities and groups in this region. It is believed that St. Thomas, the Apostle, had introduced Christianity in Travancore and had converted a good number of people into that religion.[1] In the early centuries of the Christian era, the Jews, when they faced persecution in their homeland, migrated to Kerala for asylum. The rulers of Kerala were sympathetic to those migrants and were good in their heart to grant special privileges to the Jewish trading community. Such privileges and concessions were recorded on copper plates which show the generosity and compassion towards the new settlers following a different religious system.[2] They were also permitted to construct synagogues in places like Mattanchery.

In fact the waves of Aryan religions like the Buddhism and the Jainism from the northern parts of India had found their way to this region even prior to the consolidation of Hinduism with its *chaturvarnya* division and the caste system of society. Both these heterodox religious systems with their compassionate philosophy and humane approach had organized new social institutions of medicine, education and charity in Kerala society. When those religious forces became decadent in Kerala, their institutions and centres of worship were gradually incorporated within the social structure and the cultural legacy of Hinduism.[3] The process of cultural assimilation was effective and all-embracing and the distinct identities of those religions was lost for ever in Kerala society. The assimilation was based more on the process of unity in diversity and not on the suicidal aspect of confrontation or conflict.

People living within a district geographical contour, but following heterogeneous cultural and religious trends, are bound to promote a common culture or heritage pertaining to that particular society. More often, it can be a composite culture, but absolutely leading to social integrity and unity. The social and cultural history of a region like that of Kerala stands witness to this. The people who followed different religious and cultural patterns, with their conscious or unconscious social behaviour had promoted a synthesis of cultures providing for a common heritage.

Islam as a religion and a way of life is a fine example of this generalization. As a dynamic civilization originating in the Middle East, it has spread its message throughout the world including India. Even prior to the advent of Islam, the Arabs had established regular commercial contacts with the western coast of Kerala.[4] Following those maritime contacts of trade and commerce, Islam came to the coastal towns of Kerala as early as in the time of the Prophet himself.[5] Like the Jews and the Christians, the Muslims also were well received in the social system of Kerala. The local rulers gave all possible assistance to the Arab settlers, and encouraged their settlements in coastal and interior towns.[6] In northern India, the Islamic religion had spread as introduced by the Afghan and the Mongolian conquerors, and that historical situation had led to a common animosity against its followers from the natives. However, in southern India including Kerala, it had a different process based on mutual consent and encouragement as the trading community was acceptable to the indigenous society. Centres like Calicut became a trade emporium in the eastern hemisphere, mainly because of the Muslim entrepreneurs. The bulk of the eastern trade till the advent of the Portuguese and other European nations in Asia was in the hands of the Arab merchants. Among the natives of Kerala, the Arab descendants were known by the pet name, the Mappilas. The growth of political power of the Zamorins of Calicut depended mainly on the prosperity of Arab trade. The volume of indigenous and foreign trade, mainly controlled by the Arabs and the Mappilas, made Calicut one of the major centres of foreign trade in Asia in the fifteenth century. Abdur Razszak, the Persian Ambassador, wrote in 1442 about Calicut that:

> . . . the most wealthy merchants bring thither from maritime countries considerable cargoes which they unload and unhesitatingly send into the markets and bazaars, without thinking in the meantime of any necessity of checking the account or of keeping watch over the goods.[7]

The rulers of Calicut encouraged these trading communities and settlers with liberal concessions and endowments. One of the mosques in Calicut, known as Muchundi, was given state patronage by the Zamorin. Many mosques and temples, situated in the same locality in the kingdom of Calicut, have existed with harmony and mutual respect. Some of these mosques were constructed in the same architectural style, with slight variations, as that of the Hindu temples, specifically known as Dravida. In effect, the construction style of a mosque and a temple was one and the same.[8]

In other parts of India, the Indo-Islamic architecture had its main inspiration from the Persian and Turkish traditions. However, in Kerala, the Arab tradition of simplicity of structural form had combined with the indigenous style of *Tachusastra* thereby giving rise to a new style of mosque architecture. This was probably due to the employment of indigenous carpenters and masons who knew only the temple style of architectural construction. The mosque architecture flourished in Kerala mainly between the thirteenth and sixteenth centuries when the Muslims enjoyed a prestigeous position in the maritime trade with Arabia.

Gradually, the Mappilas migrated to the interior from the coastal towns and settled as cultivators and traders. Along with such new settlements, they established their juma mosques and minor prayer halls.[9] In the long run the Mappilas became an integral part of Kerala society. This process was based on co-operation and sympathy and not on conflict and hatred. As a trading class the Mappilas enjoyed confidence and self respect from the rest of the communities.

In the sixteenth century these Arab traders and the Mappilas were the first to realize the political significance of the European expansion and the advent of the Portuguese in the Arabian waters. They started an era of native resistance against the Portuguese for establishing the right of free trade and political independence of the native rulers like the Zamorin. The role of the Kunhali Marakkars, as the defenders of Islam and the Zamorin, is a significant chapter in the history of Kerala in her fight against colonialism.[10] The Nayar soldiers of the Hindu community, and the Mappila mariners of Muslim community fought shoulder to shoulder for capturing the Protuguese fortresses of Chaliyam and Ponnani.[11] In those days of atrocities, the Hindus and the Muslims faced the Portuguese courageously and courted martyrdom in the cause of their native land and resisted its attempted subjugation by the intruders. Sheikh Zainuddin, the author of *Tuhfat-ul-Mujahideen* was a guide and philosopher of this heroic resistance against the Portuguese.[12] Religion was not a barrier in their unity and cultural integration but it strengthened its cause by encouraging martyrdom for one's own country or *Mulk*. That explains why when the Zamorin was forced to surrender the Kunhali Marakkar IV into the hands of the Portuguese, his Hindu Nayar soldiers revolted against this situation.[13]

In fact, for long centuries, Islam as a religion was deep-rooted in the soil of Kerala. The long association with the Hindu community of this region had basically restructured some of the cultural and ideological aspects of Islam. The fundamentalist sections, who are always in search of Islamic purity, will not appreciate its regional variation and the trends of change in the cultural milieu of Islamic community in Kerala. The Shariyat or the Islamic law had always recognized the primogeniture or the succession by the eldest son to property and estate. In Kerala the institution of matriliny or the succession in the female line is very commonly known by the local term *Marumakkathayam*. The ruling chieftain of Kannur or the Ali Rajas of Cannanore, the estate-owners like the Keyis of Thalassery and many other land-owning families in different parts of Kerala had adopted this local Hindu custom of succession. Here the Islamic custom and law had been dominated by the native custom which had been ratified by the court of laws. On account of such a legal situation, the Madras Legislative Assembly promulgated the Mappila Succession Act of 1919, stipulating the Shariyat rules for self-acquired properties of the Muslims who followed Marumakkathayam. The High Court of Madras held that this act, including the amendment of 1949, extending to agricultural lands also, did not purport to, nor did it abolish the rights and incidents of, the Mappila Marumakkathayam.[14] The same proposition was accepted by the full bench of the High Court of Kerala.[15] Here the court was supporting the centuries-old traditions of the Mappila community, particularly inherited by it from its Hindu counterpart. As the Mappilas wanted to strengthen their patrilineal ties, they also, like the Nayars, insisted on the partition of joint families and tarawads. Thus the Madras Legislative Assembly enacted the Mappila Marumakkathayam Act of 1939, giving permission for such partition for ensuring the operation of Shariyat laws of succession. Many wealthy Mappila families went for partition only after this act. It shows that the landed aristocracy of the Mappila community in Kerala had deeply imbibed the indigenous culture even against their religious rules and practices.

The annual *Uruz* and *Nerchas* in honour of sufis and philosophers are significant religious festivals for Islamic community in Kerala. The anatomy of those festivals resembles more often Hindu festivals like Kaliyattam, Perukaliyattam and temple festivals like *Pooram* and *Vela*. In all these festivals, the rituals and processions have common and similar elements. They are all village festivals, participated in by rural folk without any distinction of caste, creed and religion. These folk festivals are the manifestation of a common culture and heritage, and they reflect the strength of unity and oneness. The local Hindu community had always participated in the festivals of the Muslims. In the same way in many of the Teyyam festivals of northern Kerala, the ritual role as suppliers of salt and sugar is observed by the Muslims. These aspects of unity are still pursued with mutual respect. Formerly, at the time of wedding ceremonies, a brass lamp was lighted by the eldest female member in the Muslim family as is done in the Hindu family. It was also followed by the sprinkling of rice on the heads of newly wedded couples as in the Hindu custom. Another common practice is the newly to seat married couples on a white sheet spread over a blanket.

Some of the Mappila folk performances like the Kolkkali (stick play),

Oppana (a dance form) and several other items are mere imitation and modification of folk items of Hindu community. The performance of Oppana is highly indebted to a folk item exclusively performed by the Hindu women folk named after *Thiruvatirakkali*. The clapping and movement in a circle along with the gay recitation of the folk song are the main characteristics of both items. In the folk songs of Oppana, more Arabic and Persian vocabulary is used along with Malayalam words. The performance itself is rhythmic, artistic and melodius.

The classical theatres of Kerala, Koodiyattam and Kathakali, had borrowed at least some items of costumes from the Arabs and the local Mappilas. The female costumes in Kathakali are exactly the same dress as used by Mappila women. The dress known as 'Kuppayam' was a forbidden thing for a high-caste woman of Kerala who kept her upper part naked. Therefore, the model was taken from the Mappila womenfolk.

The cult of Teyyam is a ritualistic art form. Even in such performance, the Muslim characters are incorporated as boatmen of the goddesses. These characters wore fez caps and also observed the *namaz* as ritual. The famous Hindu deity, Ayyappa at Sabarimala, has a Muslim companion and saint known as Bavar. The pilgrims to the Ayyappa shrine also visit the place of Bavar. Places like the Mamburam Tangals' mosques and several Jarems of the sufis and saints are visited by the Hindus. They also bring offerings to these centres and pray for blessings and boons.

Several Christian churches like Malayattur, Kaduthuruthi, Mannarcad and Cochin and their festivals are attended by the local Hindu community also. As in a mosque, offerings are made in these churches also. Further, some of the church authorities had introduced a process of Indianization and had adopted saffron dresses for nuns and priests and lighted bronze lamps for prayers. Even much earlier, the sermons were given in the native language of Malayalam and the holy texts, like the Bible, were published in that language. Such a process had brought different communities closer and closer, thereby destroying the barriers of religion. Christianity or Islam today does not believe in proselytization as in early centuries, but exhibits tolerance and mutual respect. Such efforts had articulated their identity as Malayalee or Keralite as part of the Indian nationality.

The policy of the rulers in traditional Kerala was to encourage all religious communities and they were quite liberal in their attitude towards religious groups other than their own. Sheikh Zainuddin wrote:

> The unbelievers never punish such of their countrymen who embrace Islam, but treat them with the same respect shown to the rest of Muslims, though the convert belongs to the lowest of grades of their society. As a result of such kindly treatment, Muslim merchants of olden days used to come in large numbers.[16]

The caste system in the Hindu community had weakened its position by putting down its lower sections as untouchables for the upper sections. Christianity and Islam opened their doors for these oppressed sections who sought their liberation through conversion into those religions. Once converted, their caste grievances were largely mitigated. Such conversions in the early centuries had increased the numerical strength of the followers of those religions. The sufis enjoyed great command over the rural folk and attracted them towards the order of Islam.

The Arabi-Malayalam, a dialect of the Muslim intelligentsia, was invented for the purpose of communication among themselves and a separate branch of literature developed in that dialect. It was neither Arabic nor Malayalam but an admixture of both. Like the Urdu language and literature, this has become a language of the intelligentsia. The Muslim community were familiar with the Arabic letters and script. The language used by them was Malayalam but words from Arabic, Persian and Urdu languages were liberally borrowed into it. Even philosophical discourses like *Muhiyuddeen Mala*, authored by Khazi Mohammed in 1607, had enriched this branch of literature. The Mappila pattus (or songs) also add to the emotional integration of the Muslim mind with the Hindu ethos.[17]

As a large minority community in Kerala, the Mappilas offer many fascinating factors for study and analysis relating to historical development of Kerala society. As noted by a recent writer, 'nowhere in India have foreign trading, commercial and religious interests interacted within the indigenous socio-economic and political institutions more intimately than they have in Malabar.'[18]

An analytical study of Kerala society reveals that it had promoted a composite culture by developing an indepth harmony and tolerance among different religious communities and bringing them together in a collective experience of integration. This spirit of collectivity can be identified in her festivals, rituals and artistic performances. The boundaries of religious systems had not put the people of Kerala in water-tight compartments; rather they contributed to the matrix of a mosaic and composite culture. This culture is a product of collective human experience in the annals of history. Today, however, many of the cultural expressions of the Mappilas are under attack from both classicists and progressives. Their search for purity of Islam as part of their fundamentalist thought is prompting them to reject many ritual celebrations and processions with an indigenous character as Unislamic. These purist and classicist movements shun the folk elements of a composite culture of Kerala and lead to the polarization of religions and communities. Situations like this subscribe to the disintegration and separation which must be resisted for the well-being of an Indian society.

NOTES AND REFERENCES

1. A. Sreedhara Menon, *Cultural Heritage of Kerala – An Introduction* (Cochin, 1978), p. 17.
2. See Tarisappalli Copper-plate Grant of 849 AD issued by Ayyan Atikal Tiruvatikal, the Governor of Venad. The senior members of the Arab settlement of Quilon were asked to witness this grant.
3. There is a famous temple known as Ganapathivattam at Sultan Battery of Wayanad. Originally it was a Jaina Basti. Even now Jaina images of Tirthamkaras can be identified on the walls.
4. The Arab geographers had a thorough knowledge of such maritime centres of Malabar. See traditional account of Calicut kingdom in K.V. Krishna Iyer, *The Zamorins of Calicut* (Calicut, 1938).
5. The earliest settlements are Quilon, Kodungallur, Chaliyam, Pantalayani Kollam, Dharmadham, Sreekanthapuram, Madayi, Kasaragod, Mangalore and Barkur.
6. Then these settlements are extended to Calicut, Veliyankot, Tirurangadi, Tanur, Ponnani, Parappanangadi, Paravanna, Kappat, Tikkoti, Kannur, Baliapatam, Nileshwaram, Cochin, etc.
7. R.H. Major, (ed.), *India in the Fifteenth Century* (Delhi, 1974, reprint), p. 14.
8. Recently many of these mosques are reconstructed in concrete with minarets and domes as the Mappilas have become an affluent community with their employments in gulf countries.
9. A large number of such centres are scattered in the interior of Malabar and new settlements are effected even in the rural areas.
10. See details in K.K.N. Kurup (ed.) *India's Naval Traditions – The Role of Kunhali Marakkars* (New Delhi, 1997). Also, O.K. Nambair, *The Kunjalis, Admirals of Calicut* (Bombay, 1963).
11. A descriptive poem on this event is written in Arabic by Khasi Muhammad Bin Abdul Aziz of Calicut probably between AD 1578 and 1579. See *Fathuhul Mubeen* translation into Malayalam by Mankata Abdul Aziz, Calicut, 1996.
12. A medieval historian and sufi of Kadiriyya order of Kerala even demanded a jihad against the Portuguese. It is believed that his holy tomb is situated at the Kunhippalli mosque of Chombal, near Mahe.
13. See Nambair, in n. 10.
14. Abdu Rahiman *vs* Avoomma, A.I.R. 1956 Madras, 244. See K. Sreedhara Warrior, *Marumakkathayam and Allied Systems of Law in the Kerala State* (Cochin, 1969).
15. A.I.R. 1959, Kerala 67 (Full Bench).
16. Sheikh Zainuddin, (trans. and ed.) Sheikh Malik Hussain Nayanar, *Tuhfat ul-Mujahidin* (Madras University, 1942), pp. 51–52.
17. N.P. Muhammed, 'Reflections on Mappila Heritage', in Asghar Ali Engineer, *Kerala Muslims: A Historical Perspective* (Delhi, 1995), pp. 35–46.
18. D.N. Dhanagare, *Peasant Movements in India: 1920–1950* (Bombay, 1983), p. 54.

FIFTEEN ❖ We Calcuttans have Always Lived Together

We Calcuttans have Always Lived Together

GAUTAM CHATTOPADHYAY

INDIA, OUR VAST, COMMON motherland is, as we all know, a land where people of diverse religions, languages, cultures and ethnic groups have lived and still live. In our daily life, we speak our particular language – Bengali, Hindi, Urdu, Punjabi, Tamil, Marathi, Gujarati and so on. In our family life, during the birth of a child, a marriage or the death of a relative, we observe rituals according to our particular religion. Our songs, our poetry, our plays, and our cinema are mostly in our regional language. Even in sports we are partisans for our particular regional nationality. Yet, at all critical points, whenever there is a national crisis, danger of a threat of a foreign attack or even when we enter as competitors in sports in the world arena, we are all, invariably, Indians. In the depth of our consciousness, we realize that, despite so much diversity in the spheres of religion, nationality, language and culture, we are bound together by a great national bond – we are all sons and daughters of Mother India. An objective and analytical study of India's history throughout the ages, down to this day, proves this assertion. In this sense, in this golden jubilee of the achievement of Indian Independence, we can confidently declare that throughout the centuries, *We have Lived Together.*

However, in this article, I shall not go into a scholarly examination of India's ancient past, or of the medieval times, or even of the totality of what is known as the modern age. Instead, I shall take recourse to a micro-study of a very small area, that is also India, for the past seventy years or so, and show, from personal experience (which in every case is borne out by historical records), that despite differences, tensions and even temporary setbacks, how ultimately we have managed to live together.

The small area that I shall now speak of belongs to the south-eastern part of the great metropolis of Calcutta, where I was born and where I have continued to live for over seventy years till the present day. I was born on 9

December 1924, in a two-storied, old-fashioned house whose street number was then 43, Old Ballygunge Second Lane, but which was changed by the Calcutta Municipal Corporation in 1934 or 1935 to No. 2, Palm Place. The adjoining nearly a mile long snake-like street in 1924 was known as Ghughudanga Street but from 1935 on is now known as Palm Avenue.

From 1924, till the tragic communal riots of late 1946, this small area – a municipal ward – was bound on the west by the main road known as the Ameer Ali Avenue, on the east by the Suburban railway line, on the north by a chain of *bustees* or slums, and on the south by well-to-do, middle-class localities. Population-wise, in the twenties and the thirtees about 25,000 people lived in this small area (a population which in 1990 was approaching the figure of 1,00,000). In the colonial period, between 1924 and 1946, the break-up of the population was something like this – 90 per cent of the population were Urdu-speaking Muslim slum dwellers, migrants from poverty-stricken districts of Bihar and U.P., with a sprinkling of poor Bengali Muslims; less than 10 per cent were educated Bengali Hindus, belonging mainly to the professional classes, *viz.,* teachers, doctors, lawyers and officers in government service or private companies. There were three or four parallel roads running east to west known as Mayfair, Ballygunge Park Road, Ballygunge Park and Ironside Road, where there were a little over a hundred magnificent villas with tennis lawns and all available modern facilities; the residents of these villas were almost entirely Englishmen or at least Europeans with one or two very highly placed Indian officers of the colonial government co-existing with the rest of the population.

In our sub-area, that is, Palm Place, Palm Avenue and Mayfair, the break-up was very clear. In Mayfair lived the European lords of the Bengal Chamber of Commerce, in Palm Avenue, then known as Ghughudanga, right up to the railway line, were a score of *bustees* where lived and toiled in poverty several thousand Urdu-speaking Muslims. In Palm Place, a very short road, there were then only three Bengali households – our old-fashioned two-storied house owned by my father Khitish Prasad Chattopadhyay opposite No. 1, Palm Place, the residence of Surendra Nath Tagore, nephew of the poet Rabindranath and son of Satyendranath, the first Indian I.C.S. The third house of Bengalis completing the triangle was that of Indira Debi, sister of Surendranath Tagore, and her husband Pramatho Chowdhury, an eminent figure of Bengali literature.

Since this is not an autobiographical essay, I will skip chronological details and try to establish what I have to say. My father, who was an intimate friend and a classmate of Netaji Subhas Chandra Bose, became the first Education Officer of the Calcutta Corporation when Deshbandhu Chittaranjan Das was elected its first Mayor and young Subhas Chandra Bose was appointed the Chief Executive Officer of the Calcutta Corporation. This was in April or May 1924, several months before I was born. That was the period of great fraternization of Hindus and Muslims because of the Bengal Pact formulated by Deshbandhu and his Swarajist Party in alliance with the Khilafatists. It is to be noted for the benefit of the present generation that, while C.R. Das was elected the Mayor, the Khilafatist Shaheed Suhrawardy was elected Deputy Mayor of Calcutta Corporation, both defeating heavily the loyalists supported by the white colonial rulers.

This Hindu-Muslim confluence was not limited only to the politically conscious educated citizens but it went deep down among the sprawling poor of Calcutta. Subhas Bose was arrested in October 1924 and kept detained without trial till the end of 1927 while C.R. Das prematurely passed away in June 1925. Yet their programme remained alive. For example, the programme of a drive for mass primary education in the city went forward and in less than a decade, the number of primary schools run by the Calcutta Corporation jumped from only 3 in 1924 to 232 in 1934. The number of children of the poor, a large part of them Muslims, rose to well over 50,000 covering nearly half the slum-dwelling children of primary school age. This has been proudly recorded by Subhas Chandra in his semi-autobiographical work, *The Indian Struggle*, as also by the visiting British Labour Leader, H.N. Brailsford, in his well-known book *Subject India*. A further point to note is that in these 200 odd primary schools spread over the entire city, Hindus, Muslims, Sikhs, Christians, Bengalis, Biharis and Oriyas as children studied together, played together and grew up in reasonable friendship.

As for myself, my childhood friends who came to play with me in the afternoon in the small field inside our house were almost all slum-dwelling Muslim children and there was also one boy who was the son of our washerman who lived nearby. Nobody ever told me in the those days of glorious innocence that I was the son of a highly educated Bengali brahmin and that the washerman's son belonged to a so-called lower caste and the Muslim slum children belonged to a 'hostile' civilization! When I was somewhat older and a student of a senior class in the Ballygunge Government High School nobody told me that a few teachers as well as some classmates who used to come sometime to our home were Hindus while others were Muslims. So the forces of division, animosity and disruption were no doubt there but the point that I have tried to show is that, notwithstanding these forces, the experiences of my childhood show that the forces which helped us to live together and play together were quite strong. How strong, I shall come to that later on.

Skipping a decade, I shall now come to August 1946 to the shameful and tragic days of communal holocaust, usually referred to in history books as the Great Calcutta Killings. In those first three days of fanatical communal violence, thousands of Hindus and Muslims perished at the hands of the rioters, usually their erstwhile neighbours. Our house and the house of my maternal grandfather opposite our place were the only two houses of educated middleclass Hindus, surrounded on all sides by slum-dwelling Urdu-speaking Muslims. By 1946, they were almost all strong supporters of the Muslim League, of the pernicious Two-Nation Theory, and of the demand for Pakistan. Yet, our two houses were neither attacked nor looted nor even a single member of our two families attacked by our Muslim neighbours, although our two houses were like two small islands in a sea of Muslim population, at that time boiling with communal anger. We went through the Great Calcutta Killings without a scratch in our body and without a brick of our house being damaged.

Three months later, the Noakhali carnage took place, leading to retaliatory mass violence in Bihar. Thousands of homeless Muslim refugees arrived in our area to stay with their relatives. They were very angry to find that, while their houses had been burnt by the communal Hindus in Bihar, here their Muslim brethren had allowed two Hindu houses to remain intact. So they were planning to take 'law' into their own hands. The local leaders of the people who lived in a slum came to my father and told him all this, advising him to leave the area for the time being, as they were afraid that they would not be able to restrain the Muslim refugees from Bihar. Local Muslim activists of the Communist Party agreed that such a danger was imminent and they volunteered to occupy our house and our maternal grandparents' house as so-called tenants. The leader of this courageous band of activists was my friend Dr Maruf Hussain and a few other left-wing cultural figures. One of them, now a doyen of singers of Tagore's songs in Bangladesh, Kalim Sarafi, has recently written about this episode in a well-known Bengali monthly of Calcutta (*Nandan*), February 1997).

So we shifted reluctantly, for a year or so, to a rented house in South Calcutta and ultimately returned to our house at 2, Palm Place, just by chance on the morning of 30 January, 1948. In the evening came the catastrophic news of the assassination of Mahatma Gandhi during his prayer-meeting in defence of communal peace. Hundreds of slum-dwelling Muslims poured into our house in wild panic and sought protection from my father. We all assured them that there was no danger for them and that in any case we shall do everything in our power to preserve communal peace and amity in our area. A score of rickshaw-pullers left their rickshaws inside our residence for protection in case of an attack at night. As is well known, communal peace was preserved not only in our small area but all over Calcutta after the killing of Gandhiji and, in fact, Gandhiji's martyrdom turned public opinion against the fanatical demand of a 'Hindu-rashtra' and salvaged the ideal of a secular, democratic India.

Many years later, in 1952, or 1953, while purchasing cigarettes from a petty shop-keeper of our area, a conversation sprang up and 1946 came up. I asked the shop-keeper and his friends: 'why were our two houses not attacked nor any member of our family assaulted?' In chorus came the reply: 'That would have been a sin: Was it not your father (Khitish Chattopadhyay) who as the friend of Subhas Bose set up the first free primary school of Calcutta Corporation in this area in 1925–26 and is it not a fact that the little education that we have obtained was by studying in that school? Moreover, we slum-dwellers used to have a thousand and one quarrels among ourselves over petty issues and to avoid legal expenditure to whom did we go for arbitration?' I had no idea as to whom they were meaning and the shop-keeper told me: 'We went to your *nana i.e.* Surendranath Tagore' whose judgement they always accepted as they considered him to be a kind of *pir*. I was both amazed and overwhelmed! Then one of the friends of the shopkeeper, roughly of my age, took hold of my hand and said: 'Don't you remember that when we were young boys we used to play so many games in the field inside your house? How could we attack the house of a playmate? The Almighty would have punished us.' After another 40 years, as I look back and reflect on this incident, I feel sure that what happened in our small area was a micro-pattern of India and there must be similar episodes in all parts of our vast country. This is how we, of different religions, castes and linguistic groups have lived together for the last 50 years and more – lived perhaps not always in perfect amity, not without occasional tensions and fear, but still we did live together. This should act as a beacon of hope for the next century.

I shall now refer to a more contemporary episode. On 31 October, 1984, Mrs Indira Gandhi, then Prime Minister of India, was brutally killed by the bullets of a Sikh extremist. This led to an eruption of terrible mass violence against the Sikhs in general in the capital city of Delhi and almost throughout northern India. In Calcutta and West Bengal, practically nothing of the sort happened, barring a few negligible incidents. Most of the Sikh residents of Calcutta live in the southern part of the city. Within 24 hours, radical young men and women belonging to the Far Left had brought out a fairly big demonstration in defence of Hindu-Sikh amity, in which a large number of senior intellectuals, including myself, voluntarily participated. Hundreds of thousands of people lined the streets and applauded this demonstration. One old lady told me: 'The average Sikh is a most humane person; several years back, when I had to take my daughter in an advanced stage of pregnancy to a hospital at midnight, no taxi-driver agreed to go. Then an old Sikh taxi-driver who was passing by with his taxi took us in, reached us to the hospital and in fact, waited till my daughter had been admitted.' Other passers-by agreed and commented that we always feel very safe and secure when we board a taxi driven by a Sikh.

In even more recent times when on 6 December 1992, to our eternal shame, the Babri Masjid was demolished by organised force of Rightwing

Hindu Communalism, with the criminal connivance of the state authorities, Calcutta rose like one man to pour out its millions on the city streets in defence of communal peace and amity and in angry denunciation of the demolition of the Babri Masjid. In our micro-area, the boyhood friends, now past 60 like me, came to ask me to address one of their *baithaks* where I was received with great deal of fraternal warmth.

As the century draws to a close and when sporadic mass violence has become endemic in India, a Gujrati neighbour told me that it was only in Calcutta, despite its air pollution and traffic jams, that we feel most safe and secure, for among the average citizens of this great metropolis, communal, casteist and linguistic animosity is almost totally non-existent. Calcutta, too, had its bad patches like 1946-47, but the forces of unity and brotherhood always triumphed in the end. That is how we have lived together and how our children, our grand children and the children of centuries to come will live together as brothers and sisters in India, triumphing over the forces of religious fanaticism and all other forces of divisive violence.

SIXTEEN ❖ We Lived Together – Deccani Culture and the Qutb Shahs of Golkonda

SAROJINI REGANI

THE DECCAN HAS BEEN defined by the historians who attended the Deccan History Congress held in Hyderabad in 1945 as 'The region from the Tapti in the north to the edge of the plateau in the south', while Jouview Dubneil described it as the "large tract of the country which is bounded on the north by the Narmada and the Mahanadi, on the East by the Bay of Bengal, South by the Nilgiri Hills and 'The Penna'," which in modern geographical terms would mean the area covering the states of Maharashtra, Andhra Pradesh and the Karnataka abutting the Arcot region of the Tamilnadu and the city of Madras originally known as Chennapatnam.

In ancient times the region was referred to as Dakshinapatha. The Deccan from the very ancient times retained its unique individuality independent of the mighty empires like the Mauryans, the Guptas and the Delhi Sultanate though the Tughlaks did penetrate the Deccan. It was the Mughals who following the imperial policy laid down by Akbar, were able ultimately to make the Deccan region an integral part of the Mughal Empire under Aurangzeb in 1687. But the very conquest of the Deccan led to the undoing of the Mughal Empire, for after the death of Aurangzeb in 1707 the monolith of Mughal Empire broke up into more or less independent subahdaries like Bengal, Oudh and Hyderabad.

Deccan, from very early times, had been known for its spirit of liberalism and religious tolerance. From the third century BC onwards Buddhism and Jainism flourished in the Deccan side by side with Hinduism. Which showed the generoity and patronage of the Deccani rulers.

The Satavahana kings of Andhra (230 BC – AD 230), though followers of Hinduism, encouraged Buddhism. The proof of their religious tolerance can be seen even today in the shape of monuments like the Ajanta and Ellora Caves, the Buddhist stupa of Amaravati, and the chaityas of Dagoba.

The famous Madhyamika philosopher Acharya Nagarjuna lived at Nagarjuna Konda on the banks of the river Krishna. The Satavahana queens also were great patrons of Buddhism. Apart from the Satavahanas, the Vakataka kings of the Deccan also patronized Buddhism.

The Deccan under Ala-ud din Khilji and also during the time of the Tughlaks came under the control of the Delhi Sultanate for a short period, during the course of which the Yadava Kingdom of Devagiri in Maharashtra and the Kakatiya Empire of Warangal in the Telugu country came to an end. This resulted in the formation of a confederacy under the leadership of Kapaya Nayaka of Warangal against the Delhi Sultanate. They successfully resisted the forces of the Delhi Sultanate but it led to the establishment of several independent principalities under various Nayaks (chief) of the erstwhile Kakatiya empire. The open rebellion of the Yadava Sangama brothers Hari Hara and Bukka against the Delhi Sultanate led to the establishment of the Vijayanagara Empire in 1336, in the Karnataka country.

The Bahmani Sultanate in the Deccan came into existence under Ala-ud-din Hasan Bahman Shah in 1347, as a result of the revolt of Devagiri or Daulatabad against the Tughlak rule.

Ala-ud-din Hasan Bahman Shah chose Gulbarga as the centre of his activities. The Gulbarga included Bijapur which later became the capital of the Adilshahi rulers.

When the foundations of Bahmani Sultanate were laid in the Deccan (1318–47) the region was full of internecine warfares and bitter strife marked by Khilji intrusions and disturbances during the reign of Muhammad Tughlak, so much so that Namdev, the Bhakti saint, declared that the country was being ruled by the Daityas (Rakshasas, Demons).

However, the contemporary society retained its sanity by finding solace in the teachings of the Bhaghvata cult and the Warkari devotees of the Pandharpur cult.

It was at this juncture that Ala-ud-din Bahman Shah established his sultanate and restored peace and order in his dominions.

True to the spirit of the Deccani Culture he followed a policy of complete religious toleration, and tried to promote agriculture and animal husbandary in his dominions.

Ala-ud-din Hasan Bahman Shah followed a policy of non-discrimination between his Hindu and Muslim subjects by not imposing the *jiziya* tax on the Hindus. Thus he anticipated the policy of emperor Akbar two hundred years before Akbar. He was the first Muslim monarch in the history of medieval India who did not impose the *jiziya* tax on the Hindus.

This policy was scrupulously followed by all the successive sultans of the Deccan even when the Bahmani sultanate broke up into five independent sultanates. They also did not insist on matrimonial alliances between the sultans and the Hindu chieftains.

The policy of tolerance and goodwill set up by the founder of the Bahmani

Sultanate was followed by the successive Bahmani Sultans. Sultan Taj-ud-din Feroze Shah (1397–1422) preferred to employ local Hindu chieftains in his service rather than the Afaquis (Foreigners-Persians, Arabs and Turks) who thronged the court of the Sultans. He made Narsing of Khera one of his amirs while he conferred the Jagir of Mudhol, along with 84 villages, on one Bhairon Singh. He married Hindu ladies, participated in the local politics of the Hindu chieftains and took sides as suited him. In general he maintained cordial relations with the Hindu chieftains.

He deliberately promoted several Brahmins known for their learning and acumen to posts of honour and responsibility in his kingdom.

The arrival of the aged Hazrat Gesudaraj, the Sufi saint, during this period and his settling down at Gulbarga also brought the two communities closer. After the death of Gesudaraj the Bahmani capital was shifted to Bidar from Gulbarga.

Taj-ud-din Firoz was succeeded by his younger brother Shihab-ud-din Ahmed (1422 – 17). He was a disciple of Gesudaraj. He is remembered for his promotion of cultural synthesis between the Hindus and Muslims. Ahmad Shah's death anniversary is observed as an *urs* at Bidar in which both the Hindus and Muslims participate. The *urs* of Ahmad Shah is observed according to the Hindu calender and not according to the Hijri calender, when a 'Jangan', belonging to the Lingayat Mutt at Madhyar, dressed as a darvesh first goes to the Dargah accompanied by music and orchestra, breaks a coconut and offers flowers. Ahmad Shah is regarded by the local people as a saint or 'Wali'.

His successor, Ala-ud-din Ahmad II, is usually remembered for his fondness for Hindu philosophy. It is said that in his last days when he was seriously ill he was comforted by the saint of Gangapur, Narasimha Saraswati. When the Bahmani Empire disintegrated, in 1538 it broke up into five independent kingdoms, namely the Barid Shahis of Bidar, the Nizam Shahis of Ahmadnagar, Imad Shahis of Berar, Adil Shahis of Bijapur, and the Qutb Shahis of Golkonda.

The Sultanate of Berar (Imad Shahis) later became a part of the Nizam Shahi dominions, which in turn fell a prey to the imperialistic ambitions of the Mughals in 1636. Thus the Adil Shahis of Bijapur and the Qutb Shahis of Golkonda remained as independent states for a longer time till they too were reduced to become Mughal Provinces or Subedaris during 1686–1687.

Looking at the history of the kingdoms of Bijapur and Golkonda one finds that the two kingdoms remained true to the legacy of cultural synthesis and religious toleration of the Deccan region.

Ibrahim Adil Shah of Bijapur (1518–43) was a man of letters and he possessed an excellent library. A Hindu by name Waman Pandit was his chief librarian. Ibrahim took the title of 'Abala Bali' (protector of the weak).

He also wrote a book on Indian music called the *Kitab-e Nouras.* He was a poet who prefaced his poetical works by writing odes in praise of Goddess Saraswati and Lord Ganesha. He was generally addressed as Jagat Guru. A disciple of the Sufi Saint Gesudaraj of Gulbarga, he declared that there 'are different languages but there is only one emotional appeal be he a Brahmin or a Muslim'.

The Qutb Shahis of Golkonda also adhered to the ideals laid down by the Bahmani Sultans. When one says that the Bahmanis, the Adil Shahs or the Qutb Shahs is followed a policy of communal harmony and did not discriminate between their Hindu and Muslim subjects it does not mean that there was no breaking of temple at that time. One should remember that the constituent component kingdoms of Golkonda and Bijapur and their rulers expanded their dominions at the cost of the erstwhile Vijayanagar Empire and the various dominons of the erstwhile Naiks of Vijayanagar who after its downfall in 1565 became independent chieftains. So, while carrying on campaigns against Vijayanagar or its Naikwari territories, temples were looted for their wealth. In these attempts sometimes the Hindu generals of the Adil Shahs or the Qutb Shahs planned the looting of temples. Murahari Rao, one of the generals of Ibrahim Qutb Shah, for example looted the Ahobila Mutt.

While looting and breaking of temples did take place in the course of military campaigns outside their dominions, within their own territories these rulers observed a policy of complete toleration and gave liberal grants for maintainance of temples and also granted *Agraharas* to learned Vedic scholars. In fact the Qutb Shahi kingdom was noted for the innumerable *Agraharas* granted by its rulers to Vedic scholars, Telugu poets and artists.

Both the Adil-Shahs of Bijapur and the Qutb Shahs of Golkonda issued bilingual firmans. The former issued the firmans in Persian and Marathi, while the latter issued them in Persian and Telugu, and sometimes in Arabic and Telugu. Muhammad Quli Qutbshah issued eleven inscriptions in Sanskrit and Telugu and five in Arabic and Persian.

In the Qutb Shahi dominions both at the village and Taluq levels administration was conducted in Telugu and a number of Telugu Brahmins and some other Telugu community people were appointed as *karnams, patwaris,* accountants at different levels of administration. Generally the post of a *peishkar* was hold by a Brahmin.

The Qutb Shahis ruled over the Telugu country from 1518 to 1687 as independent rulers.

The founder of the Qutb Shahi dynasty Sultan Quli Qutb-ul-mulk was originally in the employment of the Bahmani sultans and he was appointed as the Governor of Telangana in 1495, along with the fort of Golkonda. He declared his independence from the suzerainty of the Bahmanis in 1518.

Sultan Quli, who assumed the title of Qutb-ul-Mulk, hailed from Persia and belonged to the Qara Quyunu tribe. He was a Shia by faith and when Shah Ismail Safari ascended the Iranian throne in 1501 Sultan Quli introduced the Shiah Khutbah in his dominions. Thus Shiahism became the state religion of this dyasty.

Appointed Governor of Telangana in 1495, Sultan Quli extended his dominions and ruled over the Telugu country till 1541. A devoted Muslim, he fought with frenzy in reducing the power of the local chieftains but he was by no means a missionary. He did not feel any irresistible urge to convert the Hindus to his faith and once he subdued them he allowed the local people to rebuild their temples and follow their own form of worship, provided they agreed to pay him tribute. The people referred to him with fondness as 'Bademiya'. He was the first Qutb Shahi ruler to adopt Telugu as a state language.

Sultan Quli Qutb-ul-Mulk was succeeded by his son Jamshed Quli Qutb Shah (1541–54) who in turn was succeeded to the throne by one of his brothers Ibrahim Qutb Shah (1550–80).

It was during the reign of Ibrahim Qutb Shah that the real foundation for cultural integration of Hindus and Muslims was laid.

Ibrahim, during the reign of his brother Jamshed, sought asylum in the Court of Ram Raja, the Vijayanagara ruler. True to the traditions of Indian rulers, Ram Raja not only gave Ibrahim asylum but also treated him with great honour and affection, and conferred some Jagirs on him for maintainance. He stayed at Vijayanagar for seven years. Later, after Jamshed's death, after a short interregnum, Ibrahm was invited by the nobles of Golkonda to come and ascend the throne.

When Ibrahim was returning to Golkonda, Ram Raja accompained Ibrahim upto the second stage of his journey, that is, a distance of twenty-five miles from the city of Vijayanagara and bade him a fond forewell.

But such are the exigencies of power politics that, realizing that the acquisition of the Raichur doab was absolutely necessary, Ibrahim joined the other Deccani Sultans and formed a confederacy against Rama Raja and brought about the downfall of the Vijayanagara Empire in the battle of Bannihatti or Tallikota in 1565. Rama Raja died in this battle.

During his long stay at Vijayanagara Ibrahim developed a deep attachment to Telugu literature and culture.

He married a Telugu lady, Bhaghirati by name, after whom the capital city of Golkonda was called Bhaghirati Nagaram. The contemporary Telugu poets usually referred to Golkonda as Bhaghirathi Nagar or Bhaghirati Nagaram.

Ibrahim extended great patronage to Telugu literature and gathered around him many Telugu poets and men of letters apart from Persian scholars and poets. The Telugu poets loved him and fondly referred to him as Mallik Ibharam or Vibnuram (Lord)

Ibrahim, like the Rayas of Vijayanagara and other contemporary Hindu potentates of his time, presided over literary gatherings and scholars accompanied him even during his military campaigns. Ibrahim issued several bilingual inscriptions in Persian and Telugu and these are found in several places like Koil Konda, Pangal, Rachakonda, Malkapuram and elsewhere. The local Muslim officers also issued bilingual inscriptions from this time onwards.

The first bilingual inscription in Persian and Telugu was issued even during the reign of Sultan Quli Qutb-ul-Mulk at Kondapalli in 1530.

Ibrahim was not only fond of Telugu but he also made all his six sons learn the Telugu language and literature. This knowledge of Telugu and their ability to converse in that language with the people brought the Qutb Shahi rulers closer to the people.

'Tapati Swayamvaram', a *Prabanda* written by Addanki Gangadhara Kavi, was dedicated to Ibrahim. Gangadhara Kavi was the Court poet of Ibrahim. It is from his works that one learns that Ibrahim had married the Hindu lady, Bhaghirathi, mentioned above.

Several Telugu poets flocked to the Court of Ibrahim and his capital Bhaghirati Nagaram, and Ibrahim received them and bestowed on them lavish gifts and *Agraharas*. The Telugu poets changed the word Ibrahim to Ibharama and wrote several Chatu poems in his praise, some of which run in the following way:

The Rama was the King of Monkeys

The Renuka Ram (Parashu Rama) was easily excited and became
ferocious at trivial things

While the Gopika Rama (*i.e.*, Balarama, elder brother of Srikrishna)
was a credulous yadava.

It is only Ibhiram who is incomparable
and stands in his glory as a great and
Exalted King.

Most Telugu poets praised Ibrahim for his generosity in various manners: "If he smiles on hearing your poetry he is sure to give one thousand hons, and if you are invited to his court, you (the poet) are sure to be rewarded in thousands of hons. and if you are given the honour of being seated in the Sultan's darbar you will be rewarded in lakhs and if he says 'Shahbhas' you would surely be given a crore".

Ibrahim is not only remembered for his generosity but also for his broad-mindedness and forgiving nature, for restoring to his defeated foes their former wealth and lands. These qualities of Ibrahim were clearly brought out by Gangadhara Kavi, the Court Poet of Ibrahim Qutb Shah, in his work *Tapati Swayamvaranopakyanam*, An inscription at Rendu Chintala also tells us that the village of Rendu Chintala was given as a *manyam* to one Rudra Kavi. This village is still in the possession of his descendents.

Besides Addanki Gangadhara Kavi, Kandukuri Rudra Kavi, Ganesh Kavi, Mariganti Singaracharya and several other Telugu poets enjoyed the patronage of Ibrahim, besides, of course, Persian scholars and poets. Ibrahim's elder brother Jamshed Qutb Shah was a poet in his own right. He wrote ghazals and quasidas in Persian and he expressed in his works his admiration for Indian art and sculpture.

Inspired by the liberal attitude of Ibrahim Qutb Shah, his nobles also patronized the Telugu language and poetry. Prominent among such nobles was one Amin Khan the *tarafdar* of Patancheruvu. He patronized in his court Vedic scholars like Marimganti, Appalacharya, and made him the court poet. The first work produced in pure Telugu, *Yayati Charitra*, a Yakshgana, was dedicated to Amin Khan by Ponnaganti Teluganna. Thus Amin Khan paved the way for the growth and development of pure Telugu works. The eldest wife of Amin Khan, popularly known as Badi Bibi, was known for the great interest she took in getting poor Brahmin girls married by giving the necessary support in cash and kind. Other wives of Amin Khan were also known for their good deeds.

Ibrahim Qutb Shah was succeeded by his son Muhammad Quli Qutb Shah (1580–1612). He was born to Bhaghirati Devi. He was a great personality known for his patronage of art, architecture and literature. He laid the foundation for the growth of the Hyderabad city: he beautified this city by laying gardens (Baghs) and fountains and took steps to make sure that water flowed through the canals in the city he had laid. Above all it.

Muhammad Quli Qutb Shah who was built Charminar (1592) the famous monument. The first state-owned hospital and college, the Darush-Shifa (1579), and the Jami Masjid (1597) were also built by him.

A poet in his own right, Muhammad Quli Qutb Shah is remembered for his patronage and evolution of the early Deccani Urdu in which he wrote several poems and ghazals. He used the pen name of Qutb Shah in his writings. His poem reveal a love for nature and all good things of life. He described in his poems the manner in which the various contemporary Hindu and Muslim festivals like Dassera, Deepavali, and Bathukamma were celebrated and how Muharram was observed. He described various flowers and birds and the day-to-day life of the people. We find him freely using local Telugu words in his poems in describing the daily routine in the life of a ryot during the rainy season. He also uses the word *chiguru* (tender leaves of the tamarind tree): mutton or *dal* or fish are cooked with *chiguru* to enhance their tastes. He also describes some typical Deccani Qutb Shahi dishes. The Qutb Shahi Sultans used to have separate establishments with Brahmin cooks to prepare local dishes like *kheer, chutneys*, pickles and other vegetarian dishes. The Sultan also describes the customs observed during marriage ceremonies.

On account of the cosmopolitan outlook of the Qutb Shahi rulers, the local Hindu population of Telangana and Rayalseena also observed the Muharram, revered the Sufi saints, and named their children as Hassan Ayye, Hussain Ayya, Mastan Ayya, Pir Ayya, Dastagir, Hussain Amma, Hassan Amma – a habit that continues even to this day.

Some of the notable poets who adorned the court of Muhammad Quli Qutb Shah and developed Deccani Urdu were Waghi and Ghawasi who later, during the reign of Abdullah Qutb Shah, the grand son of Muhammad Quli Qutb Shah, brought out a great philosophical work in prose entitled 'Sub-Qas' (1605), while another poet Ihhe: Nisheti wrote 'Phul-ban'.

Ghawasi, the poet laureate of Quli Qutb Shahi Court who continued even during the reign of Abdullah Qutb Shah, brought out three mathnavi *Saiful Mulk, Badtul Jamal Juti Nama*, and *Maina Satwanti*, the latter two on purely Indian floklore: *Juti Nama* was based on the popular. Indian fable of a Lorik and the pious Maina, while *Maina Satvanti* was based on the work *Sukha Saptati.*

The Telugu poet Sarangu Tammayya, who wrote 'Vaijayanti Vilasam', was a *Karnam* (accountant in the Golkonda city) and he greatly enjoyed the confidence of Muhammad Quli Qutb Shah.

Muhammad Quli Qutb Shah had no sons. He had only one daughter, Hyat Bakshi Begum, who was given in marriage to Sultan Muhammad, a son of Muhammad Quli Qutb Shah's brother.

So it was Sultan Muhammad Qutb Shah who succeed his uncle when he died. Sultan Muhammad Qutb Shahi's reign lasted from 1612 to 1626. Then his son Abdullah Qutb Shah succeeded him. Sultan Muhammad Qutb Shah was also a scholar and he encouraged historical writings. He laid the foundation for the Mecca Masjid. Among his several constructions was the Nabi Bagh. A pious man, he took care to preserve Telugu culture and traditions in his dominion.

The next Qutb Shahi ruler, Abdullah Qutb Shah (1626–72), was noted for the patronage he extended to learning and fine arts. It was during his period that several foreign amirs and scholars, after the destruction of the other Deccani sultanates, particularly Bijapur, at the hands of the Mughals, flocked to his Court for jobs. Sultan Muhammad, who favoured the Sunni faith, gave no encouragement to foreign nobles and preferred the local Deccanis for appointment to various posts. Abdullah, after his father's death, once again favoured the Shia faith. As the foreign nobles were mostly of Persian origin and were Shias by faith they found it congenial to settle down in Hyderabad.

This led to the growth of jealousy and rivalry between the local Deccanis and the foreign Afaquis.

Golkonda also lost its independent status by the treaty of 1636 with the Mughals and agreed to pay tribute to the Mughals. But the Qutb Shah kingdom of Golkonda was extremely rich. The loss of political power made Abdullah seek solace in literary activities, by holding mushairas and by patronizing fine arts like music and dance. He also spent huge amounts on charities.

He strengthened his base by restoring to the Hindu chieftains on the East coast their territories that they had lost by siding with Vijayanagar. This generous act of Abdullah won for the Qutb Shahis the loyalty of these chieftains.

Abdullah Qutb Shah, the son of Hayat Bakshi Begum, was a great poet in Deccani Urdu. He also patronized dance and music. When the great Telugu *vaggeyakara Kshetrayya* visited his court and composed some musical verses in honour of Abdullah, he was received cordially and shown much honour. The bilingual inscriptions and his Telugu inscriptions found in the Krishna district reveal that Abdullah gave several *Agraharas* to Vedic scholars and Sanskrit pandits. Gananath Pandit and Tulasi Murti were the two Telugu scholars in his court. Inscriptions of Abdullah have also been found in the Karnataka and Tamil areas of the Qutub Shahi dominoins.

Apart from Waghi and Ghawasi, the other notable scholars during the reign of Abdullah Qutb Shah were Nizam-ud-din Ahmed who wrote the Hadiqatul salatin. Allama Ibne Ahmad Khatoon wrote *Kitabul Arshad* pertaining to Jamai Abbasi. A Persian Encychopaedia was compiled by Muhammad Hussain.

Abdullah Qutb Shah had no sons. He had three daughters, of whom the eldest was married to the Mughal prince Muhammad Sultan in 1636 under the Deed of submission in 1636. It was agreed that Prince Muhammed Sultan would succeed Abdullah but as prince, Sultan Muhammed incurred the wrath of this father Aurangzeb and was put in prison along with his wife. The prince died in prison and his wife, the princess of Golkonda, is also presumed to have died in imprisonment.

The second daughter was married to Mirza Nizamuddin Ahmed of Mecca, while the third daughter was married to Abul Hasan Qutb Shah, popularly known as Tana Shah. A disciple of Shah Raju, Abul Hassan Qutb Shah (1672–87) was the last of the Qutb Shah ruler. It was during his reign that Aurangzeb finally conquered Golkonda in 1627 and made it an integral subah of the Mughal Empire. Abul Hasan was taken prisoner and was imprisoned in the Daulatabad fort where he died in 1699–1700.

Like his predecessors Abul Hasan was also a scholar and was known for his patronage to Telugu scholars and poets.

Abul Hasan came to the throne with the help of the Deccani nobles and officers led by Syed Muzaffar who was made the Mirjumla by the Sultan. Another partisan of Abul Hasan, Mustafa Hakim Khan under the name of Nekham Khan was made the governor of Chengalpat. Other important nobles who supported Abul Hasan against Mirza Nizamuddin Ahmed were Maski Miyan, Mohammad Ibrahim Khalimullah and Musakhan who was given the title of Khan-i-Khan.

Syed Muzaffar became very arrogant, after becoming the Mirjumla. He was jealous of Musakhan, the governor of Karnataka. So he recalled him from Karnataka and made him a *peishkar*, while Namdha Khan was sent as the *subedar* of Karnataka. Seeing the arrogant behaviour and corrupt practices of Syed Muzaffar, Abul Hasan replaced him by Madanna Pandit as the Mirjumla and Prime Minister in the year 1674. The appointment of Madanna as the Prime Minister was a unique event in the history of Golkonda. It speaks eloquently of the broad-mindedness of the Golkonda rulers and particularly of Abul Hasan.

It was not uncommon for the Qutb Shahi rulers to appoint Hindus, particularly Brahmins, as ministers and Mazumdars. In fact the poet Sarangu Tammayya, the writer of *Vaijayyanti Vilasamu*, says that he was the *karnam* of Golkonda and was on good terms with Qutb-ul-Mulk, the first Qutb Shah ruler.

Indapurela Narayan Raju, a Niyogi Brahmin, was a Mazumdar (1612–26) under the Qutb Shah rule and he was well known to Hyat Bakshi Begum, while Nebati Krishnamatyudu was a minister under Muhammed Quli Qutb Shah.

In fact the appointment of Hindus as ministers was on the increase from the time of Abdullah Qutb Shah. Hayat Bakshi Begum, the mother of Abdullah Qutb Shah, always consulted Hindu ministers and went by their advice so much so that, according to Thevenot, there was a rumour that she was a Hindu and a Brahmin by birth and it was due to her influence that Brahmins were being appointed as ministers and to other important posts in the administration.

But though there were several Hindu ministers who preceded Madanna, none had the honour of becoming a Prime Minister. This honour goes to Madanna alone. He assumed the prime ministership under the title of Surya Prakash Rao.

Madanna was a shrewd and strong administrator. He first tried to establish good relations with the Mughals by paying off the arrears of *Peshcush* due to the Mughal Emperor under the Ahadnama of 1636. He also made Abul Hasan send costly presents to Aurangzeb with a petition to review the relations between the two kingdoms, in reply to which Aurangzeb sent an imperial *farman* reiterating the subordinate position of Golkonda Kingdom.

Madanna, who realized that the possibility of Mughal invasion of the Deccan hung like the sword of Damocles over the heads of the Deccani Sultans, fortified all the forts in the Qutb Shahi dominions, particularly the great fortress of Kondapalli, so that the Sultan might transfer his royal treasury in case of necessity.

He evern made the Sultan visit the fortress of Kondapalli with a view to letting him realise the strategic importance of it. This fortress lay on the Vijayawada route that served as a link between the Sultan at Golkonda and the East Coast chieftains who were now loyal supporters of the Sultan.

Also, to make himself secure and have a good grip over the administration, Madanna promoted several of his relatives to high positions.

He made his elder brother Akkanna the minister in charge of armed forces, and later the Qutb Shahi Resident at Bijapur, while a nephew, Venkanna, was made a commandant of the Qutb Shahi army under the title of Rustam Rao. Another nephew, Podili Linganna, was appointed as the *tarafdar* of Poonamalil and later made the governor of Karnataka. Yet another nephew, Gopanna, well known in history as Bhakta Ramdar, was made the *tehsildar* of Bhadrachallam.

Through his nephew Podili Linganna, Madanna maintained a strict control over the English East India Company affairs at Madras. He also tried to improve the financial position of the state by avoiding wasteful expenditure and he took care to avoid oppressing the ryots unduly.

Madanna prompted the Sultan to tour his dominions during the years 1674, 1676, 1678 in the coastal regions of Karnataka and Madras so that he could familiarize himself with the latest developments in those regions. One of the major achievements of Madanna as the Qutb Shahi Prime Minister was the treaty of friendship concluded with Shivaji in 1677 making him promise to protect Golkonda from Mughal agression.

Shivaji wanted money for his Karnataka expedition, apparently to lay claim to his patrimonial share of Jagir from his step-brother Venkoji, and in return for this he agreed to protect the kingdom of Golkonda from Mughal attacks.

According to the Sabhasad Bakkar, Shivaji was received with great honour by the citizens of Golkonda with *Arti.* They displayed their happiness by painting beautiful *Rangolis* in their front courtyards.

Abul Hasan received him with great cordiality and gave him liberal financial support for the Karnataka expedition. The nobles of Golkonda also entertained Shivaji with great eclat. Thus Shivaji spent a full month at Golkonda in a congenial and cordial atmosphere of hospitality extended to him by the sultans and nobles along with the people of Golkonda.

In the words of Professor Haroon Khan Sherwani, Shivaji, by his activities, not only shut off the lands acquired by the Adil Shahs from out of the ruins of Vijayanagara, but also closed the gates of South India for the Mughals. Unfortunately for the Deccani Kingdoms of Bijapur and Golkonda, Shivaji died in the year 1680.

Prince Akbar, the youngest son of Aurangzeb, rose in rebellion against his father's relying on the Rajput support. Later his flight to the court of Shambaji, the son of Shivaji, in the Deccan made Aurangzeb personally lead an expedition into the Deccan in 1682.

The existence of the two Shiah sultanates of Bijapur and Golkonda was an eyesore to Aurangzeb. So, after putting Shambaji to death, he ordered his son Prince Azam to lay seige to Bijapur in 1685 and the sultanate of Bijapur fell into the hands of the Mughals on 13 September 1686. This naturally led Aurangzeb to turn his attention to Golkonda. Moreover, letters of Abul Hasan to his ambassadar promising military help to Bijapur fell into the hands of Aurangzeb. So he ordered his son prince Muazzam to invade Golkonda and he placed substantial Mughal army at his disposal.

Here at the Golkonda court the rivalry between the foreign nobility and the Deccanis became acute. The rise of Madanna to prominence was resented by the foreigners and this group was supported by two of the Begums of Abul Hasan whose corrupt financial dealings were brought to an end by Madanna. To add fuel to the fire Madanna's dismissal of even local Deccani Muslims from power roused the ire of the Deccanis also, but they carefully concealed their feelings and waited for a suitable opportunity to get even with Madanna.

The foreign nobility of Golkonda poisoned the ears of Aurangzeb against Madanna who at this time as Prime Minister was looking after the external affairs while his elder brother Akkanna was looking after the internal security and Home affairs.

Aurangzeb could not tolerate Madanna enjoying such a predominant position in Golkonda affairs, and so he dispatched prince Muazzam to invade Golkonda.

The Mughal forces laid seige to Malkhed. Madanna sent Khalilullah Khan, his nephew Rustam Rao to take up positions at Malkhed. This was called the first battle of Malkhed and in this Golkonda armies had the upper hand.

The Emperor, when he heard about this, was highly displeased and conveyed his displeasure to Prince Muazzam, which made the Prince enhance his efforts at the campaign leading to the second battle of Malkhed in which the Qutb Shahi army was pushed back because some of the disgruntled Qutb Shahi generals left the battle-field steathily for Hyderabad without giving a fight and the Mughals reached the capital by the beginning of October 1686. Some of the Deccani generals like Khalilullah Khan and Muhammad Ibrahim went over to the Mughals, followed by a general looting of the Hyderabad city.

Prince Muazzam now sent an ultimation to Abdul Hassan Qutb Shah, directing that he should immediately dismiss Madanna and Akkanna from their service, cede Ramgir and Sadem parganahs to the Mughals and pay to them the arrears of *peishcush*, amounting to one crore hons.

Abul Hasan Qutb Shah was completely upset at the turn of events and became demoralized. Yet it must be said to the credit of the Sultan that he did not dismiss Madanna.

At this juncture Madanna advised the Sultan to retire to Kondapalli from where he could easily procure the assistance of the East Coast cnieftains who were loyal to the Qutb Shahi Sultans. But Abul Hasan, disregarding this well intentioned advice of Madanna took refuge in the fort of Golkonda which enabled the Mughals to encircle him completely. Then, on 16 March 1686, while Madanna and Akkanna were returning to their residence after attending on Abul Hassan Qutb Shah, they were attacked by the disgruntled foreign elements and murdered. Madanna's head was cut off and sent to Prince Muazzam who in turn sent it on 3 November 1686 to Aurangzeb who was camping at Sholapur. From Sholapur the Emperor reached Bidar on the 26 and was at Golkonda by 8 January 1687.

The death of Madanna and Akkanna led to the plundering of the city. According to Bhimsen, the author of *Tarikhi Dilkasha*, Madanna's house was looted, even the doors of his house were removed. His nephew, Rustam Rao, was killed. His house was set on fire and all the inmates including the children were killed mercilessly. The death of Madanna demoralized Abul Hasan so much and he was so struck with sorrow that he behaved in an abnormal manner.

The seige of Golkonda continued from 8 January 1687 to 24 November 1687 when at last the fort fell into the hands of the Mughal Emperor through treachery. Abul Hasan was sent to Doulatabad. He died as a prisoner in the Doulatabad fort during 1699–1700.

Thus the Golkonda dominions were subjugated by the Mughals.

Abul Hassan Qutb Shah was a man of letters and a scholar with a broad vision. He was responsible for the growth and preservation of the typical Andhra style of dancing known as Kuchipudi form, for the development of which he gave the *Agrahara* of Kuchipudi in the Krishna district, to the Kuchipudi Brahmin artists who have preserved this traditional form of dance till today.

Another notable act of Abul Hasan which shows how completely free he was from religious bias and how broad his approach to religion was concerns the building of the Bhadrachalam Sri Rama temple.

Gopanna, the nephew of Madanna, was the *Tehsildar* of Bhadrachalam. Gopanna was an ardent devotee of Sri Rama. So he diverted the revenues of Bhadrachalam to the construction of the Sri Rama temple and making of costly jewellery the idols of Rama, Sita and Lakshmana enshrined in the temple.

For this diversion of the state revenue funds, Gopanna was put in prison at Golkonda. While in prison he composed several devotional songs in praise of Sri Rama which are known as Bhatla Ramdas Kirtanas.

It is said that taking pity on the sufferings of Ramdas in jail, Rama and Lakshmana went to Abul Hasan in the guise of servants of Ramdas and paid him the money due to the state. The fact is that Abul Hasan freed Gopanna from jail, and the latter became a full-time devotee of Sri Rama.

From that time onwards Abul Hassan gave several *Agraharas* for the maintenance of Bhadrachalam Sri Rama Temple. He also started the practice of sending precious pearls and costly presents to the deities at Bhadrachalam on the Rama Navami day when the marriage of Rama is celebrated. The pearls sent by the Sultan were used as Akshtalu to be showered on the dieties during the marriage ritual. This practice of sending precious pearls to Bhadrachalam on the Rama Navami day was continued by the Nizams of Hyderabad who also gave lands for the maintainance of the temple. Even now the State of Andhra Pradesh sends precious pearls either through the Chief Minister or the Endowment Minister, thus respecting the tradition set up by Abul Hasan Qutb Shah.

The Qutb Shahi rulers identified themselves with the Telugu-speaking people of their state and took pride in the cultural traditions of the people. True to Telugu tradition, the Qutb Shahi rulers from the time of Ibrahim Qutb Shah wore over their usual dress, across their shoulders, an *uttariyam* made of Himroo Silk.

The noble ladies of the Qutb Shahi court evolved a typical dress that resembled a saree, with the *dupatta* about four and a half yards long tucked with plaits into the pyjama.

Commenting on the Qutb Shahi nobles Thevenot writes: ‘All who have any considerable pay whether Moors or gentiles imitate the gentiles’. The Hindus of this period also wore Muslim dress and cultivated Muslim etiquete and manners. They also learnt Arabic and Persian. And Sufi leaders of this period not only learnt the local language but also Sanskrit.

Shah Akbar, son of Shah Raju, the spiritual preceptor of Abul Hasan, translated into Sanskrit the Telugu work on *Alankara Shastra* by Rangasayi called *Sringara Manjari.*

People in general lived in harmony with one another. Since Telangana in particular has no big rivers whose water the people could use for irrigation, the Qutb Shahi rulers dug huge tanks and encouraged irrigation using water from such tanks. These tanks were connected with one another and to the river Krishna at Pangal by the Dasabandha system of irrigation. They also preserved the ecology and maintained the greenary in their dominions by laying beautiful gardens.

The Qutb Shahis ruled over a large area comprising the entire state of Andhra Pradesh and parts of Karnataka and Tamil Nadu which included Madras.

The entire east coast of the Qutb Shahi kingdom starting from Masalipatam was dotted with textile guilds that supplied cloth to Africa, South East Asia and West Asia, and later, with the Establishment of the French and the British East India Companies to Europe as well.

The Qutb Shahi kingdom was known the world over for its diamond mines, steel, indigo, and shippping industries apart from the textile industries.

The country and its rulers were rich. Above all, rulers endeared themselves to the people and the people loved their rulers. Though it is some hundreds of years ago that the Qutb Shahs ruled over Andhra country the people still cherish their memory with love and respect.

SEVENTEEN ❖ Diversity, Heterogeneity and Integration: An Ideological Perspective

K. S. SINGH

IT IS NOT EASY to write on the theme 'We have lived together', as the media tells us almost every-day of violence, conflict, and tension among different sections of our people. And yet underlying such stories, are the complex and vibrant patterns of day-to-day interaction among groups, of their interdependence and linkages, and of living together. This paper starts with the delineation of existing ethnographic scenario covering all types of, ecological, genetic, linguistic and cultural, aspects, and the heterogeneity of groups, particularly religious groups. The paper then discusses the rooted-ness of groups in various eco-cultural niches, the processes of interdepend-ence in day-to-day life, leading to a large measure of integration of groups. Against the background of this ethnographic configuration the paper dis-cusses the ideological question, syncretism, composite culture, the freedom struggle and the post-colonial perspectives on diversity, autonomy and integration.

I

Few regions in the world have such a range of diversities as the Indian subcontinent, particularly India as it is constituted today has. There is an extraordinary range of diversities in terms of biological, linguistic and cultural traits among the people of India. Genetically, most of the Indians are a highly mixed people. The morphological and genetic variation among populations, it is stated, occurs more within a community than between communities. There are as many as 325 community-specific languages and dialects belonging to five language families and 25 scripts are in use. There are as many as 2795 communities and about 80,000 segments, synonyms, titles and surnames.

The Constitution of India categorizes most of the people in terms of the Scheduled Tribes, the Scheduled Castes, the Other Backward Classes, and the religious and linguistic minorities. Cutting across these categories are also religious, occupational groups, situated in rural and urban locations. At one level the communities are projected as homogeneous, as they also perceive themselves sharing many a common trait. But such groups are also heterogeneous, located in various regions and rooted in local kinship systems, social practices, languages and dialects, etc. These communities including castes, tribes etc. see themselves now as political communities, engaged in the struggle for a share in regional and national power structure.

The religious communities at one level consider themselves homogeneous as they follow tenets of their religion which also lays down the social norms to be followed. Religious identities are being consolidated, as they distance themselves from one another and withdraw themselves from the shared cultural space. Even a pluralistic religion such as Hinduism is being 'semitized'. At the same time, in spite of attempts at homogenization, religious conglomerations continue to remain heterogeneous [Singh, 1992, 1998b; also see Romila Thapar, 1996].

We may now discuss the structure, composition and distribution of major religious groups. Hindu communities, 3539 in all, are spread all over the country except in Lakshadweep. Hindu society, which articulates diversities of continental dimensions, is marked by division, hierarchy and linkages. The Hindu communities show an extraordinary range of heterogeneity, genetical, morphological (being a mixed group), linguistic, and cultural. Social divisions widely exist in the form of phratry, moiety, clans, sub-castes and sub-tribes. Hierarchy with divisions exists among a quarter of the communities. In Hindu society 21.6 per cent communities place themselves at high level, 46.7 per cent at the middle level and 31.1 per cent at the low level. The notion of *varna* is integral to Hinduism, with as many as 80 per cent of the Hindu communities aware of *varna* order and a larger number (61.9 per cent) recognizing their place as Brahman (10.0 per cent), as Kshatriya (20.0 per cent), Vaishya (10.8) and as Shudra (36.9 per cent). Rootedness in local cultures explains the variation in marriage practices, including cross-cousin MBD (46.2 per cent), FSD (39.6 per cent), and uncle-niece (23.7) per cent) marriages. Sororate (junior) is practised by a larger number of communities (47.6 per cent), and sororate (senior) among a smaller number (4.2 per cent). Junior levirate preponderates. Adult marriage is now mainly practised among almost all communities, but child marriage is also reported (7.4 per cent). Monogamy is the rule (99.4 per cent) but there also exist polygyny, sororal (13.4 per cent) and non-sororal (21.8 per cent), and polyandry, fraternal (0.3 per cent) and non-fraternal (0.1 per cent). All types of families co-exist on a larger scale among the Hindus, nuclear family (89 per cent), vertically extended (48.8 per cent) and horizontally extended (11.2 per cent) families. Male equigeniture is the rule among the majority of the communities (85.0 per cent). There is also the matrilineal system, with elements of female ultimogeniture (0.2 per cent) and female equigeniture (0.5 per cent). Succession generally goes to the eldest son (96.4 per cent); in a smaller number of cases (0.3 per cent) the eldest daughter inherits, as does the youngest son (0.5 per cent) or youngest daughter (0.1 per cent) or nephew (1.1 per cent). Restrictions on exchange of water and food have been extensively relaxed but they have not disappeared entirely in villages. At one level the Hindus are consolidating themselves as a religious community with a larger measure of sharing, promoted by reformists and activists and facilitated by education and communication.

The Muslim communities (584) are distributed over almost all states, in the following order: Uttar Pradesh (70), Jammu and Kashmir (59), Gujarat (87), Rajasthan (44), Andhra Pradesh (38), Bihar (41), Karnataka (27) Delhi (30), Maharashtra (25), Tamil Nadu (23), Madhya Pradesh (26), West Bengal (21), Himachal Pradesh (19), Kerala (10) and Pondicherry (10); in Lakshadweep, Assam, Haryana and Chandigarh (7 each); in Andaman & Nicobar Islands, Tripura and Daman & Diu (3 each); in Nagaland and Orissa (2), and in Manipur, Sikkim, Goa, Dadra & Nagar Haveli (one each). Even though the Muslims uniformly share the tenets of their faith, they are rooted in various ecological niches and cultural systems. The Muslim communities are also thus heterogeneous and differ from one another in biological, linguistic and cultural traits. The Muslims are mainly situated in rural-urban situations (253) followed by those living exclusively in rural (203) and urban (103) settings. Five Muslim communities such as Watal, Lalbegi, Madari / Kalander claim the status of the scheduled castes and 19 communities have been returned as the scheduled tribes. Of the total number of Muslim communities, a very large number, 60.8 per cent, have migrated to their present habitat, in recent years. While Urdu has been returned as the mother tongue by a majority of the Muslims, 46.27 per cent of the Muslims have also returned the scheduled / regional languages as their mother tongues. Social divisions among Muslims exist on a relatively smaller scale in the form of clans (22.4 per cent), sects (9.4 per cent), subcastes (10.6 per cent), bands and subtribes. Hierarchy with social divisions also exists. Differentiation is reported at social, economic, religious (sects), occupational and territorial levels. Egalitarianism in the domain of religion is a well-known feature of Muslim society. However, stratification exists; a relatively small segment of Muslim communities (15.6 per cent) perceive themselves as occupying high positions, most of them (58.6 per cent) see themselves at middle level and a smaller percentage at low level (28.85 per cent). While the norm of community endogamy operates among most of the Muslim communities, there are various levels of exogamy, such as clan exogamy (9.6 per cent), even gotra exogamy (6.7 per cent), village exogamy (7.2 per cent), and surname exogamy (3.9 per cent). Hypergamy is reported on a smaller scale (3.6 per cent), even hypogamy (1.2 per cent). It is obvious that some of the Muslim communities are rooted in local kinship system. The same is true of marriages. While parallel cousin marriages both FBD and MSD are widely practised (68.7 per cent and 65.8 per cent respectively). as per the Shariat, there are Muslim communities who prefer cross-cousin to parallel cousin marriage. The Assamese Muslims avoid both cross-cousin and parallel-cousin marriage while Meos, Tadvi, Nahal avoid parallel cousin marriage. Clan exogamy is reported from Rajput Muslims and some other converted higher groups (Siddiqui, 1993). The incidence of cross-cousin FSD is higher (81.2 per cent), as is of cross-cousin MBD (2.5 per cent) particularly in the southern states. Interestingly, both junior sororate (50.5 per cent) and senior sororate (7.4 per cent) are practised. Junior levirate also prevails (37.0 per cent); so dos senior levirate (8.9 per cent). Child marriage is allowed (7.7 per cent), and, on a smaller scale, with *gauna* (2.7 per cent). Marriage by negotiation is the common mode of acquiring mate among the majority of the communities (97.9 per cent). The other modes of acquiring mate practised by them are by exchange (20.2 per cent), by mutual consent (18.7 per cent), by elopement (2.2 per cent), by service (1.7 per cent), by purchase (0.9 per cent) – mostly among the 'tribalised groups' – and so on. The marriage symbols shared by Muslims with non-Muslims include wearing bangles (26.2 per cent), nose stud / pin (19.5 per cent), toe-ring (14.6 per cent), tali / mangalsutra (11.5 per cent), vermilion (9.1 per cent), finger ring (8.6 per cent), ear ring (6.8 per cent), nose ring (10.6 per cent) and bindi in 4.8 per cent communities. Occupationally, the Muslims are more heterogeneous than any other religious community. While land is the economic resource for many, a majority of them are landless (48.5 per cent). A smaller number depends on fishing (5.5 per cent) and on forest resources (6.3 per cent). A majority of Muslim communities are self-employed (49.1 per cent) engaged in occupations such as business (52.4 per cent) and trade (19.7 per cent). A few are employed in government service (58.2 per cent) or in private service (45.0). Various other occupations in which they are engaged include horticulture (2.9 per cent), sericulture (0.9 per cent), industry (9.1 per cent), industrial work (16.3 per cent), textile weaving (5.3 per cent), textile dyeing (2.1 per cent), masonry (6.8 per cent), woodwork (4.5 per cent), skin and hidework (2.1 per cent), metalwork (2.6 per cent), basket making 2.2 per cent), mat weaving (2.1 per cent), specialized service (5.0 per cent), skilled (14.6 per cent) and non-skilled labour (20.4 per cent) and so on. A professional middle class is emerging among the Muslims which plays a critical role in building up modern intercommunity linkages. This consists of entrepreneurs / businessmen (62.7 per cent communities), scholars including students (26.2 per cent), white-collar employees (52.9 per cent), teachers (52.2 per cent), administrators (28.9 per cent), engineers / doctors (34.6 per cent), village panchayat leaders (30.1 per cent), regional leaders (22.3 per cent) and so on.

The Christian communities are also heterogeneous like other communities, as they are drawn from various socio-religious backgrounds, and from various categories of groups such as the scheduled castes and scheduled tribes and 'other' communities in various regions. Generally, a great many pre-conversion practices survive among the Christians who share a good deal with non-Christian communities. The Christian communities (339) are distributed mainly in the southern states such as Tamil Nadu (65), Andhra Pradesh (29), Karnataka (22), Kerala (13), and in the north-eastern states such as Assam, Arunachal Pradesh (23), Manipur (23), Nagaland (19), Mizoram (15), and Meghalaya (15). They also live in Tripura (12), West Bengal (10), Maharashtra (14), Andaman & Nicobar Islands (9), Orissa (7), Goa (6), Bihar and Madhya Pradesh (5 each) and so on. Social divisions survive among most of them (76.1 per cent), such as phratry (15), moiety (9), clan 190 (56 per cent), and lineages 106 (31.3 per cent). There are sub-castes (9) and sub-tribes (23) among these communities. Hierarchy with social divisions exists among a large number. Most of the Christian communities are endogamous (95.3 per cent). Various levels of exogamy operate, clan exogamy 165 (48.7 per cent), even gotra exogamy 19 (5.6 per cent), surname exogamy 58 (17.1 per cent) and village exogamy 29 (8.6 per cent). Monogamy is the norm; however sororal polygyny (15.0 per cent) and non-sororal polygyny (23.3 per cent) are also practised. Among marriage symbols tali / mangalsutra is widely worn among a large number of communities (45.4 per cent) followed by the more popular finger-ring (30.4 per cent), vermilion (82, 24.2 per cent), toe-ring (79, 23.3 per cent), etc. There is now a wide range of occupational diversification. Some of the traditional occupations have relatively declined. Many Christian communities, mostly tribals, were engaged in hunting and gathering (29.8 per cent) which has partly declined (18 per cent); similarly fishing has declined from 101 to 86 per cent today. The communities engaged in trapping of birds and animals (43) have mostly abandoned this occupation, only 16 communities are now engaged in it. On the other hand communities traditionally engaged in horticulture (27) have increased to 49. Similarly, more of the Christian communities are now engaged in the occupations such as liquor manufacture (4.7 per cent), shifting cultivation (25.1 per cent), terrace cultivation (13.9 per cent), settled cultivation (55.8 per cent) and animal husbandry (32.4 per cent). A good number of Christian communities are also engaged in various other occupations such as business (51.9 per cent), trade (24.5 per cent), industry (10.9 per cent), government service (81.7 per cent), private service (58.7 per cent), textile spinning (4.4 per cent), textile weaving (19.5 per cent), etc. A small number of them are engaged in masonry, pottery, woodwork, salt making, skin and hidework, ivory, bone and horn-work, metalwork, etc., ranging from 1 to 5 per cent. A good number of Christian communities have returned basket making (20.9 per cent), mat weaving (8.6 per cent), specialised service (5.9 per cent), skilled labour (18.9 per cent) and non-skilled labour (35.1 per cent) as their occupations. More Christian communities are engaged in the above occupations compared to the percentage of all other religious communities. The Christian communities have reported a much higher proportion of inter-community linkages and exchange, including inter-community marriage (52). A progressive religious community, they favour education for boys (88.2 per cent) but a relatively large number of communities favour education for girls (78 per cent). Though boys are favoured for higher education, a relatively large number of communities prefer high level of education for girls as well.

There are one hundred and thirty Sikh communities living in Punjab (39), Delhi (20), Chandigarh (15), Haryana (17), Jammu & Kashmir (5), Uttar Pradesh (5), Himachal Pradesh (8), Rajasthan (4), Andhra Pradesh (3), Maharashtra (3), Assam (2), West Bengal (2) and so on. In spite of the stress on egalitarianism in Sikhism the caste system exists, and social divisions are reported (90.0 per cent) in the form of clan (76.9) per cent), sects (12.3 per cent) and subcastes (22.3 per cent). Hierarchy with social divisions is returned (26.9 per cent against 22.6 per cent). Differentiation is reported at social, economic, occupational and territorial levels. There is a perception of the three-tier hierarchy. Fifty three (40.8 per cent) communities perceive themselves as placed high, 45.4 per cent at the middle level and 13.8 per cent as placed low. A majority of Sikh communities have land as their economic resource, but a very large number are landless. They are engaged in settled cultivation (31 per cent), in labour (37.7 per cent), animal husbandry, industry, trade and business, government service, private service and self employment which is as high as 64.6 per cent against the national average of 52.0 per cent. They are reported in small numbers in other occupations such as fishing, textile weaving, masonry, woodwork, skin and hidework, basket making, skilled labour, and non-skilled labour.

The Buddhist communities (93), which constitute two per cent of all communities, are mainly distributed in Arunachal Pradesh (18), Assam (11), Uttar Pradesh (9), West Bengal (7), Himachal Pradesh (6), Jammu & Kashmir (6), Delhi (4), Andhra Pradesh (3) and so on. Most of the Buddhist communities belong to the scheduled tribes, and share the tribal characteristics. The neo-Buddhists, another important segment of the Buddhist community, consist of such groups as Mahars, Jatav, etc., who are imbued with Baba

Saheb B.R. Ambedkar's ideology stressing equality and self-respect and have pushed forward in the arena of politics and development.

The Jain communities, one hundred in all, are distributed mainly in the central and western states such as Madhya Pradesh (18), Maharasthra, Rajasthan and Gujarat (13), and sporadically in Punjab (2), Bihar (3), Uttar Pradesh (2), Himachal Pradesh (2), and even in the states of Nagaland, Meghalaya, Assam, Jammu & Kashmir, West Bengal, Andhra Pradesh, Pondicherry, Daman and Diu, Haryana and Chandigarh. They are mostly located in rural-urban situations (58), followed by their exclusive settlement in urban areas (34). A small number of them (8) also live in rural areas. Almost all of them are pure vegetarian (95 per cent against national average of 16.05 per cent). Social divisions exist among Jain communities in the form of clan (76), lineage (28), sects (16), and subcastes (38). Hierarchy with social divisions is reported among 28 communities. Differentiation operates at social (53), sectarian (26), occupational level (14), and so on. Most Jain communities (70.0 per cent) perceive themselves as placed at high and only a few at middle level. The Jains share the kinship structure of the area they are located in. Community endogamy is the norm. In the north and the west, the Jains practise cross-cousin marriages, FSD (14.0 per cent) and MBD (15) and uncle-niece marriage (6) Sororate junior is allowed (44.0 per cent) and levirate junior is in vogue in a few communities (5 per cent). The Jains are mainly engaged in business (89.0 per cent), trade (63.0 per cent), and industry (30.0 per cent). Thirty-two communities depend on land as their economic resource. Nineteen communities are mainly landowning. Forty-one of them (41.0 per cent) are engaged in settled cultivataion.

The Jains have now rapidly moved into government service (90.0 per cent), alongside of private service (66.0 per cent), and self-employment (63 per cent). A few of them are in textile weaving (3), textile dyeing (2), woodwork, glass work, jewellery making, etc. While elsewhere the Jains are traders and businessmen, entrepreneurs and merchants, the Jains in Karnataka traditionally are mainly peasant and artisan groups (Singh, 1992, 1998b).

II

The preceding discussion on diversities and on heterogeneity of religious groups, who generally project themselves as monolithic, sets the background of the discussion of the structures of interrelationship – and a few have been indicated above – of interaction at work among all groups. This is best seen at the regional level in its eco-cultural linguistic dimensions. It is here again that the rootedness of most of the communities, and the sharing of cultural-linguistic tracts by them is best explored. It is here again that the various aspects of living together in spite of occasional outbursts of tension and violence, are best seen in their enduring aspects. A few of these aspects may be briefly described:

(*i*) Most of the communities (as many as 83%) are local, situated within the existing linguistic-cultural regions (Singh, 1992);

(*ii*) Many of the communities, including the Muslims, consider themselves 'relatively' indigenous and regard others being later immigrants, as outsiders or *paradeshi, mayangs, bangal*, etc., even if they all belong to the same religious group (Siddiqui, 1993);

(*iii*) Most of the communities irrespective of their religious labels, belong to the same or similar genepools, and share morphological and genetical traits (Singh, 1992; Siddiqui, 1993);

(*iv*) Most of the communities generally speak the same language / dialects within the region, and share the folklores, folk rituals, putative kinship or ceremonial friendship, etc. (Singh, 1992);

(*v*) All share elements of hierarchy in the regional system, and forms of relationships, both vertical and horizontal (Siddiqui, 1993), even though there is a difference between inter-group relationship existing among Muslims and inter-caste relationships among Hindus;

(*vi*) The Muslims and their segments are appropriately ranged within the regional heirarchy of Communities;

(*vii*) The economic interdependence of all communities of India is closely rooted in the resource endowment and resource utilization in each region of India. This inter-dependence may assume various forms of jajmani or patron-client relationship, cultivator-tenant relationship, artisan-customer relationship and so on. This is the secular form of relationship cutting across religious divisions, an interlocking of different religious / sectarian strata in the regional context that survives all riots and all attempts to disrupt them. No religious group is functionally exclusive, and all are closely intertwined in the struggle for subsistence, survival and progress (Singh, 1992);

(*viii*) Participation in one another's religio-cultural activities is high, and in all, the incidence of sharing of traits is higher than expected (Singh, 1992).

(*ix*) While 79 per cent of the Hindus do not eat pork, 54 per cent of the Muslims do not take beef (con) and only 52 per cent eat the other beef (ox, buffalo).

Many communities of India, about 600 of them according to one estimate, are divided into religious segments. The Hindu-Sikh, Hindu-Jain, Hindu-Buddhist and Hindu-Tribals share commensal and connubial relationship – across religious divisions.

The Hindu-Muslim segments of the same lineage do not have connubial (in case of inter-marriage, they convert) or commensal relationship, but have other close links. In a cluster of villages, called Sathe, *i.e.* sixty villages lying within a 100 k.m. stretch in Ghaziabad district of Uttar Pradesh, the Hindu and Muslim segments of Chauhan lineage continue to share a unique relationship.

Some of our brothers became Muslims while the others remained Hindus. All the same, we are from the same family. Our ancestors were one, 'says Faiz Mukkadam'. . . .

The social lives of the two communities in the area are intertwined. When Ram Kali was asked to sing at the wedding in a Muslim family, she did not hesitate even for a moment as she started on *bhaiya Reghubir bhaat saware laiyo* (oh brother dear who is so like Lord Rama, bring beautiful presents when you come). Soon the strain was picked up by the women of the family. To them it did not matter that Rama was not their god. Ram Kali also relates how the Muslim women sang *Allah Allah kar ke to ye din aya, dulhan ne naya shringar rachaya* (it is by taking the name of Allah that this day has arrived and the bride has been adorned) during the wedding festivities of her daughter.

When a child is born, be it in a Muslim or a Hindu house, the words of the traditional song *tere angana mein kehlay Nandlala* (in your courtyard plays Lord Krishna) waft across the village along with the beat of the *dholak*. 'We sing the same songs; some of our ceremonies are also similar.

Everyone in the village takes part in weddings and festivites in every home', says Ram Kali. . . .

'Our style of living, dressing, weddings and other celebrations are almost the same. We hardly feel any difference. In fact, we also face the evil of dowry as the Hindus do', adds Sarvari, of a nearby village.

In the nearby hut, Kaneez is a trifle surprised when asked whether she invites Hindus to her family festivities. 'Of course, they are our relatives. We just take special care to cook separately for them because they are vegetarians. Those who are not, eat with us. We also take part in the festivities in their houses.'

Even the village temple is not out of bounds for the Muslims. Muslim children can be seen playing with their Hindu mates in the temple premises while worship goes on. Adjacent to the temple is the hut of a Muslim family. . . .

'How can we forget that we are the same blood? As long as we remember this and pass it on to our children, we will continue to live as brothers', says Mehar Ali (Saksena, Rashmi 1994).

The scholars have generally noticed that the traditionally shared cultural space is shrinking and the secularized space is growing as more and more people interact in the secular sphere. The Muslims who were very much like Hindus in many parts of the country at the beginning of the colonial period, as stated in colonial ethnography, began to look less similar as religious identities were emphasized. Islamization and *tablighi* movements stressed separateness. And yet, as the People of India project shows, in spite of sharpening of religious identities, the communities continue to share a great deal (see Singh, 1992) and their interaction in the secular sphere is growing. Stratification has survived Islamization (Zarine Bhatty 1997), as have norms of clan exogamy, cross cousin marriages among many Muslim communities (Siddiqui, 1979, 1991). The Muslims follow the rules of gotra exogamy, adopt Hindu titles or surnames, sing the same songs at life-cycle ceremonies, share the style of living, dressing, etc. There are Sathes in every corner of India.

The folklores of almost every part of India reflect a synthesis, an effortless, spontaneous intermingling of various streams. There are, no doubt, references to conflicts arising out of animosities, but towards the end of the story, all is well, all ends in harmony. Folk mind cannot stand confrontation for long. In western Madhya Pradesh and Rajasthan, Pirs blessed the founding of kingdoms by Hindu princes. Similarly, the oral epic of Devnarayan recited by the pastoral and farming communities of the Gujars, commemorates inter-caste conflict and also re-union – the Rajput chief and Gujars became dharm-brothers – the simultaneous kinship and conflict between the Gujars and Rajputs (Malik, Aditya). A similar stand of conflicts and reunion runs through many an oral tradition in different parts of the country.

The various sects in India have not only quarrelled among themselves but also closely interacted. Many medieval sects preached egalitarianism, attacked the caste system and advocated understanding and tolerance. In spite of the "polemical character" of the preachings of some of the founders of the modern sects, they too were influenced by each other, and showed a measure of respect and understanding in day-to-day dealings. There was never a time when diversity of perceptions did not exist within a religious system, even as the theologians tried to grapple with the pluralistic situation. Among the various Islamic sects in northern India are the numerically preponderant Barelvi sect which are the least critical of the little tradition in the customary practices of Muslims, as against the Deobandhis who are moderate reformists and critical of traditional elements and others who stand for purging Muslim society of extra Islamic customs (Siddiqui, 1993).

A contemporary movement, known as *Swadhyaya* or 'Study of the Self' currently underway in 12000 to 15000 villages in 12 *states* in India based on the philosophy and teachings of Panduranga Shastri Athwale or Dadaji, has addressed many aspects of social problems, such as inequality, and advocated rural development with the exploitation and enlargement of indigenous resources for the benefit of all. For our purposes, it is interesting to note that it has brought together communities divided by religion and social inequality.

The village of Hehrala in district Junagarh, Gujarat, is completely *Swadhyayi*. It comprises 40 households of Karodia Rajupts, 70 households of Harijans, and 10 households of Siddi Muslims. It had a history of discrimination against Koli Harijans and Siddi Muslims. Says Mangal Bhai, leader of the Siddi Muslims: 'We were being treated like animals, in fact a little worse. We had no rights, no dignity, no power and perhaps no life in human terms. With the coming of *Swadhyay*, all this is a thing of the distant past. There is no discrimination of any kind now, no exploitation, no quarrels, no strife and no dissent. We are all one, all children of the same god. We Siddis regularly come to the *amritalay* (temple). We have helped to build it. Likewise, our mosque was built by Hindus' (Sinha, B.K, 1998).

That syncretism is not a medieval relic, and not dying, was brought home by Saeed Naqvi's serial, *Hamari Virasat*, telecast on Doordarshan. This serial meticulously collected and vividly demonstrated the known and the not so well known living traditions of syncretism in which Hindus and Muslims interact closely at many shrines. Spread far and wide, these shrines and the practices in vogue there still continue to bear testimony to the strength of syncretism. The various streams of Bhakti, Sufism, Tantra blend in rural India. In western India the blending of these streams reached its culmination in Shirdi Sai Baba cult. In the Barak valley in Assam, the Shah Pir has a niche in every Kalibari. The story goes that the Sufis came from Silchar, exorcised witchcraft which was and is still rampant, preached Islam in local language, and showed tolerance and understanding towards mother goddess cults; on their part, the followers of these cults also showed an understanding and tolerance towards Sufism.

III

The ethnographic scenario of diversity and heterogeneity and the structure of interdependence, sharing and linkages existing among the people in various regions are now overlaid, even obscured by an acrimonious ideological debate on the nature of the identities of our people, the relationship of communities, their status and rights, being articulated in essentially religious idioms. All over the world fundamentalism is on the rise, in all religions. In this country, all religious communities who shared the common space and built up a shared heritage have now been emphasizing their separate identities, promoting their consolidation, distancing themselves from one another and seeking to protect their rights and privileges. There is very little understanding now of how religions in this country have been known to have shared the ideas of all religions being positive, equal, similar in their basics. This was emphasised in the course of the freedom struggle and the Indian renaissance but now appears to be a romantic dream. Similarly, culture – which is larger than religion – is being focused as distinct from one another. The very notion of composite culture is being questioned (Madan, 1998).

The concept of shared cultural traditions, of linkages that brought us together and that still bring us together in day-to-day life in our struggle for survival, is ignored. In fact, culture is no longer seen in its entirety, as it unfolds in everyday life or as it has existed through history. It was not a medieval phenomenon only. It could be traced to the very early times (Shrimali, 1998). It covered all aspects of life, in rural and urban; it permeated all strata of populations (Momin, 1998).

At the heart of all communal debates in India is the medieval factor. All discussions boil down to Hindu-Muslim relations. The medieval factor in Indian history has often been explored to define the current level of relations among religious communities. There is little doubt that there was considerable violence and bigotry in the early phase of encounters of different religions or cultures or civilizations in the ancient and medieval periods. Sectarian violence in the pre-Islamic period has now been well documented (Subramanyam, Sanjay). In the early medieval period Hindus and Buddhists, Hindus and Jains, Shaivites and Vaishnavites widely differed and often acted violently against each other and each other's institutions. Abul Fazal recounts the facets of sectarian conflict in the medieval period, and laments that the first encounter of sects was often bitter, and violent. Alberuni's first reaction to the Hindus was far from temperate. But as the conquerors and those who came with them settled down, a process of interaction with those who were there from the earlier period, began in all spheres of, administration, politics, languages, literature and art, and the medieval phenomenon of composite culture emerged. But by all accounts, bigotry and violence in India were on a relatively small scale than elsewhere, partly because a ruler tried to understand the pluralistic situation his regime was situated in, and the need to maintain a measure of harmony and social stability that was necessary for the exercise of political power (see Malik, Z.U., 1991). The medieval period was seminal in the further development of Indian civilization, particularly in matters of ideas, culture and technology, and efforts at spiritual synthesis (See Ali, Athar, 1990). One interesting aspect was the rise of vernacular languages, *bhasas,* and of the regional identities as defined by them within which were located groups of people known as *jati, kaum, kabila*, etc. Abul Fazl mentions the zamindars of the dominant lineages in various regions of Akbar's empire, which are strikingly similar to the dominent sections among the *jatis* and communities today. The second aspect was the understanding, gradually growing among the followers of Islam and Hinduism of respective religious tenets, and a tolerant attitude towards the religious susceptibilities of one another. The inscriptions of the distant 'tribal' Chero and Gond rulers open with a simultaneous invocation of both Rama and Allah. Rana Kumbha who defeated Sultan Bahadur Shah of Gujarat raised the Victory Tower which has the name Allah inscribed on the walls of one of its storeys

(Athar Ali, 1990). This mindset obviously acknowledged the existence of two religious streams, their equality, without giving up one's own identity. When the medieval period closed, it bequeathed this understanding of the pluralities at the religious level, and what is more important, a respect for each other's sensibilities. The princely states – and smaller *thikanas* and later the traditional zamindars of the colonial period – inherited from the Mughal rule some of the symbols of social harmony such as celebration of festivals and festivities, endowment of each other's religious centres, etc. The Gandhian movement and later the Bhoodan movement led by Acharya Vinoba Bhave emphasized common celebration of all religious festivals. A fresh understanding of the nature of the symbiosis of Islam and Hinduism is being attempted (Shamim, 1998).

The notion of composite culture was invoked by the nationalists in the course of the freedom struggle, and it received a boost through the writings, among others, of Mahatma Gandhi, Jawaharlal Nehru and Maulana Abul Kalam. The historian Gopal tells us of how Nehru approached this theme in the *Discovery of India.*

> The unity of India was an emotional reality rooted in history rather than a mere geographical creation or an imposed standardization of externals. Beneath the shared intellectual and cultural life among the educated was a common popular culture of philosophy, history, myth and legend. Existing traditions were respected, adapted and changed to meet new circumstances and ways of thought, and at the same time new traditions were developed. Every challenge of incursion of foreign elements was dealt with successfully by absorption and a new synthesis. Islam had come to India as a religion. Centuries before it came as a political force, it had been received with the usual tolerance. When later, the rulers happened to be Muslim, the essential unity of Indian life was not vitally affected and the new rulers rarely interfered with the ways and customs of the people. *A composite culture developed in such fields as architecture, food, dress and music. Even the two religions, Hinduism and Islam, influenced each other* (italics added by me, Gopal, 1986, p. 205).

Till about the middle of the eighteenth century, it was a 'predominantly syncretic culture', with no sense of social separateness (Bayly quoted by Gopal, 1986, p. 208). 'Communalism as a distinct phenomenon emerged only about the middle of the nineteenth century' (Gopal 1986, p. 208), as religious disputes mixed with economic antagonisms and political ambitions. The partition of the country, the riots and migration of populations seemed to have temporarily dealt a death blow to the notion of composite culture, that was the bedrock of Indian nationalism.

However, the nationalists were also aware of the existence of religious, ethnic and regional identities (*kaum*), and of their relationship. As Maulana Azad said to the Indian Muslims migrating to Pakistan, in 1947:

'You are leaving your motherland. Do you know what the consequences will be? Your frequent exoduses, such as this, will weaken the Muslims of India. A time may come when the various Pakistani regions start asserting their separate identities: Bengali, Punjabi, Sindhi, Baloch may declare themselves separate *qaums*. Will your position in Pakistan at that time be anything better than uninvited guests? The Hindu can be your religious opponent, but not your regional and national opponent. You can deal with this situation. But in Pakistan, at any time you may have to face regional and national opposition; before this kind of opposition you will be helpless' (quoted in Khushwant Singh, 'Seen on TV', *The Hindustan Times*, 21 March 1998).

Orientalism generated an enormous amount of interest in the ethnography of India. The colonial period with its ethnographic information and the Census data created taxonomic groups such as the tribes and exterior or depressed castes. The identities as Hindus, Muslims and Sikhs were sharply focused from the middle of the nineteenth century. Each group was generally represented as homogeneous and projected as a separate political community vying for a share in political power. The colonial administration patronized these groups and supported their attempts at homogenization in terms of the textual prescriptions and their elite's perceptions. One result of such consolidation of 'orthodox' groups and 'orthodox' norms was that the fluidity of social situation that marked the pre-colonial period was ignored and the diversities that characterized eco-social formulations in India were swept aside. Various communities of India had graduated to a strange mutual understanding in the eighteenth century; the symbols of communal harmony adopted by the Mughal court had percolated to the regional centres of power, the princely states, *thikanas* and petty chieftainships as mentioned above. The Hindus and Muslims had come to recognize and respect each other's religion even though there were generally no commensal and connubial relationships between them. All this changed in the colonial period, with the portrayal of these groups as autonomous, almost divested of commonalities of a composite culture that was evolving.

IV

The process of religious consolidation has proceeded apace in the post-colonial period. The international scenario is marked by the rise of religious fundamentalism and ethnic identities, and similar developments within the nation-state have continued with distancing of religious identities from one another, and blurring of the vision of composite culture. There are, no doubt, also countervailing processes at work. The movement for conservation of environment, the struggle of indigenous people, human rights issues, cutting across national boundaries have focused on ecological-cultural diversities, heterogeneity and identities. Historical and ethnographic studies undertaken in recent years have also highlighted linkages of groups, their close interaction and the roots of living together. Therefore the ideological perspective today should take into account diversities, heterogeneity of groups, the patterns of interaction, sharing and linkages that exist spontaneously, naturally and necessarily among various sections of people at all levels, in their day-to-day life. Secondly, the nation which grew out of the anti-colonial struggle, now embraces all identities, big and small, and should unequivocally stand for recognition of the equal rights of all groups that make up the nation. Understanding, tolerance and respect for each other's identity should be the nationalist credo today as it was during the freedom struggle and as it should be in the struggle to create a human and humane order.

The ideological currents and their impact apart, the collective life at the grassroot levels proceeds at its own rhythm and momentum. The interdependence of communities engaged in the struggle for existence continues, even grows in times of stress. The logic, the compulsion of living together in the local situation further explains the process of sharing and the structure of linkages existing among communities. The political analysts may see in occasional flareups an end to this idyllic ethnographic scenario, but ethnic traits survive catastrophies. The noted literatures, K.S. Duggal, during a recent visit to Pakistan to attend the wedding of a friends's son, was 'heartened' to hear the Muslim women sing:

Why do you stand under the Chandan tree, daughter?

I await for my father to tell him

It's time to look for a match.

What type of a match would you like, my daughter?

One like the moon in the stars,

And Krishna Kanhaiya among the gods (Duggal, K.S., 1997)

The nation-state of such diversities as ours, with a rich composite culture, should continue to re-emphasize and recreate symbols that hold us together, and should continue to explore areas of cooperation, understanding and tolerance among various sections of our people who, too, must understand and affirm pluralism. There is no alternative to living together.

References

*The data on diversity and heterogeneity of religious formations is mainly derived from the People of India Project (See below Singh, 1992, 1998b).

Abul Fazal, Allami, *Aini-i-Akbari*, vol. II, (tr.) H.S. Jarret and annotated by Jadunath Sarkar, ASB Calcutta, 1939.

Ali, M. Athar, 'Encounter and Efflorescence', Presidential Address, *Proceedings of the Indian History Congress*, Golden Jubilee, Gorakpur, 1990, pp. 1–17.

Basu, Kaushik and Sanjay Subrahmanyam (ed.), *Unravelling the Nation, Sectarian Conflict and India's Secular Identity*, Penguine Books, 1996.

Bayly, C.A., 'The Pre-history of Communalism, Religious Conflicts in India, 1700–1860', *Modern Asian Studies*, 1985, vol. 2, pp. 177–203.

Bhatty, Zarina, 'Social Stratification among Muslims in India' in M.N. Srivivas (ed.), *Caste: Its Twentieth Century Avatar*, Penguine Books, 1997.

Duggal, K.S., 'Indo-Pak Dialogue: Building Bridges of Understanding', *Mainstream*, 1 November 1997, pp. 7–9.

Gopal, S., 'Nehru, Religion and Secularism' in *Tradition, Dissent and Ideology, Essays in Honour of Romila Thapar*, (ed.), R. Champakalakshmi and S. Gopal, Oxford University Press, 1986, pp. 195–215.

Madan, T.N., 'Composite Culture: Inadequacies of Secular Response', *The Times of India*, 4 April 1998.

Malik, Aditya, 'Violence, Death and Marriage in the Oral Epic of Devnarayan', a paper presented at the national seminar on Rajasthan, Jaipur, 14–18 December 1994.

Malik, Z.U., 'The Core and Periphery: a Contribution to the Debate on the Eighteenth Century', *Proceedings of Indian History Congress*, Calcutta, 1991, pp. 169–99.

Momin, A.R., 'Composite Culture is not just skin-deep', *The Times of India*, 25 April 1998.

Sharma, Sri Ram, *The Religious Policy of the Mughal Emperors*, Munshiram Manoharlal Publications, 1940.

Saksena, Rashmi, 'Faithfully Yours, A unique relationship binds Hindus and Muslims of 60 villages of Uttar Pradesh', *The Week*, 13 February 1994.

Shahin, Sultana, 'Spritual Symbiosis, Links between Islam and Hinduism', *The Times of India*, 28 July 1998.

Siddiqui, M.K.A., *Hindu Muslim Relations*, Abadi Publications, Calcutta, 1993.

———, 'Islamization among the Tribes of Central and Western India', *Bulletin of the Anthropological Survey of India*, vol. XXXV, nos. 3 & 4, July-September 1779.

Shrimali, Krishna Mohan, 'Cultural Nationalism saps Culture, Nation', *The Times of India* 26 May 1998.

Singh, K.S. *People of India: An Introduction*, Anthropological Survey of India, Calcutta, 1992.

———, *Identity, Ecology, Social Organisation, Economy, Linkages and Development Processes: A Quantitative Profile*, vol. VII, People of India of India, Anthropological Survey of India / Oxford University Press, 1996.

———, *Communities, Segments, Synonyms, Surnames and Titles*, vol. VIII, *People of India*, Anthropological Survey of India / Oxford University Press, 1996.

———, 'The People of India: Diversities and Linkages', D. Balasubrahmanian and N. Appaji Rao (eds.), *The Indian Human Heritage*, University Press, Hyderabad, 1998a.

———, 'People of India: Diversities and Linkages', *The Indian Experience*, Indian Airlines, 1997

———, *India's Communities*, vols. IV to VI, *People of India*, Anthropological Survey of India / Oxford University Press, 1998b (forthcoming).

Sinha, B.K., 'The answers within', *Down to Earth*, 11 May 1998.

Srinivas, M.N., (edited and introduced), *Caste: Its Twentieth Century Avatar*, Pengine Books, 1997.

Subramanyam, Sanjay, 'Before the Leviathan: Sectarian Violence and the state in precolonial India', in Kaushik Basu and Sanjay Subramanyam, *op. cit.*

Thapar, Romila, 'The Tyranny of Labels', *Social Scientist*, vol. 24, nos. 9–10, September-October 1996, pp. 3–23.

EIGHTEEN ❖

Economic Life of the People of the Central Himalayan Region of India (1815–1947)

A. K. MITTAL

THIS PAPER SEEKS TO discuss some aspects of the economic history, of Kumaun during the British rule. The area taken up for the study includes the three hill districts of Kumaon, namely Nainital, Almora and Pithoragarh. Since British Kumaon also included parts of Garhwal, some sections of the paper have also included information about that region. The area under reference has a long history (Joshi 1988: 73–86). It came under the British rule in AD 1815 and remained under it till AD 1947. During the British period, this region was declared as 'Non-Regulated Area', and so the rules and regulations implemented here were quite different from those in the plains.

The picturesque terraces of the Himalayan slopes that greet the eyes of the traveller represent an extraordinary degree of strenuous toil which is surpassed in few regions of the world. Life is still hard here; whether we take herding in the pastures or working in the fields, they are back-breaking tasks, full of dreary monotony and unforeseen accidents.

The central Himalayas were an agricultural area and much of the economic life of the Kumaoni people depended upon the land and its cultivation. The village was almost entirely a self-sufficient unit and had very little contact with the outside world. Except for salt and spices for which they depended on the outside world, most of the needs of the people of the village were satisfied locally. A majority of the artisans were kind of servants of the village who had either their own plots of land which they held sometimes rent-free and sometimes at a reduced rent, or they received a fixed portion of the produce from every cultivator in the village. In exchange, they rendered their services to the village people free of charge throughout the year. Besides these artisans, there were a few others whose services were not required regularly and so they were not village servants. Weavers, goldsmiths, etc. and betel-sellers belonged to this class and served people on payment. All occupations were generally hereditary. Competition had no place in such an economic set-up; therefore, there was no incentive for change or improvement.

Industries

Tea, iron and other small products were the main industries of the Himalayan region during the colonial rule.

Tea Industry

Dr John Forbes Royle, Superintendent of the Botanical Garden, Saharanpur, recommended to the Government of India in 1827, and again in 1834 the introduction of tea plantation in the country.[1] An experimental tea garden was set up in Assam in 1835. In the North-Western Provinces, tea nurseries were set up in the Kumaon hills in 1836.[2] On 21 January 1841, the Provincial Government asked Dr H. Falconer, the Superintendent of the Botanical Garden at Saharanpur, to inspect these tea plants in Kumaon and choose suitable sites for tea plantations (Atkinson, 1882: 891). According to the report submitted, tea nurseries were located at two places – at Bharatpur near Bimtal in the hills, 4,500 feet above sea level and at Lachhmesar near Almora, 5,200 feet above sea level.[3] Dr Falconer reported that the land was 'very poor and stony'.[4] Due to the encouragement received from the officials up to 1864, besides these two nurseries, tea was planted also at Bhimtal, Nauckutiatal, Almora and Hawalbagh; the area covered by these four gardens was nearly fifty five acres.[5] In 1843, the tea plantation in Kumaon produced a good harvest of 191 lbs. of tea.[6]

In 1845, seventy-six acres of land was further added and 94,100 plants were planted. In this year, 375 lbs. of tea was produced with a profit of Rs 23,066.[7] Up to 1851, there were six nurseries in the central Himalayas and all were under the control of the Government. In 1864, on the recommendation of Dr Jameson,[8] the gardens were handed over to private capitalists and for sometime this system proved to be profitable. In 1859, the land for tea cultivation was only 166 acres;[9] by 1880, the area had increased to about 3,342 acres[10] – definitely a great improvement.

But in later years there was a sharp decline in the production of tea. There were five tea estates in Nainital district in 1928, two at Bhowali owned by Mr Newton and Mr Mullins, one at Bhimtal belonging to Mr Jones, Mr Deriaz's garden at Ramgarh and that of General Wheeler at Ghorakhal. The average output of the Ramgarh garden from 1893 to 1903 was nearly

2800 lbs. annually from 30 acres, but between 1925 to 1930 it had fallen to 783 lbs. from 21 acres; the output had been about 2500 lbs. yearly in 1930. (Walton, 1928: 53).

Similar was the condition of the tea industry at Almora. Although the manager of the Berinag Tea Company had only by a lucky chance discovered the secret of manufacturing Chinese Brick Tea, his tea was admitted by unprejudiced Bhotia traders to be far superior to the Chinese tea imported into western Tibet via Lhassa and he was able to place it on the market at a price which was 50 per cent below that demanded by the Tibetan official monopolists. In 1907 he succeeded in disposing of about 12,000 pounds, but it was probably due to the conservative prejudice of the Tibetan and Bhotia consumers and the opposition offered by the Tibetan officials that Berinag brick tea was eased out of the market altogether.

Thus, the prospects of the tea industry were very dismal. The tea-planters, in spite of the cart-road built for their benefit (Pant 1935: 125), could not compete with Assam tea which was handicapped by the same difficulty in the matter of transport (Walton 1928: 53). The Central Asian market could not be captured because of heavy Russian import duty on Indian tea and also because the monopoly of the Chinese trade was in the hands of Tibetan officials who did their best to prevent the import of Indian tea into Tibet.

Although the tea gardens did not achieve much success, the people were greatly benefited by these gardens. The tea planters changed barren tracts of Katyur into a prosperous area. Doonagiri plantations poured a vast amount of wealth into the surrounding areas from which it derived its labour.[11]

Iron

It was found that iron of good quality could be manufactured at rates below the cost of iron imported from England and a number of individuals came together under the name of Devies and Co. and they were permitted to undertake iron manufacture in other parts of the lower hills.[12] In 1858, the East India Company also took control of the factory at Khurpatal, which was later sold off to Col. Durmmond who started the work in 1861 under the name of Durmmond and Company (Sankrityayan 1959: 244). In 1862, these two steel plants amalgamated to form Kumaon Iron Works Company (Sankrityayan 1959: 244). As no coal was available in or near the area, three hundred and fifty acres of forest (from Dabaka to Makra river) was given to this Company by the Government.[13]

In 1862, the Secretary of State ordered laying of the Tramway line near Khurja station. In anticipation, Kumaon Iron Works, which was to supply iron for the rails,[14] produced a quanity of iron, but suddenly the Government dropped the idea of laying the line itself and gave a contract to the

Avadh-Ruhelkhand Railway to do the job (Atkinson 1882: 263). As a result, the Iron Works Company had to cease production in 1864,[15] although the Company tried its best to continue function until the iron already produced was disposed of. Several unsuccessful attempts were made to restart the Company (Atkinson 1882: 263). Thus, the Iron Works Company finally ceased to exist.

Small-scale Industries

Some small scale industries, such as those involving making of blankets, wool, baskets, etc., had flourished during the British period. But, unfortunately, no records are available about the history of these industries.

The weaving of cotton was the only manufacture of any importance but even this declined in consequence of the competition offered by European goods. In 1898, there were said to be some 3000 looms in Kumaon and Garhwal. Jaspur was the principal place of manufacture where a large number of Chippis or Printers found employment (Nevill 1922: 84).

Besides cotton weaving, the only other industries of any importance in the area were the manufacture of baskets and mats from the *ringal* bamboo and hemp and, to some extent, woollens. The first was almost entirely restricted to certain *pattis* of Parganah Danpur, especially Malla Danpur. Excellent matting for floors was turned out and baskets of all sorts were made, especially the box-baskets calls *kandi*. All these were sold at the annual Bageshwar fair (Walton 1928: 63).

The fibre of hemp, after extraction, was spun on a wheel into yarn and then woven into narrow strips of cloth. This cloth was very durable and bags made from it were quite stout. Apparels made from this material were much appreciated by the people of the middle hills. The hemp weavers were invariably *kolis*, a sub-caste of the Doms (Mittal 1986: 206).

The people of most of the northern *pattis* spun and wove wool from their native sheep. The staple was short and the texture of the wool coarse, so only the roughest of blankets could be woven. In 1909, a weaving school was opened at Almora, chiefly with the object of introducing an industry which might relieve the pressure on the land. By 1928, some 12000 maunds of wool was sent annually to Kanpur. Enterprising Bhotias went as far as Calcutta and Bombay to deal directly with merchants, and every year new avenues were opened for them.

A small number of people who lived by the banks of the Sarju and the Kali rivers in Kali Kumaon made catechu out of *Khaiar* tree, and derived a very meagre profit from the industry. They had also to pay a licence fee of Rs 30 to the Government.

It is interesting to note that in 1935 Thakur Joga Singh had established a factory at Gangola Kotuli for weaving that worked on water-power. It gave employment to many people and was a successful endeavour (Pandey 1937: 127).

The furniture in the hills used to be brought up from Bareilly till 1931. In that year a workshop of woodworks was opened in Haldwani by Pt. Hari Datt Joshi.[16] This industry proved very successful and many branches of this workshop are still functioning at different places.

We see that both the weaving and furniture industries were well adapted to the resources and requirements of the mountain region. The raw material, the wool and the timber are products of this region. This advantage, combined with the industrious nature of the people, made these industries eminently suitable as small-scale industries for the region.

Thus, it can be concluded that, although the wool industry prospered, encouragement was not provided by the British to other industries such as forest-based industries, for which there was great scope. Even the roads were not properly laid out and maintained in the interior parts of the hills for the convenience of the people involved in the wool industry. Secondly, the absence of coal in the hills, which was required for the establishment and functioning of a big industry, played a major role in the backwardness of this area in the matter of industries. As such most of the industries established in this area did not flourish to the extent it should have been possible.

International Trade and the Markets

The Bhotiyas carried on trade with Tibet. As a matter of fact, this trade dates back to pre-Christian era (Joshi and Brown 1987: 303–317). The primary export included foodgrains, soaps, oil, tobacco, textile, tea, sugar, *gur* and china clay, while the main items of import were salt, borax, raw wool, Tibetan tea, lambs, etc. This trade engaged thousands of people of the barren mountains, and was the mainstay of the Bhotiya economy. It was this lucrative trade with Tibet which lured the British to Kumaon. Later, the strategic importance of Tibet was realized and the Tibetan trade became a medium in the furtherance of the British policy towards Tibet, *i.e.*, of preventing Russia from controlling Tibet. Thus, under the camouflage of the Tibetan trade through Kumaon, the British kept an eye on Tibet.

There were three large towns in the Central Himalayas – Almora, Naini Tal, and Ranikhet (Goudge 1903: 7). Of these, the first was inhabited by a population of native traders and bankers, whose prosperity and mercantile interests were largely dependent on the Europeans. On the other hand, Naini Tal and Ranikhet were important only because they were headquarters of the Rohilkhand Military district. Large markets had come into existence in Naini Tal and Ranikhet (Goudge 1903: 7).

Marketing in the hills was a difficult task. The rugged and inaccessible nature of the area, the high mountains and deep watercourses, made communication very difficult. This gave rise to the holding of annual and periodical fairs throughout the hill region. As the population increased and the economic life became more varied, these fairs become more numerous and frequent. The business, formerly confined to a few principal markets, as already mentioned, gradually spread over many smaller and more frequent market places (Pant 1935: 193). The important markets in this region were Jauljibi, Thal and Bageshwar. The Jauljibi, Bageshwar and Thal marts were organized in the month of November, January and April, respectively. Nearly one hundred fairs, the attendance at which varied from 1000 to 20,000 persons, used to be held annually in the Central Himalayas (Pant 1935: 194).

Vehlcular traffic was unknown in the first half of the nineteenth century. Afterwards, continuous improvement was made in the state of roads and a network of bridle roads was laid out. The railway was also extended to the foot of the hills in 1884.[17] The facilities provided as regards communication had a direct impact upon the trade in this area. Prices showed a remarkable increase. In 1850 the finest rice was sold in Almora at 20 to 30 seers a rupee (Upreti 1903: 5). The table below shows the prices of grain in 1850 and in 1900 (Upreti 1903: 5).

Product	Rate obtaining per rupee in Almora, in 1850	Rate per Rupee in 1900
	(Seers)	(Seers)
Coarse Rice	40 to 50	7½ to 9¾
Fine Rice	24 to 30	4½ to 6¾
Wheat	40 to 50	4½ to 6¾
Atta	30 to 45	10½ to 11½
Urd	40 to 50	9½ to 11
Mandua	112 to 168	25 to 32
Ghee	4 to 5	1¼ to 1½
Tel	5 to 7	1½ to 2¾
Gur	8 to 10 Bheli	5 to 6 Bheli

Agriculture and Forests

Unfortunately, very little is known about the agricultural conditions and its development in the nineteenth century. Even Moreland in 1887 did not find agricultural records of that period as such records were not maintained during those years (Moreland 1913: 1). There is no really reliable way of knowing about the agricultural progress, except very brief accounts mentioned in various settlement reports.

Kumaon and Garhwal seem to have been agricultural areas from ancient times (Pate Ram 1916: 58). Each valley has its own peculiarities and the population had to adapt itself to these varieties of environment. There are numerous factors which make cultivation in the hills difficult. Occasional floods, hailstorms, land-slips, extensive ravages of wild animals and a high degree of mortality among both the people and the cattle are some of the special obstacles to human initiative with which the hardy hillmen have to cope. Moreover, the actual work of cultivation demands an incredible amount of labour. The hillmen have to terrace whole ridges and transport cattle, implements and manures from distant homesteads. The transport of produce by rough, precipitous paths from the fields to the homesteads and thence to the markets are arduous tasks for both men and animals(Pant 1935:76). This is the reason why Sample wrote that in the undeveloped hill tracts (like Kumaon) the problem of subsistence is very severe (Sample 1921:79). Yet, agriculture was the main source of livelihood here.

Despite these handicaps, agriculture flourished well till the beginning of the nineteenth century, when a great decline took place in its organization on account of the barbarous rule of the Gorkhas, Fortunately it lasted just about twenty-five years. After the Gurkhas, the British took over in 1815 and it benefited the area enormously and production rose sharply. From 1816 to 1822–23, cultivation increased by one-third; since then there has been a steady progress (Kennedy 1884: 242–3). Pate Ram writes that during the British period the agricultural industry had immensely improved, 'Sand Turning into Gold' and 'Desert into Garden'. (Pate Ram 1916: 216).

The cultivated area expanded largely because of the increase in population as also because of the policy of encouragement pursued by Sir Henry Ramsay* (Pant 1935:88). Agricultural population increased by 12.8 per cent within twenty years. The increase in cultivated area is quite apparent from the following table18 which shows only the statistics of three *pattis* of Chakarata, Kota and Ramnagar.

Year	Year cultivated	Area cultivable
1842–46	1,72,912 Acres	523,883 Acres
1872–73	1,85,282 Acres	810,895 Acres
1886	1,98,059 Acres	886,114 Acres

*The Commissioner of Kumaon.

The cultivable area increased by fifty per cent during the last forty years of the nineteenth century.[19]

In his settlement report of 1902, Goudge notes 'it might be said that most of the villages in the district approximate more or less to this ideal . . .'. Soil, for instance, is generally richer and deeper on slopes with a northern aspect while, on the other hand, the southern slope of a ridge gets more sunshine. When, however, cultivation extends above 6,000 feet there is marked fall in both the standard and outturn of agriculture. It is rare to find cultivation at such an altitude except inside the snows or on their border lines and there too only for a Rabi crop of potatoes if it is above 7,000 feet. The chief crops of the hills are mandua and rice in the Kharif and wheat and barley in Rabi. Upland rice of many minor varieties is grown everywhere, but it is not of any great commercial value. The best varieties of rice are basmati, hansraj and sal, the latter corresponding to the Sukhdas of lower India. Every village also has a little tobacco. In the lower villages masur is occasionally grown but chana (gram) is absolutely unknown. In the snows Himalayan barley is grown at 6000 feet and upwards, and is followed in the Kharif by phapar or chana (gram). Wheat is not found above 7,000 feet; but in the higher snow valleys close to the glaciers, a fine species of wheat, known as 'Nepal' is grown as a Kharif crop. It is sown in May and repeated in November. This is particularly the crop of the Darma Bians valleys, where it alternates with Phapar. The rotation of crop in unirrigated land is constant and uninterrupted. Rice and Jhangora are sown in the first Kharif of the series, and is followed by wheat and barley for the Rabi and by the mandua for the second Kharif. One Rabi-crop is then omitted, and the series commences anew with rice. Villages are divided into two portions, known locally as *sar*. One of these is apportioned to mandua and one to rice, so that the whole village is always cultivated for the Kharif, while the Sar, in which mandua happens to be, will remain fallow for the succeeding Rabi. Beans and vetches, such as urd, mung, bhat, etc., are sown in the Kharif, but only subsidiary to mandu and with the object of preventing exhaustion of the soil. Generally speaking, the outturn is always a good one owing to the excellence of the climate and the equable and constant distribution of rainfall. Failure of a crop is very unusual and never widespread.' (Goudge 1903: 12–13).

In Tarai, the crops showed a substantial improvement during the last decade of the nineteenth century and the first decade of the twentieth, though the cultivated area decreased. Wheat was sown and cotton extensively expanded very rapidly in Kashipur after the introduction of the railways. The staple of this crop was better than of that usually grown in the Province and the crop was popular because wild animals left it alone. In the Bhabar also production of wheat increased. (Moreland 1913: 4).

TABLE - I

Year	Rice		Wheat		Barley		Maize	
	Total Acres	Irrigated Acres	Total Acres	Irrigated Acres	Total Acres	Irrigated Acres	Total Acres	Irrigated Acres
1901–6	70,239	....	258,952	....	38,934	....	84,957	....
1906–11	400,623	185,203	336,339	129,600	64,011	29,200	91,740	1,090
1911–16	390,662	194,029	373,572	153,541	62,789	30,178	93,4419	82
1916–21	348,486	191,007	291,316	146,121	54,600	27,551	66,190	....
1921–26	168,912	107,854	259,386	106,486	42,959	19,922	43,381	103
1926–31	166,563	102,657	275,165	105,610	40,513	17,948	47,561	120
1931–36	96,781	48,703	339,198	100,136	74,148	11,220	59,761	8
1936–41	94,072	34,445	306,062	81,108	70,120	9093	52,234	23
1941–46	85,221	86	330,827	89,713	71,794	9089	56,424	6

TABLE - II

Year	Government Canals	Private Canals	Reservoirs	Wells	Other Sources	Total
	Acres	Acres	Acres	Acres	Acres	Acres
1901–6	169,602	....	207	514	2,176	172,499
1906–11	357,419	28,698	....	1,186	10,711	398,014
1911–16	366,134	36,635	....	1,199	8,674	412,688
1916–21	361,703	33,462	....	825	14,802	410,792
1921–26	346,525	18,484	....	722	12,491	378,222
1926–31	283,127	21,014	....	714	3,024	307,879
1931–36	302,417	23,294	....	684	4,136	330,595
1936–41	233,494	19,833	....	574*	4,017	248,318

*which includes 6 acres by tubewell

The accompanying table (Table I) shows the different crops and their area.[20]

For improvement of cultivation steps were taken to provide irrigation for cultivable land. A network of canals was laid out in the Tarai and Bhabar (Moreland 1913: 4). In the hill *pattis* also irrigation was an accomplished means of costly channels (Goudge 1903: 14).

Table II shows different sources of irrigation as well as the area irrigated by them.[21]

Out of the total irrigated area in 1950–51, 92.3 per cent was irrigated by canals, 0.1 per cent by wells and 7.6 per cent by other means.[22]

Forests

The Central Himalayan forests extended from the Ganges in the West to the Sarda in the East, covering the lower spurs and ridges of the Himalayas (Pearson 1869: 1). In the Himalayas, the forests play a most important part in the economic life of the people. They provide them with cheap-fuel, leafage, fodder and timber for agricultural implements.

The contract arrangement for felling trees continued in the hills until the year 1858 since no conservation measures had been introduced till then. Between 1855 and 1861, due to the tremendous demand for railway sleepers, uncontrolled felling of Sal went on in the more accessible forests. The havoc caused by reckless destruction of valuable forests for railway sleepers proved a blessing in disguise by drawing the attention of the Government to the need for conserving the national timber resources. Ramsay, the then

Commissioner of Kumaon and the first Conservator of Forests, was quick to recognize the gravity of the situation and he soon took energetic measures to stop this wanton destruction of forests.

From this time, conservation of forests progressed with vigour. Ramsay, on his own initiative, checked the indiscriminate felling of trees and enforced rotational working of forests as well as the practice of hammer marking of trees prior to felling.[23] In 1861–62, the cultivation in forests was stopped by assigning land to the people below the hills in the Bhabar; next, the cattle stations were broken up and all herds of buffaloes were removed from the forests. This operation took three years from 1862 to 1865. In 1867–68, forest fires were successfully eliminated from most of the hill forests (Pearson 1869: 10). Forest boundaries were more clearly demarcated (Webber 1902: 3).

The forest department in this region was organized for the first time in 1868 with a Conservator of Forests as its head. However, the work of building up a forest estate proved a long and uphill task. The early pioneers had to survey, examine, describe and demarcate extensive areas of trackless forests, much of it in unhealthy and broken country inhabited only by wild animals. They had to do it in order to organize the protection of forests against fire and other disasters; to count and number their valuable trees and arrange for their judicious exploitation, to record minutely, in collaboration with civil authorities, all existing rights and, on top of everything, to wage a perpetual and often thankless war against the customs and malpractices of generations, e.g., uncontrolled grazing and lopping, indiscriminate felling, incendiarism, the vested interests of get-rich-quick timber contractors – in fact against all the various activities that had reduced the more accessible and valuable forests of the State to a state of semi-ruin.[24]

For several decades, the Forest Department remained engaged more in 'conservation' than exploitation. The forests were impoverished and required careful nursing. And this essential Conservation Policy, which was the key note of the forest administration then, created ample discontent among the people of Kumaon (Pant 1921: Introduction).

The people of Kumaon had so far quietly borne the encroachment into their sacred rights, but these violent shocks which came in quick succession proved too much for them and forced them to give vent to their anguish. There was a wide-spread feeling of discontent and the forest policy of the Government was criticized and condemned all over the area.[25]

In response to this agitation, Lt. Governor Sir John Hewett made a declaration on the 2 November 1908[26] that 'the Government had no desire to make money out of the forests in Kumaon; and intended to spend for the benefit of the people of Kumaon, the amount by which the receipts exceeded the expenses.'[27] But his basic idea was that in order to check the 'reckless destruction of wooded area' it was imperative to bring the waste lands within the purview of the Forest Act (Pant 1921: 11).

In 1917, a fresh settlement was made which divided forests into the following categories:[28]

(*a*) Reserved Forests: (*i*) Old reserve, (*ii*) New reserve;
(*b*) Protected Forests or Civil forests.

Civil forests continued to be under the control of the Deputy Commissioner while the old and new reserves were managed by the Forest Department.

The aftermath of the settlement gave rise to vehement protest all over the area. Angry villagers set fire to large areas of forests. In 1916, the Kumaon Association came into existence to deal with the forest problems of this area.[29] The late Shri G.B. Pant worked as its General Secretary for a number of years. This Association believed that even the prescriptive and indefeasible rights, which were recognized in theory even by those who initiated the forest policy, were denied. From the point of view of the local villagers, the settlement operations could be summed up as follows:

> 'For want of a nail the shoe was lost, for want of a shoe the horse was lost, for want of a horse the man was lost and for want of a man the kingdom was lost' (Mittal 1988: 256).

Compelled by the exigency of the situation that then provided, a committee was appointed in 1921, the report of which is popularly known as the Kumaon Grievances Committee Report.[30] On the recommendations of this Committee, another Committee was appointed in 1930,[31] which was called the Kumaon Forest Committee, popularly known as the Parliament of Kumaon as far as the forest administration in Kumaon is concerned. The members of this Forest Committee were the presidents of the District Boards of Almora, Naini Tal and Garhwal. This Committee had extensive powers. But the people were not satisfied since they wanted to enjoy the same rights they had enjoyed before the settlement of forests was made. After the formation of a popular ministry in U.P. in 1938, the representatives of Central Himalayan region raised the question of their forest rights. The Government requested the Kumaon Forest Committee to look into the matter. On the recommendations of this Committee, some facilities were provided to the people, vide G.O. No. 605/AF/XIV–240 dated 22.9.1941, but these were far from the expectations of the people, and they remained dissatisfied.[32] This situation continued till 1947.

Today, when we talk about the protection of forests, and people support the Chipko Movement, we should note that the change in the views and attitudes of the people towards forests has come after independence. When the British adopted the same policy of conservation of forests, almost one hundred years ago, they were severely criticised and movements were launched against their policy. Mr G.B. Pant had written, 'The policy of the Forest Department can be summed up in two words, namely encroachment and exploitation' (Pant 1921: 36). Although there is no doubt that people had to face certain problems due to the forest policy of the British, the growing needs for the forest produce and the vast development of communication in the hills had turned forests into potentially valuable national assets. And the valuable national assets could not be left open for just such things as grazing, gathering of fuel, etc. For conservation of forests it was necessary for the British administrators to encroach upon the traditional rights of the people in the forests. The illiterate people of Kumaon then could not quite understand the importance of the forests. But the British cannot be exonerated from the charge that there were some glaring flaws in their forest policy. They did not give any importance to the preservation and protection of oak trees which greatly help in retaining the soil cover. The British made no efforts to inform the people about the utility and value of the forests. Instead of removing the misapprehensions of the people they tried to suppress the voice of the people. Further, when the people were denied the right to cut forests, the British should have applied the same policy for government purposes also. But that was not done. At the same time while implementing their forest policy, the British also did not think of providing some substitute fuel to the people and no information was sought about the requirements of villages before enforcing the policy. And no compensation was given to the people whose rights were disregarded under section 29, clause 3 (Pant 1921: 37). There was also resentment against the British policy of fire protection. The burning of pastures and forests was a traditional practice in hills, and the people believed that it promoted the fertility of land. (Mittal 1988: 264)

Tenancy Rights and Land Revenue Settlements

Under the native kings the proprietory right in land was vested in the sovereign. The property in the soil was called 'THAT' and grant in 'THAT' conveyed a freehold in the soil as well as the produce. The rent of these lands had at subsequent periods been almost wholly presumed to be the Rent-Roll, but the property in the soil generally remained with the heirs of the grantee. It was on grants of this nature that the rights of a large body of the occupant land-holders were founded. (Stowell 1907: 2f)

Traill has written, 'The occupant Zamindars (Thatwan) hold their estates in heriditary and transferable property' (Stowell 1907: 2) The resident tenants were divided into two classes, the *Khaikar* and the *Kaini*, If the land granted was already held as property by others, the occupant proprietors, if they continued on the estate, sank into tenants of the new grantee, and according to the custom of the country, the grantee was permitted to take one-third of the estate into his own immediate cultivation,[33] but the right of cultivation rested with the original occupants, who were called *Khaikars*. Besides the government revenue (*sirti*), the *Khaikar* was called on to pay to the proprietor various dues known as *Bhent, Dastur* (dues in kind) and '*Pithai* (an annual cash rent). (Pauw 1896: 41) The rent of the *Khaikar* could not be increased under any circumstances during the settlement period.

The *Kaini*, under the native government, held a position like that of a slave, or at least that of a vassal. He was bound to the estate of his lord. Gradually, the *Kainis* assumed the character of tenants permanently resident on their master's estate, and by virtue of long continued occupancy they came to be considered like the *Khaikars* except in the nature of the rent they had to pay.

The *hissadari* right was introduced by the British. The idea of any land without a private owner was repugnant to the British administrators and so, as in the plains, the proprietory right was conferred on the zamindars. The cultivators were then called *hissadars* or co-sharers in the estate and were allowed full rights of transfer in the cultivated land of the village. These rights were never extended to the waste land.[34] Another kind of resident tenants, who had no right of occupancy either acknowledged or prescriptive, were those who rented the land which the proprietors themselves could not cultivate due to their being absent or due to some other reason. The tenants paid their rents either in kind (1/3 of the produce) or in money according to existing rates. In case no resident cultivators offered to cultivate the land, the owner was free to let it out to any inhabitant of the surrounding villages. This was known as *palkasht* cultivation. This type of cultivation was, because of the uncertainty attending it, subject to a lower rate of cess than other kinds of land.[35]

In an ordinary village the shares of various recorded *hissadars* in all or the greater part of the village land were separately held and recorded under a system of imperfect partition. There was usually some jointly held common land (*gaon-sanjait*) which was owned by the whole body of *hissadars* in proportion to the amount of their separate shares. Any *hissadar* could have his proportionate share of the *gaon-sanjait* separated by imperfect partition, and when this was done the remainder of the land ceased to be strictly *gaon-sanjait* and remained *sanjait* of certain specific *hissadars* only. The portions partitioned off became amalgamated with the already existing separate shares of their owners.[36] Where the proprietors were a coparcenary body, the tenure was usually called *bhai-bhant*, in which the proprietory right was in an extreme state of subdivision, each estate being shared amongst all the coparceners.

Thus a community of petty cultivating proprietors existed during the British rule, each with full proprietory right over his own specific share and his fractional share in common land, and united only by a common liability for land revenue.

The first settlement here was made by Gardner in 1815. Before the settlement some interchanges of villages were made with Garhwal[37] and then the land revenue was assessed, on the basis of the actual receipts of the Gorkhas during the preceeding year.

The next settlement was made in 1817 (Saksena 1956: 18) by Traill, with the help of padhans or headmen of each village for their respective villages. This was a new mode of collection introduced in this area and since the powers and responsibilities of padhans were not yet defined, this arrangement was introduced partially only and the leases were restricted to one year. The settlement was made at Rs 89,539 (Atkinson 1886: 465–66). The third settlement was the first technical settlement. It was effected in 1818 and was based on the principles similar to the previous settlement. 'The assessment was slightly increased. The increase demanded from each village was too small to render it as an object to the village proprietors to protect the settlement by making unfounded objections' (Atkinson 1886: 466). The settlement had an assessed revenue of Rs 98,991.38

Some local poets have severely criticized these settlements (Paliwal 1966: 99), for example Shri Krishan Pandey, who was a contemporary of Traill. He described the pathetic scene of the society in a poem. (Paliwal 1966: 100). But it appears that the poet had expressed biased opinion against the British and his only aim was to criticize and deplore the British administration, since the condition in Kumaon had certainly improved after the British rule replaced the Gurkha regime (Mittal 1986: 43).

In the next settlement, Bisi was taken as the standard of land measurement. It was found impossible to prepare a Record-of-Right of every village owing to the number of shares, but an effort was made to protect the proprietory body, by placing them entirely under their own Padhan and by forbidding the Kamins to interfere in collection of the revenues of any village. (Atkinson 1886: 467–68) With the help of Parganah records, Records-of-Rights of every village were prepared. Earlier, the record of cultivable area was based on the quantity of seed sown, which obviously could not be the exact measurement of the cultivated area. In this settlement, therefore, in assessing the revenue of a village, the number of inhabitants of that village was considered more important than the arable area. In this settlement, in 1820, the total revenue demand amounted to Rs 108, 327 only.[39]

Due to these settlements, the value of the land increased to a great extent. A good area of waste land was brought under plough, prices of grain rose and kept rising and the land owners were taxed lightly.[40] All these measures certainly improved the condition of the people.

For the first time, a field survey was attempted in 1823 and a guess measurement was taken. (Baden 1892: 309) Native officers wrote down the names and areas of estates (*thoks*) and the settlement was based on these areas. Philip Woodruff writes (Woodruff 1954: 230) that Traill's men went from village to village and wrote down where the boundaries lay. Traill wanted to know how many villages there were in the division, what the fields could reasonably pay, and where the peasants thought the boundaries ran between one village and the next. Traill had certainly done a tremendous work, even though it was sketchy, and any one who thought of making a better job of it later had to take it into account.

Besides the guess measurement book of 1823, a Revenue and Rent-Roll was prepared showing how the *Padhans* collected revenue and where the rent was due on *Asamis.* It should be noted that in the previous settlement, Records-of-Right were made on the basis of *parganah* records, but here the Revenue and Rent-Roll was formed by field survey. (Baden 1892: 309) In this settlement, which is also known as *Assi Sala Bandobast* or *San Assi Bandobast* (as it was made in Samvat 1880) revenue assessed was Rs 119, 430 only.[41] This settlement was extended for a second period of five years starting from 1828. (Atkinson 1886:470) The net revenue assessed in this settlement was Rs 122,495 only. (Atkinson 1886: 470) Traill recommended a settlement for five years only, which on assessment resulted in Rs 124,729 only. (Mittal 1986: 46)

The ninth settlement was made by Batten in 1842, and it was for a period of twenty years.[42] No reasons have been given for fixing the term of the settlement at twenty years. It appears that Gowan had succeeded in preparing the minds of the people for accepting a settlement for such a long term.

The Record-of-Right, which was framed for each village, was the characteristic of Batten's settlement.[43] This Record-of-Right contained a complete description of the rights of every occupant, the past history of the assessments, the boundary arrangements; the engagement paper (*ikrarname*) of the inhabitants in regard to the remuneration of the Padhan and the collections of all sorts to be made under the heads of the *thokdari, sayanchari* and his *hissedari* dues, and also binding themselves down to a conformity with certain rules in regard to the public service and good administration and the *phard-phant* (Rent-Roll) showing the name of the *Padhans*, the distribution of the revenue payers amongst several *Padhans,* where more than one were elected; the quotas of revenue payable by shareholders or occupants; the division of the non-proprietory tenancy amongst those recorded as proprietors and the liabilities of the *pahikasht* and other cultivators, whenever discovered. (Atkinson 1886: 477)

It appears from the available records that this settlement improved the condition of the people. As no village had manorial rights in this settlement which authorized them to dispose of timber, claim pasturage fees or exclude their neighbours who from olden times had enjoyed the priviledge of grazing their cattle, cutting wool, gathering leaves, etc., this system may be considered as one of the chief causes of the increase in cultivation since 1840. Small hamlets became large villages and villages sprang up where only cattle sheds had existed formerly. Sir Ramsay, the Commissioner, in his report[44] said that, Batten's settlement had paved the way for more accurate details. The people came to know that they had some rights which could be defined and secured. They learned by degrees to assert those rights; they also learned methods of the British that applied to field measurement. The people were acquainted with Khusrah measurement and quite prepared to accept it as the basis of new settlement, and thus they were by degrees taught to understand that their rights ought to be correctly recorded.

It should be noted that, although Batten compiled a detailed Revenue-Rent-Roll, in which the details of the revenue paid by the share-holders and the rentals paid by the permanent tenants (*khaikars*) were entered, these statements cannot be taken as completely reliable, as they were prepared by the villagers themselves whose main object was to make themselves out as poor as possible in order to cut down the revenue to be paid (Beckett 1874: 1). Tewari goes on to write that this virtually was a Record-of-Rights, not of the people but of the tea planters and the Government. (Tewari 1923: 60)

The tenth settlement was effected in 1863-64 by Beckett, and it was fixed for thirty years. At the time of that settlement, however, no actual measurement of the land was taken. Therefore, so far as estimate was concerned this settlement was not reliable – the last estimate having been made by Traill in 1823, for that was also of little use except for boundaries. It was prepared by native officials who summoned the *Padhans* of the village and noted down from them the boundaries and estimated areas. This afforded some very rough idea of the size of each village. The main principles[45] on which the measurements were carried out in the tenth settlement were as follows:

1. All terraced land was to be measured unless it had relapsed into forest, but forest clearing and slopes cultivated only after the lapse of eight or ten years, known as *khil* or *kaunla* were not to be measured and each enclosure of a field was to be measured separately.[46]
2. The whole of the terraced land was to be shown under four heads – (*a*) Irrigated, (*b*) Good dry, (*c*) Second rate dry and (*d*) Casual cultivation or Irjan.

It was not practicable for surveyors to adhere to these instructions and they classified all the cultivable area under three (Beckett 1874:1) heads: (*a*) Permanent cultivation, (*b*) Casual cultivation, and (*c*) Waste.

After the measurements were taken by surveyors, Beckett introduced an ignenious procedure to bring all the land in the village to one common standard of quality (known as second quality dry land), as that would greatly help in fixing the revenue. Each of the other three classes were brought to this standard by trebling the irrigated land and then by adding one-half to the first quality dry and by reducing casual cultivation by one-half.

Thus taking every thing into consideration, an average rate of one rupee per *bisi* (Beckett 1874: 3) was fixed to be the average rate in the second quality dry land, and in this way, the good land was made to help the bad land in the assessment of rates. Beckett took great pains in fixing the rates. He personally inspected each village and had before him its history; due to this procedure he succeeded in making modifications in the statistical rules. There was considerable revision of the *pattis* and parganahs at the recent settlement which altered the area so much that in the preparation of records of a parganah and its revenue at the time of Batten and Traill, it did not represent the area known under the same zone after this settlement.

For the first time, in this settlement, the land which was underestimated earlier was assigned a fair value on the Revenue-Roll. Beckett, by way of a check on the surveyors, gave each occupier an extract from the survey record, relating to his own holding. This enabled the occupier to bring before the settlement officer any omissions prior to the final record in the books on which the assessment was based. Beckett also took care to omit from his calculations all the waste land already described. The people were awarded full powers to use such land. This must certainly have extended the cultivation. The most significant feature of the tenth settlement was the regular field measurement as made in the plains, a real cadastral survey.

In the absence of many necessary records that have been weeded out from the Commissioner's office at Naini Tal, it is difficult to make any accurate assessment. However, it can be concluded that in so big a task as the making of a settlement, minor flaws are not uncommon and that too in a hill region, where it is more difficult than in the plains.

The next settlement was made by Goudge in 1900. That was the eleventh settlement during the British occupation. Economy, simplicity of procedure and moderation in assessment were the principles followed by Goudge.

The new revenue stood at Rs 2,67,559 for the Almora district – an increase of 22.47 per cent and at Rs 50,314 for the Naini Tal *pattis* – an increase of 30.68 per cent. The increase in the cultivated area was 22.12 per cent. The incidence of the new demand per soil unit was 12 annas 6 paise in Almora and 14 annas 8 pies in Naini Tal, against 12 annas and 13 annas 6 pies respectively at the previous settlement.[47] The list of revenue-free and assigned revenues remained the same as it was in Beckett's settlement. (Goudge 1903: 12)

After the maturity of this settlement in 1930, the government once again tried to enhance the revenue rates by 33 per cent and work for the new settlement was started,[48] but the public raised their voice against the proposed enhancement and the government had to abandon the idea of not increasing the revenue rates. Consequently no settlement was made in 1930 in Kumaon.[49]

It may be concluded that, although the revenue administration of the British in this region was far better than that of the Gorkhas (who were the predecessors of the British) and was very well laid out and systematic, they (the British) cannot be acquitted of the charge of exploiting the people of the Central Himalayan region, as was their policy in every colony. The British were proud of having increased the revenue which was due to the expansion of cultivated land (as they say). According to the British administrators, the revenue was always realized without trouble and no severe coercive measures were ever used which ostensibly proved that the increase of revenue (in every settlement) was always reasonable. The table[50] below shows the continuous increase in the assessment in every settlement:

Name of the District	Assessment in the Settlement				
	1815	1816	1817	1820	1823 (Rs)
Almora Nainital Hill Pattis	85,328	89,689	99,228	1,08,599	1,19,730
	1,828	1,853	1,845	1,872	1,902
–do–	1,22,829	1,25,121	1,30,633	2,50,264	3,17,874

From this table it is clear that revenue assessment increased in every settlement. In fact, it was not due to the expansion of cultivated area only, but also due to the increase in the revenue rates*, which the people paid quietly not because the rates were reasonable but because of two reasons: firstly, they had not forgotten the cruel rule of the Gorkhas; and secondly, the people were illiterate and were not aware of their rights. When the people got educated they became conscious of their rights and when, in 1930, the government tried to increase the revenue they opposed it tooth and nail and succeeded in their endeavour.

The British authors have mentioned that 'the universal rise in the standard of comfort is a sign of the great general increase of wealth throughout the district. Huts have been replaced by masonry houses.' (Goudge 1903: 18) But this seems to be an exaggerated claim. There is no doubt that the non-agricultural income of the people increased and perhaps Goudge's opinion is

*For example, revenue assessed in the tenth settlement had showed an increase of 81 per cent over the previous settlement while the new area brought under cultivation was very small. Further, in the eleventh settlement an increase of 22 per cent was made in the assessments.

based on that fact. But it cannot be denied that the adoption of non-agricultural professions was forced upon the hill people by the smallness of their holdings. Although agriculture was the main source of subsistence for the people, cultivation had failed to keep pace with the increasing population and the British did not provide any loans or advances for improvement of the land. In Nainital District the cultivated area per capita had gone down during the British rule. This is clear from the table below:[51]

Year	Population	Area sown (Acres)	Area of cultivation per capita
1921	276,875	249,004	90.0
1931	277,286	225,727	81.4
1941	291,861	233,690	80.1
1951	335,414	222,354	66.2

It meant that every man, woman and child got less food and other items of agricultural produce in 1951 than in 1921.

Even today, most of the people of the Central Himalayan region live far below the poverty line. The legacy of the British rule is perhaps responsible for this poverty and the economic backwardness of this area.

Notes and References

1. House of Commons, *Fourth Report Select Committee on Indian Affairs* 1852–53, vol. XXXIII (National Archives, New Delhi).
2. Home, *Public Proceedings*, no. 7 of 29 June 1842 (National Archives, New Delhi).
3. *Falconer's Report* dated April 21, 1841,Vide Home Public Proceedings, no. 5 of 2 June 1841 (National Archives, New Delhi)
4. *Ibid.*
5. *The Nurseries in the Hills* Vide Home, Public Proceedings, no. 23 of May 1844 (National Archives, New Delhi).
6. *Robertson's Minute* of January 3, 1843, Vide Home, Public Proceedings no. 5, March 8, 1843 (National Archives, New Delhi).
7. Home, *Public Proceedings*, F. no. 2.
8. Home, *Public Proceedings,* no. 14 of 20 May 1864 (National Archives, New Delhi).
9. *Tea Plantation Report*, File no. 12, State Archives, U.P. Lucknow.
10. *Ibid.*
11. Ramsay, Sir Henry, *Report on the Settlement of Kumaon* (Govt. Press, Allahabad, 1874), p. 22.
12. *Report on Durmmond and Company* (Unpublished), Regional Archives, Nainital.
13. *Ibid.*
14. *Ibid.*
15. *Ibid.*
16. *Records, Haldwani Furniture Mart*, Haldwani.

17. Vide Home, *Revenue and Agricultural Proceedings*, letter no. 2815, 13 September, 1885 (National Archives, New Delhi).
18. *Ibid.*
19. *Imperial Gazetter of India*, vol. XVIII, (Oxford), p. 328.
20. *District Census Handbook (1951) Nainital District,* pp. 184–87, (Allahabad).
21. *Ibid.*, pp. 200–3.
22. Ibid, Introduction, p. III.
23. *Uttar Pradesh Forest Administration Souvenir* (1861–1961), p. 36, R.C. Soni (ed.) 1961, Lucknow.
24. *Almora Akhbar* (Almora), 10 October 1907
25. *Almora Smarika* 1976, S.C. Tripathi (ed.), (Almora), p. 103.
26. *Annual Report on the Forests of U.P.*, 1909 (U.P. State Archives, Lucknow), p. 66.
27. *Ibid.*
28. Papers related to the Forest Settlement Report (State Archives, Lucknow), p. 32.
29. *Almora Akhbar*, 1 October 1917, Almora.
30. *Shakti Saptahik*, 8 February 1921, Almora.
31. *Swadhin Praja*, 8 January 1930, Almora.
32. *Report of Kumaon Forests Fact Findiang Committee* (Office of Chief Conservator of Forest, Lucknow), pp. 37–41.
33. *Revenue Letters Issued*, vol. 71, Book 3 (National Archives, New Delhi), pp. 80–81.
34. *Miscellaneous Records regarding Agra and North-Western Provinces*, vol. 489 (National Archives, New Delhi), p. 65.
35. *Ibid.*
36. *Ibid.*
37. Revenue Letters Issued, *op. cit.* F. No. 33.
38. *Letter* dated 21 June 1818, from Traill to the Board of Revenue, Records of Kumaon Division, Board of Revenue, Allahabad.
39. *Revenue Letters issued*, vol. 89, Book No. 2, 114.
40. *Ibid.*
41. *Letter* dated 1.6.1823, from Traill to the Board of Revenue, Kumaun Records, Board of Revenue, Allahabad.
42. Batten, J.H., *Official Report on the Province of Kumaon: Introduction* (State Archives, Lucknow).
43. *Ibid.*
44. Ramsay, Sir Henry, *Report on the Settlement of Kumaon* (Govt. Press, Allahabad, 1874), p. 2.
45. *Ibid.*
46. *Ibid.*
47. *Letter No.* 101/I-719-A dated 28.1.1904 from the Secretary to the Board of Revenue, Kumaon Records, Board of Revenue, Allahabad.
48. *Karma Bhumi Visheshanka*, 26 January 1956 (Kotdwara), p. 42.
49. *Shakti Saptahik*, 2G January 1950, Almora.
50. Data collected from various settlement reports.
51. *District Census Handbook*, Nainital, 1921, 1931, 1941 and 1951, Allahabad.

NINETEEN ❖ The Empire's Proletarian Army: Indian Indentured Labour Migrants

MARINA CARTER

INDIAN INDENTURED LABOUR MIGRATION was brought into being to offset the consequences of terminating the slave trade in British colonies. The demand for labour determined rates of immigration to particular colonies, but it was socio-economic conditions in India which influenced the overall volume of indentured recruitment. While many migrants were already seeking work away from home when recruited, overseas indenture implied mobility on a grander scale than before, and the time lapse away ensured that around two thirds of all emigrants settled overseas. The movements of these small, eclectic populations and their installation in already heterogeneous societies, provide a fascinating insight into the transplantation of Indian cultural and social mores overseas and the processes of adaptation required of villagers hitherto unused to inter-caste and inter-region cohabitation and marriage.

The Scale and Timing of Emigration

Government-regulated indentured migration was undertaken as a rescue package for British sugar plantations. The scheme began in 1843 when Mauritius was the sole beneficiary, and was expanded to include the West Indies, the French sugar colonies, Natal and Fiji. Mauritius was offered the opportunity to become the first site for this 'great experiment' in the use of free Indian labour to harvest sugar because of its previous experience with Indian workers, its virgin lands and proximity to the source of supply. It was to be the model for other British sugar colonies to follow. The island had been leading the way since 1834 when the regular importation of indentured Indian workers first began. Almost immediately the scheme became a subject of concern to capitalists elsewhere in the British Empire. When Bettington & Co. of Sydney, Australia, expressed an interest in Indian labour, the Mauritian capitalists encouraged them with details of the success of their immigration scheme:

> The experiment of free labour has been entirely successful; we have 50 free Indians on our own estate . . . they are quiet, docile and industrious. The total cost, including passage here and back, at the end of their apprenticeship, which is generally five years, together with food, clothing, etc. . . . is no more than 5 shillings per week, which you will allow is cheap labour in any country. . . . It seems to us, that in New South Wales the deficiency of agricultural labour might be beneficially supplied from Bengal.[1]

Accordingly, 61 male labourers were shipped to Sydney on 22 August 1837 and a further 28 in December of that year. Around 400 men, and a handful of women and children, also embarked for Demerara and Berbice on the ships Whitby and Hesperus in January 1838. During the years 1837 and 1838, Mauritius, for its part, imported more than 5,000 male labourers, but only around 100 women. Around this time, however, the emigration of so-called 'coolies' was brought to the attention of the British Parliament by the Anti-Slavery Society and its sympathizers. A series of debates between them brought the whole issue into the public domain and led to the suspension of migration, until it was resumed to Mauritius alone and under government control in 1843.

It was not until two years later that the question was decided in favour of re-opening migration to Mauritius, with the passing of Act XV of 1842. This law established an Emigration Agent for that island at each of the principal ports in India and migrants began to arrive from 1843. After a huge influx of immigrants to Mauritius from the three Presidencies in that year, emigration was restricted to Calcutta. In 1844 migration to the West Indies was recommenced, and the agents at Calcutta and Madras were authorized to send 5,000 emigrants each to British Guiana and Jamaica and 2,500 to Trinidad.[2] The West Indies experienced difficulties in securing its annual supply and began to cast envious glances at the volume of the Mauritius emigration and the apparent popularity of the island amongst recruits. In 1850, their agent took a close look at the working of the Mauritius emigration depot in Calcutta and reported to the Governor of British Guiana as follows:

> All the emigrants intended for the Mauritius present in the yard about 500 in number were brought up for my inspection. I found that a considerable number of them were returned emigrants: men who had previously been to Mauritius and who had returned from there at the expiration of the five years or who had anticipated that period by paying themselves a portion of the return passage money. In physical appearance and muscular development and perhaps also in intelligent expression these men appeared to me somewhat superior to the others and were evidently returning to Mauritius with the conviction that their situation there would be preferable to their situation in India.
>
> Of these returned emigrants a few were men who having acquired the confidence of the proprietors or managers of the plantations on which they had been located in

Mauritius, were now employed by them as agents for the collection of fresh emigrants in India. These having all their expenses paid, and the prospect of remuneration proportioned to the number and quality of the emigrants they should bring back with them to Mauritius, had procured labourers in the villages and districts of country to which they belonged. . . . I found a vessel (the Mohassur) preparing to take emigrants. Her complement would be about 260, and of this number 45, or rather more than one sixth, were men who had previously been in Mauritius and were now returning there with the view of bettering their fortunes or of settling permanently in the island . . . emigrants of all classes and castes were, on their first emigration, averse to removing their families from this country, as they looked forward to returning here after the lapse of a few years.[3]

The pertinent observations of the West India agent, notably the knowledge disseminated about the island by its large group of returnee recruiters, was to constitute a special feature of the indenture system in Mauritius throughout its operation, and one which other islands tried with varying degrees of success, to emulate. The envy of the West Indies labour exporters was very soon to turn to open rivalry. In 1858 St Lucia also commenced recruiting operations in India and Act XLVI of 1860 brought the French colonies into the arena of labour exportation, thus adding Reunion, Martinique, Guadeloupe and French Guiana to the ranks of rival colonial interests. In the same year acts were also passed permitting emigration from St Vincent and Natal. In 1862 the Seychelles were given the right to recruit in India.[4]

By the start of the1860s, with a number of colonies thus competing for indentured labour, emigration agents began establishing sub-depots upland from the port towns, in order to prevent rival exporters interfering with their recruits. The Protector of Emigrants at Calcutta explained that the old system of supplying the wants of the colonies 'through the agency of old return Emigrants and other Native Recruiters, who were duly furnished with funds in advance by the Emigration Agent in Calcutta, to enable them to defray the outlay incurred in bringing the people to the Depot' had fallen into disarray owing to the difficulties experienced en route to Calcutta. It was now considered necessary to employ the services of paid local Agents, stationed in the mufassil, to protect each colony's interests and to receive such emigrants as they were able to procure from the arkatis who went into the recruiting districts. In 1861, for example, there were five offices located at Raniganj, one each for Mauritius, Jamaica, Demerara, Trinidad, and Reunion. Raniganj was an important site because of its location on the main road leading from Bihar and Hazaribag, along which, it was reported, 'numbers of poor persons travelling down the country in search of employment are intercepted and prevailed upon to accept food and clothing on the road . . . when once they take assistance from the Agents, they are entirely in their power, and the Agents offer them to any of the Offices without much choice on the part of the Coolies themselves'. On arrival in Raniganj, the migrants were taken by rail to Calcutta.[5]

During the 1860s there occurred what seemed to be an endless succession of accusations and counter-accusations as colonies blamed each other for decoying away recruits. The Mauritius Emigration Agent recounted one such clash between his agency and French recruiters:

> a man named 'Solum', a return Emigrant from the Mauritius, had collected in his own District a band of eighty-four souls in all, and was proceeding in charge of them . . . when he was met on the way by several Emissaries of the Bourbon Agency, and from what these Emissaries stated to the laborers, the latter were led to infer they would be escorted by them direct to my Depot for ultimate shipment to the Mauritius, for which place they had left their homes . . . on the party of Emigrants reaching Raneegunge, railway tickets were taken for the whole number to Howrah, but the most singular fact in the case is that, instead of being brought on to Howrah, as the Coolies believed they would be, they were taken out of the railway carriages at Chundernagore, a French settlement, detained there some little time, fed with sweetmeats, and then put on board boats and brought to a Ghat at Garden Reach (within a few hundred yards of the Bourbon Depot), and there landed in the middle of the night. The coolies themselves say that it was so dark they were unable to discover in which direction they were being taken, or to what Depot.[6]

In 1864 a consolidating law was passed which was designed to remove major discrepancies in legislation governing emigration to different colonies, to regulate recruitment and depot procedures for the better protection of migrants, and to define the duties of the Protectors of Emigrants. In the same year, heavy mortality on the passage from Bombay to Mauritius led to a suspension of emigration from that Presidency. Following the passing of this act, the indentured labour importing colonies complained about competition from inter-Asian migrations, such as those to the tea plantations. They decried the increasingly tough laws regulating the collection and despatch of their migrants, whilst countries like Ceylon and Malaysia which shipped even larger numbers of workers were not subject to the same provisions. After the implementation of Act XIII of 1864, it was pointed out that the depot accommodation of the Ceylon Agency in South India was inferior, and that Ceylon recruiters could bring 'their coolies down the coast in frail country coasting vessels called dhonies . . . we are required to bring our coolies down the coast by steamers or first class sailing vessels'. The West Indian and Mauritius agents had to pay registration fees to Magistrates and Protectors, and employ a Surgeon whilst the Ceylon Agent, relieved of all these expenses, was thus 'able to pay a much higher premium to contractors and recruiters . . . and thus obtain coolies more readily than ourselves.[7]

By the mid 1860s the longer established colonies were also feeling the effects of competition from Natal because of the high price paid to their contractors at 35 rupees a head. Natal recruited principally in the southern districts of the Madras Presidency. The French continued to operate from their settlements of Pondicherry, Yanam and Karaikal, having closed down their Madras agency some years earlier. Once again, it was represented that the contractors preferred the French service because they were permitted 'under the pretence of supposed advances, to extort Rs 13 from each emigrant out of the Rs 15 which he receives prior to embarkation'. The Indian Government was exhorted to place the French Agencies also under the operation of Act XIII of 1864 in all respects. In 1866–67 the prevalence of epidemic fever in Mauritius, and the resulting mortality provoked the temporary suspension of emigration operations.[8] Mauritius had seen the peak years of its immigration strategy and now became a minor player, as other colonies, like Fiji, moved in to tap the Indian labour market.

In 1871 Act VIII was passed to consolidate the laws relating to the emigration of native labourers from British India. Many previous regulations were restated, and further measures instituted, particularly relating to the operations of recruiters. Under the act Emigration Agents were subject to approval by the Government of India, and their remuneration to be a fixed annual salary. The Indian Government was to appoint a Protector of Emigrants at each port whose duties were outlined by the Act. Emigration was authorized only from the three ports of Calcutta, Madras and Bombay, and migrants were required to register with the magistrates of their home districts before leaving their region. The magistrate was to ascertain their comprehension of the contractual terms offered them; in the port towns, the Protector himself was expected to examine emigrants. If emigrants were considered by the Medical Inspector to be unfit or if found to be irregularly recruited, Emigration agents were required to pay the amount necessary to return the migrant to his home and to maintain him until he was fit to make the journey. Ships proposing to transport migrants were also required to be licensed and for this they had to fulfil a number of requirements. The passing of the act brought howls of protest from emigration agents concerned who thought the licensing and registration provisions would hamper their work.[9]

As the supply of labour to the West Indies and Mauritius dwindled or levelled out, complaints about obstruction and competition gave way to considerations of cost, and attempts to pare the expenditure of the agencies. In 1873 the governments of Natal, the West Indies and Mauritius were informed of proposals to amalgamate the agencies. However, the Government of Bengal stressed that the case of Mauritius was 'quite apart from the West Indian colonies, and under different conditions which are well known to the Indian population' so that it should be kept separate from the proposed West Indian Colonies Amalgamated Emigration Agencies. In later years, in fact, the Mauritius agency was to be amalgamated with that of other colonies.

Mauritius was generally treated as in a class of its own insofar as emigration was concerned. In his report on the working of the emigration depots in 1874 the Protector noted that a special feature of the Mauritius depot was that 'there are always in the Mauritius depot a comparatively large number of old returned emigrants about to re-emigrate with their families and friends' who cooked for themselves and did not require the same level of care as that bestowed on new migrants travelling alone.[10] Despite this praise, by the 1870s Mauritius was no longer the Model colony of the Indian indenture diaspora, and the true state of affairs was revealed by Sir Arthur Hamilton Gordon who, having completed a stint in Trinidad, was able to compare the West Indian colonies with Mauritius, when he arrived as Governor there. Protective legislation was revealed to be better honed in the West Indies. The less well-regulated Mauritian system was perhaps symptomatic of a colony which was no longer really in need of imported labour and could rely on the circular migration of returnees to maintain migrant levels.

The Migrants and their Mobilizers

In the recruiting districts, the vital role of return emigrants was revealed by the Magistrate of Patna who explained:

> The coolies who emigrate to Mauritius and elsewhere generally return with comparatively handsome fortunes, and their good luck is noised abroad. Coolies working in the Colonies send information of their well-doing to their friends and relatives by the return Coolies, and the first information called for by those who feel inclined to emigrate is as to the climate of the country they have served in. Intending Emigrants being satisfied on that point have no objection to cross the 'Black Water' and sell their labour in the dearest market. Irish Emigrants remit money to their friends in Ireland and send information of their well-doing. The Indian Coolie does the same, only his love of country is as great as he always returns to it, after putting by a handsome provision for his old age.[11]

The important role of returnees is paradoxically demonstrated by the problems they created for labour exporters at times of competition when returnees from one colony were lured into the recruiting service of another. Differential rates of emigration naturally tempted recruiters to take the highest offer. In 1861, the Mauritian agent confronted Marriott, the British Guiana representative, with the contention that 'there is not on your establishment a single recruiter who has not been employed by this agency for the last 17 years in recruiting coolies for the Mauritius'. The Mauritian Governor drafted a note in which he deprecated the departure of recruiters into the service of other colonies.[12] However, if Mauritius had always relied on return migrants, did this make the island a special case, or was this feature shared by other indentured labour importing colonies?

By the 1870s the Demerara migration was certainly beginning to exhibit some of the same features as the Mauritius indenture system with increasing numbers of returnees featuring in annual emigration. In his report for 1873–74, the Calcutta Protector speculated,

> the fact that 96 were found willing to return to Demerara during the year may be explained by the large remuneration which labour finds there, the average sum brought back to this country by each emigrant having been no less than Rs 293 during the past year. It is a new feature that among the returned emigrants to Demerara several should be found proceeding to the colony as private passengers and paying large sums for their passage.[13]

It seems plausible that the information networks which operated in the recruiting districts had registered the declining economic position of Mauritius and the harsh legislation recently enforced there against time-expired immigrants, and that British Guiana was usurping the favoured position of Mauritius. If further research proves this to be the case for the West Indies and other colonies, we might need to consider the redefinition of the indenture system in terms which bring it closer to the kangani model of Sri Lanka.

Returnees worked alongside the local recruiting hierarchy: agents, sub-agents, duffadars, arkatis and maistries. Their operations stretched across three distinct zones: the recruiting districts, the mufassil half way stations where sub-depots were located, and the port towns where the main depots were sited and from where migrants were embarked for the various colonies. The emigration agents were usually European officials who liaised with contractors and sub-agents, and employed returnees and local recruiters. In the mufassil the duties of the sub-agents included superintending the operations of the recruiters, providing for the lodging and feeding of emigrants, their registration before the local magistrate, and despatching them by railway to the depot. The ordinary recruiters came from a range of backgrounds: visiting the Demerara depot in Shahabad in the early 1880s, Grierson met with four recruiters whose previous employments had been respectively as a peon to a zamindar, a servant to a mahajan, a watchman, and a return emigrant from Mauritius.[14]

Recruiters worked within the constraints of a profession which was not always appreciated. According to Grierson, 'they dare not go into the bustees to recruit for fear of being maltreated, or of having false cases brought against them. It is for this reason that they can never leave the bazars or open streets.' Recruiters also reported that the police frightened intending emigrants away. However, this was due less to their disapproval of emigration as to their greed for bribes. Thus Grierson's informants noted that at the Howrah bridge in Calcutta constables stationed themselves, refusing to let bands of recruits pass unless a bribe of 2 or 3 rupees was paid. Other obstacles placed in the way of recruiters included the intervention of Europeans whose servants had been kidnapped, the delaying tactics of sceptical magistrates and the anti-emigration lobbying of Indian capitalists, anxious to prevent the flow of labour overseas. In 1856, for example, the West India Emigration Agent complained that the Assistant Collector of Salem refused to pass the emigrants collected to his petty Maistry (Morla Meerah) and put a peon as a guard over the maistry until they were dispersed. In his reply the Magistrate explained that he did not pass the coolies referred to because the Maistry represented that he had engaged them to go Mauritius. The British Guiana agent complained in 1867 that the Collector at Kanpur would not register his recruits 'saying that I was sending all the strong people out of India, and that I had taught the people to speak all in one tongue', meaning that the intending emigrants had been all taught to express their willingness to emigrate, and their satisfaction with the terms of the engagement. In 1871 the Jamaica agent reported that some of the magistrates kept intending emigrants waiting for two and three days before they would register them:

> Obstructions are thrown in the way of registering the emigrants, and at times it has been with the greatest difficulty that they could be got registered at all; so bad has it become in some districts that it has been reported to me that batches of coolies have been removed from the district in which they were collected and taken to another, where the magistrate had the reputation of being a fair dealing man and one who attended to his duties himself without the intervention of subordinates.[15]

The large-scale emigration and rising number of colonies competing for labour in mid-nineteenth century India did not go unnoticed by local capitalists. The Landholders' Association, in 1861, viewed 'with alarm the strenuous efforts which are being made by the various Agencies established in Calcutta, for the encouragement of Native Emigration to the West Indies, Mauritius, and the French Colony of Bourbon', and plans to grow cotton in Australia using cheap Indian labour. They considered that an 'erroneous impression appears to exist in these various Colonies, and in England, that India is overpopulated'; this they refuted, adding that natives of India disliked sea travel and accusing the overseas agencies of deceiving

> the simple agriculturist, who in many Districts is little removed from the ignorant condition of savage life. He is not made to understand, he is wanted to labor in countries only to be reached after a long sea voyage, but with specious promises, or other less justifiable means, is induced to proceed to the Capital and there shipped off in comparative ignorance of his destination and engagements.[16]

The Landholders' Association in Bengal therefore sustained its anti-emigration campaign by casting doubts on the real willingness of migrants to proceed overseas. Their representative asserted that the Protector of Emigrants could not in practice ascertain the actual knowledge possessed by the intending migrants, and described the process of confirming consent thus:

> The intending Emigrants, prior to embarkation, are usually asked in gangs if they are willing to proceed to Mauritius, Demerara, or other parts for which they are recruited, and mixed in those gangs or around them are Native decoys who vociferate loudly their willingness to proceed to the Port they are wanted for, the rest or some of them ignorantly join in the cry, and thus the general assent is considered as given and the people are embarked.[17]

Were local capitalists and magistrates justified in their desire to prevent unrealistic promises being made to naive villagers? The labour exporters issued notices for intending emigrants which described average wage rates, contractual terms and working conditions. While not strictly inaccurate, they continued to paint a rosy picture of the indenture system. The Trinidad agency promised the following terms:

> Emigrants will be provided with a free passage from Calcutta to Trinidad for themselves and their families, with proper food, clothing, and medical attendance during the voyage.
>
> The Island is exceedingly fertile, and the rates of wages for work, which is principally . . . by piece work, vary from ten Annas to one Rupee, and an industrious laborer can easily earn double the latter sum in a day. In no case is the daily pay less than ten annas; during the crop(the season for manufacturing the Cane juice into Sugar) the ordinary wages for all employed are thirteen and a half annas, those laborers employed in keeping up the fire for boiling the juice of the Cane, superintendents of work, and trenchers, are paid at a higher rate as those varieties of work require greater attention.
>
> Whilst ill the Emigrants are provided with Medical attendance, medicine, and nourishment gratis. They are provided at all times with houses rent free, and in most instances with as much garden ground as they can cultivate at their leisure hours for their own benefit. The climate and soil are favorable to the production of every description of grain and vegetables grown in this country.
>
> Emigrants can always communicate with their relatives and friends in India through the medium of the protector of Emigrants in Trinidad and the Agent here. Great care is taken by the Protector of Emigrants in Trinidad in locating the Emigrants on their arrival, not only not to separate blood relations but to respect as well the more distant ties of kindred and of even local acquaintances. Whole families, men women and children can go together.
>
> Trinidad Emigration Agency Office,
> Trinidad Emigration Agent,
> Calcutta, 186.

What kind of people were tempted by such notices into registering as migrants? Individual explanations for migration reveal an intriguing blend of economic necessity, chance encounters, trickery, and traditions of labour mobility in defining causative factors.[18] However, these decisions or circumstances cannot be considered in isolation from the broader defining features of indentured migration. The characteristics of the overseas Indian populations depended on the location and networks of recruiters, the level of influence of returnees in the targeting of specific villages, externally imposed restrictions on the migration of certain case or ethnic groups, and gender requirements, to name only some.

The legislation governing sex ratios in indentured migration is a good example of the effect of externally imposed requirements on the make up of the migrant population. In 1843 when Mauritius began to recruit labour, on average only 13 women were despatched per 100 men. A year later, when the West Indies joined the ranks of the labour importers, women formed around 21 per cent of migrants, this fell to 16 per cent at the close of the 1840s, but following legislation which prevented ships from departing without a required proportion of women, the annual percentage rose to 30 and 40 per cent of male emigrants.[19] However, the problems of legislating for a desired sex ratio in immigration were outlined by the Land & Emigration Commissioners in their report on migration in 1866:

> In the course of the year a question arose as to the minimum proportion of females to males to be required in the emigration. This question is attended by considerable difficulties, because, on the one hand, a small proportion of women gives rise to strifes and jealousies, if not to worse crimes among the men, while, on the other, to require a large proportion leads either to the acceptance of a very inferior class, or to an injurious limitation of the whole number of emigrants.[20]

The greater the migration, the more difficult it was for the colonies to achieve the legally fixed ratio. In 1872 when the 40:100 female / male ratio was applied, the West Indies only managed an average proportion of 37.83 to 100. Eventually, the rule was relaxed to provide for a 25 per cent sex ratio of women to men.

The ratio of women to men in migration was thus a function of the encouragement given to family resettlement in the colonies and the imposition of quotas, but it was also influenced by the level of activity of returnees in bringing female relatives overseas, and the type of labour required – tea cultivation employed a greater proportion of women than cane planting. The requirements of employers, as articulated in their requisitions or in the instructions given to emigration agents by the colonial states, helped to define the characteristics of indentured populations by restricting recruitment to certain castes, age ranges and ethnic groups. For example, the British Guiana agent at Calcutta was instructed to reject all intending migrants who showed signs of disease, were aged more than 35 if male or 30 if female, or who were of the castes of Fakirs, Kayeths, Brahmins and Baniahs. This did not stop high caste migrants from concealing their real status. When Grierson made his survey of the castes of 1,226 migrants and found that only one-third could be characterized as of a low social position, he noted that this contradicted what he stated was the universal belief: 'I have been assured by every native from whom I have enquired, and by most Europeans, that only the lowest castes emigrated.[21]

Characteristics of migrants might also be determined by specific crises: Whilst a natural disaster might bring members of more prosperous communities to the agency gates, a conflict such as the 1857 Uprising, prompted some disaffected soldiers to take the overseas escape route. A member of the Police Enquiry Commission in Mauritius reported the presence amongst immigrants of mutineer sepoys, and claimed that this explained high vagrancy levels:

> I have met many old soldiers who, to my personal knowledge, must have been actively concerned in 1857 in the mutiny of an army in which they and their forefathers had for a century eaten the salt of the Honorable East India Company . . . it requires but little knowledge of the Bengal sepoy and his history to show he would not emigrate to work as a coolie from choice, on the contrary, he would, if he did leave his country, naturally finding the work distasteful, I may almost say impossible, run off, and pass his time vagabondising, preying on his neighbours.[22]

As with caste, the nineteenth century officials did not tire of speculating on regional differences in migration and ascribing preferences for particular colonies in explanation. Thus in his report for 1873–74 the Calcutta Protector noted:

> the detaied returns given show that the native of Oude, as a rule preferred to emigrate to Demerara: while natives of Bengal and Behar preferred the Mauritius, which also attracted a large number of men from NWP. It is noticeable that of the lower provinces of Bengal, the eastern districts with their large population supply but a very trifling quota to the emigration agencies for the colonies. The probability is that these districts find a nearer and more convenient field for their surplus labour in the tea plantations of Assam and Cachar.[23]

The Magistrate of Patna believed it was the Biharis' repugnance for the climate of Assam and Syllet that led them to prefer Mauritius as a labour destination. The Commissioner of Chota Nagpur also had his theories as to what motivated the denizens of the district to migrate:

> The country is capable of supporting a very much larger population than it contains, but in bad seasons the Ryots are unable to meet the heavy rent demand in some parts of it and [are] reduced to poverty . . . they are in that condition easily persuaded to accept the tempting offers of the Agents of the Emigration Companies. The Subordinate Agents of those Companies have no scruples about suiting these offers to the wishes of the Ryots, always recruiting for whatever place they are most likely to agree to go

to. The Mauritius, as best known, is most popular, and. . . . I have myself come across agents for the French Emigration Committee unscrupulously recruiting for the Mauritius.[24]

Geoghegan, whose region of origin data was compiled from information provided by the Calcutta Protector of Emigrants, observed that the earliest recruiting grounds for the colonies were in the so called 'hill coolie' or adivasi areas of Bihar and Chota Nagpore, but that the proportion of tribals in overseas migration had declined as a result of heavy mortality in their shipment and their recruitment for local tea plantation production. Geoghegan also observed that 'recruiting operations seem to have been pushed further westward into the North West Province below Cawnpore, and, since the suppression of the mutiny, into Oudh. The tracts which now figure most largely in the lists are Arrah, Gyah, Patna, Allahabad, Ghazipur and Oudh. As regards southern India, the largest recruiting districts were considered to be Godavery, Vizagapatam, Ganjam, Madras and Chingleput. Geoghegan had little data concerning Bombay. A decade later, Grierson reported that few residents of Calcutta or its neighbourhood were recruited, most migrants being drawn from the ranks of 'up country men who have come down here for work'.[25] The relative importance of eastern, western and southern India as zones of recruitment depended on a number of factors: local competition for labour and attitudes of Presidency governments towards colonial emigration (favourable in Bengal, and disapproving in Bombay), legislation which decreed the opening or suspension of various ports for emigration, and preferences expressed by labour importers all played a part in defining and circumscribing recruiting operations. Between 1844 and 1850, for example, Madras and Bombay were closed to the Mauritius emigration, who recruited only from Calcutta, and after 1862, the West Indies also took its recruits chiefly from that port, but when Natal began to recruit labour in 1860, it was almost exclusively from Madras. The French colonies took a large proportion of their recruits from ports in the French Indian comptoirs.

Despite the statistical evidence of circular and returnee migration, it is clear that throughout the period of recruitment for indenture, migrants were often either unaware of their real destination or unable to reach the colony of their choice. As late as 1883, Grierson was reporting: 'I have heard of coolies who were enlisted for Natal, imagining that they were going to Nattore in Rajshahye.' Relatives had difficulty in following pioneer migrants to specific destinations and returnees were frequently prevented from reaching specific colonies or estates by misrepresentation arising from competition between labour exporters, or poor labour allocation practices.[26] It is not unrealistic, therefore, to conclude that indentured migration could at one and the same time be a calculated decision and a reluctant leap into the unknown.

Processes of Migration and Settlement

At the sub-and port-depots, and on the ships which took them overseas, migrants began their induction into unfamiliar living conditions and routines. On the voyage, commensality was difficult to avoid. Many high caste migrants were punished for refusing to take cooked food. Others tolerated the temporary sojourn on the ship by likening it to a 'temple of Juggernauth' where caste differences could safely be ignored. But there were other, unseen traumas. Ship mortality rates reflected both the debilitation of famine-driven recruits and the dangers of exposure to unfamiliar epidemiological environments. Once at their destination, migrants began the long process of adapting to new work routines, and reordering their personal lives.

The experience of the indentured labourer depended very much on the provisions enshrined in the contract he or she had signed and the manner of its enforcement. Contractual terms were not uniform across all labour importing colonies. In Grenada, Antigua, St Lucia and St Vincent, immigrants were paid wholly in money, no rations being alloted to them. In Demerara they were fed for the first four months after their arrival, in Trinidad for the first two years, and in Mauritius they received rations for the entire period of the indenture. Women immigrants who were invariably indentured in the West Indies, were not indentured in Mauritius and consequently did not receive rations. In 1860 when the French colonies were legally authorized to ship migrants from British ports in India the system adopted was slightly different from that employed by the British colonies. Labourers were pre-engaged in India with fixed wages and rations. The period at which wages were paid also differed between colonies: in Jamaica and Demerara they were paid weekly, in St Lucia and Trinidad fortnightly, in Mauritius, monthly. All colonies were required to provide housing for indentured immigrants, but the modes of enforcing it, as also the estimate of what constituted suitability and sufficiency, varied. In Trinidad and Demerara the Governor could remove immigrants from estates where their accommodation was bad or insufficient, whilst in Mauritius the law depended on the opinions of the various local magistrates, who could order that lodgings be repaired. Medical care was better defined and elaborate than housing provisions in colonial legislation. By 1871 immigration law in all the West Indian colonies and Mauritius provided for a hospital on estates, and for medical attendants; in Mauritius and most of the West Indies these were appointed by the proprietor of the estate, but in Jamaica and Trinidad the attendants were government officers. Immigrants in Demerara were bound to work for five days a week and seven hours a day, in Trinidad for 280 days of nine hours, in St Lucia, Grenada, and Jamaica six days a week, excluding holidays and in Mauritius, to work seven days (two hours on Sundays).[27]

Absence from work was punished in Trinidad by imprisonment for seven days, whilst five days' absence in Demerara could lead to two months' imprisonment. In Mauritius the labourer, absent without justifiable cause, lost double his wages, and if absent for more than three days could be declared a deserter and imprisoned for up to three months. Mauritius and British Guiana came in for special scrutiny in the 1870s when concerned individuals – De Plevitz in Mauritius and Des Voeux in Guiana – drew the attention of the authorities to abuses in the law and administration of those colonies concerning Indian immigrants. In both colonies Royal Commissions were appointed to assess the truth of the allegations, and it was found that vagrancy legislation and the intervention of the judiciary had been used to pressurize immigrants to re-engage and to limit their opportunities for mobility.

Insofar as the return passage was concerned, in the West Indies immigrants were entitled to a free passage home after ten years' residence, or to a small grant of land; in Mauritius this right was withdrawn in 1853. The colonies thus also differed in their attitudes to labourers once the indentures were terminated. In the West Indies no re-engagements were allowed until the previous contract had expired. In Mauritius the labourers had been 'exposed to many acts of petty tyranny' if they refused to re-engage with some months of their indenture left to run. The British Guiana Commission recommended that no re-indentures run for longer than 12 months. In Natal, many time-expired Indians were repatriated; in Fiji, Indians were barred from purchasing land. In the West Indian colonies the immigrant received, on the expiration of his contract, a certificate of industrial residence, by which he became free to work on his own account or to re-engage. The re-indenture was optional and the immigrant at this stage was, in theory, 'as free a man as any other inhabitant'. In Mauritius, although a certificate was given, this had to be purchased and he then had a week in which to re-engage. Any labourer who declined to re-engage, had to pay a tax of £1.

Reports were annually or twice yearly compiled to indicate the size of the Indian population in the colonies, the mortality rate on estates, and the numbers reindenturing or returning to India. In 1870 the Indian population on estates in British Guiana numbered 52,598 of whom 40,220 were under indenture and 12,378 were not. In 1868 it was reported that the death rate of Indian immigrants there stood at 29.4 per 1,000 per annum. The Emigration Commissioners pointed out that this return dealt only with 'the lowest class of unskilled labourers' and comparing it with the available urban mortality returns of all classes in Britain, which was apparently about 24.56 per 1,000, concluded that 'the mortality of the lowest class of the labouring population, if taken by itself, would scarcely be less than that of the Indian immigrant in British Guiana'. This comfortable conclusion, however, failed to take into account the more restricted age range of the Indian overseas population at this period. Since most of the statistical surveys of indentured populations have used data which identify the Indian only at the onset of the indenture, much research remains to be done in this field.[28]

The records regarding the prosperity of indentured labourers as measured by their remittances and declared savings on returning to India, were considered by Geoghegan to have 'been too laxly kept' to be of much use. However, he did report that over the first three decades of government emigration, returnees from British Guiana brought home ten lakhs of rupees, averaging 300 rupees per person. The comparable figure for Trinidad was 166 rupees.[29] Of course, not all of those who returned were prosperous time-expired migrants. There were also many who, through infirmity or other causes, were sent back in an indigent state. By 1872, the Indian Government was considering the advisability of alleviating their distress, particularly as some migrants found it difficult to be reintegrated into their own communities:

> In some cases, no doubt, they return poor and helpless, in consequence of their own imprudence in the colony; nevertheless their condition, aggravated possibly by the loss of their relatives and caste in this country, gives all of them a claim to consideration. It would be a great boon if a fund could be raised for their support.[30]

When the Indian Government queried whether the colonies should not be made responsible for the relief of emigrants permanently injured in that colony, or otherwise unable to maintain themselves, they received a firm no from the British Secretary of State for the Colonies. Kimberley was of the opinion that this would be quite contrary to the usual principles on which emigration was carried on from one country to another. He stated:

> If a debtor and creditor account is to be struck between the colonies and India, it would be necessary to estimate the value of the advantage which India derives from emigrants who leave India, practically paupers, and return with considerable sums of money amassed in the colonies, by means of which they become contributors to the wealth and revenue of India . . . if the liability of the colony were admitted in the case of loss of limb it might on similar grounds be extended to cases of ill health from disease contracted in the colony, and a colony might become responsible for the maintenance in India of an indefinite number of paupers without having any means of knowing whether they were making reasonable efforts to procure a livelihood.[31]

By the close of the 1860s, when indentured migration to the West Indies and Mauritius had been in operation some three decades, attention was turned to the numbers of Indians who had not exercised their option of return passages, and could therefore be considered as having settled overseas. Guiana was calculated to have a population of around 15,000 Indians who had declined to exercise their right to a free return passage, while in Trinidad an equivalent figure of 7,887 immigrants was estimated. Mauritius had received 220,000 immigrants by 1871, and around one third of the Indian population returned home. The concern of officials was now redirected towards assessing the social conditions of these overseas Indian populations. Violence on estates, particularly the crimes of wife-murder and the high rate of suicide, preoccupied colonial officials and generated a voluminous correspondence. Statistics revealed that the overseas Indian populations were committing a greater number of wife-murders and suicides than other ethnic groups in their various territories. Officials in this Victorian age of scientific racism then debated whether this was a statistically significant phenomenon, a peculiarity of the Indian people, or a by-product of socially dysfunctional living conditions within the indenture system. The Presidency governments were called upon to provide statistics. It was difficult to compare rates between India or between colonies themselves, but the data demonstrated that the early years of indentured immigration saw higher than average figures. On the issue of wife-murders, the conclusions which the Government of India drew from the material collected were that 'the statistics bearing on the question of murders of women in the cooly importing colonies are so absolutely fragmentary, that we are not in a position to form any opinion as to the relative frequency of woman-and wife-murder amongst the people of India and amongst the Indian emigrants in those colonies'.[32]

It was felt that the presence of women had a bearing on the incidence of these melancholy data, but surprisingly little research had been conducted on the marriage patterns of the first generation immigrants. How did they adapt to finding partners in an environment where caste endogamy was presumably more difficult to achieve? My own research on the settlement of Indians in Mauritius indicates that while caste endogamous unions were more difficult to arrange, immigrants adapted by looking for partners from among the caste communities to which they were most closely related. Endogamy was in most cases replaced by the most acceptable alternative: hypergamy, which in the Indian context enabled high caste males to take wives from lower castes. A common language and region of origin continued to influence partner selection in marriages contracted at Mauritius by immigrants. From a sample of 165 marriages between first generation north Indian immigrants where the caste status of both parties is listed, there were numerous cases of Chamar females marrying up to Brahman, Ahir, and Gowala males. Similarly, women from the Vaish categories, for example Koiri, were also considered acceptable wives for Brahman males. Those individuals, who belonged to castes for which there were numerous potential partners, were in many cases able to contract intra-caste marriages. Thus, Chamars, Nonias, Koiris, Kurmis, Burryeks and others were able to find suitable marriage partners of the same caste. Significantly, these are among the caste groupings which remain important in Mauritius today, reflecting the strength and continuity of the larger socio-religious units to which many migrants belonged.[33]

Did indenturing Indians therefore lose all contact with India? Grierson believed that even those individuals who returned to India had often broken 'with all their home ties'. In proof of this he cited the West Indian emigration agent's comment that returning Indians from those colonies were required to make a will and that they left their property to a wife or relation in the colony rather than to a person in India.[34] It could be argued instead that many migrants created two sets of ties rather than replacing the old social obligations with the new. A study of letters between migrants and their families in India reveals that in many cases, despite absences of several decades, the acquisition of new families and property overseas, migrants continued to be involved with and interested in the domestic squabbles, financial and marital arrangements of their relatives in India.[35] Frederick Mouat, a Bengal civil servant who visited Mauritius in the mid nineteenth century, extolled the virtues of the migrants he met, describing,

> the intelligence, freedom from prejudice, knowledge of improved modes of agriculture, and habits of industry brought back by the return coolie to his benighted home. I had frequent opportunities of conversing with many of this class on my voyage back to India, and perceived that there was a shrewdness, spirit of independence, and worldly wisdom about the most intelligent of them, that would never permit them again to submit quietly to the crushing, heartless oppression, and utter selfishness of native zamindars, of whose tender mercies they had acquired a most correct and wholesome estimate. . . . In my wanderings I fell in with a few who had given up all hope and wish to revisit their native soil; they seemed comfortable and well to do, and spoke in high terms of the country of their adoption.[36]

Of course, not all migrants returned to India on completion of their indentures. Time-expired labourers in Reunion went to Mauritius, old immigrants in Mauritius went to Natal and Madagascar, Indians in the West Indies travelled between the islands, and some overseas Indians even journeyed from Mauritius to Brazil and China. It was obviously cheaper for employers to import Indians who were already working in neighbouring colonies rather than to recruit them from India. For their part, the governments where the ex-indentured labourers were settled, would be freed from the obligation of providing a return passage to India. As one diaspora spawned another, the indenture experience paved the way for new forms of labour migration in the British Empire and into the postcolonial era.

Notes and References

1. Parliamentary Papers (PP) 1837–38 (669) Thomas Blythe & Sons to Bettington & Co., Sydney, 22 April and 7 October 1836.
2. 7th General Report of the Colonial Land and Emigration Commissioners (GRCLEC), 1847; Geoghegan Report, pp. 9–15.

3. 12th GRCLEC, 1852, Appendix No. 42, Extract of a Report from Mr White to the Governor of British Guiana, 8 November 1950.
4. Geoghegan Report, pp. 16–28.
5. Bengal Emigration Proceedings (BEP), Range 15 vol. 76, Eales to Rivers Thompson, 13 March 1861; J.H. Young, Esq., Commissioner of Burdwan, to the Secretary to the Government of Bengal, 6 February 1861.
6. BEP 15/77 A.M. Monteath to H. Bell, 17 February 1862, encl. Caird to the Magistrate of the 24-Pergunnahs, 19 January 1861.
7. BEP 432/17 correspondence with the Indian Emigration Agents, 1865.
8. BEP 432/20 Baker to Secretary, Government of Bengal, 8 May 1869.
9. 32nd GRCLEC, 1872, Appendix: Act no. VII of 1871.
10. BEP vol. 171 Protector of Emigrants report 1st September 1874.
11. BEP 15/77 E.F. Lautour to G. F. Cockburn 31 January 1862.
12. CO 167/426 Caird to Marriott, 8 November 1860; BEP 15/76 Colonial Secretary, Mauritius to Secretary, Government of Bengal, 6 February 1861, encl. Governor's Minute of January 1861.
13. BEP vol. 171 Protector of Emigrants report 1st September 1874.
14. BEP vol. 432 W.J. Jeffrey, Esq., Emigration Agent for British Guiana and Jamaica, to Captain C. Burbank, Protector of Emigrants, 11 March 1867; Report on Colonial Emigration from the Bengal Presidency, G. Grierson, 1883, Diary, p. 34.
15. India Public Proceedings Range (IPP) 188 vol. 45 Magistrate of Salem to Chief Secretary to Government 3rd December 1856; BEP 432/18 Emigration Agent of British Guiana to Protector of Emigrants Calcutta, 8 July 1867; BEP vol. 168 Extract of a letter from the Agent General of Emigration for the Government of Jamaica, to the Protector of Emigrants, Calcutta, 28 April 1871.
16. BEP 15/76 W.F. Fergusson to E. H. Lushington, 30 December 1861.
17. BEP 15/77 W.F. Furgusson to E.H. Lushington, 7 March 1862.
18. For petitions and letters of immigrants, see the author's *Voices from Indenture Experiences of Indian Migrants in the British Empire*, Leicester University Press, 1996, and *Lakshmi's Legacy*, EOI, 1994. For an example of a district with a tradition of migration, see G. Yamin, 'The Character and Origins of Labour Migration from Ratnagiri District, 1840–1920' *South Asia Research*, vol. 9, no. 1, May 1989.
19. PP. 1859 xvi (2542) Russell to Higginson, 25 May 1855; Russell to Wodehouse 23 June 1855.
20. 27th GRCLEC, 1867.
21. Report on Colonial Emigration from the Bengal Presidency, G. Grierson, 1883, p. 35 and Appendix p. 5.
22. Report of J. Gorrie on the dissent of J. Fraser from the Police Enquiry Commission, 1872.
23. BEP vol. 171 Protector of Emigrants report 1st September 1874.
24. BEP 15/77 E.F. Lautour to G.F. Cockburn 31 January 1862; Major E.T. Dalton to H. Bell, 14 March 1862.
25. Geoghegan Report, p. 67; Report on Colonial Emigration from the Bengal Presidency, G. Grierson, 1883, Diary, p. 69.
26. Report on Colonial Emigration from the Bengal Presidency, G. Grierson, 1883, p. 33. For example, two boys, rejected by the West Indian and Mauritian agents were sent on to Cachar tea plantations: BEP 15/77 S. Wauchope to Secretary, Government of Bengal, 3 July 1862.

27. 11th GRCLEC, 1851, Report of Hugon, Protector of Immigrants.
28. 31st GRCLEC, 1871. See the age and mortality data reproduced in the author's *Servants, Sirdars and Settlers: Indians in Mauritius, 1834–1874*, Oxford University Press, Delhi, 1995.
29. Geoghegan Report, pp. 68–69.
30. BEP vol. 169 Protector of Emigrants, Calcutta to Secretary, Government of Bengal, 29 February 1872.
31. BEP vol. 170 Herbert to Secretary of State for India, 8 July 1873.
32. 32nd GRCLEC, 1872; Indian Emigration Proceedings, vol. 691, 1871–72, Secretary, Government of India to Secretaries, Governments of the Presidencies, 30 August 1872; Government of India to Secretary of State for India 2 September 1872.
33. Carter, M. *Servants, Sirdars & Settlers*, *op. cit.*, pp. 258–59.
34. Report on Colonial Emigration from the Bengal Presidency, G. Grierson, 1883, p. 36.
35. Carter, M. *Voices fro Indenture*, *op. cit.*, *passim.*
36. F. Mouat, Rough Notes of a Trip of Reunion, the Mauritius and Ceylon, Calcutta 1852, p. 96.

TWENTY ❖

The Crisis of Indian Polity: A Historical Perspective

DWIJENDRA TRIPATHI

IT REQUIRES NO GREAT insight to conclude that India at present is passing through a deep crisis, if not the deepest ever. When an American journalist suggested in 1960 that the coming decades might turn out to be the most dangerous for the country as a nation[1], most of us scoffed at it as the wishful thinking of an unfriendly observer. India had just emerged from a long colonial oppression as the result of a combined effort of all its people. There seemed to be no earthly reason to suspect that the unity of purpose demonstrated during the struggle for freedom was in any danger of evaporation. However, even a casual survey of the national scene today would suggest that our smugness was greatly misplaced.

Nothing seems to be working right. Practically all the instruments we had created to ensure the unity and progress of the nation are under great deal of stress – almost to the breaking point. Social tension has perhaps never been more severe in our entire history. Communal relations have reached the nadir – reflected glaringly among other things in the emergence of Muslim ghettos in the major cities, something that even the British, despite their policy of 'divide and rule', could not achieve. Caste wars in some parts have become endemic; revolt against established authorities is the order of the day everywhere; insurgency and violent secessionist movements are a common feature of our national life; law and order situation is out of control practically everywhere. As a result, no other democratic country has committed the might of its armed forces to quell internal disturbances or ensure domestic peace as often as India has done in the last few decades. Political instability, for long a regular feature of the state governments, has extended itself to the Centre, and the entire political class, supposedly the custodian of the political system, stands bereft of all credibility and relevance in the eyes of the ordinary citizen. Corruption at every level, self aggrandisemeant at the cost of common weal, and blatant disregard for all civilized means in pursuit of power and pelf have penetrated our body politic so deeply that they neither occasion shame from the perpetrators nor derision or contempt from the rest of the society. In short, all symptoms that are commonly associated with a national crisis of the first magnitude are present in today's India; all those conditions that had preceded the breakup of the country on numerous occasions in the past seem to be testing the resilience of the nation once again.

How have we come to this pass? What has caused this crisis? It is tempting to attribute this to the duplicity of our politicians, to the absence of sagacious leadership, to the greed of our people, to the rising consumerism, to the disappearance of morals from our public life, to the dynamics of development or to the travails of maturation of a relatively young nation. Most nations during their development phases have experienced some chaos, some disruption before stabilizing, and it may be argued that what we are witnessing in India is a normal process of change. In other words, it will be tempting to explain away the Indian crisis with reference to the birthpangs of a nation or look upon it merely as a temporary aberration. However, the fact that what we are witnessing in India today is essentially a recurrence of what the country has experienced periodically almost at regular intervals in its long sweep of history would militate against any attempt to locate the roots of the present convulsions in the immediacy of circumstances. We need a more rational explanation.

I

The facts are well known but they bear repetition in the interest of providing a proper perspective for our analysis. The process of state formation, in the present sense of the term, did not start until long after the Aryan society had attained a certain measure of stability and begun to have a vague sense of a pan-Indian consciousness. This is clear from the fact that while the scriptural literature belonging to the early phases of our history sings to the devotion of Bharatkhand and Jumbudvipa, obviously referring to the entire Indian land mass, the polity of the age was characterized by innumerable tribal formations, independent of one another, scattered through the length and breadth of the subcontinent. It is not until around the beginning of the sixth century BC that somewhat larger political formations began to emerge. Though of modest sizes by present standards, they were known as *mahajanapadas* (giant states) which unquestionably they were in comparison with the tiny entities of the earlier period. As many as sixteen of them were in the north India alone in addition to a number of autonomous republics of relatively smaller sizes. The southern peninsula must have had its own subdivisions, although we do not know the actual position. So fragmented was the Indian polity, it is doubtful if any of the rulers presiding over the destinies of these states dreamt of expanding his sway over the entire sub-continent, although the concept of *chakravartin* (universal king) had already developed as the literature of the period indicates. In fact the emergence of the first all-India empire, or something close to it, had to wait for another two hundred years when Chandragupta Maurya (322–298 BC) laid a strong foundation by subjugating practically all the principalities, big and small, of the north India and his grandson Ashoka completed the task by extending his sway to the entire south except the southernmost tip of the peninsula.

The first ever territorial integration of India, however, did not outlive Ashoka. The empire created by him could not, like Ulysess' sword, be managed by weaker hands and soon broke into smaller principalities. India once again became a geographical expression as it had been before the rise of the Mauryan power, and remained so until the rise of the Guptas almost more than five centuries later. One of the rulers belonging to this dynasty, Samudragupta (330–80), once again brought practically the entire land under his hegemony. Although he did not rule over the whole subcontinent directly, he forced, through conquest or diplomacy, the rulers of the principalities, out of his direct domain, to accept his suzerainty and pay him tribute. This imperial unity too, like the one achieved by Ashoka, did not last long and disappeared within three generations of Samudragupta's death. King Harshvardhan (606–647) tried to emulate Ashoka and Samudragupta, but succeeded in uniting only a part of northern and western India under him, and even this partial unity did not survive long after his death.

The territorial dismemberment that followed Harsha's death lasted for almost six centuries until Alauddin Khalji carved out another all-India empire. But this too perished with his death, heralding another long spell of political disintegration that lasted almost up to the emergence of Mughal Emperor Akbar (1556–1605), with only Muhammad bin Tughalaq providing an all too brief interlude of unity in between. The territorial integration achieved by Akbar, however, was partial as he did not exercise control over a large part of the south. In view of this it will be fair to conclude that not until the reign of Aurangzeb (1659–1707) did India witness another imperial unity in the real sense after the break up of the Khalji empire. And history repeated itself once again after Aurangzeb's death: within a few years the territorial unity achieved by him vanished, yielding place to innumerable independent political units almost perpetually at war against one another. Taking advantage of the perennial dissension among the rulers of these successor states, the British in gradual stages brought the whole subcontinent under their control by 1818, almost hundred years after the disintegration of the Mughal empire.

Our survey of the imperial unities in Indian history may give the impression that their durations coincided with the entire span of the reigns of their respective architects – extending into the reigns of their successors as well in the case of Samudragupta and Akbar – right from their accession. We, of course, know that this was hardly the case. Most of these empire-builders took some time to settle down in their new roles before setting off on a conquest course to expand their boundaries, and remained engaged in the task almost until the end of their reigns. Also, it is inconceivable that their imperial edifices crumbled all of a sudden on the morrow of their deaths; the process of disintegration took at least a few years to complete itself except in the case of the Tughalaq empire, the decline of which began in the life-time of its architect, Muhammad-bin-Tughalaq himself. Even if we ignore these finer points of calculation, the total duration covered by all the empires that emerged with some semblance of a pan-Indian character between the early sixth century BC when the process of state formation gained momentum, and the early nineteenth century, when the British established their undisputed sway over the entire subcontinent, would not exceed five hundred years. In other words, even under a generous estimate, all the imperial unities in Indian history put together can claim less than one-fifth of a span of 2500 years long history. A more precise estimate, allowing for the fact that durations of the imperial unities in question were somewhat shorter than the reigns of the empire-builders (and their successors in a few cases), would bring down the aggregate still further.

Our account of India's imperial unities must be read along with two more caveats. One, boundaries differed from empire to empire; no two empires had the same boundaries. And two, in addition to these big empires, there arose from time to time large kingdoms in various parts of the subcontinent which have left their imprint on the course of India's history and culture: Shunga, Kushan, Shatvahana, Chalukya, Chola, Pratihar, Vijaya Nagar, Bahamani, Maratha to name only the most notable ones. Although they were regional powers at best, some of them regarded themselves as empires, and have been regarded as such by later commentators. These two caveats taken together would suggest that empire was an elastic concept and did not signify a definite territorial boundary. By the same token, titles such as *chakravartin, samrat*, or *shahanshah* which were adopted by the Indian rulers, holding territories of varying sizes, had only a notional value; they did not connote an all-India jurisdiction. If we accept that, sporadic emergence of imperial unities or large kingdoms at different times in Indian history cannot be viewed as stages in the progressive evolution of an Indian nation-state. India remained more of a geographical expression than an integrated political entity all through these centuries.

II

A pan Indian culture, however, continued to take shape, despite territorial fragmentation being a rule rather than an exception well up to the first quarter of the nineteenth century. The process started at a very early stage of our history when the Aryan immigrants embraced some of the beliefs and rituals of the earlier inhabitants such as the Shakti and Shiva worship. Being devotees primarily of natural forces and without the constraints of an organized church to befog their thinking, it was easy for them to have an open mind about a variety of precepts and practices, subject only to some broad moral parameters. As a result there developed a remarkable degree of freedom of thought and even of action in the early Aryan society. Conflicting schools of thought prevailed among different groups of Aryans who made no attempt to stifle the intellectual freedom of others, whether within or out of their fold. In later years as the Aryan power and influence expanded, their religious ideas and practices became much more elaborate and organized, but intellectual freedom remained a cherished legacy with them. That the ancient Indian scriptures, including the Vedas, have differing positions on a host of major issues is a proof in point. So divergent are the views expressed in them that a number of religious sects that later emerged in India can trace their respective doctrines, mutually conflicting though they are, to one or the other canonical text of the ancient Aryans. More importantly, the early Aryan society tolerated dissent from even those who challenged the very foundation of its religious-spiritual edifice: the belief in a supreme being, the theory of *karma*, and the transmigration of soul.

The examples of the Ajivikas and Charvakas would suffice to illustrate this point. Although we are not quite sure of their times, it is certain that both these systems of thought came in existence before the birth of Buddhism and Jainism. Though differing in many essential details with regard to their philosophical base and principles, both these schools denied the moral consequences of action and the existence of non-material substance in man or universe. Both were godless and ridiculed ruthlessly practically every tenet of the conventional Aryan thought; and for both, the material well-being was the only goal of life. With a view to denying the existence of a creator for the universe, they emphasized that perception was the only true source of knowledge, rejecting the validity of inference, the other source of knowledge according to the ancient Indian system of reasoning.[2]

Ajivikas and Charvakas, it must be stressed, were not isolated systems. They represented a tradition of heretical thinkers which continued at least up to the sixth century BC – the age of a veritable intellectual revolution. We do not know how influential they were or how large their following was. But this is beside the point. What is important is that these heretical preachers were allowed to propagate their views without let or hindrance. Even if we accept the argument that the Aryan society probably ignored them because their influence was too limited to pose any threat to the establishment school, the same cannot be said about the Buddhism and Jainism which flourished around the sixth century BC, and attracted a large segment of the population into their fold – and which too were heretical in their basic character. The conclusion is inescapable that the Aryan commitment to intellectual freedom – freedom of thought and expression – was so deep that it could not be denied even to those who openly sought to demolish the very philosophical base without which the Aryan superstructure of ethos and beliefs could not stand.

In fact, the early Aryans seem to have had a relatively flexible attitude to religion, subject to some general parameters. The world '*dharma*' signifying the body of their religious precepts and practices strongly suggests this. Loosely translated as 'duty to oneself and society', it had a much broader connotation than the narrow sense in which 'religion' is used, and implied a much greater scope for individual judgement in matters spiritual – and even temporal. The stress in the Smriti literature on *shravana*, (listening), *manana* (reflection) and *yoga* (application)[3] as the three principal props of learning also indicates that there was very little room for religious regimentation in the early Aryan society. For, what the above-mentioned learning process implied was that receiving the lesson from the teacher was only the first stage; to complete his education, the pupil must apply his own mind and come to an independent judgement. A system of education based on these principles would have been inconsistent with a less catholic socio-cultural system than the word '*dharma*', according to us, connotes. No other word seems to have signified the Aryan religion in general at least up to the sixth century BC, when a number of sects began to come to the surface with more distinctive proper names. Of the heterodox sects, the Jainism and Buddhism emerged as the most dominant, while the Shaivism and Vaishnavaism a little later turned out to be the most important in the orthodox category. The word '*dharma*', however, continued to be used for the Aryan religion in a generic sense for several centuries until Hinduism displaced it.

A society where the flexibility implied in the open-ended concept of '*dharma*' set the norm of social-cultural interaction, and well-entrenched tradition of intellectual freedom ensured that the dissent even of the most radical nature would be tolerated, must have found it relatively easy to accommodate within its fold a great variety of groups and communities, or peaceably coexist with them without causing much social tension. This explains why most of the later immigrants coming from various places and belonging to various racial, linguistic and socio-cultural backgrounds – the Sakas, the Kushans, the Greeks, the Parthians, the Huns – who came as invaders, adventurers or simply intruders were so easily absorbed in the Aryan society. Admittedly, the fact that the size of these later immigrant groups was small and most of them did not have much of a distinctive culture to boast of, must have helped the process, but it was primarily because of the

Aryan catholicity that the assimilation was so complete as to leave no definite mark of their identity in the country of their adoption. Again, it is because of this kind of catholicity that the Aryans found it easy to accommodate, even assimilate, those segments of the Indian population whom they encountered in the course of their expansion in the subcontinent – particularly in the south which could boast of an equally developed civilization.

Another important factor that influenced the process of accommodation and absorption was the caste system. Although its original character, signifying a social division of labour, had already been eroded and the system had become hereditary for all practical purposes, new castes could still emerge – in fact, never ceased to emerge throughout our entire history – on occupational basis. This could easily help situate the immigrant groups as well as the non-Aryan segments of the Indian population in the new society that was taking shape as a result of intermingling of peoples and cultures. Most of the Rajput clans, for instance, identified themselves with ancient Kshatriyas to signify their position as ruling classes, and came to be accepted as such, although they probably originated with a number of foreign tribes that intruded into the subcontinent after the break-up of the Mauryan Empire.

It is important to remember that the new society that was emerging, transcending the Aryan stock, did not comprise only those who could be accommodated within the Aryan scheme of things; even groups and communities which came to India with very strong ties of deeply entrenched socio-cultural traditions – such as Jews and Zoroastrians found India to be eminently hospitable. The Jews are believed to have entered India as early as AD 70, following a devastating fire at Jerusalem, and they have continued with their religious-cultural pursuits to this day without an iota of persecution which, otherwise, has been their fate elsewhere. Likewise, the Zoroastrians who fled their original homeland, Persia, to escape conversion to Islam in the eighth century have maintained their racial purity and cultural distinctiveness with remarkable success. Strangely enough, even a proselytizing sect – neither Judaism nor Zoroastrianism is one in a strict sense – such as Christianity had no difficulty in making an unhindered entry into India as early as the first century AD when St. Thomas, one of Christ's apostles, is believed to have come to the country, won converts to his faith, and established a church in south India which continues to exist to this day.

It would have been a miracle if the cohesiveness that characterized the early Aryan society had remained unaffected by all these changes. The heterogeneity that set in was evident more or less in almost every walk of life, but there were two areas that reflected the new trend most visibly. These were language and religion. As the new immigrant groups belonging to the non-Aryan stocks came under the Aryan socio-cultural umbrella, and the Aryan influence expanded to the whole of the subcontinent, a number of colloquial dialects began to replace Sanskrit, the language of the Aryans, as media of common interaction in the northern and western regions. Although all these were offshoots of Sanskrit, they in due course assumed independent identities, developed their own literature and for all practical purposes became the languages of common discourse in their respective regions. Besides, there were four languages of the Dravidian family – Tamil, Telugu, Kannada, and Malayalam – that had already attained considerable maturity and could boast of highly developed literature. An inevitable consequence of these developments was that Sanskrit, the *lingua franca* of the early Aryans, ceased to be the language of the common man and remained limited to the elite; it also remained the only link language in the subcontinent.

As regards religious heterogeneity, we have already noted that out of the many sectarian systems that emerged from the intellectual upheaval of the sixth century BC, Jainism and Buddhism were the most dominant in the heterodox category while Shaivaism and Vaishnavaism grew to be the most important among the orthodox sects. Although the philosophical roots of all these four religious orders lay in the ancient Aryan texts, they differed from one another with regard to the supreme objects of devotion, modes of worship, religious rituals, and the roads to salvation. And these differences appeared to be so irreconcilable to their adherents that the Brahmans, the interpreters of the orthodox sects, advised their followers to keep away from Jain temples – one should prefer being crushed to death under an elephant's feet to visiting Jain temples – and ridiculed the Buddhists in no uncertain terms. In the eyes of the Jains and Buddhists, on the other hand, the orthodox sects were perpetrators of inequity and exploitation. Strangely, the Shaivaits and the Vaishnavaits too had violent differences between them so that they would keep away from one another's places of worship and refrain from mentioning the names of one another's supreme deity even inadvertently.[4] To add to the complexity of the situation, the two heterodox sects got divided into factions – Jainism into two major denominations, Shvetambar and Digambar, and Buddhism into three, Hinayana, Mahayana, and Vajrayana. Shaivaism and Vaishnavaism, on the other hand, while retaining their unity on the surface, developed characteristics peculiar to different regions. While a sizeable section of the subcontinental population followed one or the other of these sects or their factions, and a few isolated religious orders claimed the allegiance of a small fraction, the majority perhaps still clung to the original concept of *Dharma*. With the passage of time, the animosity between the orthodox and heterodox schools ceased to be a factor. For, the orthodox sects became much more tolerant of Jainism, which never attracted a very large following, and Buddhism virtually disappeared from the land of its birth and ceased to be a serious threat, so much so that the orthodox school was magnanimous enough to incorporate the Buddha among its pantheon. Strangely enough, the chasm between the orthodox school, particularly Shaivaism and Vaishnavaism, remained still unbridged.

Thus despite centuries long intermingling of races and cultures, the subcontinental populace was still divided into a congeries of religious-linguistic pluralities with very strong regional or even local affiliations, when the Muslim conquerors laid the foundation of the Delhi Sultanate at the beginning of the thirteenth century. Even though the philosophical roots of these pluralities lay in the ancient Aryan texts, they could hardly claim to have a common identity. There was no generic nomenclature to refer to the different pluralities, the allegiance of their followers to a common land was limited to their attachment to the centres of pilgrimage associated with their sects scattered all over the subcontinent, and their reference to Bharatkhand and Jambudvipa in their prayers was simply the continuance of a tradition and signifying little else. For the Muslim immigrant, however, all inhabitants of Hindustan – the name the Persians had given long ago to the entire land mass beyond the River Sindhu (whose name they could not pronounce correctly because of phonetic limitation of their language) – were Hindus. Somehow, however, this title was never applied to the Jews, Parsees, and the Christians here. 'Indian' became a common appellation for the rest of the population, comprising a variety of groups, sects and races, including the untouchables and the tribals. It is not realized very often that it was the Muslim immigrant who, ironically enough, provided a crucial base for the revolution of what is now popularly considered to be the majority community in India.

III

The rise of Islam in the wake of Muslim immigration offered probably the most serious challenge to the two basic strategies that had characterized the approach to dealing with earlier immigrant groups. Assimilation was out of the question, for Islam, unlike the earlier groups, represented a resurgent culture, acutely conscious of its identity and destiny. And accommodation or co-existence was rendered difficult by the manner in which Islam made its entry into the subcontinent. The entry of even those of the earlier immigrants who came originally as invaders did not hurt in any manner the susceptibilities of the common man, as their engagements were limited to rulers alone. In contrast, the early Muslim invaders – Mahmud of Ghazni in particular – also destroyed Hindu places of worship. They did so to satiate their greed for wealth, supposedly hidden in the temples, but justified their act in the name of religion. This left a bad taste in the mouth of the ordinary Hindu, the hangover of which would continue to vitiate the Hindu-Muslim relations for centuries to come. It is worth remembering that much before Mahmud's invasions, Arab traders had commercial interaction with their counterparts on the western coast and some of them had even settled down there.[5] It is also noteworthy that the relations between the Hindus on the one hand and the Christians, Jews or Parsees on the other never took a communal colour, and the Hindus and Muslims in south India, unaffected by Mahmud's misadventures, continued to live in greater harmony.

And yet, accommodation did take place although the process was necessarily slow. In the next six hundred years, many Hindu customs and rituals would creep into the Muslim social world and vice-versa. A large number of Arabic and Persian words, the languages that the Muslim immigrants brought with them, became a part of the vocabulary of regional languages. A new language, Urdu, was born from the synthesis of Hindi, the language of a large part of the north, and Arabic and Persian. Practically no sphere of life – dress, manners, customs, food and architecture, literature, music and so on – remained free from the imprint of interaction between the Muslim and Hindu communities. Even in the realm of religion, where the scope for accommodation appeared to be the least, a number of Sufi saints and Bhakti poets like Kabir and Nanak attempted to bridge the gulf by stressing the commonality of the apparently conflicting systems. The fact that both the Hindus and Muslims still pay respects to the *dargahs* (mausoleums) of Sufi saints all over the country and that there are shrines, howsoever few, where both the communities offer prayers indicates the measure of the success these messengers of unity had achieved. Encouraged by the prospects of synthesis between Hinduism and Islam, Emperor Akbar even attempted to found, though unsuccessfully, a new religion drawing on the commonalities of both, and Prince Dara Shikoh's love for ancient Aryan scriptures is well known. In many instances, Hindu converts to Islam carried into their new religion some of their pre-conversion practices, even though inconsistent with the Shariat, and some elements of Hindu caste system made inroads into sections of Indian Muslims,[6] despite their allegiance to perhaps the most egalitarian religious system in the world.

Though no other Muslim ruler except Akbar actively promoted accommodation between the two systems of religion, none consciously or deliberately hindered the process either. We can cite three facts to support this observation. For one thing, there were few cases of forced conversion. Some Hindu chieftains led their subjects into Islam with an eye on the benefits derivable from affinity to the religion of the sovereign power and a small section of high caste Hindus was motivated by the hope of being a part of the power structure. But a large majority of the converts came from the low caste categories whose position in the Hindu caste structure was none too enviable. They were naturally lured by the relatively egalitarian character of Islam.

Secondly, no Muslim ruler ever tried to establish a theocratic state. Admittedly, some rulers did impose *jezia* (tax chargeable from infidels under

Islamic law) but in all other matters, Hindu law was applied to decide cases involving the Hindus. And *jezia* in all probability was simply an economic measure or a means to placate the fundamentalist clergy. In fact, the basic framework adopted by the successive Muslim rulers for governance represented a remarkable continuity of the essential features of the administrative systems developed under the Hindu rulers. And thirdly, instances of direct religious persecution of the Hindus were few and far between; armed conflicts in most cases were political in nature – a war of conquest or a response to a rebellion or a threat to the sovereign power, the kind of situation that no governing system can afford to ignore regardless of the religion of the opponent. No proper count has been made, but on a rough reckoning, armed conflicts between Muslim rulers probably out numbered those between the Muslim and the Hindu rulers in Indian history.[7] It is also not without significance that the communal riots were a rare phenomenon in pre-British India.

While mutual accommodation between the Hindus and the Muslims was understandably slow under the conditions prevailing after the emergence of the Muslim kingdoms in India, the process of synthesis between the orthodox sects, particularly Shaivaism and Vaishnavaism also continued to be slow. The rise of Islam could not provide a strong enough impetus for these sects to discover common grounds between them. Perhaps they had not yet exhausted their capacity for conflict and were still far from reaching a point of consensus – a process through which all religious-cultural movements in India have arrived at syntheses. Whatever the case, it took another couple of centuries before the orthodox Hindu sects could leave behind their traditional animosities, discover the essential commonalities between them and regard one another as complements and not adversaries. Some of the Bhakti poets, notably Tulsi, contributed significantly to this welcome development.[8] Although another two centuries would elapse before the generic expression 'Hinduism' would emerge to signify all different denominations having roots in ancient Aryan scriptures – and this would be the contribution of the Europeans who coined the phrase for the first time around 1830 – by the middle of the seventeenth century, sectarian differences between them had ceased to be of consequence.

The Indian Islam, in contrast, appeared to be somewhat more fragmented than Hinduism when the destiny of India passed into the British hands. The descendants of original immigrants were regarded superior to the later converts, and distinctions, based on the pre-conversion castes continued to divide the latter group. Besides, there were divisions based on almost irreconcilable differences in the interpretation of Islamic philosophy and tradition even though the sources of Islamic theology were much less varied and perhaps more authentic than those of Hinduism. With Sunnis, Shias,

Bohras, Khojas – and a little later Bahais and Ahmadiyas – the Muslims were no less a divided lot than the Hindus. And then the distinctive regional characteristics impacting on the socio-cultural life of the people in the subcontinent affected the Muslim society as much as they did the other constituents of India's population. Neither the Hindu nor the Muslim society, thus, was a cultural or even a communal monolith.

India, thus, was still a fractured society when the British rose to supremacy, despite all the synthesis that had taken place. Numerous multicentric circles of caste, religion, sect, language, region, custom, and tradition still characterized this politically fragmented land mass. And yet, there were unmistakable signs that the gathering momentum of the process of fusion, or at least accommodation, among these pluralities was leading inexorably on to the emergence of a composite culture. In other words, the pan-Indian consciousness had made definite strides. This is what commentators of practically all persuasions from Vincent Smith to Jawaharlal Nehru had in view when they stressed on the cultural unity of India.[9] Some recent writers refer to the same thing by calling India a civilzation state. It must be added, however, that the identification of the different constituents of this cultural unity or civilization state with India as a political unit was no stronger than that of various regions of Europe with Christendom in the Middle Ages. The pan-Indian consciousness was still not strong enough to sustain a pan-Indian state.

The British control over India for well over hundred and twenty-five years both facilitated and hindered the process of unification – territorially as well as emotionally. For one thing, the entire subcontinent now was under a single paramount authority. And then the new rulers took a number of steps to govern this country smoothly and exploit its resources efficiently for the benefit of their own people: introducing a common currency as a legal tender throughout the land; dismantling the numerous trade barriers such as custom *chowkies*; promoting the learning of English; building an extensive railway network; expanding the road system; developing modern communication systems, such as posts and telegraph; setting up an elaborate machinery for the administration of justice; and so on. While achieving their intended objectives, these measures also produced some unintended and welcome results. Together, they tied up the existing congeries of local markets into a sort of national market, bridged the distances, both physical and emotional, between places, and created much greater facility for interaction between people living in different parts of the country. Regional or local loyalities, of course, did not disappear, but they now had to increasingly contend with a growing sense of identification with the entire land. If the British were the first to accomplish the territorial unification of the entire country, ironically, they can also claim the credit for giving a much greater impetus to the pan-

Indian consciousness than any other governing system in the past. Exposure to western liberalism through imperial connection and English education provided further reinforcement to the process.

The British ruling presence, at the same time, interrupted the autonomous process of accommodation through which various socio-cultural pluralities had discovered a measure of common identity until then. This process in all probability would have gained momentum and reached its logical conclusion in due course, had not an external arbiter intervened – an external arbiter that had its own axe to grind. This arbiter fully exploited the situation to serve its own interest wherever the level of accommodation was still fragile and, if allowed to consolidate beyond a point, might jeopardize the future of the Indian Empire.

The way the colonial authorities dealt with the Indian freedom movement illustrates their role both as unifiers and disruptors. Perhaps the most emphatic expression of the pan-Indian consciousness generated during the British rule was the national movement. Founded by a small group of the elite, the Indian National Congress was a harmless organization, demanding nothing more than some minor political concessions, at the time of its birth. The colonial authorities welcomed the development and even blessed it. They, however, became uneasy when the organization began to speak in an increasingly radical language, reflecting the growing sense of interdependence and common destiny among the Indians, cutting across regions, religions, castes, or languages. Realizing the threat that this development, if unchecked, would pose to their imperial interest, and aware that the mutual suspicion and mistrust between the Hindus and the Muslims had not yet completely disappeared, the alien custodians of India's destiny did everything possible to widen the gulf between them. Beginning with the attempt to partition Bengal, which would have upset the balance of population in the province as it existed then, they never stopped their clever divisive machinations that even a leader of Gandhi's sagacity and sensitivity could not quite cope with. It is no accident that the All India Muslim League was founded barely a year after Lord Curzon's abortive attempt to divide Bengal, and the principle of communal representation, providing for the election of Muslim representatives to the Indian legislatures by the Muslim electorate alone, was introduced just a couple of years later. This principle, it may be recalled, remained an integral part of all the constitutional schemes the British devised for India before their departure.

Separate representations for Hindus and Muslims had already become a *fait accompli* when Gandhi emerged on the Indian political firmament. But when the British tried a similar trick some time later to divide the scheduled castes from the rest of the Hindu community, he, by this time the tallest leader in the country, foiled their strategy by using all his strength including the threat of a fast unto death. For him the struggle for freedom had to proceed alongside the effort to create a sense of nationhood by tying up the loose ends that still existed in the pan-Indian consciousness, by uniting Indians of all hues under a common umbrella against the colonial domination, and by generating a sense of emotional bond among them, transcending regional, religious or linguistic barriers. Hence the stress on mass action, Hindu-Muslim unity, integration of the untouchables and the tribals with the mainstream of the Indian population, and development of Hindustani as a link language. Gandhi, thus, was looking beyond freedom; he was preparing his people to attend to the common task of reconstruction, following the British departure, lest the fissiparous forces that had overpowered the forces of unity on numerous occasions in the past might prevail once again.

And in this aim he succeeded to a very large extent. For, the Congress which was still an elite organization before Gandhi came to the helm, became under his leadership a truly national movement representing practically all Indians except the separatist Muslims. And fighting against a common adversary, Indians became much more aware of the common bonds that united them than at any time before. For the first time in the entire history of India, the unifying forces appeared to have gained an upper hand against the forces of division. Gandhi's leadership also provided a sense of empowerment to the depressed sections, that had remained all these centuries condemned to the wretchedness of their position thanks to the inequity of the caste system. By the time freedom came, a broad consensus had already emerged in favour of an affirmative action to improve the lot of the scheduled castes and tribes. In short, Gandhi not only won freedom for India but also succeeded in making the numerous pluralities, in which the Indians were divided, much more conscious of their common destiny than anytime before. Some conquerors in the past had created simply territorial unities in the subcontinent; Gandhi, for the first time in Indian history, laid the foundation of a nation. Quite justifiably, Subhash Chandra Bose, despite his differences with Gandhi in the matter of strategies, called him the 'Father of the Nation'[10] even before the country was free. The popular enthusiasm that greeted the advent of Independence, despite the division of the subcontinent, and the optimism with which the Indians belonging to all sections looked into the future was a pointer to what this remarkable leader had achieved during his thirty-year leadership of the freedom movement.

IV

What the above survey indicates is that the divisive forces have always been more potent than the factors of unity throughout out history. Admittedly, some measure of unity was achieved on occasions, but it always happened under exceptional leadership, and could not survive once the quality of leadership declined. The fate of empires created by rulers from Ashoka to Aurangzeb bears this out. These imperial unities, at any rate, did little to generate a meaningful sense of identification with a single nation. This to a certain extent was achieved during the freedom movement, particularly during the Gandhian era. But it was still a young, fragile, vulnerable unity. It needed careful nursing so that it could attain requisite maturity to prevent the centrifugal forces from gaining an upper hand once again. This is where the post-Independence custodians of India's destiny have been found grievously wanting. Instead of consolidating, the free India has been progressively dissipating the gains made during the struggle for independence. Ironically, the nation's constitution, its basic instrument of governance, has been made a tool for this dubious achievement.

The constitution that came in force in 1950 was not a perfect document. Its preference for a parliamentary form of government was primarily due to the founding fathers' exposure to and fascination for the British model. In view of the fact that Indians had no meaningful experience in running democratic institutions it would have been better to opt for some other system requiring a more flexible political morality and party discipline than the parliamentary form demands. The choice of the federal structure was, however, based on a more practical consideration: the need to provide sufficient scope for regional diversities to express and flourish, and keep under effective check at the same time the fissiparous tendencies that had shown remarkable tenacity all through India's history. The provision for a strong centre, however, was a significant departure from the traditional position of the Congress which had consistently pleaded for more powers for the provinces in the past.[11] Perhaps the developments immediately prior to Independence, culminating in the partition of the country, forced the founding fathers to review their traditional position. The division of powers between the centre and the states was such as to invest the constitution with a much more unitary bias than the founding fathers would have intended, had they followed the traditional Congress position. Out of these, the one relating to the dismissal of a state government on a mere assertion of the governor, a centre's appointee, that the constitutional machinery had broken down had the potential to strike at the very root of the federal structure.

The founding fathers could not perceive the serious threat to the federal scheme that would come from the organizational structure of the Indian National Congress, the ruling party at the centre as well as in the States for most of the time after the Constitution came into force. The president of the Congress during the pre-Independence days, when it functioned as a national movement rather than as a political party, enjoyed enoromous powers. This perhaps was necessary to ensure a unity of command, as in a war-like situation, but the structure of the party ought to have been changed after it became a ruling party so that its internal functioning conformed to, and thus reinforced, the federal character of the polity the nation's constitution intended to foster. However, the party remained as centralized in its internal functioning as before and its president continued to be the 'High Command', as during the pre-Independence days.

Despite these limitations of the constitution and the party structures, the Indian democracy functioned fairly well during the Nehru era (1947–64). Three general elections for the central and state legislatures were organized successfully and the manner in which governments at every level were formed and functioned conformed to the principles of parliamentary democracy both in letter and spirit. The federal principles suffered little strains. Except on one single occasion, when the Communist government in Kerala was dismissed on doubtful grounds in 1959, the Centre seldom stretched the constitutional provisions to interfere with the functioning of state governments. And this despite the fact that the same person – Jawaharlal Nehru – was the Prime Minister under a constitution with a unitary bias and also the head of a ruling party with a unitary character for most of the time. This combination could have proved deadly for the young Indian democracy.

If it did not and the parliamentary system within a federal framework functioned smoothly during this phase, it was because of three reasons. First, the generation participating in the democratic experiment then had just emerged from the crucible of the freedom struggle, and the idealism of the Gandhian era had not yet entirely disappeared. Elections were by and large peaceful and orderly and the use of unfair means for electoral success was still within the tolerance limit. Secondly, the freedom movement had thrown up a large number of leaders with national stature who had a mass base in their respective regions. Most of these leaders were at the helm of affairs in the various states and could not be pushed around by the party high command. And lastly, Nehru himself was a great respecter of democratic norms and institutions. As a principal framer of the Constitution, he must have considered it his sacred duty to ensure that its provisions were honoured both in letter and sprit. No surprise, then, that during this phase, the chief ministers were the leaders of the legislature parties in their respective states in the true sense of the word. They held the post because they enjoyed the support of the legislators belonging to the majority party in the state assemblies and not because of the blessings of the central leadership of the party. With the legitimacy this provided to their position, coupled with their personal standing, these leaders functioned as a countervailing force against the unitary biases in the constitutions of the country and the ruling party. Matters affecting their states were settled through the process of mutual accommodation. Solutions for regional problems thus could be sought in a national perspective, reinforcing the sense of common identity and interindependence in a multi-cultural society.

All this began to change after the general elections of 1967 which was a watershed in the history of Indian democracy. It marked the end of the Congress hegemony on the nation's polity and it heralded the entry of a new generation of Indians into politics for whom the idealism of the freedom movement was a distant phenomenon, for whom the electoral success and the power that came with it was too tempting a goal to be risked by undue concern for the means employed to achieve it. This trend gained momentum as the years passed resulting in the growing use of money power, intimidation and force to win elections, and lack of concern for party loyalties to acquire governmental power or benefit by it. Violence became so endemic to our political life that hundreds of persons have lost their lives in practically every election held since 1967 (until T.N. Seshan, the Chief Election Commissioner from 1991 to 1996, brought some improvement). And in no other parliamentary democracy had defection ended prematurely the tenures of so many governments so often as in India since 1967.[12] A political system where the electorate have to risk their lives in the process of appointing their government, where they have to contend with many extraneous factors while expressing their will, and where their elected representatives thwart the mandate given to them with impunity – this is what defection in essence amounts to – can hardly be considered an effective instrument of governance.

The federal structure, the other pillar of the Constitution, did not fare better than the parliamentary system during this phase. Although the Congress recovered from the setback it had received in the elections of 1967, it no more had the benefit of such leadership at the state levels as could act as a countervailing force to the unitary biases in the structures of the government and the party. Some of the old leaders with firm political base in their states were either dead or sidelined because of the split in the party in 1969. As the political rejuvenation of the party, reflected in the resounding success of Congress in the general election of 1971, was rightly attributed to Indira Gandhi, who like her father remained Prime Minister as well as party president, she had no fear of challenge from any quarter in the party or the government. But unlike her father, she frequently tampered with the state governments – removing the chief ministers, using the power of the central government if they belonged to the opposition, or her prerogatives as the Congress President in case they were from her own party – as if they were the vassals of the Centre. The practice continued under Rajiv Gandhi too, except that he demonstrated still greater proclivity for changing the heads of state governments belonging to his own party! Tampering with the state governments was not a Congress habit alone; the short-lived Janata Party government at the centre in 1977 too dismissed a number of Congress governments in the states on the specious plea that the defeat of that party in the parliamentary elections of 1977 indicated that it had lost the mandate to rule over the states where it was already in power!

This is not the occasion to analyse the merits and demerits of the specific cases of tampering with the state governments by the central authority. What is of substance is that such acts hampered the process of the growth of a healthy federal polity. A provision meant to be invoked sparingly to meet special exigency has been used so often and sometimes so nonchalantly that it has made a mockery of the federal structure. No wonder then that the central government very often is the target of resentment and attack regarding matters which come within the purview of state responsibilities. Consequently, the kind of advantage a truly federal structure could have provided to a vast country like India in containing the impact of regional issues on the national polity has never been fully realized. In many cases, resentment against the failure to find acceptable solution to local-regional issues, falling within the jurisdiction of state governments, has been allowed to go so much out of hand as to threaten the unity of the nation itself. The Ayodhya issue is an excellent example.

If the parliamentary system within a federal framework became a caricature of what it was intended to be, the founding fathers' approach to improving the lot of the hitherto neglected sections of the Indian population was twisted beyond recognition by the post-Independence generation. The framers of the Constitution divided these sections in two categories: (*i*) scheduled castes and scheduled tribes, and (*ii*) backward class of citizens or weaker sections of the population. The first category was an easily identifiable lot, and a broad national consensus had already emerged, thanks largely to Gandhi's relentless efforts, in favour of some immediate action to eliminate the sense of alienation among the people in the category. The founding fathers' prescription for them was unambiguous, direct and clearcut: constitutional abolition of untouchability, reservation of seats for scheduled castes and scheduled tribes in the central and state legislatures, and an enabling provision authorizing reservation of jobs for them in central services. Aware, however, as they were that these privileges if continued beyond a point would be counter-productive and hamper national integration, they placed a limit of ten years for their operation. Reservation thus was meant to be a purely transitory expedient.

As for the backward classes or the weaker sections, they were not easily identifiable as backwardness could be caused by a host of factors and might have regional or even local characteristics. The constitution, therefore, contained simply a general, enabling clause investing the Indian state with the authority to take whatever legitimate steps it deemed fit to ameliorate the condition of people in this category. Apparently, the founding fathers were clear neither about the composition of the backward classes, nor about the action to be taken for their benefit. Also, they did not attach the same degree of urgency for action in this regard as in the case of the scheduled castes and tribes. No wonder that this enabling clause was included in the directive principles of the constitution, the primary purpose of which was simply to define and delimit the parameters of state action for social change.[13]

There can be no doubt that the manner in which the provisions to ameliorate the position of the weaker sections in both the categories specified above have been implemented has resulted in a serious distortion of the original intent behind them. The reservations for scheduled castes and tribes have been extended every ten years with the result that even after half a century the end of what was meant to be a purely temporary measure does not seem to be anywhere in sight. No attempt has ever been made to assess whether the scheduled castes and tribes still require the crutches of reservation, whether the provision has not outlived its utility, or whether it is not fragmenting the beneficiary groups themselves. As no political party has the courage to abolish it for fear of losing the votes of the beneficiary castes, the privilege is likely to become a permanent feature of our polity.

But this is nothing in comparison with the distortions in implementing the provision for 'backward classes'. As the framers of the constitution did not consider it necessary to identify these classes, the Government of India appointed in 1953 a commission for the purpose headed by a well – known freedom fighter – Kaka Kalelkar. Submitted three years later, its report conceded that caste could not be the basis to determine backwardness, and yet specified more than two thousand groups largely on the basis of caste for reservation of jobs in central services and some other benefits, such as admission to professional institutions. The Nehru government virtually ignored the report as the Home Ministry concluded that the Commission had failed to come out with 'positive and workable' criteria to identify backward classes. A few years later, the government gave up the idea of drawing up a Central list, but advised the States to identify backward classes within their own respective jurisdictions, using economic test instead of caste criteria. If there was still any ambiguity about the Union government position on this issue, this was made amply clear in the course of the discussion on Kalelkar Commission report in the Lok Sabha which, having gathered dust for nine long yeas, was placed before the house in 1965, a few months after Nehru's death. Condemning the report, the government averred that the caste criteria for determining backwardness ran counter to the freedom movement's stress on the need to establish a casteless society. Around the same time, the Supreme Court also declared that determining backwardness on the basis of caste was violative of the constitutional provision. It is thus clear that by the mid 60s, it had been fairly well established that caste *per se* could not be the basis to identify backward classes.[14]

With the decline in the political fortunes of the Congress and the emergence of a new class of leaders at the State levels, the situation began to change drastically. Some of the States, particularly in the South, had already extended the benefits of reservation in jobs and educational institutions to weaker sections, in addition to the scheduled castes and scheduled tribes, using a variety of criteria not excluding caste. As the political scenario changed, reservation began to be increasingly used as a medium to expand political base. It caused resentment among the higher castes, particularly the younger generation which saw a serious threat to their future in this process, and several States witnessed violent resistance against the reservation policy pursued by their governments. Gujarat, in particular, had to contend with rioting students for weeks in 1985 when the State government sought to increase the quota for certain specified castes in admission to technical and professional institutions and government jobs on the eve of the elections to the State assembly.[15]

The Congress government at the Centre in the meantime showed little enthusiasm to get involved with drawing up a list of backward classes. It continued to stick to the position taken by the Nehru government that there was no need to have a Central list. However, when the Janata Party formed the government in 1977, it perceived a great deal of potential political advantage in drawing up a Central list, and appointed a commission under the chairmanship of a Bihar politician, B.P. Mandal, for the job. By the time the report of the commission was submitted, however, the Congress had returned to power at the Centre. On the basis of criteria many experts considered questionable, the commission had identified about 4000 castes across the land to be categorized under backward classes and to be entitled to the benefit of reservations. The report, discussed in the government circles and in a meeting of the chief ministers, evoked serious misgivings. This is where the matter rested until the Janata Dal government came to power after the general elections of 1989.

Given this background the announcement of Prime Minister V.P. Singh, heading a minority government, in 1990 to implement the Mandal Commission Report came as a complete surprise to the nation, including even the two major political parties supporting his government from outside. A national consensus on caste-based reservation was still a far cry, and if the reservation riots in many states during the 1980s were any indication, the nation was terribly divided on the issue. Even the report of the Mandal Commission had never been meaningfully discussed either inside or outside the parliament. The conclusion, therefore, is inescapable that the motive behind the

Prime Minister's sudden announcement was to outwit his political opponents in his own party for momentary political gain, pious rhetorics refuting the charge notwithstanding.

Whatever the case, the decision did not have even the semblance of the kind of national consensus to back it up that had preceded the adoption of the reservation clauses for the scheduled castes in the constitution. And by no stretch of imagination or logic can it be considered consistent with the ethos of the freedom movement which aimed at establishing a casteless society. Although the Supreme Court, contrary to its earlier judgements,[16] has given qualified support to the decision, there is no doubt that the implementation of the Mandal Report in whatever form would expand the scope of and perpetuate a system of privilege that the founding fathers intended to be only a temporary expedient.

The reorganization of states on linguistic basis effected in 1956 contravened, *prima facie*, neither the intentions of the founding fathers nor the programme of the freedom struggle. In fact, this had remained a major plank of the Congress programme ever since 1920. The silence of the Constitution on this issue, however, suggests that the framers were none too enthusiastic about it, or else a document that left no major national issue without some guideline for the future generation could not have been totally indifferent to it. Perhaps the holocaust at the time of the birth of free India and the partition of the country, caused by the exploitation of religions-cultural differences, acted as a warning against a territorial rearrangement based on a single cultural variable, lest it might give impetus to sub-nationalisms of an unhealthy kind and impede the process of national integration.[17] Pressure from various quarters, more particularly the death through hunger strike of a state level political leader demanding the creation of Andhra Pradesh by bifurcating the existing Madras State, forced the hands of the government.[18] Viewed thus, the linguistic reorganization of the country would appear to be yet another example of the founding fathers' intent being flouted by the later generation.

We have dwelt upon only the major areas where the post-Independence generation has acted against the spirit of the constitution, or the intent of the founding fathers, while ostensibly remaining within its boundaries. But the matter does not end here. Wherever the constitutional provisions have proved less flexible or the judiciary has tried to protect them from being manipulated, they have been amended to suit the will of the executive. It is not very often noticed that between 1950 and 1994, a period of less than fifty years, the constitution has been amended not less than seventy-six times, sixty times during the post-Nehru era. No other written constitution in the world has ever been treated so mercilessly. Admittedly, some of the amendment have been of a routine nature, but most of the substantiative ones were directed to bypassing or overriding court orders, as a chief justice of Supreme Court once ruefully remarked.[19]

It is nobody's case that the Constitution should have been treated like a holy cow. What is being stressed here is that a document which represented the accumulated and collective wisdom of a generation that witnessed, and in fact was the architect of, the maximum degree of national unity and cohesion in our entire history, should have been treated with greater respect. And at any rate the intent of the founding fathers ought not to have been sacrificed to narrow parochial gains or personal aggrandisement. Practically all the problems, vitiating our polity, can be attributed to the tendency on the part of the post-Independence generation to twist and mutilate the intent of the Constitution or thwart the spirit of the freedom struggle.

True, the formation of linguistic states has not yet created a chain reaction many feared it would, but the distortions in the federal structure and the parliamentary form are directly responsible for uncontrolled corruption, caste wars, religious fundamentalism, distrust of the governing system and the political class, and for the debasement of practically every institution created by the founding fathers for the efficient management of our polity. In other words, the ethos and values that had helped us achieve a measure of national unity, never witnessed any time before in our history, and that were enshrined in the Constitution have been allowed progressively to dissipate themselves. The Constitution of 1950, as has been noted earlier, suffered from many imperfections,[20] but a faithful adherence to the spirit of even this imperfect document would have served us better.

The crisis of the Indian polity, thus, is basically due to the same factor that caused the disintegration of the imperial unities on numerous occasions in the past. The empires crumbled because those who succeeded their creators failed to display the qualities and virtues necessary for nurturing their inheritance. Likewise, the post-Independence generation has been moving away from the spirit and ethos generated during the freedom movement and thus throwing away the gains made during that glorious period of our history. India possesses remarkable resilience which it has demonstrated on numerous occasions. But even India's resilience may find it hard to cope with a continuing string of divisive policies and actions. And there may not be another Gandhi to repair the damage once the nation's unity is fractured beyond a point.

Notes and References

1. Seling S. Harrison, *India: The Most Dangerous Decades* (Princeton: Princeton University Press, 1960).
2. Debiprasad Chattopadhyaya, *In Defence of Materialism in Ancient India* (New Delhi:

People's Publishing House, 1989), pp. 24–25; also K Satchidanand Murty, *Philosophy in India* (New Delhi: Motilal Banarasidas, 1991), pp. 15–17.

3. For further discussion see A.S. Altakar, *Education in Ancient India* (New Delhi: Motilal Banarasidas, 1948).
4. A staunch Vaishnava in Gujarat, for instance, would ask the tailor to 'make' his clothes because the word for stitching in the local language sounded like 'Shiva'.
5. S.T. Lokhandwala, 'Indian Islam, Composite Culture and Integration' in *Composite Culture of India and National Integration,* (ed.) Rasheeduddin Khan (Simla: Indian Institute of Advanced Study, 1987), pp. 1031–107 has discussed this point in greater details.
6. Ibid; M. Mohiuddin, 'The Elements of a Composite Culture, in *Composite Culture of India,* (ed.) Khan (cited under note 5 above), pp. 84–102; also S.C. Misra, 'Medieval Trader and His Muslim World' in *Business Communities of India,* (ed.) D. Tripathi (New Delhi: Manohar, 1984), pp. 41–48; S.A.I. Tirmizi, 'Muslim Merchants of Medieval Gujarat' in *ibid.*, pp. 59–68.
7. Mohiuddin, 'The Elements of a Composite Culture' (cited in note 6 above) claims that this in fact was the case.
8. It is significant that Tulsi's *Ramcharita Manas* starts off with Shiva telling the story of Ram, an avatar of Vishnu, to Parvati, and Ram has been portrayed praying frequently at the feet of Shiva. To further underline the Shaiva-Vaishnava amity, the poet makes Ram declare at one place: 'No enemy of Shiva can ever be my devotee – not even in dream.'
9. Vincent Smith, *The Oxford History of India,* (ed.) Percival Spear (New Delhi: Oxford University Press, 1994), Introduction; Jawaharlal Nehru, *The Discovery of India* (New York: John Day & Co. 1946), Chapt. 3.
10. Bose had used this expression for Gandhi in his address from the Singapore Radio, beamed to India, soon after the fall of the British colony to the Japanese forces during the Second World War.
11. See the following articles in Nirmal Mukerji and Balveer Arora (eds.), *Federalism in India: Origins and Development* (New Delhi: Vikas, 1992) for elucidation: K.A. Ramasubramanian, 'Historical Development and Essential Features of the Federal System', pp. 105–24; Mohit Bhattcharya, 'The Mind of the Founding Fathers, pp. 84–104; Ashish Bannerjee 'Federation and Nationalism: An Attempt at Historical Interpretation', pp. 41–63.
12. It may be instructive to recall that in post-war Britain there were occasions when governments having wafer thin majority functioned smoothly without any fear of defection. Harold Wilson's government that came to office after the elections of 1964 was one of these.
13. Originally, a special case clause for 'weaker sections' was included in the Directive Principles (article 46). Later in 1951, it was stated through an amendment to the Fundamental Rights section (article 15–4) that the special measures to improve the lot of 'socially and educationally backward classes' would not be violative of the right to equality under law.
14. For details see M.L. Madan, *Indian Political System*, (New Delhi: Ajanta Publications, 1989), pp. 270–90.
15. For a flavour of contemporary debate on caste-based reservation see the following articles in the *Economic and Political Weekly*: I.P. Desai, 'Should Caste be the Basis of Recognizing Backwardness? vol. 19, no. 28 (14 July 1984), pp. 1106–16; Ghanshyam

Shah, 'Caste, Class and Reservation', vol. 20, no. 3 (19 January 1985), pp. 132–36; Upendra Baxi, 'Caste, Class and Reservation', vol. 20, no. 10 (9 March 1995), pp. 426–28. Also, Marx Gallanter, *Competing Equalities: Low and Backward Classes in India* (New Delhi: Oxford University Press, 1984).

16. The Supreme Court had ruled in Balaji vs. State of Mysore and Chitralekha vs. State of Mysore that caste *per se* as the basis of reservation was violative of the constitution. *All India Reporter* (1964), Supreme Court, p. 1827.
17. It may be pertinent to recall how another multicultural society approached the problem of territorial reorganisation. Informed by the principles embodied in a report prepared by Thomas Jefferson in 1784, the United States decided to divide the entire West by the parallels of latitude and longitude on the map of the country. The states, thus, created had population with a variety of socio-cultural and even linguistic backgrounds.
18 That Prime Minister Nehru resisted the formation of linguistic states is well known. A recent book confirms it. See Robert D. King, *Nehru and the Linguistic Politics of India* (New Delhi: Oxford University Press, 1996).
19. Quoted in M.M. Singh., *The Constitution of India* (Calcutta: World Press, 1975), p. 1195.
20. Soon after the constitution of 1950 had come into force, M.C. Mahajan, a former Chief Justice of the Supreme Court, had written to the Prime Minister: '. . . the constitution had made no contribution towards consolidating the people of India into a single nation; on the other hand it was tending to take the country back to the age of separate kingdoms. The appetite for power among politicians of different varieties was becoming intense and the desire to rule within certain geographical boundaries was assuming dangerous proportion.' Quoted in Verinder Grover (ed.), *Essays in Indian Government and Politics* (New Delhi: Deep and Deep, 1988), pp. 340–41. This is, of course, an extreme view and an overstatement but it does underline the imperfections of the document.

TWENTY-ONE ❖ Surviving Through Culture Encounters: India and Globalisation

KAMLESH MOHAN

THE HISTORICAL MEMORY OF India's forced exposure to the global market forces and its cultural encounter with the West under the banner of the British raj for almost two centuries provides a concrete starting point for hypothesizing about the emerging cultural scenario in the wake of the inexorable communication and commercial revolution throughout the world. Recent developments, particularly the rise of reform movements in the Soviet Union and Eastern Europe, have been described as the 'end of history' by Francis Fukuyama. In his view, we are witnessing the end-point of mankind's ideological evolution and universalization of Western liberal democracy as the final form of human government.[1]

However, we have to concede that the 'end of geography' is a hard reality. The communication revolution has made distance and geographical divisions irrelevant. The lightening speed and ease of information flow through digital bit streams have impinged upon the politico-economic sovereignty and cultural specificities of the Third World countries. In view of the fast-paced globalization of trade and commerce as well as recent trends towards universalization of food-habits, modes of dress, patterns of behaviour, there is a wide-spread anxiety about saving our cultural heritage and richness of spiritual life.

Globalization has more comprehensive agenda and a formidable pool of economic resources (underwritten by multinational capital) than the British colonialism whose cultural domination and impact remained confined to the educated elite of Indian society in the absence of the powerful network of the electronic media. Among its long term objectives are the acquisition of a decisive role in the formulation of politico-economic and social policies relating to education, health, water, electricity, etc. and systems, especially, infrastructure for liberalization of the Third World countries through huge but conditional investments in the agricultural and industrial sectors and also through loans by International Monetary Fund and World Bank.

The major argument of this paper is that the Euro-American project of globalization of open market and free trade through the dissemination of its consumerist culture and its artifacts has serious socio-cultural implications, in relation to the preservation of Indian cultural ideals, public perception of sexual relations, gender roles, women's status and empowerment. I shall argue that in the present multi-pronged East-West encounter, Indian women, in the first instance, are likely to become not only the bearers and signifiers of tradition but also the tradition itself. The fear of the loosening of the patriarchal structure and control over women owing to the full-scale cultural-religious intrusion and the anxiety about the threat to religious / communal identities are likely to result in zealous imposition of domestic ideology, the glorification of the cult of 'genteel lady', as happened during the course of industrial revolution in Britain.[2]

Secondly, I fear that women may not only be commodified but also used as an agency by the capitalists. The proponents of consumer capitalism regard cultural conquest either through electronic media or through beauty pageants, fashion shows and other pompous extravangazas as the facilitator of the economic process, *i.e.* open market and free trade.

For a coherent and meaningful discussion of the problem of 'cultural invasion', I shall divide this paper into six sections: (I) Conceptualizing Culture, (II) Ideals of Indian Culture, (III) Indian Response to the Onslaught of Westernism / Modernity, (IV) Ideals of Modernity, (V) Globalization, Consumerism and Mass Culture, and (VI) Conclusion.

I. Conceptualizing Culture

At the outset, it is helpful to refer to the different trajectories of the word culture as it is, according to Raymond Williams, 'One of the two or three most complicated words in the English language'.[3] In the Indian context, its use for entirely contradictory purposes during the colonial and the post-independence period has added to its complexity and ambiguity. Its early use was made primarily for agricultural operations – 'cultivation', 'tending' and 'growth'.

The career of this word became multi-directional with its gradual shift to the particular and the personal in terms of cultivation of mind and personality and later its application to describe a process or the product of a process in the late eighteenth and early nineteenth century.[4] Its polysemic character and modernity (used synonymously with westernism) has to be kept in view. A variety of processes and institutions have been grouped under the banner of modernity – industrialization, expansion and consolidation of colonialism, democracy and modern nation-states.

A few common assumptions about culture – its organic wholeness, continuity and growth – were shared by thinkers, literary critics and anthropologists of varied hues in the late nineteenth century in Europe. For example, E.B. Taylor's anthropological conception of culture as 'a complex whole' and its characterization by Mathew Arnold as a domain of highest human values and creations of mankind, which can be conceptualized as enduring, traditional and structural values,[5] still dominate the theoretical perspective of social sciences, humanities and even casual discussions. Its organic and transcedent attributes were later elaborated by T.S. Eliot and F.R. Leavis and incorporated in English literature.

However, for understanding the full implications of Euro-American cultural invasion, it is relevant to refer to the complementary use of two other notions of culture – 'residual' and 'dominant' (terms coined by Raymond Williams) in the British writings during the late nineteenth century for politico-economic domination of the colonial people. The Orientalist and Utilitarian, particularly anthropological, projects for studying the organization and functioning of 'native' societies and their cultures exemplified pursuit of knowledge for hegemony rather than for pure intellectual/scholarly curiosity and considerations.[6] For example, Edward Said's seminal work, *Orientalism* (1978), has enabled us to understand how construction and projection of the 'Orient' as Europe's 'Other' in racial and cultural terms was geared to fix the colonial people in a subordinate position in relation to the 'master races' of Europe.[7] The primitive societies were regarded as the museum of mankind where the past of advanced western societies could be recovered.[8]

Integration of these two senses of culture in the entire project of knowledge about ancient societies, their people and culture was effected skillfully in the Orientalist writings. While one set of writers advertised the glories of ancient Vedic-Aryan civilization of India, the other presented its people as irrational, immature, depraved and lazy 'natives'.[9] Sharing the negative assumptions of the second group of Orientalist writings, the anthropolgical studies, which used the paradigm of cultural relativism, utilized ethnography for creating numerous stereotypes about various socio-religious groups and qualified the divisions among them not only in terms of 'inherent' and 'intrinsic' divisions among them but also in terms of their civilized or barbaric attitude and treatment of women.[10]

In fact, indictment of the 'degenerate Indian civilization', 'effeminacy of Indian men' and of the 'abject' position of women, who required 'protection' and intervention on humanitarian grounds,[11] was ingrained in the colonial ideology and social policy of the raj. The entire argument was crystallized into a rational justification of the British rule in India on grounds of moral superiority.[12] This supercilious approach towards India, appropriated by the

Euro-American capitalists, surfaces in their pronouncements and economic policies towards the Third World countries. They continue to condemn, bully and inferiorize, interpersed by occassional pats, the Asian and African nations for their inability to control poverty, population, resolve socio-political problems and protect human rights of terrorists, minorities and women. Regarding these as legitimate grounds for western intervention, the First World has pressurized the poorer nations into moulding their economic policies according to their dictates.

The reappearance of the overt western dominance is regarded as potentially more dangerous to cultural autonomy as there is now more powerful conjunction between the highly sophisticated communication technology, state power and multinational capital. It has facilitated the circulation of particular definitions of national, communal, caste and gender identities suiting the Euro-American agenda of global capitalism. Cultural penetration, increasingly viewed as an adjunct of any sustained system of global exploitation, is an extension of counter-insurgency through non-military means.[13]

In such a situation, culture has become the site of politco-economic battles between the First World and the Third World countries. The people regard it as an identity-marker in order to relate themselves with the nation and the world and a guide for individuals to school them into a specific pattern of behaviour. In fact, members of various communities learn to respond to different situations individually or collectively in accordance with their cultural orientation through shared symbols, codes, language and behaviour patterns as well as modes of dress.

Communication, which is not only transmission but also reception and response, plays a central role whether in 'cultural invasion' or 'cultural defence'. The task of 'cultural defence' requires an indepth understanding of the nature of Indian tradition and its essential ideals.

II. Ideals of Indian Culture

It is not easy to generalize about Indian culture for three reasons: Firstly, it is an amalgam of diverse traditions (Hindu, Islamic, Buddhist and Jainist), religious symbols, languages and creative products of multiple ethnic imaginations. Secondly, it is constantly in the making, strenuously contested and reconstituted. Being dynamic and open-ended, it is best described by the Persian world *ravayaat*, *i.e.* flowing or constantly in motion. Indian culture is constantly engaged in the process of experimentation, and self-renewal; it has been redirecting its social energy throughout its evolution from ancient to modern times. Thirdly, production of knowledge about India's society and culture by Indians and others remains burdened by the assumptions of

Orientalist scholarship. For example, the dominant ideology of Hindutva has appropriated the homegenizing agenda of the Orientalist and thus glossed over the complexity of our cultural/ideological formation. But projecting the Indian culture as monolithic and unchanging, its protagonists have distorted its true nature. The Euro-American academicians have also stereotyped understanding of caste, gender inequalities, nationalism or communalism through dominant paradigms such as 'hierarchy' for Indian society, 'filial piety' for China and 'honour and shame' for circum-mediterranean.[14] Despite these problems, caused by different trajectories about culture, and the complex nature of Indian tradition, it is possible to identify its essential ideals: (*a*) Communitarian Ideal, (*b*) Spiritual Ethos-Worldly Concerns, (*c*) Moral Values and (*d*) Creativity and Spirit of Accommodation.

(a) Communitarian Ideal

The most striking feature of Indian culture, which survived its encounter with the West, is the location of individual in the network of powerful communitarian relationships: family, kinship, and caste and their primary use for social cohesiveness,[15] now transformed into a political asset. For example, the partiarchal family being the reproductive unit, has continued to be used as a site for the socialization of the girl-child and for the transmission of cultural values, practices and traditions of major religions. The entire complex of community networks was utilized not only for schooling its members for discipline, work-culture, social and religious values but also for protecting and reinforcing the structures of land-relations. The major reason underlying the communitarian orientation and practice was the country's agrarian economy. Primarily comprising huge stretches of well-irrigated plains and the advantage of ample sunshine for the greater part of the year, India has maintained an agrarian economy over the past five thousand years. The British government exploited and developed this potential with minimum financial investment and technological inputs in order to feed and expand its industrial empire. Such a policy introduced many complexities in the stratification of the peasant society.

A major characteristic of the peasant society is that it values the communitarian ideal and cultivates this orientation. Historically speaking, Indians are known for their deep loyalty to the village, family and *jati*. Another major feature of this society is its relatively peaceful and closer relationship with nature and its effortless adjustment with nature and its rhythm of cyclic seasons. A distinct emphasis upon co-existence, peace and harmony rather than obsession with overpowering, controlling and exploiting nature characterizes the attitude of an agricultural community.

(b) Spiritual Ethos-Worldly Concerns

The second important dimension of Indian cultural heritage is its emphasis upon the realization of the ultimate spiritual ideal, *i.e.* unity with cosmos without undermining material achievements. The pervasive presence of spiritual ethos in the Indian life does not imply negation of the other aspects of life. The characterization of Indian outlook (used synonymously for Hindus) as pessimistic and other-worldly by western scholars is exaggerated. In fact, one of the main concepts underlying the ancient Indian civilization was the coordination of spiritual life with worldly life. For example, Hindu religion has emphasized a balanced, albeit a gender-biased, approach to the four ends of man: *dharma, artha, kama,* and *moksha. Dharma*, which refers to an ideal principle or norm to which man should conform in the course of his worldly activities, is assigned the first place as it is the regulating factor in the pursuit of material gains and pleasure.[16] Referring to *rajdharma* (king's moral duty), the *Lawbook* of Yajnayalkya states that where there is conflict between the principle and policy, righteousness and material gain / advantage, *dharma* and *artha*, the former should prevail.

As for *kama*, *i.e.* love or pleasure, its control by *dharma* is obligatory. The Hindu ideal does not preach abstinence from pleasure for all or at all stages; it rather preaches, universally, the ideal of chastened love or pleasure, regulated by considerations of both morality and well-being. In more than one authoritative text, the householder's life is considered to be the greatest of the four stages of life. Hinduism does not hold up monasticism or eremitism as a common ideal for all. It is these strains and trials of household management, family life and social obligations that discipline man and prepare him for *moksha*.

The pursuit of *moksha i.e.* liberation from the cycle of death and rebirth, is placed as the last phase of life; it is the life of retirement and spiritual endeavour and is the final and ultimate aspiration of man in the Hindu scheme of values. It is evident that no aspect of life was originally considered unimportant and none was denied or repressed. Instead, all that appears to be lower could be integrated with the higher according to Hindu philosophy. There was no distinction between the sacred and the profane.

Islam, which had developed a positive interaction with Hindu culture from the thirteenth century onwards, was firmly rooted in the material world, despite its dominant spiritual ethos.[17] As the 'field of action and the farming ground for the world to come', the present world is of great importance and value to man. What *Quran* emphasizes is that from the relative point of view of man, the world is as real as he himself is. The affirmation of life and of physical world is peculiar to Islam.

Contemporaneous with the ongoing cultural ferment throughout India,

Guru Nanak launched his crusade for the spiritual and moral purification of both the Hindus and the Muslims. The Sikh tradition, as it evolved from the fifteenth to seventeenth century AD, aligned religious goals with worldly concerns.[18] In the Sikh, especially the *Khalsa*, world-view, salvation could be attained while living in the world and pursuing secular objectives, such as the acquisition of political power or the accumulation of economic resources in the form of agrarian land. These secular objectives had, however, to be attained within the particular framework of beliefs and religious practices. Paramount among these beliefs was the *Khalsa* normative order-*kirt karni, vand chakna te namu-japna* (to labour for one's keep, to share with others and to practice the repetition of the Divine name). Obiviously, Sikh religion has remained functional in its approach.

(c) Moral Values

All major religions have concerned themselves not merely with the generation and transmission of moral values for the individual but also with social values. The extent to which they have done this has varied from religion to religion. As for Islam, a detailed statement of not only social values but even State and social laws are incorporated in the *Holy Quran* itself; as regards Christianity, Jesus himself separated the two by the statement 'Render unto Caeser what is Caeser's and unto God what is Gods's'. However, it is difficult to compartmentalize these two aspects in practice because of the scope given to interpretation in Islam and the extent of Church's involvement in State affairs. The Hindu scriptures also deal with social and individual moral values. However, the position of Hinduism on this issue is as ambiguous as on any other matter owing to the wide variety of these scriptures and the breadth of interpretation accepted by various authorities.

In the present situation created by globalization, it is increasingly difficult to avoid intermeshing of individual and social values and priorities. The efficient functioning of a market economy requires a minimum base of moral infrastructure just as it requires a minimum base of physical infrastructure. 'Honesty is the best policy' is not so much a moral dictum as a cost effective method of organizing inter-human relationships whether for personal concerns or large-scale business purposes. The consequences of all round deceit prove more costly in the long run than the consequences of straight dealing.

(d) Creativity and Spirit of Accommodation

The great strength of Indian culture is its dynamism, its creativity, its ability to accommodate and synthesize the multiple currents and traditions. A close scrutiny of the process of its evolution shows that the resilience of the inner core has helped it to protect its fundamental values. Its openness has enabled it to respond to new currents of thought, and transform them into a source of energy for new patterns of development and growth. Many voices of dissent have enriched its fabric. While Indian culture learnt important lessons from Buddhism and Jainism, it was influenced in a different way by the challenge of Islam.[19] Islam's message of social egalitarianism, democracy, rights for women, though within a patriarchal framework, had been incorporated in the social vision of Hinduism and made it more responsive to the changing cultural ethos and popular aspirations.

Passing through the initial phase of hostility and ideological conflict, caused by power struggle, interaction between Hinduism and Islam led to several unique cultural innovations in Indian society. Sufism is the best example of this creative fusion. The ongoing cultural movement gained in richness and breadth of vision through the intervention of sufis and saints. For example, Ramanand, Tulsidas, Kabir and Guru Nanak challenged orthodoxies and went beyond the trappings of forms and rituals.

Perceiving the fundamental unity of all religions, the sufis had preached the message of unity and devotion to one God whom they liberated from the monopolistic hold of religious priests of all denominations. Most of them conceived of and preached divine unity in terms of idealistic monism. Their greatest achievement was to enable the masses to experience spirituality and God's unbounded love without the mediation of external agency and rituals. Representing 'a revolt against blind conformism, social injustice and suppression of the individual', Sufism functioned as a liberating force for the human mind against the restraints of an imposed system. However, towards the end of the eighteenth century when it came into contact with the western ideas and civilization, it had lost its capacity to imbibe new currents and transform them into a stimuli for creativity.[20] It may partly be explained in terms of the peculiar nature of the East-West encounter – first in the form of trade, then of armies and administrators.

The accommodative spirit was also evident in the aesthetic consciousness of Hindus and Muslims. Architecture was the main field which afforded the greatest opportunity for the Muslim and Hindu minds to influence each other. What now remains of the first great buildings of the Delhi Sultans, such as the Jama Masjid of Ajmer and the Quwatul-Islam mosque near Delhi, shows that from the very beginning, the Islamic conceptions of architecture had to be adopted to the genius of the Indian environment, Hindu architects and artisans. Fergusson has pointed out that the design of the Jama Masjid in Ajmer was taken from the Jain temple on Mount Abu. The creative impulse and the spirit of mutual give-and-take percolated to the popular speech in the thirteenth century – a mixture of Persian with a dialect of western Hindi gave rise to a new language called Urdu. In due course of time, Urdu became the vehicle of a rich literary tradition, evolved by Hindu and Muslim writers and poets. It travelled to Deccan as the *lingua franca* in which the Hindu and Muslim advisers / companions from the north conversed with one another. It was in the Deccan that this language increasingly became not only a popular medium of communication but also the vehicle of expression for creative minds.

It may be said that these three ideals of Indian culture ought to be regarded as the ideals to be aspired for. I would not argue that Indians were always community-oriented, peaceful, spiritual and tolerant. India also passed through phases of violence, hatred and war; nor was there in India any lack of people with materialistic and individualist ambitions. However, in times of cultural upheaval caused by the British conquest, primacy of the cultural ideals bound the people together, irrespective of differences in religious faith and practice.

III. Indian Response to the Onslaught of Westernism / Modernity

With the coming of West through the British colonialism in India, radical departures occurred in the manner of redefinition of society, polity, family and gender, rendering the eighteenth century praxis irrelevant. A drastic change in the balance of politico-economic power against Indians and blockade of channels of socio-cultural communication made them insular and robbed them of creative thinking for more than a century.

Confronted with the colonial state's systematic programme of cultural hegemonization as a part of its strategy for political control, the Indian people responded in a variety of ways. Their response ranged from grateful acceptance of westernism as an agency for rejuvenating the Indian tradition to Gandhi's protest against its attitude of arrogant superiority because of its material achievements, mindless mechanization and irreligiosity.

I wish to focus briefly on the predicament of the nineteenth-century reformers, whose development as an intellectual community had been facilitated by the objective conditions created by the colonial rule but their bonding matured in the course of their social struggles.[21] It is likely to give us a clue about responses to the present cultural crisis, caused by the onrush of westernism / modernity on the heels of liberalization.

In the nineteenth century, the British highlighted the weaknesses of Indians' traditional social order, inferiorizing their culture, epistemology and the people as a race; and this obliged the Indians to launch cultural-ideological struggles on two planes: against the traditional order on the one hand and against cultural hegemonization by the colonial state on the other. While the reformers had found traditional culture inadequate to meet the challenge of western modernity, they were not inclined to adopt the bourgeois liberal model in *toto* as the cultural and intellectual engineering had caused anxiety among many of them about the survival of tradition itself. Thus ambivalence and contradiction in their attitude towards tradition and modernity, which is characteristic of colonial consciousness, surfaces repeatedly in their ideological formulations throughout the nineteenth and early twentieth century.

It is not surprising that the reformers of all hues – a 'liberal' Ram Mohan Roy or a 'rationalist' Akshay Kumar Dutt or 'revivalists' like Dayanand and Swami Vivekanand – had based their political, economic and social thought on the premises of western liberal discourse such as constitutionalism, rationalism, individualism and capitalism. Their utter dependence upon the West for social and moral regeneration is illustrated by their version of India's idealized past and its bourgeois future. Its impact was also reflected in their image of 'new' woman who combined the bourgeois virtues of orderliness, thrift, personal hygiene, cleanliness, sense of responsibility, literacy and accounting with the traditional feminine virtues of chastity, self-sacrifice, service, submissiveness, devotion, patience, etc.[22] The reformers' ideal of *sahadharmini* or companion in a monogamous marriage also suited the work-culture of a capitalistic economy, envisaged in the liberal framework. Obviously, the creation of a new social ethos was to complement the emerging bourgeois order.

The current debates between the liberals and the revivalists about the multiple consequences, particularly cultural, of globalization of economy tend to reproduce the past arguments, sense of urgency and perceptions of contemporary situation. One such example is the adoption of language of socio-cultural reform in the late nineteenth and early twentieth century, which was inscribed with the discourse of 'crisis' having frequent allusions to 'continuity and change', 'new times' and 'tradition and modernity'. The second example is the vigorous defence of the bourgeois ideology which reflects a perpetual fascination for Western (now Euro-American) practice of consumer capitalism, its tantalizing visions of prosperity and modernity.

However, critical temper has not been completely lacking. Nearer our own times, Gandhi's insightful and creative reading of Indian and Western tradition in the context of hegemonic British rule in India had urged him to reject social reformers' alternative. Thus, he launched a 'transcultural' protest against the materialist and hyper-masculine world-view of colonialism.[23] I shall return to his critique of Western civilization and its claim to modernity a little later. At this juncture, let me discuss briefly the ideals of Western modernity whose renewed onslaught in the wake of economic liberalization has aroused fears of cultural invasion.

IV. Ideals of Modernity

The present-day connotation of Western modernity, which signified 'new' in life-experiences rather than social totality and emphasized its transitory nature, its arbitrariness and its sense of opposition to unilinear time in the nineteenth century, regards it as a 'fixed end-state' of progress or development.[24] As advocates of this view, Euro-American nations, like the British imperialists, not only equate modernity with westernization but also claim their monopoly of transformatory role. It is from this angle that the West continues to define the ideals of modernity, which are strikingly different from the ideals of Indian culture. Though an integral part of the Enlightenment project, modernity subsumes many currents – democratic liberalism, Marxian socialism, rationalism, expansionism, industrialism, post-colonialism, urbanism, etc. Despite its complex nature, it is possible to define the salient features of this world-view:

(*a*) It is conceived as a closed monolith incapable of being shaped or changed by modern man. Berman has pointed out that 'open visions of modern life have been supplanted by closed ones.'[25]

(*b*) In this world-view, modernity as a 'fixed end-state of progress or development divides societies or social entities into either traditional or modern. In the case of non-western societies, modernization has become synonymous with Westernization. This theory offers no alternative for understanding change in any way other than Westernization and moving to that stage in the universal history of secularism and differentiation.[26]

(*c*) According to the exponents of modernity, history advances in a linear direction. Everything being dynamic, human beings are always engaged in improving the world they live in. Thus, it is future-oriented and evaluates achievement in material terms.

(*d*) Being modern implies the acceptance of value-neutral, scientific, universalistic rationality and rejection of emotional / affective relationships and religious beliefs. It is secular as it regards psychic and mystic explanations irrelevant for understanding the phenomenal world.

(*e*) Modernity has become gender-biased by not only continuing the gender-division of labour but also the monopoly of men in public affairs: administration, politics, science and art.[27a] Its dominant feature being the rationalization of economy, politics, culture and knowledge, it was perfectly logical to justify exclusion of women from public sphere on grounds of 'genderification' of rational and emotional capacities of people. 'Values such as rationality, objectivity, logical thinking and matter-of-factedness', in Tijssens' view, came to be considered as primarily masculine.' This mindset was integrated into the ideology that legitimized the role of middle class women as wives and mothers. In all European countries, the presupposition of this ideology was that these nurturing capacities have been instilled into women's nature[28] – equating biological function with mental capacity. Thus the need of bourgeois businessmen for a secure retreat from the harsh and competitive world,[27b] which became central to the project of domesticity in the Victorian Britain, is likely to assume a great value for the entrepreneurs of the Third World, pitted against the multinational consumer capitalism on their own home ground.

(*f*) According to modern world-view, scientific, progress should be measured in terms of man's capability to master the secrets of nature, and control and exploit its resources. Harmonious relationship with nature has been regarded as a sign of primitive rather than advanced societies until recently.

Obviously, such a world-view is based on the notion of hierarchical relationship between West as the teacher and East as the taught.[29] The West (and now Euro-American nations) with all its Enlightenment experience regards itself as superior in all respects – cognitively, materially and culturally – to the non-West. In order to become modern, a nation and its people must learn the knowledge system of the West, its life-style and its behaviour patterns. In short, the East must become the mirror-image of the West. Undoubtedly, India's first encounter with modernity under the British rule had already exposed her to the bitter experience of a hierarchical relationship, having its terms defined, elaborated and fixed in the course of two centuries of colonial domination. Indian people have yet to forget how hyper-masculine values of Westernism had been used as a criteria to denigrate their eugenical fitness for self-rule and dub their epistemology, technology and culture as static and primitive in the scale of world-civilisation. Britain also claimed to use it as an agency to modernize its people in the role of a self-appointed teacher.

However, the colonial state was not particularly keen on modernizing Indian economy, culture and society as it never wanted another dynamic rival. It is evident from its policy of limited application of technology for agricultural development[30] and its alliance with feudal / traditional elements against the weaker sections of society, particularly women. Its social policy, particularly the codification of customary law which deprived women of right to agricultural property and access to economic resources in general, showed its feudal orientation.[31] In addition to its political manouvering, systematic dissemination of Western ideals was instrumental in the colonization of Indian consciousness which was a knotted combination of ambivalence and resentment against the cultural invasion in the garb of modernization.

Indian attitude towards modernity had acquired more criticality, clarity and sharpness when Gandhi pulled the intellectual community out of the orbit of bourgeois values through his powerful critique of Western civilization. In his pamphlet *Hind Swaraj* (1909),[32] he indicted the West for its stance of arrogant superiority over its material achievements, mindless mechanization, barbarity and irreligiosity. His cultural agenda was based on such principles as seldom coincide with the ideals of Western modernity. For example, Gandhian action for recasting gender relations was far more original and comprehensive in scope than the social reform movements we have already discussed. The strength of his project for social and moral regeneration of India lay in three areas. Firstly, it did not compartimentalize social and political domains. Secondly, his understanding of the dynamics of social-change, power-equations as it affects gender relations was far more perceptive and realistic than was true of the earlier movements in any part of the world. Thirdly, it was neither limited by scriptural injunctions, nor by considerations of class, community or religion, while rectifying inequity in gender relations.[33] It may be pointed out that Gandhi had tried to reach out to every section of Indian society as is evident from the response of women, scheduled castes and tribal communities to his movements. Above all, his sensitivity to the untapped potential of India's rich cultural resources, particularly folk resources, and relevant elements of modernity has been conceded not only by the advocates of Western modernity, particularly feminists, but also by the traditionalists.

However, the decolonization process initiated by Gandhi has lost much of its force as his thought and practice could not capture fully India's urge for 'relevant' modernity in terms of the multiple needs of its fast-growing population and its national aspirations. The changing parameters of global economy and the inability of India to resist multinational pressures for liberalization have once again made people vulnerable to the tantalizing visions of Western modernity.

Obviously, 'inevitability of modernity' is posing a real threat to the three great ideals of Indian culture we have already spoken of. Firstly, the ethos of an ultra-urban / industrial orientation militates against the ethos of an agricultural society – its close identification with local communities and family-kinship ties. The mindset for a future-oriented and achievement-based view of life disrupts the relatively peaceful character of a non-modern community-living.

Secondly, the externalization of modernity, its secularity, its logic of technological manipulation of nature for man's continual, material well-being goes against the spiritual ethos / ideal of Indian culture. The process of objectification of nature – the most fundamental feature of modern / scientific / technological enterprise – has not been integrated into Indian outlook and way of life. Even a casual reading of *Vedas* and *Upanishads* shows that the Indian sages approached nature with a spirit of humility and self-surrender. In short, our cultural tradition viewed nature as an expression of cosmic order and not something to be objectified, controlled and exploited. As it had put premium on being environment-friendly, its relevance for modernity cannot be doubted.

Thirdly, the ethos of Western modernity – its cognitive arrogance, scientism and universality – is not comfortable with heterogeneity, plurality and differences. Thus, there is an inherent clash between the homogenizing impulses of modernity and accommodative spirit of our cultural ideals. The practice of theological disputation which formed an integral part of Indian intellectual quest, showed that Indian society favoured fairplay and freedom in propagation of the principles of various religions and thereby encouraging co-existence of plurality of faiths. This was why activities of Christian missionaries had continued for centuries without attracting any serious opposition. However, an open-ended approach to religion was gradually replaced by construction of rigid polarities, sealed boundaries and organized and enumerated religious communities with the establishment of a nexus of government officials and missionaries.

It can be said that the powerful current of Western modernity, which accompanied colonization, Christinization and anglicization, is now hitting us with full force. Thus, the spectre of cultural invasion is no longer imaginary but real.

V. GLOBALIZATION, CONSUMERISM AND MASS CULTURE

In the present discussion of 'globalization and cultural invasion', the project of Western modernity, which seeks to standardize cultural patterns, perceptions, expectations and responses in the Third World, has remained central as it underpins the philosophy of consumer capitalism. In other words, modernity as a grand system relies for the success of globalization, upon the efficient inter-connections between world-wide dissemination of 'global culture', telecommunication and deregulated markets and free trade in the Third World. Thus globalization, despite its obvious economic agenda, poses a serious threat to cultural autonomy as conditioning and directing of human choice and value facilitate economic process. The era of liberalization is forcefully changing the existing value system by linking the tastes of the average Indian, particularly the young and the adolescents in middle classes, with those of their counterparts in the West. The underlying logic is: global market economy shall create inter-linkages between 'forward' and 'backward' societies.[34]

This argument has special significance, for, according to a recent survey by International Board for Rural Development, India's burgeoning middle class forms about one-third of the country's population. This chunk of population is more than the total population of Europe, leaving out the erstwhile Soviet Union. The thrustful purchasing power of this middle class makes India a country with a vast potential market. This possibility prompts the West to clamour for the Indian domestic market which, they believe, is largely untapped. The process of capturing it will work only when there is a corresponding change in the value pattern of the targeted society. The target groups of people have to be attuned to the ethos of 'global culture'. Even more tactical requirement is to capture the hearts and minds of the adolescents and the young for mounting a full-scale cultural invasion.

A study of the cultural invasion obliges us to discuss various aspects of 'global culture' and its universalistic mission that seeks to play down, even suppress, all cultural differences and specificities. With their tremendous techno-economic power, the Euro-American nations are privileged to define and dictate the contents of 'global culture', popularly known as consumerist culture. Claimed to be based on the ideals of modernity and Western rationality, it seeks to bridge the gap between all cultures and generate a set of uniform responses and expectations. Using the latest communication technologies as an instrument, the Euro-American industry, in collaboration with multinational business-managers, is transmitting words, images and symbols of a consumerist culture into our world.

What is this consumerist culture? Consumerism assumes the form of a culture when the desire and necessity of consuming are stretched beyond the fulfilment of basic needs of each member of a society, arising from biological demands. Its salient features may be specified as follows:[35]

(*a*) Consumer needs are artificially generated. Limits on them are determined by intellectual and cultural motivation which education can help to generate and foster. Since our education system does not train and build refined tastes and desires, the electronic and print media would manipulate our choices and preferences to serve commercial interests. Obviously, the seductive and colourful advertisements of consumerist products/items, promising more sexual thrill, fun and pleasure, play a vital role in moulding the tastes of consumers in that direction. More and more newly created needs generate ever-growing craving for consumption.

(*b*) Consumerism means multiplication of possessions for material comforts, luxuries and possessions which signify a way of living. One may buy a new model of a car not to satisfy need for transportation but as a status symbol. Hence, consumerism means more than just the consumption of things and commodities.

(*c*) Consumerism, which is the culture of late capitalism, depends for its success on the numerical strength of the middle class having more than ample leisure time and extra purchasing capacity.

(*d*) The ethos of consumerism thrives on the perversion of the acquisitive instinct of men and women. As a successful life is equated with having everything, not having something implies failure and loss of status. Obviously, the people, living in the ethos of a consumerist culture, perpetually suffer from a sense of insecurity, anxiety, nervous tension and an incessant craving for the latest models, fashions and fads. In the long run they get addicted to the excitement of instant achievement and success and are alienated from their history, culture and particularly folk-memories.

(*e*) The target of consumerism is the creation of mass culture[36] which requires standardisation of perceptions about fun, life styles, behaviour patterns, choices of products for daily use on the basis of opinion polls. The mass culture, while moulding and catering to average taste, de-individualizes techniques as required for mass production and marketing. In fact, it is the product of an industrial society which has more equally distributed income, mobility, education and leisure.

(*f*) In mass culture, gregariousness is internalized owing to the high psychological costs of individuality and privacy. People fear solitude and unpopularity, popular approval becomes the only moral and aesthetic standard. The love for art and learning gradually becomes restricted to a small number of people. To put it succinctly, the growing lure of mass markets for both producers and consumers diverts potential talent from the creation of works of art and literature.

(*g*) As mass culture creates addiction to prefabricated experience of emotions, a majority of the people are deprived of the 'remaining possibilities of autonomous growth and enrichment, and their lives become ever more boring and unfulfilled' as pointed out by Earnest van den Haag.[37]

At this juncture in our discussion, it may be useful to review briefly the changing perspectives on massification of culture since the end of World War as we are hypothesizing about the attendant ill-effects of such a phenomenon with the adoption of 'open door' economic policy in India. With increased impetus to industrialization, urbanization and the development of 'mass' media, especially television, regarded as the major factors for the development of mass culture in America during 1930s[38], we are getting anxious about the destruction of cultural diversity and deterioration of taste-levels to the lowest denominator. For example, in late 1950s, Rosenberg, while reiterating the shrill warning of American research studies regarding the misuse of tools of mass persuasion for social control, underlined the dangerous possibilities of the use of culture by totalitarian regimes.[39]

Actually, this approach had become the intellectual base for motivation research in the advertising industry by the 1950s and in the 1960s; these developed techniques were applied to the American political process.[40] At present, these tools of mass persuasion are being used by the multinational capitalists in collusion with the Euro-American governments and the Indian ruling elite not only to capture untapped markets but also to reorient economic, social, and science and technology policies to facilitate their penetration and hegemony. From this perspective, the mass audience is a 'huge, inchoate, socio-cultural compost in which everything is mixed up together.'[41]

This concept of massification had been challenged by Edward Shils at the Taminent Institute Seminar on mass culture in 1961; he asserted that mass culture actually enhanced individuality owing to the availability of increasing number of consumer choices.[42] Bypassing the interpretations of the other advocates of this approach,[43] I shall focus on a more relevant hypothesis for visualizing the Indian situation. Peterson and Maggio have broken the mass-culture argument into two parts:[44] (*i*) that the forces of modernization significantly reduce cultural diversity; (*ii*) that an increasingly homogeneous mass culture has emerged. While it is true that much cultural diversity of ethnic, regional and folk type has been destroyed in post-industrial American society, in India, a different course of development may be chartered as it is far from being an industrial society and may skip various stages in search of 'relevant' modernity. As Indian society is not a monolith, existence of several 'taste cultures'[45] is likely to resist the total massification of culture. The selectivity of choice, which has been empirically documented in the American case, shows that development of a homogeneous culture may be uneven in such a vast country as India.

However, it may be conceded that consumerism has gradually tightened its grip over the Indians, especially the middle classes, during the past one decade. What are the long-term implications of consumerism for Indian society and culture? For a realistic assessment, three specificities of Indian situation must be kept in view. Firstly, the presence of one hundred million illiterates in the age-groups of 15 to 35 years makes India an ideal ground for testing the power of tele-advertising in moulding the mental ethos of such a chunk of population whose sense of discrimination shall gradually be blunted owing to its narcotic effect over time. Secondly, the equal number of Indian middle class especially the impressionable adolescents and the young women are seen by the commercial interests as the potential purchasing agents whose systematic conditioning would ensure long-term market control. Thirdly, new communication technologies, in the hands of ruthless and avaricious multi-national capitalists, are no longer amenable to check or control either by the developed or developing countries, especially when illiteracy rules out the intervention by books.

The power of books and the power of television may be differentiated in three different ways. Firstly, entry to the world of books requires a certain level of intellectual and literary skill. For watching television, no such mental training is required. Any one can watch and enjoy visuals, whether at home or in the market-place and also play electronic games. Unlike printed words, visual images are much more effective in spreading values of the 'global culture'. Secondly, watching television is a relaxed, passive and, to some extent an uncritical exercise. Reading a book demands some response in the form of thinking and argument with its author. Obviously, constant viewing of television does not develop the critical faculty. Thirdly, colourful and glamorous images while talking and smiling are intensely seductive but unreal. These images make the viewers uncritically and blindly receptive. Thus, penetration of visual media into the humblest home has made the possibility of cultural invasion real and serious.

It may be pointed out that the foreign television with its attractive cultural package is not the only threat to the ideals of Indian culture. It has an ally within the country itself in the form of Doordarshan, Star or Zee TV, 21 channel and ABCL (Amitabh Bachchan Company Ltd.). In its eagerness to survive in the competitive market, the Indian television is beaming a diluted version of Euro-trash, musical extravaganza, beauty-contests, fashion shows, soap serials, etc. Thus, the spread of consumerist culture is being aided by the commercial market-managers in India.

Anyone familiar with the media scene knows how easy it is to captivate the hearts and minds of uncritical viewers and persuade them to regard the consumerist culture as their own. Constantly exposed to the values and outlook of a dominant culture, the illiterate and impressionable adolescents as well as the young tend to copy sexual behaviour and life-styles of glamorous men and women. By watching images and advertisements of expensive clothes, cars, gadgets and luxurious houses on television, members of middle classes with limited means and the poor people get frustrated as this 'hyper-real' world, to use Baudrillaud's phrase,[46] is beyond their reach. Free circulation of visions of affluence in the absence of democratization of economic resources breeds imitative tendencies, violence, sexual crimes and all sorts of pathological complexes among the economically weaker sections who happen to be also illiterate.

With their growing consumerist orientation, the viewers tend to shun the basic simplicity of life-ethos which used to be the major feature of an agricultural society. Their blunted sensibilities fail to find joy and meaning in harmonious relationship with nature's rhythm and beauty. Their growing dependence upon artifacts and external agents for entertainment and enjoyment weakens the will-power of the majority of the people to mobilize their inner resources for enrichment of life such as introspection, reflection and contemplation.

Despite the potential importance of electronic media for promoting social communication and bonds, *i.e.* improvement in the depth and breadth of harmonious interpersonal and intergroup communication, it seems to have become instrumental in the dissemination of consumerist culture. People in the developed societies have got so addicted to mass media that they have very largely withdrawn themselves from community life. The programmed life dished out by the television has weakened social bonds and alienated people from their neighbours, friends and even family members. The proliferation of video-culture has led to the development of a new brand of narcissism in the Indian middle class.

Obviously, this narcissistic ethos of consumerist culture militates against the communitarian orientation of Indian culture which values fulfilment of individuality within familial and kinship network. It does not imply that a positive grounding in culture has helped the Indian people to become models for the quality of family values and interactions, social solidarity, public order and safety. But so far it has kept in check the number of divorces, desertions and separation cases, parent-child clashes, vagrancy, delinquency, indulgence in crazy thrills and mindless addiction to video-games, crime and violence, and scale of social anomie and alienation. However, increasing exposure to Euro-American modes of behaviour, glamorous life-styles and materialist values extolling consumption-linked pleasure, have brought a noticeable change in public perceptions. Repeated bombardment of messages through commercials and teleshopping regarding products and artifacts ranging from home-appliances, designer clothes and jewellery to computers does block other inputs and gradually the task of decision-making is increasingly taken over by media, jointly controlled by innovative advertisers, industrialists and capitalists.

The proliferation of consumerism-generated mass culture leads to the regular establishment of 'culture industry'. It manufactures culture like any consummable item. Like any other industry it uses every new form of technology to improve its product. Technology touches almost every aspect of mass culture. Music, film and industry, sports and eveything else get reduced into a great technological spectacle. People are seen talking more and more about technics but little about life. Their tastes and evaluation of performing and plastic arts are guided by attractive packing. They buy cultural artifacts like any other commodity – food, soft-drinks or cosmetics.

The process of commodification of art and culture in a consumerist society affects attitudes to human relations – especially gender-relations – and public perception of women. The woman of the consumerist era is not idealized either as an enlightened mother nor as a self-fulfilled working person, nor as the equal partner and companion of man, deriving fulfilment from creativity – both physical and spiritual. A consumerist society (representing the essentialist view of Euro-American-sponsored culture) projects woman as the glamorized sex-object and as a source of pleasure. The major purpose of her existence is to provide titillation to the over-stimulated sensuality of the male-dominated world. Software producers in such a society are motivated to innovate infinite variety of forms and methods of voluptuous entertainment for men whose overstimulated and overstrained organism seeks lower forms of thrill, excitement and relaxation for their life. This indicates a powerful, though invisible, alliance between managers of communication systems and the kings of vast industrial empires. The former stimulate the appetite and greed for infinite variety of goods and services, towards which the latter channelize the economic resources and technical skills.[47]

Indian women are being increasingly seen as purchasing agents for their family by the multinational commercial interests which seem to utilize their American experience in the course of globalization of consumerist culture as a part of the Euro-American project of carving out politico-economic empires. The domestic division of labour has long positioned women as the primary consumer in Western and Eastern societies. The level of consumption of products and services by unpaid housewives and single women in their homes is indeed critical for recreating and maintaining a production style and pattern that functions to support the capitalist economy. In this respect, consumption activity would promote both gender and economic-stratified forms of exploitation.

Studies on Euro-American television and women yield enough evidence to show that consumer capitalism has substantial stake in reinforcing domestic ideology. Several programming genres, such as quiz-shows, some talk-shows and cooking-slots recognize women as the target-viewers as well as the target consumers. Each programme is divided into slots for sponsoring advertisers of various products to whom audience is sold in return. Take, for example, soap-opera, the melodramtic serial which is usually considered to be almost exclusively a women's genre though many boys and men watch this as well. While commenting upon the contradictions built into the enjoyment of television soaps by women, Michle Mattelart has insightfully pointed out that for the politically aware viewers, the soap-operas can be seen as a tool of capitalism. Its social function is to colonize women as consumers by preying upon their loneliness and desperation over being excluded from the production process. Ironically, such pleasures are trivialized both by the feminists and the popular press.[48] However, the videos of American soap operas, films and Euro-trash beamed by Doordarshan in late-night slots and by the cable-operators and Zee and Star TV – generously interspersed with advertisements of multinational products – have now been using Indian housewives and teenaged girls as their target guinea-pigs.

Globalization of consumer capitalism has long-term negative implications for cultural, especially religious, practice. These implications are likely to be two-fold. Firstly, the plea of cultural defence shall increasingly result in the manipulation of religion for electoral gains and in competitive fundamentalism for preserving religious patriarchies. Secondly, the colonization of religion by the money-power of big multinationals and the powerful Indian commercial houses, which has already converted it into an object of glamorization, shall lead to the negation of spirituality and the dominance of material over spiritual goals.

Turning to the argument of cultural defence, it may be said that the proponents of Hindutva have unwittingly projected the role of religion as divisive. Taking their cue from colonial ethnographers, they have reinforced the conceptualization of religion as enumerated community which may be used for electoral politics. Unlike Gandhi, who utilized his creative interpretation of various religious traditions for forging tools of political protest, *e.g. Ahimsa* and *Satyagraha*, they have manipulated the notion of cultural diversity, religious precepts and idioms for homogenizing Hindus, engineering communal riots and activating hatred and intolerance. Instead of promoting egalitarian values, movements against gender and caste injustice and oppression, instead of creating an ethos of tolerance, spirituality and fairplay, the religious leadership of the Hindus and Muslims has encouraged the growth of exclusivist identities and hierarchical relationship. Their greed for power has exacerbated social tensions, inter-religious conflicts and egoistical drives rather than the spread of sanity and a spirit of mutual accommodation. Take, for illustration, the violence and bloodshed caused by flamboyant *rath yatras* and the so-called liberation movement of Ram Janam-bhoomi of Ayodhya.

Let me refer briefly to the implications of globalization of capitalism and its nexus with State and religion for gender justice. The new policy of economic liberalization has prompted the minority and majority community leaders to protect male privilege with the help of the State, which has been called upon to legislate new laws regarding labour, wages, property rights and active involvement of women in the economic and political processes in order to appear just and progressive in Western eyes.

For the success of new economic policy, the Asian values of family cohesiveness, discipline and education are likely to assume new importance. Instead of re-casting gender-equations in the family, the minority communities are advocating the preservation of personal laws and the majority is clamouring for the legislation of uniform civil code. Neither of them is interested in conceding real conjugal guardianship and custodial and property rights to women. The Indian State is, obviously, acting in collusion with these religious leaders and capitalists for politico-economic reasons. This is evident from its withdrawal from its welfarist functions, the maintenance of which could have mitigated patriarchies operating in the family, the community and the work-place. For all of them the restriction of women to domestic roles is crucial.

Secondly, colonization of religion by money power has diluted its positive role in socio-cultural life of the Indian people. The growing reliance of religious leadership on their wealthy constituency for displaying their organizational strength has reduced spirituality to gorgeous rituals. This is evident from the competitive sponsorship of religious festivals by some of the big multinationals and the Indian industrial /commercial concerns. Anyone who has witnessed the gorgeous spectacle of Durga Puja in Delhi and Calcutta would feel disgusted by the quantification of religion in terms of money power. Thus, the fast-growing trend of measuring success in proportion with its external trappings has led to de-spiritualization and erosion of the noblest cultural ideals and strengths. Naturally, it is affecting the daily behaviour and religious practices of the people in a negative manner.

V. Conclusion

The growing awareness of cultural invasion and acute sensitivity to the threat to Indian culture implies neither insulation from fresh ideas and refusal to interaction with other cultures nor defence of regressive values, outdated social customs and resistance to change. It means critical exploration into our past and contemporary history and retrieving those components of our knowledge and culture as well as institutions as can serve as a nucleus for constructing a framework of relevant modernity for India.

The first question to be asked is whether India's earlier experience of politico-economic and cultural domination has equipped the present political leadership and intellectual community with foresight and historical imagination to differentiate between the purely rapacious motives of Euro-American nations and their professed fraternal concern for economic, scientific and social development of the Third World countries which are also together known as the South. The opposition / ruling party's commitment to implement the new economic policy – privatization, marketization and free trade – and the ruling party's advocacy of 'swadeshi' and 'protectionism' seem to rest on the considerations of electoral politics because the new economic policy orientation is geared towards the generation of wealth without clarifying the social purpose for which wealth may be used. Their policies do not appear to be based on a realistic assessment of the strengths and weaknesses of existing infrastructure, social institutions and cultural resources, requisite for formulating a long-term strategy for revitalizing the country's economy. No serious exercise has been undertaken to devise ways and means for the utilization of foreign capital or investment and expertise as a catalytic agent.

The intellectuals, who at best form a dispersed intellectual community at present, have fortunately seen through the underlying linkages between the Euro-American lobbying for global culture and its relentless pressure on the Third World to give them access to their resources and markets. While commenting upon M.I.A. (Multilateral Investment Agreement), the latest instrument on the anvil for economic domination, Martin Khor (Director, Third World Network, Malaysia) has rightly dubbed it as 'a return to a colonial era situation'. The European Community has already introduced other instruments or concepts for controlling rivals and decreasing their competitiveness such as I.P.R.A. (Intellectual Property Rights Agreement) T.R.I.M.S. (Trade-related Investment Measures) and others but M.I.A. has the most serious cultural implications. The proposed treaty would not allow exclusion on cultural or moral grounds or for the media, communication and information sectors. Foreign companies in these sensitive areas would be allowed to enter and be treated at par with local firms. Thus, cultural imperialism is inbuilt in the long-term strategy of globalization of capitalism. Obviously, the target group is the country's around 250 million upper and upper-middle class population, whose crass consumerism is the best bet for the neo-imperialists.

The present situation is particularly piquant, for the adolescents and the young (whether hailing from poor and illiterate sections, or from the educated and well-to-do middle classes), who are forced to live in a transitional world because new cultural sensibilities, social values and reference-points have not yet been created even after five decades of independence. With the removal of literacy and geographical barriers through the ever-widening reach of television, including cable culture, it is a challenging task for the impressionable viewers to resist cultural conditioning by the soap operas, visual images of opulence coupled with glowing descriptions of Western superiority in epistemological, social, political and material advancement. Thus, democratization of images without the democratization of resources has caused bewilderment, resentment and anger against the social institutions and political system which are unable to satisfy its people's needs and craving for quality consumer goods and cultural artifacts. In the absence of an education system, which can inculcate a deep understanding, appreciation, and sense of pride in the Indian culture, imitative tendencies in dress, food-habits, behaviour, life styles, values, and perceptions are increasingly visible among boys and girls. Such a situation has been used as a tangible evidence by sociologists like Ernest Gellner and political scientists like Fukuyama to argue that no culture can remain indifferent to the 'superior Western industrial culture' and bourgeois ideology.

However, this argument about the inevitability of Western modernity must be contested. It is not surrender to it but a critical reflection and voice of dissent against pathologies of modernity which is desirable. We need to focus our creative energies on formulating a new cultural agenda which ought to retain its criticality in order to have a meaningful dialogue with the West. In this agenda, definition and investigation into all aspects of 'relevant' modernity for India must be given top priority. The relevant modernity for our country neither advocates the rejection of a rich cultural heritage nor withdrawal from community-based social life which draws its sustenance from constant interaction with the folk-culture. In our pursuit of modernity, we must fully realize the emancipatory potentials of the cultural ideals discussed in Section III. For example, the peaceful communitarian ideal, that our culture emphasizes, can rescue the world from devitalizing competitive mentality, its aggressive individualism and the resultant social alienation. Similarly, the accommodative spirit of our culture can serve as an antidote against the ruthless drive for universalization of tastes, behaviour-patterns and homogenization of culture.

The paradigm of modernity for India does not ignore material aspect of human existence. It acknowledges the need to multiply generation of wealth from industry as well as agriculture through the sophisticated but labour-intensive technologies of production. As India can never hope to attain either the targets of production or consumption in the Western societies, its pursuit of modernity has to set its sight at 'sustainable development' which avoids five distortions identified by *Human Development Report 1996:* jobless growth, ruthless growth, rootless growth, futureless growth and voiceless growth. It may be possible to avoid these distortions if the economic policy adopts the bifocal strategy of accelerated economic growth and a broad focus on the social sectors—health, women's welfare, education, credit to low-income groups and small-scale entrepreneurship, as has been done in the Far East and South-East Asian countries.

To follow the economic ideals of global capitalism is not beneficial for India because it equates development with consumerism and application of advanced technology to every sphere of life with progress. It is urgent to prevent the market forces from colonizing our mind and life once again. Cultural recovery is impossible without formulating an alternative agenda for politico-economic development which should give priority to the development of human resource capital and the construction of a civil society – gender-sensitive, communitarian, ecologically friendly, morally mature and cultured. It is apt to end this discussion of globalization and cultural invasion with Gandhi's sensitive observation:

> I don't want my house to be walled in on all sides and my windows to be stuffed. I want the cultures of all lands to be blown about my house as freely as possible. But, I refuse to be blown off my feet by any.

In short, neither traditionalism nor Westernism but a third alternative can save us from cultural take-over, leading to economic and political hegemony which is the ultimate target of globalization.

Notes and References

1. Francis Fukuyama, 'End of History Debate', *American History Review*, 34, 3, 1990, p. 8.
2. Catherine Hall, 'The Early Formation of Victorian Domestic Ideology', in Sandra Burman (ed.), *Fit Work For Women* (London, 1979), p. 23.
3. Raymond Williams, *Keywords* (First printed 1976, London 1983), p. 87.
4. For a review of the career of 'culture' particularly from the angle of literature, see Raymond Williams, *The Long Revolution* (London, 1961), pp. 41–71; also see his *Culture and Society* (London, 1996), pp. 295–338.
5 James Clifford, *The President of Culture* (Cambridge, 1988), p. 235.
6 For a discussion of anthropology's relation to colonialism, see Talal Asad (ed.), *Anthropology and the Colonial Encounter* (London, 1973); James E. Marcus, *Writing Culture: The Poetics and Politics of Ethnography* (Barkeley, 1986); Johannes Fabian *Time and other: How Anthropology Makes Its Object* (New York, 1983).
7. Edward Said, *Orientalism* (London, 1978), p. 87 Although Said's argument and illustrations are based on the Middle East (now known as West Asia), his conclusions are also applicable to other colonial societies, particularly India.
8. Bernard Cohn, 'The Command of Language and the Language of Command', in Ranajit Guha (ed.), *Subaltern Studies*, iv (New York, 1985), p. 325.
9. *Edward Said*, n. 7.
10. E.A. Gait, *Census of India 1991*, Report, i, pt. I, p. 120: Robert Burn, *Census of India 1901*, North-West Provinces and Oudh, Report, iv, pp. 75–76.
11. James Mill, *The History of British India* with notes by H.H. Wilson (London, 1840), pp. 312–13.
12. Kamlesh Mohan, 'Clamping Shutters and Valorizing Women: Tensions in Sculpting Gender Identities in the Colonial Punjab in Pritam Singh and Shinder Thandi, *Globalisation and the Region: Explorations in Punjabi Identity* (London, 1996), pp. 175–76.
13. Samit Kar, 'Miss World '96: Cultural Invasion of the Worst Kind,' in *Mainstream*, 23 November 1996, p. 8.
14. Arjun Appadurai, 'Theory in Anthropology: Centre and Periphery,' *Comparative Studies in Society and History*, 28:2 (April, 1986), p. 357.
15. My discussion of the communitarian ideal is based on David G. Mandelbaum, *Society in India* (First printed 1972: Bombay, 1984), pp. 33–180.
16. For a sympathetic angle on this issue see Theodre de Bary ed., *Sources of India Tradition* (First printed 1958; Delhi, 1988), pp. 211–366.
17. S. Abid Hussain, *The National Culture of India* (First NBT Edition, 1978: Delhi, 1992), p. 66, Mohammed Sahib's sayings, Compiled in Hadith, repeatedly emphasize *i.e.* the present world is a preparation for the next world.
18. For a detailed discussion of this aspect of Sikhism, see Upinder Jit Kaur, *Sikh Religion and Economic Development* (Delhi, 1990), pp. 70–159.

19. For information on Islam's influence upon Indian Society, especially its cultural implications, see: M. Mujib, *Indian Muslims* (London, 1967); S.A.H. Abid, *Sufism in India* (Delhi, 1992), pp. 81–121.
20. M. Mujeeb, *Islamic Influence on Indian Society* (Delhi, 1972, p. 65..
21. For a discussion of the process of the formation of the intellectual community in the nineteenth century, see K.N. Panikar, 'Culture and Ideology: Contradictions in Intellectual Transformation of Colonial Society in India' in *Economic and Political Weekly*, 5 December 1989, pp. 2115–20.
22. Kamlesh Mohan, *n.* 12, p. 194.
23. Ashish Nandy, *The Intimate Enemy: Loss and Recovery of Self under colonialims* (Delhi, 1983), p. 48.
24. David Frisby, *Fragments of Modernity* (Cambridge, 1986), p. 13. For a detailed discussion of difference of approaches to modernity between nineteenth-and twentieth-century sociological thinking, see M. Berman, *All That is solid Melts into Air* (London, 1983).
25. M. Berman, *n.* 24, p. 24.
26. Aysegul Baykun, 'Women between Fundamentalism and Modernity' in Bryan S. Turner, *Theories of Modernity* (New Delhi, London, Newsbury Park, 1990, 1991), p. 138.

27*a*. Cited in Lieteke van vucht Tijssen, 'Women between Modernity and Post-modernity', in Bryan S. Turner, *Theories of Modernity and Post-modernity* (New Delhi, London, Newsbury Park, 1990, 1991), p. 151.

27*b*. E. Wilson, *Women and Welfare State* (London, 1977), p. 22.

28. Tijssen, n. 27a She has based her argument of 'genderification' on L. Braun's exposition (1901: 190) whose writings are not available in English.
30. For illustration see Rai Bahadur Ganga Ram's failure to experiment with tube-wel technology owing to Punjab Government's uncompromising stand on the limited modernization of agricultural and irrigation technology. It has been discussed in Imran Ali, *The Punjab under Imperialism 1885–1947* (First printed 1988; Delhi, 1989), pp. 219–22 and 231–36.
31. David Gilmartin, 'Women, Kinship, and Politics in Twentieth Century Punjab' in Gail Minault (ed.), *The Extended Family: Women and Political Participation in India and Pakistan* (Columbia, 1981).
32. *Hind Swaraj*, published in Gujrati in the *Indian Opinion* of 11 and 18 December 1909, was issued as a booklet in January 1910. Its proscription by the Govern-ment of Bombay in March 1910 hastened Gandhiji's decision to publish its English translation (with his foreword written on 20 March 1910), which was issued by the International Printing Press, Phoenix.
33. I have borrowed these ideas from Ravinder Kumar, 'On Gender Theory, the Social Sciences and "Relevant" Modernity' in *Manushi*, no. 68, p. 26.
34. For an insightful sociological perspective on the cultural dimensions of contemporary global capitalism, see Max Weber, *The Protestant Ethic and the Spirit of Capitalism* (New York, 1958), Samit Kar, *n.* 13.
35. My discussion of the features of consumerist culture is based on Susan George, *How the Other Half dies* (London, 1985).
36. For a critical view of Edward Shil's theory of three-tier classification of culture, see Earnest van dan Haag, 'A Dissent from the Consensual Society', in Bernard

Rosenberg & David Manning White, *Mass Culture Revisited* (New York, 1971), pp. 85–92.

37. *Ibid.*, p. 92.
38. For an understanding of the theory of the development of 'mass culture' in America, see Y. Gasset, *Revolt of the Masses* (New York, 1932); D.Mac Donald, 'A Theory of Mass Culture', in Rosenberg and D.M. White eds., *Mass Culture* (New York, 1957).
39. B. Rosenberg, 'Introduction', in B. Rosenberg and D.M. White, *n.* 38.
40. Mc Ginnis, *The Selling of the President* (New York, 1968, 1969).
41. R. Clausse, 'The Mass Public at Gripps with Mass Communication', *International Social Science Journal*, 20, p. 624.
42. Edward Shils, 'Mass Society and its Culture', in N. Jacobs (ed.), *Culture for the Millions*? (Boston, 1961).
43. For example, see T. Parsons and W. White, 'The Mass Media and the Structure of American Society', in *Journal of the Social Issues*, 16, pp. 67–77, Harold Wilensky, 'Mass Society and Mass Culture: Interdependence or Independence?' in *American Sociological Review*, 29, pp. 173–97.
44. R.A. Peterson and P. Di Maggio, 'From Region to Class: The Changing Focus of Country Music, in *Social Forces* 53, pp. 497–560.
45. I have borrowed this term from Tom Wolfe, *The Kandy Colored Tangerine Flake Streamline Baby* (New York, 1965), p. xv.
46. J. Baudrillard, *Simulations:* Trans M. Foss (New York, 1983 a); In the shadow of the silent Majorities: Trans M. Foss (New York, 1983 b), p. 27.
47. The idea expressed in the foregoing three paragraphs are borrowed from Lisa A. Lewis, 'Consumer Girl Culture: How Music Video Appeals to Girls', in Mary Ellen Brown, *Television and Women's culture: The Politics of the Popular,* (London, 1990), pp. 89–101.
48. Mary Ellen Brown, 'Consumption and Resistance', in Brown, *Ibid.*, pp. 203–4.

Index

Contributors

1. A.K. Mittal
   Professor, Department of History
   University of Gorakhpur
   Gorakhpur (U.P.)
2. A.R. Kulkarni
   SHRI
   992/993-23, Rajendranagar
   Pune-411030
3. Dwijendra Tripathi
   'Munish Kutir', 134, Goyal Park,
   Vastrapur, Ahmedabad-380015
4. Eugenia Vanina (Ms)
   Centre for Indian Studies
   Institute of Oriental Studies
   Moscow
5. Gautam Chattopadhyay
   President, Paschim Banga Itihas
   Samsad
   2 Palm Place
   Calcutta 700019
6. Haraprasad Ray
   Flat A-3, ONOBUIN Apartments
   64, Santoshpur Avenue
   Calcutta-700075
7. J.S. Grewal
   622, Phase-III-A, Mohali
   Chandigarh
8. Kamlesh Mohan
   Professor, Department of History
   Punjab University, Chandigarh
9. K.A. Nizami
   Nizami Villa, Sir Syed Road
   Aligarh-202001
10. K.K.N. Kurup
    Vice-chancellor
    University of Calicut
    Calicut-673635 (Kerala)
11. K.N. Chitnis
    A1/23,
    Rambag Colony, Navi Path
    Pune-411030
12. K.S. Singh
    A-40/3, S.F.S. Flats, Saket
    New Delhi-110017
13. K.S. Mathew
    Professor, Department of History
    Pondicherry University
    Pondicherry-605014
14. Marina Carter (Ms)
    92 Greenfield Road
    London-N15 5ER.
15. M.K. Dhavalikar
    33, Navketan Society, Kothrud
    Pune-411029

Attention: Readers/Authors

This checklist includes all recent and forthcoming titles in the field of Social Sciences, History, Philosophy and Literature.

We welcome your comments which will be valuable to us to improve the quality of publications.

Invitation to authors: If you are working on a manuscript now or planning to write one in near future—maybe a textbook or a monograph—we shall be glad to receive your proposal for its publication.

If you want to receive our publication information sheet regularly please send your name

INDIA COUNCIL OF HISTORICAL RESEARCH
MONOGRAPH SERIES

Archaeology of Seafaring
EDITED BY HIMANSHU PRABHA RAY
x + 352 pp Rs 795

Indo-French Relations
EDITED BY K. S. MATHEW AND S. JEYASEELA STEPHEN
x + 330 pp Rs 795

We Lived Together
EDITED BY S. SETTAR AND P. K. V. KAIMAL
x + 368 pp Rs 795

Jallianwala Bagh: Masscrace (Forthcoming)

Second World War: As catalyst for Social Changes in India
S. B. SINGH
Demy 8vo xii + 208 pp Rs 395

Indigo and the Raj
PRABHAT KUMAR SHUKLA
Demy 8vo 210 pp Rs 250

Tarikh-i-Akbari
MUHAMMAD ARIF QANDAHARI
An annotated English translation with introduction by
TASNEEM AHMED
Demy 8vo 315 pp Rs 350

The Politics of Bhutan
PARMANAND
Demy 8vo viii + 260 pp Rs 250